The Scope of
Bargaining in
Public Employment

Joan Weitzman

The Praeger Special Studies program—
utilizing the most modern and efficient book
production techniques and a selective
worldwide distribution network—makes
available to the academic, government, and
business communities significant, timely
research in U.S. and international economic, social, and political development.

The Scope of Bargaining in Public Employment

PRAEGER SPECIAL STUDIES IN U.S. ECONOMIC, SOCIAL, AND POLITICAL ISSUES

Praeger Publishers   New York   Washington   London

Library of Congress Cataloging in Publication Data

Weitzman, Joan.
    The scope of bargaining in public employment.

    (Praeger special studies in U.S. economic, social,
and political issues)
    Bibliography: p.
    Includes index.
    1. Collective bargaining—Government employees—
United States.   2. Collective bargaining—Government
employees—New York (State)   3. Collective bargaining—Teachers—United States.   I. Title.
KF3409.P77W44   344'.73'0189041353   74-11926
ISBN 0-275-05760-7

PRAEGER PUBLISHERS
111 Fourth Avenue, New York, N.Y. 10003, U.S.A.

Published in the United States of America in 1975
by Praeger Publishers, Inc.

Printed in the United States of America

In Memory of

My Beloved Mother,

Ann B. Parker

One of the most controversial issues in public sector labor relations concerns the appropriate subjects for collective negotiations. What subjects should be open for discussion at the bargaining table, what subjects should be determined exclusively by public management, and what subjects should be regulated through legislation are questions that have sparked highly diverse opinions among collective bargaining participants, practitioners, and observers.

In recent years much has been written on collective bargaining in public employment, but few attempts have been made to discuss in depth the scope-of-bargaining issue and its implications for the development of public sector labor-management negotiations. In this study I attempt to acquaint the reader with the meaning of the scope of bargaining and to analyze the problems associated with it in public sector labor relations.

This study is not intended to be exhaustive, and I am confident that more issues have been raised herein than have been resolved. However, in reviewing and analyzing the historical background of the scope-of-bargaining concept, the variety of scope-of-bargaining definitions that have been written into public employee bargaining laws, the contrasting legal opinions concerning appropriate bargaining subjects, the effect of civil service codes on bargaining laws, the relationship between professionalism and the scope of negotiations, and the views of the parties concerning the scope of bargaining, I make an exploratory attempt to study an issue at the very heart of collective negotiations that is in need of additional research.

I have tried in this project to maintain a scholarly neutrality toward certain controversial points of view, although I must confess what the reader will eventually discover for himself—that I bring to my research my background as a student of industrial and labor relations, participant in teacher-school board negotiations, and staff member of a labor relations agency. I have studied and engaged in (sometimes, quite stumblingly) the art and science of collective bargaining, and I believe in its value as a means of institutionalizing labor-management conflict in modern industrial society. I believe that all employees, be they privately or publicly employed, should have the statutory right to organize and bargain collectively with their employers through representatives of their own choosing. But I also maintain that both private and public employers must not be denied the right to manage their business and government enterprises effectively and efficiently.

Having confessed my biases, I wish to acknowledge my debts of thanks to those individuals who provided valuable assistance in the research and preparation of this study.

To my friends and former colleagues of the New York State United Teachers, I am very indebted. Emanual Kafka, Dean Strieff, Robert I. Allen, Ronald Crawford, and especially Bob Manners helped me not only by providing valuable research materials but, more importantly, by giving me my first opportunity to serve as a professional at the collective bargaining table. For their assistance and confidence in my ability, I shall always be grateful.

I also want to express appreciation to the faculty of the New York State School of Industrial and Labor Relations at Cornell University, whose members stimulated and challenged me always to do my best during both my undergraduate and graduate years of study. I am very grateful to Professors Lawrence Williams and Kurt Hanslowe, members of my graduate committee, who with much patience and encouragement guided me through my courses and doctoral research. And I am especially indebted to Professor Jean McKelvey, my respected mentor and graduate committee chairman, who has inspired me to follow her example as both a scholar and a successful practitioner of industrial and labor relations.

Thanks go also to my newest teacher and present employer, Arvid Anderson, chairman of the New York City Office of Collective Bargaining, who, during our association, has given me greater insights into the issues discussed in this book and who has shown me how much I still need to learn. I shall always be grateful to him for being a patient and instructive "boss" and for allowing me to benefit from his vast experience in labor-management relations.

For my husband, Allan, I have a special, personal feeling of gratitude. His support has been unwavering, his helpfulness unlimited, and his love unbounded.

CONTENTS

Appendix

LIST OF ABBREVIATIONS

AASA	American Association of School Administrators
AFSCME	American Federation of State, County and Municipal Employees
AFT	American Federation of Teachers
HERB	Hawaii Public Employment Relations Board
HSTA	Hawaii State Teachers Association
MERC	Michigan Employment Relations Committee
NASSP	National Association of Secondary School Principals
NEA	National Education Association
NLRA	National Labor Relations Act
NLRB	National Labor Relations Board
NYSSBA	New York State School Boards Association
NYSTA	New York State Teachers Association
PERA	Public Employment Relations Act
PERB	Public Employment Relations Board

I

THE CONCEPT: ITS PRIVATE AND PUBLIC SECTOR DEVELOPMENT

What subjects are appropriate for collective bargaining in the public sector? Arvid Anderson notes that public employee organizations are pressing hard to bargain on and for "more."[1] Public management, on the other hand, fears an expansive scope of bargaining, for it implies bilateral determination of issues traditionally exclusively within managerial control. In the private sector the meaning of the phrase "wages, hours, and working conditions" has gradually been defined through National Labor Relations Board (NLRB) and court decisions. Today there is occasional disagreement about the "outer limits" of the scope of bargaining, but there is a broad area of agreement on the extent and range of subjects appropriate for collective bargaining. In public employment, however, we are just beginning the process of refinement in definition.

Public sector managers often see in collective bargaining the dissipation or abrogation of their authority. They also resist the process because in government, many managerial decisions are defined and shaped through the political processes to which their agencies are subject. Decisions about the extent and quality of agency services, and the priorities to be established among them, often are affected by interest groups that influence these decisions through the political process.[2]

Other scope-of-bargaining problems arise because, in many states, collective bargaining is superimposed on an existing civil service structure. This structure involves the establishment of local commissions that are authorized to promulgate rules and enforce compliance with the merit system. Over the years, however, merit systems have grown to encompass many aspects of labor relations and working conditions other than recruitment, classification, and promotion. These aspects include the processing of grievances, employee training, salary administration, and safety—subjects that most labor organizations consider appropriate for collective bargaining.[3] Bargaining difficulties frequently occur because many state laws do not specify whether control over these matters rests exclusively with civil service commissions, or whether public employee bargaining statutes empower local government executive officers to negotiate on these matters that are also "terms and conditions of employment."

The scope of bargaining is also a controversial subject because of the demands of some employee groups to bargain on issues that public managers have traditionally considered to be the sole prerogative of management. The issue of bargainable subject matter and the important distinction between "policy questions," on the one hand, and "working conditions," on the other, are very crucial where professionals are concerned.

Professional employees frequently want to bargain on professional standards and to participate in making decisions that affect their work and "clientele." They believe that their training and experience entitle them to have a voice in the determination of organizational policies. Teacher spokesmen, for example, have stated that there should be no restrictions on negotiable subject matter. As one teacher advocate contended, ". . . school boards will be forced to share authority to determine educational policies [as] teachers exert a claim of special competence to participate in decision-making over educational programs and services."[4]

There have been various responses to these developments. One has been to define, sometimes very narrowly, either by law or by administrative order, what subjects may be negotiated. However, it has been argued that if the scope of bargaining is too restricted, employee concerns are ignored, disputes arise over whether a subject is negotiable, and these items that are determined to be non-negotiable often appear in a different guise under a negotiable heading.[5] Moreover, too limited a scope will encourage employee organizations to press for statutory or administrative changes to expand the area of bargaining.

Another response has been to allow bargaining on the traditional "wages, hours, and working conditions" but to exclude from negotiations, through statutory management rights clauses, such policy issues as the mission of the agency. Although this approach may eliminate some controversies, problems still arise in determining which subjects fall within or outside the ambit of the management rights clause.

Experience indicates that neither of these responses is sufficient to cope with the demands that are made by public employee organizations, especially those of professionals. Besides, the answer to scope-of-bargaining problems does not lie in merely devising ways to prevent employee representatives from bringing their demands to the bargaining table. Employee organizations often have good ideas regarding the aims and operations of public agencies. To deny them the opportunity to voice their concerns may be as undesirable as allowing them to bargain about every item that strikes their fancy.

Lewis Kaden once related an incident that highlighted the need to resolve scope-of-bargaining problems:

I have heard a teachers' union president talk of his frustration at the bargaining table in dealing with the scope of negotiations. When he suggests that the discussion turn to wages, the Board of Education responds that they do not

4

control the purse. When he suggests that they negotiate
about room assignments, study hall responsibilities and
patrol obligations, the Board responds that these are subjects within the management prerogative. When he indicates
the teachers' desire to negotiate over curriculum development and experimental programming, the response is that
these are matters of policy.[6]

If collective bargaining is to be viable, the scope of negotiations must
include subjects that are relevant to employees. Placing excessive
restrictions on the scope of bargaining limits the institution of collective bargaining as a means of guaranteeing public employees a
voice in the determination of their working conditions. On the other
hand, too broad a scope of negotiations also can be detrimental to
meaningful bargaining. "Negotiating too many subjects may weaken
management's operating power, thus making it difficult, if not
impossible, for management to operate the organization."[7]

Private sector experience demonstrates that a precise line cannot be drawn between proper and improper subjects for collective
bargaining. Economic and technological developments have gradually
changed the status of certain subjects in the private sector. This
also may occur in the public sector, especially under the pressure
of the labor organizations representing professional workers. To
reconcile this pressure with our political process and the separation
of powers in government will present a difficult task during the next
few years.

The chapters in Part I of this study provide a conceptual background and a review of the laws and literature regarding the scope
of bargaining. The first two chapters trace the development of the
duty and scope of bargaining in the private sector. They also review
the important doctrines of sovereignty and of illegal delegation of
power, and their influence on the growth of public sector bargaining.
Chapter 3 summarizes state legislation with respect to the scope of
bargaining, and Chapter 4 analyzes the recommendations of various
expert study commissions as to how the scope of negotiations should
be defined in public employee bargaining laws. Chapter 5 is a review
of the literature on the scope of bargaining and a presentation of
alternative approaches that have been advocated by labor relations
experts, management, and labor organizations. Chapter 6 is an
intensive inquiry into the development of the scope of bargaining in
New York State under the Taylor Law. The chapter reviews the
legislative history of public employee bargaining and analyzes significant decisions of the Public Employment Relations Board and
courts concerning the scope of bargaining.

NOTES

1. Arvid Anderson, "Public Employees and Collective Bargaining: Comparative and Local Experience," in Thomas Christensen, ed., Proceedings of New York University Twenty-First Annual Conference on Labor, May, 1968 (New York: Matthew Bender, 1969), p. 464.

2. Arvid Anderson, Milton Derber, W. Donald Heisel, Martin Wagner, and Frank P. Zeidler, "Pending and Emerging Issues and Implications," in Committee on Executive Management and Fiscal Affairs, National Governors' Conference, 1970 Supplement to Report of Task Force on State and Local Government Labor Relations (Chicago: Public Personnel Association, 1971), p. 49.

3. Charles M. Rehmus and Russell A. Smith, "Labor Relations in State and Local Government in Michigan," ibid., p. 26.

4. Quoted in Wesley Wildman, "Collective Bargaining with Professionals in Public Employment," in Public Employee Relations Library, Perspective in Public Employee Negotiation (Chicago: Public Personnel Association, 1969), p. 48.

5. Anderson, Derber, et al., loc. cit., p. 49.

6. Lewis B. Kaden, "Collective Bargaining in the Private and Public Sectors, a Comparison," in Harold S. Roberts and John B. Ferguson, eds., Collective Bargaining and Dispute Settlement in the Public and Private Sectors, Proceedings of a Conference, July 31, 1969 (Honolulu: Industrial Relations Center, University of Hawaii, 1970), p. 20.

7. Michael H. Moskow, J. Joseph Loewenberg, and Edward Clifford Koziara, Collective Bargaining in Public Employment (New York: Random House, 1970), p. 239.

1

THE CONCEPTS OF
SOVEREIGNTY AND
ILLEGAL DELEGATION
OF AUTHORITY

SOVEREIGNTY AND THE ILLEGAL DELEGATION
OF AUTHORITY

For many years the Hobbesian concept of sovereignty provided the basis for the prohibition of collective bargaining in the public sector. The concept emanated from the English common law doctrine that the "king can do no wrong" and that no individual citizen could sue the state without its consent. Traditionally, sovereignty has been defined as the "supreme, absolute, and uncontrollable power by which any independent state is governed."[1] The sovereign, in turn, has been defined to mean the "person, body, or state in which independent and supreme authority is vested."[2] In this country the people historically have been regarded as sovereign, although their democratically elected federal, state, and local governments have, through practical necessity, exercised the sovereign will in their name.

Simply stated, the sovereignty doctrine holds that, as the sovereign employer, the government cannot be forced to accept any obligations it shuns or to continue to respect an agreement if it ultimately determines that it cannot or ought not. The government employer, therefore, contrasts sharply with the private employer, who must obey the law and cannot claim to represent a higher authority that permits him to define his own responsibilities.[3]

Collective bargaining has been regarded as inimical to the concept of sovereignty because it involves joint, rather than unilateral government, determination of employment conditions.[4] Moreover, unionization has been regarded as impermissible in public employment because a labor organization divides an employee's allegiance between itself and the government of which he is a loyal servant. This sentiment was expressed by Virginia's former governor, William M. Tuck:

7

> Unionization of the public service diverts the loyalty,
> allegiance and obligations of the employees from the
> people and their government which are entitled to them,
> to the union. . . . Such an intolerable situation is utterly
> incompatible with sound and orderly government. It
> constitutes a threat to state sovereignty.[5]

It also has been contended that there is a fundamental conflict between collective bargaining and the sovereignty doctrine because of the government's unique responsibility to act on behalf of all citizens within its jurisdiction. To the extent that collective bargaining can interfere with the governmental responsibility to maintain uninterrupted operations that promote the public weal, it is thought to be intolerable. The New York Supreme Court pointed this out in 1943 when it stated:

> Nothing is more dangerous to public welfare than to admit
> that hired servants of the State can dictate to the govern-
> ment the hours, the wages and conditions under which they
> will carry on essential services vital to the welfare,
> safety and security of the citizen. To admit as true that
> government employees have power to halt or check the
> functions of government, unless their demands are satis-
> fied, is to transfer to them all legislative, executive and
> judicial power. Nothing would be more ridiculous.[6]

In essence, then, sovereignty, as it applies to labor relations, refers to the government's power to fix, through law, the terms of its employees' employment. This power in unique, unalterable, and unilateral.

In reality, however, the strength of the sovereignty doctrine has slowly been ebbing. Legislation passed over the years by Congress and state legislatures has given individuals the right to sue government for redress of alleged injuries. New York's 1939 Court of Claims Act, for example, provides:

> The state hereby waives its immunity from liability and
> action and hereby assumes liability and consents to have
> the same determined in accordance with the same rules
> of law applied to action in the supreme court against
> individuals and corporations.[7]

Even without the benefit of legislation, the courts have eroded the sovereign immunity rule. As the Supreme Court of California observed:

The rule of governmental immunity for tort is an anach-
ronism, without rational basis, and has existed only by the
force of inertia. . . . The doctrine . . . was originally
court made. . . . Only the vestigial remains of . . . immunity
have survived; its requiem has long been foreshadowed.
For years the process of erosion . . . has gone on
unabated.[8]

In labor relations, too, the sovereignty doctrine has been stren-
uously attacked. Critics ask: If government grants the courts the
right to adjudicate certain types of disputes between the state and
private citizen and to award damages, which the state must pay, is
there really a much greater surrender of sovereignty when a legislature grants an arbitration tribunal, for example, the right to bind
the government in an agreement with its employees?
    A rather simple kind of logic has begun to emerge with respect
to sovereignty and labor relations. Inasmuch as the state is, indeed,
empowered to make policy in order to discharge its functions, there
is no reason why it cannot adopt a public personnel policy embodying
collective bargaining. As one critic of the sovereignty doctrine
writes, collective bargaining can be analogized to the situation in
which the sovereign authority has consented to suit—"an act which
in reality is a partial abdication of its sovereignty through the exercise of its sovereign power. To deny state governments this right
would be to deny their sovereignty."[9]
    The argument can be stated in yet another way. Since, in a
democracy, sovereignty reposes in the people, their elected representative in the legislature may authorize collective bargaining in
government without violating the sovereignty doctrine. The passage
of legislation specifically authorizing collective bargaining in the
public sector, therefore, represents the will of the polity.
    The arguments in favor of public service collective bargaining
become more compelling when one reflects on the progress of bargaining in the private sector during the past century. In The Case of
the Twenty Journeymen Tailors, People v. Faulkner, in New York
(1836), the court warned that if collective bargaining in the private
sector were "tolerated, the constitutional control over our affairs
would pass away from the people at large, and become vested in the
hands of conspirators. We should have a new system of government,
and our rights [would] be placed at the disposal of a voluntary and
self-constituted association."[10]
    Such sovereignty-rooted arguments against private sector col-
lective bargaining have long since been abandoned in favor of a
national labor policy supporting bargaining. Today those who argue
against collective negotiations between public employers and

employees may be accused of basing their conclusions on outmoded concepts (dating back to an era when government opposed all forms of employee organization and collective bargaining), adopting exceedingly narrow interpretations of governmental authority, or using the sovereignty doctrine as an excuse to avoid collective bargaining with unions. The proponents of public sector bargaining are correct in recognizing the inequities of granting full bargaining rights to private employees while simultaneously denying similar rights to public servants. As the American Bar Association has stated: "A government which imposed upon private employers certain obligations in dealing with their employees may not in good faith refuse to deal with its own public servants on a reasonably similar basis."[11]

In many states the sovereignty doctrine, at least with respect to labor relations, has been narrowed as new public employee collective bargaining laws have been passed. (See Chapter 3.)

This doctrine has not, however, been the only hindrance to the introduction of collective bargaining in the public sector. The related concept of the illegal delegation of power has proved even more elusive than, yet as fundamental as, the sovereignty doctrine to the understanding of governmental authority. Kurt Hanslowe states the concept thus:

> The argument is that for government to contract with a union or other employee organization concerning conditions of public employment constitutes an improper sharing, delegation, or abdication of governmental authority.[12]

Thus, whereas the sovereignty doctrine focuses on the issue of whether and to what extent government's power is supreme, the concept of illegal delegation of power refers to how government, as an employer, ought to exercise that power.

Those subscribing to this concept emphasize that the state, in fulfilling its duty to further the good of the polity, cannot share its governmental power with a private group. Moreover, the state cannot, in reality, bind itself in agreements with private associations because it must retain the legal authority to repudiate any of its commitments for the benefit and safety of the commonweal.[13] It is this interpretation of governmental responsibility that renders unlawful the notion of collective bargaining by public employers and employees, for the state can neither bargain away its power to govern nor give up its discretion in exercising its sovereignty.

Traditionally, however, government has entered into contracts with private parties; and the law, at all levels of government, has recognized this practice as necessary. In many respects the government resembles a business; it, too, must purchase supplies and contract for services necessary to maintain efficient operations.

But, as Hanslowe explains, the law, with respect to municipalities, for instance, distinguishes between contracts involving the "legislative" or "discretionary" powers of government and the "business" or "proprietary" contracts to which government may be a party:

> . . . where governmental discretionary powers are involved, a governing board can make no contract which would bind its successors in office with respect to the exercise of the discretion." This is not true of so-called proprietary contracts. "Generally contracts with gas, electric, water, telephone, and street railway services and rates are considered proprietary. . . . So, too, contracts for printing supplies, the removal of garbage, and sewage disposal. . . . Teachers and school administrators may ordinarily be employed for periods beyond the term of the contracting body. [14]

From this example it appears that the practical requirements of running government sanction the permissibility of proprietary contracts. If, however, a government agency may contract for garbage collection and for the employment of a school administrator, why should it not be free to do so for the services of teachers through an organization representing the latter?[15] Teachers sell a service that schools need and if, as the above quotation implies, contracts for the employment of teachers and administrators are proprietary, the real question is whether such contracts can be collective. At least one critic writes, "If a state can contract with one employee, there is no good reason to deny it the power to contract with two or more employees as a group."[16]

Moreover, whether or not a government employer bargains with individual workers or with their representative is an irrelevant consideration in determining whether or not the employer is illegally delegating its power. Failure to recognize this has led to the misuse of the doctrine of sovereignty as a prohibition against collective bargaining in the public sector. An employee of government may be called a public servant, but he is not a possession of government; government must buy his services just as it buys other goods and services. That government makes this purchase of employee services through an agent speaking for the collectivity does not mean that it has delegated its sovereignty or allowed a private party to act in its place. Admittedly, government may not legally delegate its authority on matters properly within its discretion, as defined by statute, nor abdicate its responsibilities to private parties. The negotiation of contracts for the salaries and services of personnel through an employee representative, however, lies within the discretion of a government employer. Additionally, the joint determination of conditions of employment need not compel a public employer to restrict its discretion to such an extent that it abdicates its duty to manage a public entity. The signing of a collective bargaining agreement does not represent a usurpation of the governmental authority but merely an agreement stipulating what compensation and conditions the employer will provide in return for the services its employees render.

THE MEANING OF THE DUTY TO BARGAIN

Additional light is shed on the subject of illegal delegation of authority if one reviews exactly what is required of a public employer under the duty to bargain. Assuming, for the moment, that an employer is obligated to bargain in good faith with respect to "wages, hours, and other terms and conditions of employment," it is helpful to look at the NLRB and federal court decisions specifying the behavior required by the dictate of good faith bargaining under the National Labor Relations Act (NLRA).[17] A review of these decisions, and the good faith criteria they have developed, will enable one to judge whether such standards, if imposed in the public sector, would infringe on government's legislative power.

Section 8(d) of the NLRA obligates employers and employee representatives to meet at reasonable times and confer in good faith with respect to wages, hours, and conditions of employment. Under the Taft-Hartley amendments, the following language was added to Section 8(d): ". . . but such obligation does not compel either party to agree to a proposal or require the making of a concession." Even under the Wagner Act, which did not contain this pronouncement regarding the making of concessions, the courts maintained that good faith bargaining did not require either party to concede. The law was interpreted, however, to require the parties to make efforts to reach agreement. As the Fourth Circuit in NLRB v. Highland Park Manufacturing declared:

> [T]he act, it is true, does not require that the parties agree;
> but it does require that they negotiate in good faith with the
> view of reaching an agreement if possible; and mere discussion with the representatives of employees, with a fixed
> resolve on the part of the employer not to enter into any
> agreement with them even as to matters as to which there
> is no disagreement, does not satisfy its provisions.[18]

This basic requirement still holds true. The duty to bargain in good faith is an "obligation . . . to participate actively in the deliberations so as to indicate a present intention to find a basis for agreement. . . ."[19] This implies both "an open mind and a sincere desire to reach an agreement" as well as "a sincere effort . . . to reach a common ground."[20]

Early cases also focused on the question of whether good faith bargaining required that each party make counterproposals in response to the other's demands. In 1941 the Third Circuit said that parties should justify their demands "on reason"; and if such reason fails to convince, the parties must be ready to compromise. But, it added, agreement through compromise cannot be effected unless the party rejecting his adversary's demand offers a counterproposal. "Refusal of an employer to make counterproposals on invitation of the union after rejecting the union's proposals may go to support a want of good faith on the part of the employer and hence a refusal to bargain. . . ."[21]

A review of the cases concerning failure to make counterproposals as evidence of bargaining in bad faith, both under the Wagner Act and later, reveals that an employer's refusals to counterpropose may indicate bad faith; but it is just one piece of evidence in the totality of employer conduct that may demonstrate that the employer did not come to the bargaining table with a genuine desire to reach agreement. As the Fourth Circuit noted in NLRB v. Stevenson Brick and Block Company,[22] except in the cases where the conduct fails to meet the minimum requirements established by law or constitutes an outright refusal to bargain, all the relevant facts of a case are studied in determining whether the employer or the union is bargaining in good or bad faith. The "totality of conduct" is the standard through which the "quality" of negotiations is measured.

In the area of good faith bargaining, the Board has experienced considerable difficulty when it has had to infer the employer's state of mind from the content of its bargaining proposals. This type of case raises delicate problems, because if the Board assumes that bargaining demands may indicate bad faith, it may involve itself too deeply in determining the desirability of certain items for inclusion in a bargaining agreement. In other words, what the Board considers a reasonable proposal is questionable as a standard for judging a party's good faith.

This issue was squarely confronted in NLRB v. American National Insurance Company,[23] a landmark decision involving management rights. In that case, during collective bargaining the union proposed a broad arbitration provision. Rejecting this proposal, management responded by proposing a management rights clause stipulating that all matters concerning hire, discharge, discipline, promotions, and work schedules would remain within management's exclusive control. The parties continued bargaining and eventually reached agreement on all other issues. The employer, however, remained adamant on the management rights clause; and the union subsequently filed charges with the Board, alleging the employer had violated Section 8(a)(5). The Board held that the employer's insistence on the management rights clause was per se violative of Section 8(a)(5), regardless of its good or bad faith. The Fifth Circuit refused to enforce the Board's decision;[24] and the Supreme Court affirmed the Fifth Circuit, holding that the employer's position represented neither a per se violation of its bargaining duty nor an indication of bad faith.

Chief Justice Fred Vinson, writing for the Court, reasoned that the parties' inability to reach agreement resulted not only from the employer's refusal to concede its proposal but also from the union's firmness in resisting the management rights clause. He noted that management functions clauses were contained in many collective agreements and were accepted solutions to labor disputes. According to the Court, the degree of employee participation in the setting of standards regulating negotiable subjects must itself be a bargainable issue. Although the Court recognized that an excessively broad management rights clause might reflect an employer's efforts to avoid its statutory bargaining duty, it argued that such occasional abuse did not warrant a blanket prohibition against the negotiability of all management functions provisions.

American National Insurance is significant because it reaffirmed the principle that a party's subjective intent must be judged, not only on the basis of its hard bargaining on a crucial issue but also on the totality of its conduct. Of even greater importance, however, was the Supreme Court's confirmation of the Board's lack of authority to regulate the substantive terms of a bargaining agreement. As one commentator noted, the Court by implication reiterated the Board's role: "Somewhere between the bargainer's right to remain adamant and his obligation to bargain in good faith is a grey area in which the content of his proposals is relevant, and the Board must devise flexible standards that are based on this conception."[25]

Applying these private sector determinations to public employment, one may argue that unless a government employer demonstrates through various actions that it has no intention of negotiating an agreement, it may, without violating the good faith duty, refuse to make a concession or counterproposal in response to a union demand. Furthermore, it may propose and bargain hard on a management functions clause. Resistance on one or more items when the whole record indicates no intention to avoid the duty to bargain is not a violation of the good faith obligation. In this sense collective bargaining per se does not infringe upon governmental authority or compel a delegation of governmental power to a private party.[26]

The decisional law on the duty to bargain indicates that an employer need not always show that it bargained in good faith but, rather, that at least it did not bargain in bad faith. This reasoning is in line with the concept that an employer may violate Section

8(a)(5) if its behavior indicates "a desire not to reach agreement." This reasoning also establishes a collective bargaining "mood," to use Harry Wellington's word,[27] that respects the statutory duty to bargain and, at the same time, "is gentle to freedom of contract." Judge Calvert Magruder, commenting in Reed and Prince, also focused his concern on bad faith bargaining:

> . . . Thus if an employer can find nothing whatever to agree to in an ordinary current-day contract submitted to him, or in some of the union's related minor requests, and if the employer makes not a single serious proposal meeting the union at least part way, then certainly the Board must be able to conclude that this is at least evidence of bad faith.[28]

Bad faith has also been inferred from a party's refusal to supply necessary and relevant information to the other party, from the adoption of a "take it or leave it" attitude, and from a party's declaration that it will not sign an agreement unless it includes certain or all of that party's demands.

In NLRB v. White,[29] the Fifth Circuit dealt with the following question: Can employer bad faith be inferred if the employees' bargaining agent completes negotiations having gained little of value? The court said no, referring to American National Insurance, wherein the Supreme Court said that the Board could not sit in judgment of the substantive terms of a bargaining agreement. The Fifth Circuit did, nevertheless, qualify its decision by stating that it did "not hold that under no possible circumstances can the mere content of the various proposals and counterproposals of management and union be sufficient evidence of want of good faith to justify a holding to that effect." The Court thus recognized that occasionally demands are so unreasonable or objectionable as to frustrate any serious negotiation.

If the state courts adjudicating public employment disputes adopt reasoning similar to that developed in the private sector with respect to good faith bargaining (and there is much reason to assume they will in many cases),[30] a government employer may bargain hard; and unless its offers to a union are flagrantly unreasonable or humiliating, it will not be found guilty of refusing to bargain in good faith. The basic test to determine whether the techniques required by the duty of good faith bargaining constitute an invasion of governmental authority, and a consequent illegal delegation of power, is whether the public employer must capitulate to all union demands. Clearly, collective bargaining does not compel capitulation, even in the private sector, where the employer is not the guardian of the public welfare.

If the doctrine of illegal delegation of power should not persist as a bar to all collective bargaining in public employment, what aspects of governmental authority, if any, should this doctrine govern? Harry Wellington and Ralph Winter offer a meaningful comment:

> The doctrine of illegal delegation commands that certain
> discretionary decisions be made solely on the basis of
> the judgment of a designated official.[31]

According to Wellington and Winter, because collective bargaining implies some sharing of control by management and union, there is a possibility that an item of crucial importance to the public interest could be sacrificed to the politics and power struggles of the collective bargaining process. Therefore, some public policy limitations are necessary to prevent the sharing of those powers that must, for the good of the commonweal, reside in the government alone.

Wellington and Winter correctly define the doctrine of illegal delegation of power; they do not contend that it should prevent all bargaining in public employment, but only that it should regulate the subjects over which public employers and unions may bargain. But this correct definition of the doctrine of illegal delegation does not, necessarily, speak for the validity of the concept. Other students of labor relations contend that in the public sector, as well as in the private sector, the only rational determinants of the scope of bargaining should be the relative strengths of the parties and their desires. Whether or not the scope of bargaining in public employment should be limited, whether such limitations should be statutorily or contractually specified, and what specific subjects should be excluded from the scope of bargaining are questions that this study will explore.

NOTES

1. Black's Law Dictionary, rev. 4th ed., p. 1568.
2. Ibid.
3. Felix A. Nigro, Management-Employee Relations in the Public Service (Chicago: Public Personnel Association, 1969), p. 26.
4. See Wilson R. Hart, Collective Bargaining in the Federal Service (New York: Harper & Row, 1961), p. 44.
5. Allan Weisenfeld, "Public Employees—First or Second Class Citizens," 16 Labor Law Journal 685, at 687 (1965).
6. Railway Mail Ass'n. v. Murphy, 180 Miss. 868, at 875, 44 N.Y.S. 2d 601, at 607 (Sup. Ct. 1943); rev'd. on other grounds sub. nom. Railway Mail Ass'n. v. Corsi, 267 App. Div. 470; aff'd., 293 N.Y. 315, 56 N.E. 2d 721; aff'd., 326 U.S. 88 (1945).
7. Kurt L. Hanslowe, The Emerging Law of Labor Relations in Public Employment (Ithaca, N.Y.: New York State School of Industrial and Labor Relations, Cornell University, 1967), p. 18.

8. Muskopf v. Corning Hospital District, 55 Cal. 2d 211-221 passim, 359 P. 2d 457-463 passim (1961); quoted in Hanslowe, op. cit., p. 19.

9. William J. Kilberg, "Appropriate Subjects for Bargaining in Local Government Labor Relations," 30 Maryland Law Review 179, at 181 (1970).

10. Courier and Enquirer, May 31, 1836, reproduced in 4 Commons and Gilmore, A Documentary History of American Industrial Society 315, at 322 (1910), as quoted in H.H. Wellington and R.K. Winter, "The Limits of Collective Bargaining in Public Employment," 78 Yale Law Journal 1107, at 1109-10 (1969).

11. American Bar Association, Second Report of the Committee on Labor Relations of Governmental Employees (1955), p. 125.

12. Hanslowe, op. cit., p. 21.

13. Hart, op. cit., p. 53.

14. Hanslowe, op. cit., p. 22.

15. Ibid., p. 23.

16. Kilberg, loc. cit.

17. Except in 8(d) the Act does not define what kind of behavior is required under the duty to bargain or what is meant by "good faith." In the private sector the concept of good faith bargaining has been evolving for almost a generation, as the NLRB and courts have, through hundreds of cases, attempted to read meaning into the law's requirement to bargain in good faith with respect to "wages, hours, and other terms and conditions of employment." Numerous legal essays have also been written on this topic. See, for example, Archibald Cox, "The Duty to Bargain in Good Faith," 71 Harvard Law Review 1401 (1958); R.P. Duvin, "The Duty to Bargain: Law in Search of Policy," 64 Columbia Law Review 248 (1964); Nathan Feinsinger, "The National Labor Relations Act and Collective Bargaining," 57 Michigan Law Review 807 (1959); Fleming, "The Obligation to Bargain in Good Faith," 16 Southwest Law Journal 43 (1962); Note, "Adamant Insistence on a Management Functions Clause as a Refusal to Bargain Collectively," 52 Columbia Law Review 1054 (1952).

18. 110 F.2d 632, at 637, 6 LRRM 786 (CA 4, 1940).

19. NLRB v. Montgomery Ward and Co., 133 F.2d 676, 12 LRRM 598 (CA 9, 1943).

20. Ibid. at 686. See also NLRB v. Reed & Prince Mfg. Co., 205 F.2d 131, at 134-35, 32 LRRM 225 (CA 1, 1953), where the court said:

[W]hile the Board cannot force an employer to make a concession on any specific issue or to adopt any particular position, the employer is obligated to make some reasonable effort in some direction to compose his differences with the union, if section 8(a)(5) is to be read as imposing any substantial obligation at all.

17

21. NLRB v. George P. Pilling & Son Co., 119 F.2d 32, at 37 (CA 3, 1941).

22. 393 F.2d 234, 68 LRRM 2086 (CA 4, 1968).

23. 343 U.S. 395 (1952).

24. 187 F.2d 307, 27 LRRM 2405 (CA 5, 1951).

25. Robert P. Duvin, "The Duty to Bargain: Law in Search of Policy," 64 Columbia Law Review 248, at 261 (1964).

26. Of course, it is probable that once a party enters into good faith negotiations, it will voluntarily make counterproposals. But since no compulsion is involved, there can be no issue of violation of governmental authority. For further elaboration of this argument, see Reynolds Seitz, "School Board Authority and the Right of the Public School Teachers to Negotiate—A Legal Analysis," 22 Vanderbilt Law Review 239 (1969).

27. Harry Wellington, Labor and the Legal Process (New Haven: Yale University Press, 1968). Professor Wellington is concerned about collective bargaining law and its occasional restriction of the parties' freedom of contract. At one point he notes that although the NLRB cannot ignore the reasonableness of proposals, a party can be unreasonable without violating the NLRA. "By and large only the party bargaining with a desire not to reach agreement is guilty of an unfair practice. From time to time concern with freedom of contract allows even such a wrongdoer to escape without sanction."

28. NLRB v. Reed & Prince Mfg. Co., at 134.

29. 255 F.2d 564 (CA 5, 1958).

30. As one commentator suggests, ". . . it is conceivable, based upon . . . the common law of labor relations, that a court will decide that a refusal to bargain is an unfair labor practice not permitted to any employer, including the states and their political subdivisions." Note, 19 Catholic Law Review 361, at 365 (1970).

31. Wellington and Winter, op. cit., p. 1109.

2

LEGISLATIVE HISTORY

Section 8(5) of the Wagner Act imposed upon employers a duty to bargain but did not specifically define the subjects of collective bargaining. It simply referred to Section 9(a), which provided, inter alia, that representatives designated or selected by the employees in an appropriate unit would be exclusive for the purposes of collective bargaining in respect to "rates of pay, wages, hours of employment, or other conditions of employment. . . ." Because the law went no further in clarifying the scope of bargaining, the NLRB very early assumed the responsibility for determining what were compulsory subjects for bargaining.[1] For example, in 1940, the Board held in Singer Manufacturing Company:

> . . . paid holidays, vacations, and bonuses constitute an integral part of the earnings and working conditions of the employees and . . . are matters which are generally the subject of collective bargaining. . . . [I]nsistence upon treating such matters as gratuities to be granted and withdrawn at will constitutes a refusal to bargain. . . .[2]

During the Wagner Act period the Board also held that the following subjects were mandatory bargaining items: discharges, pensions, profit sharing, work loads and work standards, insurance benefits, union security clauses, subcontracting, shop rules, work schedules, rest periods, and merit increases.[3]

Congressional concern regarding the Board's determinations prompted the House of Representatives to approve a proposed section of the Labor Management Relations Act of 1947 enumerating the compulsory subjects of bargaining.[4] The list was thought necessary to narrow the expansive scope of bargaining, which the Board had been developing, to those items of "mutual" concern to employers and unions. The aim was to curb labor's encroachment into the traditional realm of unilateral, managerial decisions. A minority on the House Committee on Education and Labor believed, however, that such a list, if enacted, would preclude bargaining about "a host of other matters" that traditionally had been negotiated in several industries.[5] The NLRB also urged the exclusion of such a list from the Act. In a statement made in 1947 to the Senate committee considering amendments to the Wagner Act, NLRB Chairman Paul Herzog said that the scope of bargaining "depends upon the industry's customs and history, the previously existing employer-employee relationship, technological problems and demands, and other factors." He also noted that the scope might "vary with changes in industrial structure and practice."[6] He suggested that the task of defining the scope of bargaining should remain with the Board, subject only to judicial review.

The language ultimately adopted in the 1947 amendments to the Act, with respect to subjects of bargaining, closely resembled the original provisions. Eliminating the redundant term "rates of pay" and adding the word "terms" to conditions of employment, Congress defined collective bargaining in Section 8(d) to include "wages, hours, and other terms and conditions of employment." In so doing, Congress preserved for the NLRB the task of defining the subjects of bargaining.

DECISIONAL HISTORY

NLRB v. Borg-Warner

The landmark decision of NLRB v. Wooster Division of Borg-Warner Corp.[7] established, for the first time, a distinction between mandatory and permissive subjects of bargaining. In this case the employer had insisted, during collective bargaining, upon the union's acceptance of proposed "recognition" and "ballot" clauses. The recognition clause would have denied recognition to the local union's parent international union, which had been certified by the Board, and granted contractual recognition to the local union only. The ballot clause stipulated that with respect to nonarbitrable disputes, after a negotiation period a secret ballot on the employer's last offer would be held among employees in the bargaining unit. If the employees rejected this offer, the employer would have had 72 hours to alter his offer. If the employees rejected the new offer after a second vote, the union would have been allowed to strike.

The Board found that although Borg-Warner's insistence on these two clauses did not indicate bad faith, it was a per se violation of Section 8(a)(5). Holding that the employer's proposed provisions were only permissive subjects of bargaining, the Board equated Borg-Warner's insistence on them with a refusal to bargain on a mandatory subject. The Sixth Circuit refused to enforce this aspect of the decision;[8] but the Supreme Court, in a five to four decision, reversed and upheld the Board's determination.[9] Confirming the Board, the Court said:

> . . . good faith does not license the employer to refuse to enter into agreements on the ground that they do not include some proposal which is not a mandatory subject of bargaining. . . . [S]uch conduct is . . . a refusal to bargain about the subjects that are within the scope of mandatory bargaining. This does not mean that bargaining is to be confined to the statutory subjects. Each of the two controversial clauses is lawful in itself. . . . But it does not follow that, because the company may propose these clauses, it may lawfully insist upon them as a condition of any agreement.[10]

Thus, from the Borg-Warner decision there emerged three categories of bargaining subjects: statutory, or mandatory, subjects about which the parties must bargain; nonstatutory, or permissive, subjects about which the parties may bargain; and illegal subjects about which the parties are legally prohibited from bargaining.[11]

Reading Sections 8(a)(5) and 8(d) together, the Supreme Court held:

> These provisions establish the obligation of the employer and the representative of its employees to bargain with respect to "wages, hours, and other terms and conditions of employment. . . ." The duty is limited to those subjects, and within that area neither party is legally obligated to yield. . . . As to other matters, however, each party is free to bargain or not to bargain, and to agree or not to agree.[12]

Justice John Harlan, writing the dissenting opinion, opposed the Court's conclusion that bargaining prohibited a party from insisting on a permissive subject. He wrote:

> The Act sought to compel management and labor to meet and bargain in good faith as to certain topics. This is the affirmative requirement of section 8(d) which the Board is specifically empowered to enforce, but I see no warrant for inferring from it any power in the Board to prohibit

bargaining in good faith as to lawful matters not included in section 8(d). The Court reasons that such conduct on the part of the employer, when carried to the point of insistence, is in substance equivalent to a refusal to bargain as to statutory subjects, but I cannot understand how this can be said over the Trial Examiner's unequivocal finding that the employer did in fact bargain in "good faith," not only over the disputed clauses but also over the statutory subjects. . . . It must not be forgotten that the Act requires bargaining, not agreement. . . .[13]

Justice Harlan admitted that insistence on certain permissive subjects might "be so extreme as to constitute some evidence of an unwillingness to bargain"; but in such circumstances, he maintained, the good faith standard could have disposed of the issue.[14]

The Borg-Warner decision also may be criticized in that the Court failed to provide either sufficient rationale to support the mandatory-permissive-illegal categorization or specific criteria for determining under which category a subject will fall. The only criterion clearly spelled out is that a provision that "regulates the relations between the employer and the employees" is a mandatory subject, whereas a clause that "deals only with the internal relations between the employees and their unions" is permissive.

In the private sector the scope of bargaining is tightly interwoven with the duty to bargain. The phrase "wages, hours, and other terms and conditions of employment"

. . . fixes not only the subjects about which the employer and the union are compelled by law to bargain but also the field in which (1) the employer is barred from unilateral action and (2) the employee is excluded from making his own individual agreement with the employer. . . .[15]

Thus, an employer's unilateral changes concerning mandatory subjects of bargaining during the life of a collective bargaining agreement have been held to be per se violations of the duty to bargain. The Board and courts have ruled similarly in cases in which an employer bargained directly with his employees, such actions having been interpreted as attempts to undermine a union's status as bargaining representative.[16] While such employer actions bypassing the union may be strong evidence of a lack of good faith, the Board and courts have tended to view them in terms of the per se rule. Under this approach, it has been held that inasmuch as the NLRA authorizes collective representation, any repudiation or circumvention of the basic requirement can constitute an independent unfair practice, regardless of a party's state of mind (good or bad faith).*

Although the per se analysis was used often after the passage of the Taft-Hartley Act, it was not until the 1962 case of NLRB v. Katz[17] that the Supreme Court expressly recognized the existence and validity of the per se doctrine. In Katz the employer during negotiations unilaterally changed sick leave policy, general wage increase policy, and merit wage increase policy—all conditions of employment that have been held to be mandatory subjects of bargaining. The Supreme Court, upholding the Board's determination that such changes per se violated Section 8(a)(5), declared:

> The duty "to bargain collectively" . . . is defined by Section 8(d). . . . Clearly, the duty thus defined may be violated without a general failure of subjective good faith; for there is no occasion to consider the issue of good faith if a party has refused even to negotiate in fact—"to meet . . . and confer"—about any of the mandatory subjects. A refusal to negotiate in fact as to any subject which is within Section 8(d) and about which the union seeks to negotiate, violates Section 8(a)(5) though the employer has every desire to reach agreement with the union in an over-all collective agreement and earnestly and in all good faith bargains to that end.[18]

The phrase "wages, hours, and other terms and conditions of employment" has proved deceptively simple, and for the last 35 years the Board and courts have been determining what and how much are embraced by this statutory provision. Frank McCulloch, Chairman of the NLRB during the Kennedy and Johnson administrations, has noted that the phrase "wages, hours, and other terms and conditions of employment" has been consistently expanded, but not on the basis of any hard and fast rules:

> Lying at the heart of our Act is the requirement that employers and unions engage in good faith bargaining concerning "wages, hours, and other terms and conditions of employment." All agree that this statutory phrase was not intended to permit one party to handcuff the subjects of collective bargaining to conditions existing at the time of

---

*During the Wagner Act period this same category of cases existed, but the distinction did not begin to emerge until the passage of the Taft-Hartley amendments added the good faith requirement separately from the general duty to bargain requirement.

the law's enactment. The content of this term expands with time.

Obviously no rubric or rule of thumb can demarcate the line between mandatory and permissive bargaining. No verbal niceties, no system of metes and bounds, will do justice to the needs of our pulsating, industrial society. Again we resort to the pragmatic, ad hoc approach. . . .[19]

Hours of employment have caused little difficulty in the area of mandatory subjects of bargaining, and there have been few cases on this topic. The category of wages has been broadly interpreted to cover every form of compensation for labor performed: piece rates, incentive plans, shift differentials, paid holidays, severance pay, overtime pay, Christmas bonuses, pensions, profit sharing plans, stock purchase plans, and merit wage increases. Distinguishing between mandatory and permissive subjects of bargaining under the phrase "other terms and conditions of employment" has been the Board's most demanding task regarding the scope of bargaining. It is beyond the boundaries of this chapter to embark on a detailed review of Board and court decisions. Suffice it to say that the Board has held mandatory subjects of bargaining to include provisions for grievance and arbitration procedures, layoffs, discharge, work loads, vacations, holidays, sick leave, work rules, a no-strike clause, use of bulletin boards by unions, seniority, retirement age, and union security.

A management rights clause also is a mandatory subject of bargaining, although the decisional law on this issue indicates that an employer's insistence on such a clause can, if interrelated with other factors, lead to a finding of bad faith. Admittedly, American National Insurance held that an employer who insists on a management rights clause covering terms and conditions of employment does not commit a per se violation of Section 8(a)(5), and the Board may not rule on the desirability of the substantive terms of an agreement. The Board must determine in each case whether the good faith requirements of Section 8(d) have been met.[20] Nevertheless, in Dixie Corp.,[21] an employer who had insisted on unilateral control of all subjects of bargaining as a condition precedent to agreement, in the context of refusing to supply relevant data to the union and refusing to accept the appropriate bargaining unit, was found guilty of refusing to bargain in good faith. In another case an employer who insisted on a detailed management rights clause that reserved absolute unilateral control of virtually every significant term and condition of employment, coupled with a limitation of grievances and arbitration to the express terms of the contract and a waiver of bargaining, was held in violation of Section 8(a)(5).[22] These cases indicate that although management rights clauses are mandatory subjects of bargaining, they may justify a finding of bad faith if they are excessively broad or are proposed in conjunction with other sweeping demands.

Permissive subjects of bargaining may be negotiated and included in a collective agreement. A party's decision to bargain on such a subject waives neither his right to claim later that the item is, in fact, permissive rather than mandatory nor his right to refuse to include the item in the final agreement. As the Fourth Circuit stated:

> A determination that a subject which is non-mandatory at the outset may become mandatory merely because a party had exercised this freedom [to bargain or not to bargain] by not rejecting the proposal at once . . . might unduly discourage free bargaining on non-mandatory subjects.[23]

Although even in its early days, the Board held that parties were permitted, but not legally obligated, to negotiate on certain issues, since Borg-Warner the Board has dealt extensively with the matter of permissive subjects of bargaining. Items that it has ruled permissive include definition of a bargaining unit, parties to a collective bargaining agreement, performance bonds, internal union affairs, and union label.

Fibreboard and Its Progeny

Few labor relations issues have sparked as much controversy in recent years as has the question of whether or not an employer must bargain with the union about decisions to subcontract work. In Fibreboard Paper Products Corp. v. NLRB,[24] the Supreme Court answered this question affirmatively, upholding the Board's decision that subcontracting was a mandatory subject of bargaining that an employer must bargain to impasse with the union before unilaterally contracting out work that could be done by his own employees. Prior to this decision the Board had generally held that an employer was not obligated to hold discussions with the union on economically motivated decisions to subcontract work. Although its decisions were not always consistent, the Board most often held that an employer's unilateral decision to subcontract work violated Section 8(a)(5) only when the purpose was to discourage union membership or completely avoid his obligation to negotiate.[25] In the absence of antiunion animus, the employer's only duty was to bargain about the effects of the decision on his employees and not about the decision itself.[26] The Fibreboard decision therefore represented a shift in the Board's policy regarding nondiscriminatory, economically motivated decisions to contract out work.

The employer in Fibreboard, having determined that the subcontracting of its maintenance work could result in significant savings, informed the union representing the maintenance employees of its decision to subcontract the work. Soon afterward

25

the employer terminated the employment of all of its maintenance workers, and the union responded by filing charges of an unfair labor practice against the company, alleging violations of Sections 8(a)(1) and 8(a)(5).

When the Board first ruled on Fibreboard, it followed established precedent and dismissed the union's charges because the company's motive in subcontracting was economically based rather than discriminatory. A year later, however, the Board again faced a subcontracting problem, and in Town and Country Mfg. Co.[27] it reversed its Fibreboard decision. Although in Town and Country the employer's decision to subcontract its hauling operations was prompted by a desire to avoid bargaining with the union, the Board held that even if the subcontracting decision had been economically motivated, the unilateral decision constituted a violation of Section 8(a)(5). The Fifth Circuit affirmed the Board's decision, but only on the grounds that the employer's subcontracting decision was motivated, at least in part, by a desire to avoid its bargaining duty; the court was silent on the latter issue.

In light of Town and Country, the Board, on rehearing, reversed its first Fibreboard decision and ordered the company to reinstate the terminated maintenance employees and to bargain with their union. Both the D.C. circuit court and the Supreme Court affirmed the Board's decision and order.

Interestingly, although the Supreme Court was unanimous in affirming the Board, the decision for the Court, written by Chief Justice Earl Warren, and the concurring opinion, written by Justice Potter Stewart, indicate that the justices were not of one mind with respect to the larger problems posed by the case.

Chief Justice Warren gave three major reasons for upholding the Board. First, subcontracting fell "well within the literal meaning of the phrase 'terms and conditions of employment.'" Fibreboard's decision resulted in the termination and replacement of employees who were capable of doing the subcontracted work. Clearly, management's decision to contract the maintenance work substantially affected its employees' job security. Although the company viewed subcontracting as a means of achieving savings through a reduction of the work force, decreased fringe benefits, and lower wages, the unilateral decision was, in effect, an abrogation of its duty to bargain about such matters with the representative of its employees. An employee's right to have a voice in the determination of wages and benefits is reduced to naught if the employer is allowed unilaterally to replace its employees with others to perform the same jobs for less.[28]

Second, the Court believed that the ability of collective bargaining to mitigate the adverse impact on union members of an employer's decision affecting their employment is adequate reason for subjecting that decision to the bargaining process. Warren emphasized that because the company was concerned about reducing the costs of its maintenance operation and little else (that is, there was no capital investment involved and the plant's basic operations were not to be altered), collective bargaining might have resulted in an agreement that would have satisfied the company's objective and, at the same time, been acceptable to the union. As Warren explained, one of the major purposes of the Act was to encourage peaceful settlement of disputes by subjecting labor-management controversies to the mediatory influence of negotiation:

> To hold, as the Board has done, that contracting out is a mandatory subject of collective bargaining would promote the fundamental purpose of the Act by bringing a problem of vital concern to labor and management within the framework established by Congress as most conducive to industrial peace.[29]

Third, the Chief Justice suggested that the "conclusion that 'contracting out' is a statutory subject of collective bargaining is further reinforced by industrial practices in this country. While not determinative, it is appropriate to look at industrial bargaining practices in appraising the propriety of including a particular subject within the scope of mandatory bargaining."

The Chief Justice maintained that the Fibreboard holding was limited to "the facts of this case." He emphasized that the Court's decision "need not and does not encompass other forms of 'contracting out' or 'subcontracting' which arise daily in our complex economy."

The language and rationale of the Court's decision were, nevertheless, broad and conducive to expansive interpretation. As one critic remarked, "It is difficult to understand why most subjects that meet the Chief Justice's industrial practice test would not be classified as mandatory. Most subjects that are likely to be raised during collective bargaining can be brought within the literal language of the statute; and the industrial peace rationale applies across the board."[30]

Perhaps a similar recognition of the broad implications of the Court's decision prompted Justice Potter Stewart to write his concurring opinion (joined by Justices John Harlan and William Douglas):

> Viewed broadly, the question before us stirs large issues. The Court purports to limit its decision to the "facts of this case." But the Court's opinion radiates implications of such disturbing breadth that I am persuaded to file this separate statement of my own view.[31]

Justice Stewart's concurrence rested on the fact that Fibreboard involved the replacement of one group of workers with others who performed the same jobs under similar conditions. The facts in Fibreboard therefore resembled those of a case in which the employer, to avoid his bargaining obligation, terminated workers and replaced them with others willing to work for less compensation—in violation of Section 8(a)(5).[32] Management decisions "which are fundamental to the basic direction of a corporate enterprise or which impinge only indirectly upon employment security" were, in Justice Stewart's view, excluded from the bargaining area defined by Section 8(d). Referring to the facts in Fibreboard, he stated:

> This kind of subcontracting falls short of such larger entre-
> preneurial questions as what shall be produced, how capital
> shall be invested . . . or what the basic scope of the enter-
> prise shall be. In my view, the Court's decision in this case
> has nothing to do with whether any aspects of those larger
> issues could under any circumstances be considered sub-
> jects of compulsory collective bargaining. . . .[33]

Thus, the actual meaning of the Fibreboard decision emerges through a conjunctive reading of the Warren and Stewart opinions. The holding of Fibreboard is that an employer must negotiate in good faith with the union about subcontracting of the sort that occurred in that case. An employer who acts unilaterally prior to bargaining commits a violation of Section 8(a)(5). At the same time, however, the Fibreboard decision indicates that the union, in bargaining over subcontracting, should attempt to present an alternative that satisfies management's needs or accept management's decision and confine itself to negotiating on ways in which the detrimental effects of management's decision can be reduced. Furthermore, under Fibreboard the parties do not have to reach agreement; if they cannot, once management has fulfilled its bargaining duty, it can act unilaterally. Finally, the American National Insurance decision, applied in conjunction with Fibreboard, indicates that the employer has the right to bargain in good faith for unilateral control of future subcontracting, should the need arise.[34]

Although it is herein maintained that the Fibreboard holding was a narrow one, many have interpreted it to mean that all management decisions having "substantial impact on any of the union's traditional concerns are proper subjects for mandatory bargaining."[35] Indeed, the Board has been criticized for opening the way for practically unrestricted infringement on management rights.[36] The post-Fibreboard record of cases, however, indicates that the Board has not given an expansive reading to the Fibreboard holding. It has proceeded cautiously, using a case-by-case approach, in an effort to adopt a flexible system adaptable to the facts of each case. The Board described this approach in Shell Oil:[37]

> The principles of [Fibreboard] . . . are not meant to be
> hard and fast rules to be mechanically applied irrespective
> of the circumstances of the case. In applying these prin-
> ciples, we are mindful that the permissibility of unilateral
> subcontracting will be determined by a consideration of
> the setting of each case.[38]

This declaration recognizes that occasionally the duty to bargain
over subcontracting is extremely burdensome to an employer, particularly if the company lets many subcontracts per year (the Westinghouse Electric Corporation, for example, subcontracted more
than 5,000 pieces of work in a single year[39]) or if the company must
act quickly on a decision in order to meet an emergency. From the
Fibreboard line of cases have emerged, therefore, a series of circumstances that, if present, will excuse an employer from bargaining
on a subcontracting decision during the contract period:[40]

1. The contract included either a "management rights" clause
or a provision that could be interpreted as an indication of the
parties' intention to allow unilateral subcontracting by management.[41]

2. The subcontracting in dispute complied with the traditional
means by which the employer operated his business and did not vary
in degree or kind from subcontracting other work under the firm's
established past practice.[42]

3. The union had a chance to negotiate about changes in existing
subcontracting practices at the regular bargaining sessions with
the employer.[43]

4. The subcontracting involved had no demonstrable adverse
impact on the employees in the bargaining unit.[44]

5. The exigencies of the particular business decision required
unilateral action.[45]

All of these factors do not have to be present in a given case;
the presence of only one, however, may not be sufficient to excuse
an employer from the duty to bargain about a subcontracting decision.
What is necessary is a showing that the union has waived its right to
bargain on subcontracting because of the existence of a contractual
management rights clause, that the union has traditionally acquiesced
to unilateral management decisions on subcontracting, and/or that
the union was at least given sufficient notice about the subcontracting
plans so that it could have raised any objections during the preceding
contract negotiations.

On the other hand, in order to prove that an employer has violated Section 8(a)(5), a union must, at the very least, satisfy the
threshold requirement of detriment.[46] A showing that management's
subcontracting decision has inflicted substantial harm on employees
of the bargaining unit is, logically, the most important consideration
in a subcontracting case. Because negotiating a decision is generally
more costly than making a decision unilaterally, it would not make

sense to force the employer to negotiate unless (1) employees would actually be harmed if management subcontracted the work in question and (2) this adverse impact on the employees could, through bargaining, be mitigated.

One very controversial case in the Fibreboard line (although it actually was first litigated prior to the Supreme Court's decision in Fibreboard) is Adams Dairy Company.[47] The employer there had been engaged in selling milk and dairy products to retail outlets through both driver-salesmen and independent contractors. In the face of severe competition, however, it decided to change its entire distribution system to an independent contractor arrangement. It informed the union of its decision and terminated the employment of all of its driver-salesmen. Though the Board conceded the economic justification for this change, it ordered Adams to reinstate the drivers with back pay and to bargain, upon union request, over the decision to transfer its delivery operations to independent contractors.[48] The Eighth Circuit reversed the Board, and the Supreme Court remanded the case to the Eighth Circuit with instructions to reconsider its original holding in light of Fibreboard. The Eighth Circuit sustained its original decision, however, holding that, unlike Fibreboard, in Adams Dairy (1) the company changed basic operations and eliminated a part of its business (rather than merely substituting for its own employees those of another employer) and (2) there was a change in capital structure and a recoupment of capital investment. The court also exonerated the employer because its decision was economically motivated and not stimulated by anti-union animus.[49]

The Board and courts also have disagreed on whether an employer must bargain over subcontracting during a strike. In Hawaii Meat Company[50] the Ninth Circuit overruled the Board and held that an employer did not have to negotiate with a union over subcontracting during a work stoppage. In a subsequent decision the Board held that an employer was not obligated to negotiate over subcontracting work of a bargaining unit during a strike if the facts indicated that the employer viewed the arrangement as a temporary action taken to maintain existing business relationships.[51]

Several cases involving the question of whether under Section 8(a)(5) an employer must bargain over a partial closing of its business or a plant relocation have hinged on interpretations of the Fibreboard and Darlington Manufacturing Company[52] decisions. In Darlington the Supreme Court held that an employer may close his entire business for any reason, including anti-union motivation. However, a partial closing intended to "chill unionism" violates Section 8(a)(3). The Supreme Court's decision did not specifically rule on whether an employer must bargain about an economically motivated decision to close part of a business.

However, in Adams Dairy, as noted above, the Eighth Circuit relied on the employer's lack of anti-union animus as one of the reasons for not requiring him to bargain over his economically motivated decision to "close part of his business" and subcontract the work in question. In a similar decision, NLRB v. William J. Burns International Detective Agency,[53] the Eighth Circuit again reversed the Board and held that an employer who had unilaterally closed a division for economic reasons did not have to bargain, because it had neither engaged in subcontracting per se nor demonstrated an anti-union animus. The court held that under the Darlington rationale,

> . . . the finding of lack of anti-union motivation in closing
> the Omaha division for economic reasons precludes a
> finding of unfair labor practice in refusing to bargain with
> the Union.[54]

In Royal Plating and Polishing Company[55] the Third Circuit ruled that an employer was not obligated to bargain over whether to close one of its two plants. In the court's view, the employer's decision to shut one plant instead of moving to another location was a managerial decision to recommit and reinvest funds in the business. This decision was economically motivated, and it involved a significant change in the economic direction of the business. The court therefore concluded that nothing in Fibreboard required bargaining about such managerial decisions, which, in the words of Justice Potter Stewart, "lie at the core of entrepreneurial control." The employer did, however, have to negotiate over the effects of its decision.

In Ozark Trailers[56] the Board disagreed with the views of the Eighth and Third Circuits. Rejecting the Darlington decision as inapplicable, the Board relied on Fibreboard and concluded that an employer must bargain about an economically motivated decision to close part of its business. In closing one of three corporations in an integrated operation, without first negotiating with the union, the employer violated Section 8(a)(5) because it did not bargain with the union regarding either its decision to close the plant or the shutdown's effect on the employees. Since the company's decision was based, in part, on the excessive labor costs of the plant in question, the Board felt that the issues involved (inferior workmanship, poor productivity, and others) should have been discussed in negotiations, just as it had ordered bargaining over labor-cost issues in Fibreboard. The Board stressed the "mediating influence of collective bargaining" and observed that the widespread bargaining about subcontracting indicated that negotiation could solve difficult problems. It concluded that there "is no justification for interpreting the statutory bargaining obligation so narrowly as to exclude plant removal and shutdown from its scope."

In General Motors Corporation,[57] however, the Board adopted a less expansive interpretation of Fibreboard. The employer in this case had sold a factory-owned retail sales and service outlet to an independent dealership. Although it bargained with the union as to the effects of the sale, it refused to negotiate the decision to sell the facility in question.

In a split decision the Board reversed the trial examiner and held that Fibreboard was inapplicable because the present case involved a sale rather than subcontracting.* The Board relied substantially on Justice Stewart's concurring opinion in Fibreboard that not every managerial decision terminating an individual's employment is subject to the duty to bargain, and on the opinions of the circuit courts with respect to plant closings. The majority stated:

> Consistent with the expressly restricted scope of Fibreboard, the courts have sustained the Board's position in subcontracting cases, but rejected Board decisions requiring bargaining over more elemental management decisions, such as plant closings and plant removals.
>
> It appears that the Board has not dealt definitively with the specific question whether the Act imposes a duty to bargain over a decision to sell an employing enterprise. We believe, however, that this issue is controlled by the rationale the courts have generally adopted in closely related cases, that decisions such as this, in which a significant investment or withdrawal of capital will affect the scope and ultimate direction of an enterprise, are matters essentially financial and managerial in nature. They thus lie at the very core of entrepreneurial control, and are not the types of subjects which Congress intended to encompass within "rates of pay, wages, hours of employment, or other conditions of employment."[58]

There was agreement among the Board members that bargaining on the effects of management decisions on employees was still mandatory. The Board held, however, that on the facts of this case, the employer had bargained in good faith over the effects of the sale.

In their dissenting opinion members John Fanning and Gerald Brown argued that since Fibreboard, the Board had consistently found a duty to bargain about decisions involving subcontracting, plant removal, and plant closure. Disagreeing with the majority's reliance on Justice Stewart's opinion in Fibreboard and the dicta

---

*The majority was composed of Chairman Edward Miller and members Howard Jenkins and Ralph Kennedy. Members John Fanning and Gerald Brown dissented. Ozark Trailers was unanimously decided by the then Chairman Frank McCulloch and members Fanning, Brown, and Zagoria.

therein with respect to managerial decisions, the dissenters contended:

> The fact is that the Supreme Court has not addressed itself
> directly to the issue here involved, and Fibreboard, while
> it may be considered limited in scope, remains the only
> Supreme Court pronouncement in this area. We therefore
> would adhere to the Board's development of those prin-
> ciples, especially as set out in Ozark Trailers.[59]

Thus, the dissenters did not distinguish a partial business sale from
any other cessation or transfer of certain business operations and
would have adhered to the line of Board cases that held that refusal
to bargain over a decision to terminate a portion of a business is a
violation of Section 8(a)(5).

The Court of Appeals for the District of Columbia, with Chief
Justice Bazelon dissenting, upheld the Board,[60] agreeing that the
business transaction in General Motors was properly characterized
as a sale made without anti-union animus and as a decision "fundamental to the basic direction of a corporate enterprise." Therefore
it was not a mandatory subject of bargaining.[61]

At first blush it may have appeared that General Motors sapped
the vitality of Ozark Trailers. Post-G.M. decisions have indicated,
however, that the General Motors holding is to be narrowly construed
and applied only in cases involving sales of businesses. As the Board
recently held in Royal Typewriter Company:

> In General Motors, the Board held that an employer was
> not obligated to bargain with a union concerning an economic
> decision to sell an independent dealership. It did not over-
> rule Ozark Trailers . . . and other decisions in which the
> Board, notwithstanding court decisions to the contrary, held
> that an employer operating two or more plants was obligated
> to bargain with respect to a decision to close one of those
> plants. Decisions since General Motors have reached the
> same result. Accordingly, we hold that Respondents were
> required to bargain in good faith concerning the decision
> to close the plant.[62]

Apparently the Board still clings to Ozark Trailers, although
the scope of that decision has now been more carefully defined. The
Ninth and Tenth Circuits have, however, joined the Third and Eighth
in refuting the Board's approach.[63] Although the courts agree that
an employer should notify the union and should bargain about the
effects of a managerial decision to partially close or relocate a
plant, they maintain that there is no duty to bargain about the basic
decision, made purely for economic reasons. If this Board-court

rivalry persists, the controversy regarding the duty to bargain over partial closures and business reorganizations probably will not be conclusively resolved unless the Supreme Court rules on the issue or the NLRB adopts a new position.[64]

NOTES

1. For discussion on the legislative history of the NLRB's power to define mandatory bargaining subjects, see Archibald Cox and John Dunlop, ''Regulation of Collective Bargaining by the National Labor Relations Board,'' 63 Harvard Law Review 389, at 391-401 (1950).

2. 24 NLRB 444, 6 LRRM 405 (1940); enforced, 119 F.2d 131, 8 LRRM 740 (CA 7, 1941).

3. On discharges, see NLRB v. Bachelder, 120 F.2d 574, 8 LRRM 723 (CA 7, 1941); on pensions, Inland Steel Co., 77 NLRB 1, 21 LRRM 1310 (1948); enforced, 170 F.2d 247 (CA 7, 1948); cert. denied, 336 U.S. 960 (1949); on profit sharing, Union Mfg. Co., 76 NLRB 322; enforced, 179 F.2d 511 (CA 5, 1950); on work loads and standards, Woodside Cotton Mills Co., 21 NLRB 42, 6 LRRM 68 (1940); on insurance, W. W. Cross & Co., 77 NLRB 1162 (1948); enforced, 174 F.2d 875 (CA 1, 1949); on union security clauses, Winona Textile Mills, Inc., 68 NLRB 702 (1946); enforced, 160 F.2d 201 (CA 7, 1947); on subcontracting and shop rules, Timken Roller Bearing Co., 70 NLRB 500 (1946); enforcement denied on other grounds, 161 F.2d 949 (CA 6, 1947); on work schedules, Inter-City Advertising Co., 61 NLRB 1377 (1945); enforcement denied on other grounds, 154 F.2d 244 (CA 4, 1946); on rest periods, National Grinding Wheel Co., 75 NLRB 905 (1948); on merit increases, Aluminum Ore Co. v. NLRB, 131 F.2d 485 (CA 7, 1942), enforcing 39 NLRB 1286 (1942).

4. Sec. 2(11) of H.R. 3020, as passed by the House, contained the following language regarding the scope of bargaining:

> Such terms should not be construed as requiring that either party reach an agreement with the other, accept any proposal or counterproposal in whole or in part, submit counterproposals, discuss modification of an agreement during its terms except pursuant to the express provisions thereof, or discuss any subject matter other than the following:
> (i) Wage rates, hours of employment and work requirements;
> (ii) procedures and practices relating to discharge, suspension, lay-off, recall, seniority, and discipline, or to promotion, demotion, transfer and assignment within the bargaining unit;

  (iii) conditions, procedures, and practices governing
    safety, sanitation, and protection of health at the
    place of employment;
  (iv) vacations and leaves of absence; and
   (v) administrative and procedural provisions relating
    to the foregoing subjects.

H.R. 3020, 80th Cong., 1st sess. 2(11)(B)(vi)(1947), in 1 NLRB, Legislative History of the Labor Management Relations Act of 1947, at 166-67 (1948).
  5. Referring to Section 2(11), the Minority Report stated:

> This section attempts to limit narrowly the subject matter
> appropriate for collective bargaining. It seems clear that
> the definitions are designed to exclude collective bargaining concerning welfare funds, vacation funds, union hiring
> halls, union security provisions, apprenticeship qualifications, assignment of work, check-off provisions, subcontracting of work, and a host of other matters traditionally the subject matter of collective bargaining in some
> industries or in certain regions of the country. The appropriate scope of collective bargaining cannot be determined
> by formula; it will inevitably depend upon the traditions of
> an industry, the social and political climate at any given
> time, the needs of employers and employees, and many
> related factors. What are proper subject matters for
> collective bargaining should be left in the first instance
> to employers and trade-unions, and in the second place,
> to any administrative agency skilled in this field and competent to devote the necessary time to a study of industrial
> practices and traditions in each industry or area of the
> country, subject to review by the courts. It cannot and
> should not be strait-jacketed by legislative enactment.

Ibid., at 362.
  6. Hearings before Senate Committee on Labor and Public Welfare on S. 55 and S. J. Res. 22, 80th Cong., 1st sess. 1914 (1947).
  7. 356 U.S. 342 (1958).
  8. 236 F.2d 898 (CA 6, 1956).
  9. The Court held that the ballot clause related only to the procedure to be followed by the employees before the union acted to reject a final offer or to call a strike. It therefore dealt only with relations between the employees and their union. ". . . [B]y weakening the independence of the representative chosen by the employees . . . [i]t enables the employer, in effect, to deal with its employees rather than with their statutory representative."

The recognition clause was also deemed a nonmandatory subject because it was considered an evasion of the duty to bargain with the certified representative for the employer "to insist that the certified representative not be a party to the collective bargaining agreement." 356 U.S. at 350.

10. 356 U.S. at 349.

11. Illegal subjects are those requiring action that is unlawful or inconsistent with the basic policy of the Act. These subjects may not lawfully be included in an agreement, regardless of the parties' intent or their efforts to waive or acquiesce with respect to such inclusion. Furthermore, in Meat Cutters Union (Great Atlantic & Pacific Tea Co.), 81 NLRB 1052 (1949), the Board said: "When . . . one of the parties creates a bargaining impasse by insisting, not in good faith, that the other agree to an unlawful condition of employment, that party has violated its duty to bargain."

12. 356 U.S. at 349, citing NLRB v. American National Insurance Co., 343 U.S. 395 (1952).

13. 356 U.S. at 357-58. Emphasis in original.

14. The dissenting opinion received substantial support from commentators, and several legal experts have urged that Borg-Warner be overruled. See, for instance, H.H. Wellington, Labor and the Legal Process (New Haven: Yale University Press, 1968), pp. 66-90.

15. Charles J. Morris, ed., The Developing Labor Law (Washington, D.C.: American Bar Assn., 1971), p. 389.

16. See Medo Photo Supply Corp. v. NLRB, 321 U.S. 678 (1944); Wings & Wheels, Inc., 139 NLRB 578 (1962).

17. NLRB v. Katz, 369 U.S. 736 (1962).

18. 369 U.S. at 742-43.

19. Frank McCulloch, "Role of Federal Government in Labor Relations: Labor Relations Philosophy of Kennedy Administration NLRB," 49 LRRM 74 (1962).

20. Morris, loc. cit.

21. 105 NLRB 390 (1953).

22. Stuart Radiator Core Mfg. Co., 173 NLRB 27 (1968). See also Vanderbilt Products Co., 129 NLRB 1323 (1961), enforced, 297 F.2d 833 (CA 2, 1961), wherein it was held that an employer who made such extreme demands that no "self-respecting" union could accept them was found guilty of violating Section 8(a)(5).

23. NLRB v. Davidson, 318 F.2d 550, at 558 (CA 4, 1963).

24. 379 U.S. 203 (1964).

25. See New England Web, Inc., 135 NLRB 1019; enforcement denied, 309 F.2d 696 (CA 1, 1962).

26. Brown Truck and Trailer Mfg. Co., 106 NLRB 999 (1953).

27. 136 NLRB 1022 (1962); enforced, 316 F.2d 846 (CA 5, 1963).

28. Note, "The Scope of Collective Bargaining," 74 Yale Law Journal 1472, at 1476 (1964-65).

29. Fibreboard Paper Products Corp. v. NLRB, 379 U.S. 203, at 211 (1964).

30. Wellington, op. cit., p. 69.

31. Fibreboard Paper Products Corp. v. NLRB at 217-18.

32. Ibid. at 223.

33. Ibid. at 225.

34. Wellington, op. cit., p. 73.

35. Note, "Collective Bargaining and the Professional Employee," 69 Columbia Law Review 277, at 284 (1969).

36. For a discussion of these problems, see Margaret K. Chandler, Management Rights and Union Interests (New York: McGraw-Hill, 1964).

37. 149 NLRB 26, 57 LRRM 1279 (1964).

38. Ibid., 58 LRRM at 1280.

39. Westinghouse Electric Corp., 150 NLRB 136, 58 LRRM 1257 (1965).

40. For discussion on these circumstances, see Elihu Platt, "The Duty to Bargain as Applied to Management Decisions," 19 Labor Law Journal 143 (1968); "The Scope of Collective Bargaining," op. cit.

41. International Shoe Corp., 151 NLRB 693 (1965); Kennecott Copper Corp., 148 NLRB 1653 (1964) (management rights clause); Ador Corp., 150 NLRB 1658 (1965) (management rights clause giving employer the right to eliminate production of any of his products and to lay off employees no longer needed); Fafnir Bearing Co., 151 NLRB 332 (Board noted that trial examiner gave insufficient weight to the presence of a management rights clause in the agreement).

42. Westinghouse Electric Corp., 58 LRRM 1257. Westinghouse was not guilty of violating Section 8(a)(5) since, as the union knew, the company had been engaging in extensive subcontracting for many years.

43. Ibid.

44. Fafnir Bearing Co.; Superior Coach Corp., 151 NLRB 421 (1965); Shell Oil Co., 57 LRRM 1279; Kennecott Copper Corp.

45. In Shell Oil the Board declared:

> [T]he amount of time and discussion required to satisfy the statutory obligation "to meet at reasonable times and confer in good faith" may vary with the character of the subcontracting, the impact on employees, and the exigencies of the particular business situation involved.

57 LRRM 1279, at 1280.

46. "The Development of the Fibreboard Doctrine: The Duty to Bargain over Economically Motivated Subcontracting Decisions," 33 University of Chicago Law Review 315, at 318 (1965).

47. 322 F.2d 553 (CA 8, 1963).

48. 137 NLRB 815 (1962).

49. In its second decision the Eighth Circuit applied the Darlington partial closing test to the Adams Dairy case. See Platt, op. cit., for sharp criticism of the Eighth Circuit's imposition of a Darlington principle on a Fibreboard situation.

50. Hawaii Meat Co. v. NLRB, 321 F.2d 397 (CA 9, 1963).

51. Empire Terminal Warehouse Co., 151 NLRB 1359 (1965).

52. 380 U.S. 263 (1965).

53. 346 F.2d 897 (CA 8, 1965).

54. Ibid. at 902.

55. 350 F.2d 191 (CA 3, 1965).

56. 161 NLRB 561 (1966).

57. 191 NLRN 149, 77 LRRM 1537 (1971).

58. 77 LRRM 1537, at 1539 (1971).

59. Ibid. at 1541.

60. Automobile Workers, Local 864 (General Motors Corp.) v. NLRB 470 F.2d 422, 81 LRRM 2439 (CA D.C., 1972).

61. In reaching its decision the court looked to the decisions of the courts of appeals in similar cases. It noted that if an employer's decision

> . . . appears to be primarily designed to avoid the bargaining agreement with the union or if it produces no substantial change in the operations of the employer, the courts have required bargaining. . . . If the decision resulted in the termination of a substantial portion or a distinct line of the employer's business or involved a major change in the nature of its operations, no bargaining has been required. . . . The difficult cases have been those involving a small but not insubstantial proportion of the employer's business; in these cases, the results have often hinged on hints of anti-union animus. (81 LRRM 2441-42)

In General Motors the court concluded that the evidence supported the company's assertion that its transaction was in fact a sale and a decision lying "at the core of entrepreneurial control." (81 LRRM 2442)

62. Royal Typewriter Co., 85 LRRM 1501, at 1509 (1974). See also American Needle & Novelty Co., 84 LRRM 1526, wherein the Board stated:

> The fact that here the Respondent transferred the work from one location to another, rather than subcontracting the work as in Fibreboard, does not change the result. It is well settled that an employer has an obligation to bargain concerning a decision to relocate unit work. . . .
> In General Motors the Board was concerned with a decision which involved a significant investment or with-

drawal of capital affecting the scope and ultimate direction of the enterprise. Here there was no sale or arm's length transfer or any other transaction which could be said to rise to the level of the transaction the Board was concerned with in that case. (84 LRRM 1526, at 1529 [1973]).

63. NLRB v. Transmarine Navigation Corp., 380 F.2d 933 (CA 9, 1967); Thompson Transport Co., 165 NLRB 96 (1967); enforcement denied, 406 F.2d 698 (CA 10, 1969).
64. Morris, op. cit., p. 422.

Wisconsin in 1959 was the first state to enact comprehensive legislation concerning collective bargaining for all public employees, with the exception of those employed by the state. Since then collective bargaining in the public sector has become a widely accepted practice. By mid-1974, 40 states had authorized all or some public employees to participate in the determination of working conditions beyond the constitutional right to petition the legislature. The only states without any legislation or attorney general opinions authorizing bargaining or collective discussions for at least certain public employees are Arizona, Arkansas, Colorado, Louisiana, Mississippi, North Carolina, Ohio, South Carolina, Tennessee, and West Virginia. Additionally, several local jurisdictions, including Baltimore, Los Angeles, Eugene (Oregon), New York City, and San Francisco have enacted laws authorizing bargaining for public employees.

Several different types of collective bargaining relationships are created by the state laws. Mandatory negotiations, in either the "meet and confer" or the collective bargaining form, are required in 34 states. The remaining states have enacted either statutes permitting bargaining or meeting and conferring, or laws merely allowing the presentation of proposals to the employer.

"Meet and confer" laws reflect the legislative assumption that the private sector bargaining model is not appropriate for the public sector and that the unique aspects of public employment entitle public employers to greater managerial discretion. Thus, under the "meet and confer" framework "the outcome of public employer-employee discussions depends more on management's determinations than on bilateral decisions by 'equals.'"[1] In contrast, laws requiring "negotiations" or "collective bargaining" imply that the parties at the bargaining table are equals and that contract language will be bilaterally determined. Several local jurisdictions and states, including California, Georgia (firemen), Kansas, Missouri, Oklahoma (police and firemen), Oregon, South Dakota, and Wyoming (firemen), have passed "meet and confer" laws. Most state laws, however, embody the negotiations approach. The trend, as one commentator notes, is away from the "meet and confer" approach and toward the negotiation requirement. "In fact," he states, "the 'meet and confer' approach can and perhaps should be viewed as an interim measure between no collective bargaining and full collective bargaining."[2]

With the statutes enacted by Massachusetts and Montana in 1973, and by Iowa in 1974, 28 states now have reasonably comprehensive statutes of general applicability: Alaska (all public employees), California (all municipal and state employees), Connecticut (all municipal employees), Delaware (all public employees), Hawaii (all public employees), Idaho (firemen and teachers), Indiana (teachers), Iowa (all public employees), Kansas (all public employees; local option as to coverage), Michigan (all public employees except classified state employees), Minnesota (all public employees), Missouri (nurses, teachers), Montana (all public employees), Nebraska (all public employees), Nevada (all local government employees), New Hampshire (state employees, police, municipal employees at local option), New Jersey (all public employees), New York (all public employees), Oregon (all public employees), Pennsylvania (all public employees), Rhode Island (all state and municipal employees), South Dakota (all public employees), Vermont (all public employees), Washington (all public employees), and Wisconsin (all public employees).*

There is wide variation among the states with respect to employee coverage. Some states favor all-inclusive statutes, while others have enacted separate laws for each classification of employee or, more often, laws granting bargaining rights to local employees only. Teachers, covered in several states under general laws, are more frequently covered by special statutes, as are firemen and, less often, police.[3]

Most of the state laws governing public employee bargaining have adopted the language of the National Labor Relations Act (NLRA) in defining the scope of bargaining to be "wages, hours, and other terms and conditions of employment." As was explained in Chapter 2, in the private sector this language has been broadly interpreted to include most matters that affect employee working conditions and employer-employee relations. Whether or not the courts and employment relations boards in the public sector adopt equally broad interpretations of the scope of bargaining remains to be seen. It is already

---

*As of mid-1974 there are, however, 72 laws, municipal ordinances, and personnel rules and regulations that provide for collective bargaining or meeting and conferring among public employers and public employee representatives.

41

clear, however, that despite the passage of comprehensive bargaining legislation, the scope of public employee negotiations is often restricted by the presence of civil service codes and preexisting state laws defining the powers and duties of public employers. How conflicts between these laws are resolved will be a crucial factor in the development of the scope of bargaining in public employment.[*]

LIMITATIONS ON THE SCOPE OF BARGAINING

Fifteen jurisdictions expressly limit the scope of bargaining by including in their statutes management rights provisions enumerating those prerogatives retained by public employers: the City of Baltimore, Hawaii, Indiana, Kansas, Kentucky, Minnesota, Montana, New Hampshire, New York City, Nevada, Pennsylvania, Texas, Vermont, Wisconsin, and the District of Columbia. A typical management rights clause is the following provision of New Hampshire's statute:

> The State retains the exclusive right through its department heads and appointing authorities . . . (a) to direct and supervise employees, (b) to appoint, promote, discharge, transfer or demote employees, (c) to lay off unnecessary employees, (d) to maintain the efficiency of government operations, (e) to determine the means, methods and personnel by which operations are to be conducted, and (f) to take whatever actions are necessary to carry out the mission of the agency or department in situations of emergency.[4]

This clause, and others like it, reflect the influence of the federal Executive Orders 10988 and 11491, both of which included strong management rights provisions.

In addition to the specific collective bargaining restrictions provided by statutory management rights clauses, the rules and procedures of a merit or civil service system limit the scope of bargaining in many states. Connecticut, Kansas, and Maine, for

---

[*]It is worth noting that several states, including Nebraska and New Jersey, apparently determined that the language of the NLRA was inappropriate for public employee bargaining legislation. The laws of these states define the scope of negotiations to be "grievance procedures and conditions of employment," leaving doubt as to whether hours of work and monetary issues are negotiable. While it is arguable that the phrase "conditions of work" includes working hours and wages, such statutory language indicates that the legislatures in question may have intended a narrower definition than that used in the private sector.

example, exclude from negotiations the conduct and grading of merit examinations and the appointment of candidates from lists based on such examinations. The laws of Hawaii, Rhode Island, Vermont, Washington, and Wisconsin also exclude various aspects of the merit system from the realm of negotiations. The Hawaii statute, for instance, stipulates that the parties "shall not agree to any proposal which would be inconsistent with merit principles."

Matters covered by state laws (other than bargaining legislation) or executive orders also are frequently nonnegotiable. Wisconsin excludes compensation and "other actions provided for by law"; and Hawaii excludes classification, retirement benefits, the salary ranges, and the number of incremental and longevity steps currently provided by law, although the wages paid in each step and the length of service for steps are negotiable.

Some state laws require an appropriate legislative body to approve negotiated contract provisions, either because these provisions contravene existing law or because an appropriation of funds is necessary to effectuate the agreement. New York and Connecticut stipulate that an agreement requiring either an amendment of law or additional funds is not to be implemented until the appropriate legislative body approves and acts upon the agreement. The Connecticut statute adds that if the legislative body rejects a negotiated provision, it must remand the item to the parties for additional bargaining. Hawaii and Massachusetts have similar provisions, limited to appropriations for cost items.[5] If there are conflicts between contract provisions and existing laws or ordinances, four jurisdictions provide that the laws or ordinances shall prevail.[*] In contrast, Connecticut, Massachusetts, and Hawaii, among other jurisdictions, provide that negotiated agreements will take precedence over conflicting laws.[‡]

The scope of bargaining also is often limited with respect to union security. Some statutes specifically prohibit union security clauses, while other laws are silent on the issue.

Michigan's law formerly was silent on union security. But after a Michigan Supreme Court decision banned the negotiation of agency shop agreements in the absence of express statutory authorization, the legislature amended the Public Employment Relations Act to permit bargaining on this form of union security.[6] Rhode Island in 1973 amended its bargaining law covering state employees to provide for negotiation of agency shop contracts. New York's Taylor Law is silent on union security, but the Public Employment Relations

---

[*] See Delaware teachers' law, Kansas nonteachers' law, New Hampshire state employees' law, and New Mexico regulations.

[‡] See also Prince Georges County Ordinance, Texas Fire and Police Relations Act, Vermont Municipal Employee Relations Act, and District of Columbia regulations.

Board and the New York Supreme Court, Appellate Division, have held the agency shop to be illegal and, therefore, nonnegotiable.[7]

The checkoff of union dues on a voluntary basis is authorized by statute in several states and may be permitted in others without express statutory authorization.[8] Those states that presently permit some form of union security include Hawaii, which permits the collection of a service fee from all members of a bargaining unit; Pennsylvania, which allows maintenance of membership; Washington, which permits maintenance of membership for port district employees; and Wisconsin, which in 1971 amended its municipal bargaining law to permit the negotiation of "fair share agreements," or agency shop clauses, in contracts between city employers and employee organizations.[9]

HIGHLIGHTS OF 1973 LEGISLATIVE DEVELOPMENTS

There was a substantial amount of legislative activity in 1973. Twelve states enacted or amended public employee bargaining laws; at least two local jurisdictions adopted bargaining ordinances; and Illinois' Governor Dan Walker issued an executive order granting employees in the executive branch of state government the right to organize and bargain.

Indiana passed its first bargaining law. It covers teachers and mandates bargaining on salaries, wages, hours, and salary- and wage-related fringe benefits. Contracts may contain a provision for binding arbitration of grievances. Employers need not bargain but may discuss

> . . . working conditions, other than those provided in
> Section 4 [subjects of bargaining]; curriculum develop-
> ment and revision; textbook selection; teaching methods;
> selection, assignment, or promotion of personnel;
> student discipline; expulsion or supervision of students;
> pupil-teacher ratio; class size or budget appropriations;
> provided, however, that any items included in the 1972-73
> agreements between any employer school corporation and
> the employee organization shall continue to be bargainable.

The Indiana law contains a management rights provision establishing the responsibility of school employers to direct the work of employees; establish policy; hire, promote, demote, transfer, assign, and retain employees; suspend or discharge employees; maintain efficiency of school operations; relieve employees for lack of work; take actions necessary to carry out the mission of public schools. Contract provisions may not conflict with federal or state

44

laws or employer or employee rights under the act. An employer also is prohibited from signing an agreement that would place it in a position of deficit financing.

The act prohibits the right to strike. It also enumerates six employer and four employee organization unfair practices, including interfering with employees' rights, refusing to bargain or discuss, and refusing to comply with provisions of the bargaining law. Procedures to settle disputes include mediation and fact-finding. School employers and employee representatives also may voluntarily submit any disputed issues to final and binding arbitration.

1973 also saw Texas adopt its initial piece of public sector bargaining legislation. Under the law police and firemen may organize and bargain on wages, hours, and working conditions—but only if voters in local jurisdictions petition their governments for a referendum and adopt the bargaining law by a majority vote. Strikes are prohibited, and unresolved disputes may be submitted to arbitration, if mediation fails. The act states that it supersedes any conflicting laws and preempts any local ordinances adopted by the state or municipalities through personnel boards and civil service commissions. Any negotiated contract provisions take precedence whenever the contract "specifically so provides." Additionally, any existing benefit provided by law that relates to police or firefighter compensations, pensions, hours of work, and other conditions of employment shall not be repealed or reduced by the act.

Massachusetts significantly amended its comprehensive bargaining statute. The law defines the scope of bargaining as wages, hours, standards of productivity and performance, and any other terms and conditions of employment. In contrast with the original statutory language, the law now permits negotiated agreements to prevail over any conflicting ordinance, bylaw, rule, or statutory provision.

Another important change relates to the adoption of new "final offer" arbitration procedures in police and firefighter disputes. Final and binding interest arbitration also may be invoked voluntarily in impasses involving other categories of public employees. The new law also stipulates that all employees in a certified unit must pay a fee to the union that is "proportionately commensurate" with collective bargaining and contract administration costs—where such agency shop agreement has been approved by a majority of employees in the unit.

Minnesota's comprehensive public employee bargaining law, effective in 1972, authorized negotiations, allowed professional employees to "meet and confer" on policy matters, banned strikes, established a tripartite public employment relations board, and gave county courts the right to enjoin unfair labor practices.

In 1973 the law was amended to grant nonessential employees the right to strike if an employer refuses to submit an impasse to binding arbitration or to comply with a binding award. The amendments also included a fair share provision, which requires nonmembers of an exclusive bargaining agent to pay a fair share of negotiating and grievance processing costs.

The amendments make the duration of a contract negotiable, but a three-year maximum is maintained. The scope of bargaining continues to be defined as grievance procedures and terms and conditions of employment, including hours of employment, compensation, fringe benefits, personnel policies affecting employee working conditions. With respect to professional employees, mandatory subjects include hours, compensation, and economic aspects relating to employment—but not educational policies. A public employer must meet and confer, however, with professional employees on policies and those matters relating to their employment that are not included under the definition of terms and conditions of employment. The law also states that employers are not required to bargain on matters of inherent managerial policy, which include, but are not limited to, functions and programs of the employer, overall budget, utilization of technology, organizational structure, and selection, direction, and number of personnel.

Montana enacted a new comprehensive law covering all public employees except teachers and nurses, who are covered by other statutes. Parties may bargain on wages, hours, fringe benefits, and other conditions of employment, including the agency shop and binding grievance arbitration. The act, however, contains a management prerogatives provision that preserves the right of public employers to operate and manage their affairs, which include directing, hiring, promoting, transferring, and laying off employees for lack of work or funds; maintaining efficient government operations; determining methods, means, job classifications, and personnel by which government operations are to be conducted; taking necessary actions to carry out the mission of the agency in emergencies; and establishing the processes by which work is to be performed. Dispute settlement procedures include mediation, fact-finding, and binding arbitration if agreed to by the parties.

Under Oregon's comprehensive bargaining act, employees may bargain on "matters concerning employment relations," including fair share agreements and binding arbitration provisions to cover both rights and interest disputes. Employees other than policemen, firemen, and guards at mental and correctional institutions have a qualified right to strike following exhaustion of statutory impasse procedures and in the absence of a clear and present danger to public health, safety, and welfare. Unresolved disputes involving police, firemen, and guards must be submitted to final and binding arbitration.

Cities with collective bargaining ordinances may continue to operate under their own systems if the Public Employment Relations

Board determines they do not conflict with the new state law and if they incorporate the new procedures.

South Dakota's state and local employee bargaining law also was amended in 1973. The amendments lessen strike penalties, add employer and union unfair labor practices to the statute, and specify that the bargaining obligation includes a duty to negotiate on matters that are, or may be, regulated by a state or local agency and to submit agreements reached on these matters to the appropriate legislative body. The South Dakota law defines the scope of bargaining as grievances procedures and conditions of employment. There are no statutory restrictions on the employer's authority to bargain.

Vermont replaced its municipal bargaining law with a new statute covering municipal employees, police, and firefighters. The scope of bargaining is defined as wages, hours, and conditions of employment, including binding arbitration of grievances and the agency shop. Excluded are "matters of managerial prerogative," which are defined as "any nonbargainable matters of inherent managerial policy."

If any collective agreement is found to conflict with "any state law, charter, or special act, such law shall prevail," except as provided to the contrary in the section concerning binding arbitration of tenure grievances. However, if a collective agreement conflicts with an ordinance, bylaw, or regulation adopted by a municipal employer, the vote of the legislative body approving the agreement shall validate the agreement and supersede such ordinance, bylaw, or regulation.

The act permits a limited right to strike in the absence of danger to public health, safety, or welfare. Dispute settlement procedures include mediation, fact-finding, and voluntary submission to binding arbitration.

In 1973 Washington joined other jurisdictions in amending its local employee bargaining law to establish compulsory binding arbitration of police and firemen's disputes that are not resolved through mediation or fact-finding. The civil service law and state university classified employee statute also were amended to allow the agency shop, provided a majority of the members in a bargaining unit vote in favor of it.

Finally, as noted above, Michigan and Rhode Island amended their bargaining laws to authorize the negotiation of agency shop provisions.

In addition to these state jurisdictions, the city of San Francisco and Prince Georges County, Maryland, adopted local labor relations ordinances.

In San Francisco city and county employees may organize and meet and confer on wages, hours, and conditions of employment. Charters, ordinances, and civil service rules, however, supersede collective agreements. The ordinance establishes mediation and fact-finding procedures to resolve disputes. Parties also may voluntarily select final and binding arbitration; and if a dispute involves employees in vital services affecting public health, safety, or welfare, their dispute must be submitted to binding arbitration after mediation and fact-finding procedures have been exhausted.

Prince Georges County, Maryland, adopted an ordinance granting county employees the right to unionize, bargain, and strike in limited circumstances. The ordinance provides means for selection of appropriate units; requires parties to negotiate on wages, hours, and other conditions of employment; preserves certain merit principles; and establishes procedures for handling disputes and strikes. Negotiation of agency shop agreements is permitted. Contracts also may contain binding grievance arbitration provisions, and the ordinance also allows employees to authorize "voluntary binding arbitration with respect to [a] negotiation impasse."

An approved contract's terms prevail over conflicting merit system or personnel rules, and the County Council must appropriate funds to implement a contract that it approves. The ordinance also states:

> The employer shall have the obligation to bargain on matters
> which, although otherwise within the scope of bargaining,
> require action by a body, agency, or official other than the
> county executive or county council. In addition, the employer
> shall have the obligation to bargain on the question of whether
> it should request such a body, agency, or official to take
> such action or support such request, provided, however,
> that no impasse panel . . . shall be empowered to recom-
> mend that the employer make or support such a request.

In addition to the legislative actions reviewed above, Illinois Governor Dan Walker issued an executive order granting employees in the executive branch of state government the right to organize and to elect representatives to bargain with state agencies. The scope of bargaining includes wages, hours, and other terms and conditions of employment "so far as may be appropriate and allowable under applicable law and subject to laws regarding the appropriation and expenditure of state funds and the rules of the department of personnel." Additionally, the state is not required to bargain on the merit principle and competitive examination system; an agency's policies, programs, and statutory functions; its budget and structure; decisions on standards, scope, and delivery of service; utilization of technology; the state retirement system; life and health insurance; and "anything required or prohibited by law."

PUBLIC EMPLOYEE BARGAINING LAWS: THE EMPLOYEES COVERED AND THE SCOPE OF BARGAINING

Appendixes A and B set forth the state statutory provisions on the scope of negotiations. Appendix A indicates the public employees covered in each state and the type of authorization for collective negotiations. Appendix B summarizes the scope of bargaining for each classification of employee covered by public sector bargaining laws.

State Employees

Several states, including New Hampshire, Rhode Island, Vermont, and Wisconsin, have separate laws governing collective bargaining for state employees. Generally these laws authorize bargaining on wages and salaries (except for Wisconsin), work schedules, leaves, vacations, grievance procedures, and other working conditions. Most of the laws, however, place civil service matters, such as recruitment, classification, and promotion, outside the scope of bargaining. Moreover, several jurisdictions—New Hampshire, Vermont, and Wisconsin—have management rights clauses that specifically enumerate those management prerogatives not to be abrogated through collective bargaining.

Municipal Employees

There are at least 15 laws specifically governing municipal employees. These generally include local government employees and teachers, and mandate collective bargaining between local public employers and employee organizations.

In Maine municipal employee organizations may bargain over wages, hours, and working conditions; however, the act specifies that "public employers of teachers shall meet and consult but not negotiate with respect to educational policies. . . ." The act also excludes "the conduct and the grading of merit examinations, the rating of candidates and the establishment of lists from such examinations, and the appointments from such lists." But if certain other merit system matters—such as demotion, layoff, reinstatement, suspension, discharge, or discipline—are arbitrated in a negotiations dispute and the resulting bargaining agreement is in conflict with merit system regulations, the provisions of the agreement shall be controlling. Connecticut's law is similar to that of

49

Maine in that it permits the terms of an agreement, subject to the approval of the appropriate legislative body, to override any existing local laws, rules, or regulations that may be contrary to the bargained agreement.

The Nevada and New York City laws contain management rights clauses relieving management of the duty to bargain over the hiring, promotion, classification, transfer, direction, layoff, suspension, discharge, and discipline of employees; the maintenance of the efficiency of government operations; the determination of the methods, means, and personnel by which operations are conducted. However, New York City's statute states that questions concerning the "practical impact" of managerial decisions on employees, such as questions of manning and work load, are negotiable. Thus, if the Board of Collective Bargaining or the parties determine that a managerial action has impact on municipal employees, and the city is unable to relieve that impact through the exercise of its statutory management prerogatives, the parties may have to bargain over the action to be taken in order to relieve or reduce this practical impact. The requirement to bargain concerning the impact does not, however, reduce the city's continuing management rights in the specified matters; and those matters remain excluded from the scope of mandatory bargaining.

Police and Firemen

Many states have general laws or attorney general opinions establishing bargaining rights for safety employees. In addition 12 states have separate laws applying to bargaining by police and firemen: Alabama (firemen), Florida (firemen), Georgia (firemen), Idaho (firemen), Kentucky (both), South Dakota (both), Texas (both), Wyoming (firemen), and Vermont (firemen). Most of these laws list wages, hours, and working conditions as the scope of bargaining; only the Kentucky and Texas statutes contain specific limitations on the realm of negotiations.

Teachers

Twenty-nine states have enacted legislation that authorizes negotiations by school teachers.* Of these, 17 have statutes specif-

---
*
There is more legislation applicable to teachers than to any other type of public employee. Irving Sabghir suggests that this reflects the fact that teachers have been the most militant public employee group in recent years.

ically applying to teachers: Alaska, California, Connecticut, Delaware, Florida, Idaho, Indiana, Kansas, Maine, Maryland, Montana, Nebraska, North Dakota, Oklahoma, Rhode Island, Vermont, and Washington.

On the whole the statutes that cover teachers separately from public employees specify a relatively broad scope of bargaining. Perhaps this reflects legislative recognition that the professional status of teachers endows them with a legitimate concern with educational objectives and professional standards. This element of professionalism, not found in many other occupational groups, is a crucial factor influencing teacher views of collective bargaining. In line with the above remarks, it is readily observed in Appendix B that the scope of teacher negotiations often encompasses more than the customary "wages, hours, and working conditions."

The California statute (Education Code 13085) is a "meet and confer" law that enumerates the major areas of teacher concern. It states:

A public school employer . . . shall meet and confer with representatives of certificated and classified employee organizations upon request with regard to employment conditions and employer-employee relations, and, in addition, shall meet and confer with representatives of employee organizations . . . with regard to procedures relating to the definition of educational objectives, the determination of the content of courses and curricula, the selection of textbooks, and other aspects of the instructional program to the extent such matters are within the discretion of the public school employer or governing board under the law.

Washington's law also permits a wide scope of teacher bargaining. Under the act the designated employee organization ". . . shall have the right . . . to meet, confer and negotiate with the board of the school districts or a committee thereof to communicate the considered professional judgment of the certified staff prior to the final adoption by the board of proposed school policies relating to, but not limited to, curriculum, textbook selection, in-service training, student teaching programs, personnel, hiring and assignment practices, leaves of absence, salaries and salary schedules and non-instructional duties."

Other states—Alaska, Kansas, Oklahoma, Rhode Island—give recognition to the added areas of teacher concern by inserting the word "professional" into the standard language covering scope of bargaining. For example, Alaska's statute states that each school board, as well as the state board of education in behalf of state-operated schools, "shall negotiate" with its certificated staff "in good faith on matters pertaining to their employment and the fulfillment of their professional duties." Similarly, the Kansas law grants teachers' organizations the right "to participate in professional negotiation with boards of education . . . for the purpose of establishing, maintaining, protecting or improving terms and conditions of professional service." On the other hand, 18 states do not provide in their statutes for negotiations of professional subject matter. This is due, in part, to the inclusion of teachers with state and local employees under a single law.[10]

Limitations on Scope

It is noteworthy that most of the laws applicable solely to teachers do not contain a management rights clause. This does not mean there are no areas legitimately lying within the exclusive province of management. It merely confirms the difficulty of clearly delineating where professional standards and working conditions end and management rights begin.[11] Moreover, certain items—for example, class size—seem to involve matters both of policy and working conditions. Three states—Montana, Maine, and Minnesota—attempt in their laws to distinguish between educational policy and traditionally negotiable items by specifically excluding from bargaining curriculum, policy of operation, selection of teachers, and physical plant matters (in Montana), or by limiting the bargaining strictly to wages, hours, and working conditions (in Maine) or to economic aspects of employment (in Minnesota). The Maine statute, for example, states that public employers of teachers "shall meet and consult but not negotiate with respect to educational policies," and "educational policies shall not include wages, hours, working conditions or contract grievance arbitration."

Several laws that include teachers with other public employees do contain a management rights provision that also applies to teacher negotiations. In these states it seems likely, however, that the scope of bargaining for teachers may be broadened by interpretation, that is, by giving a liberal definition to the term "conditions of employment."

NOTES

1. Advisory Commission on Intergovernmental Relations, Labor-Management Policies for State and Local Government, 51 GERR Reference File 101, at 109 (Mar. 1970).

2. Lee C. Shaw, "The Development of State and Federal Laws," in Sam Zagoria, ed., Public Workers and Public Unions (Englewood Cliffs, N.J.: Prentice-Hall, 1972), p. 28. Although the "meet and

confer" statutes impose a lesser duty upon public employers than do mandatory collective bargaining laws, the practical distinction between "meet and confer" statutes and stronger bargaining legislation is not always as great as it would at first appear—especially if a written agreement is required after meeting and conferring. The 1970 amendments to California's Winton Act (School Employer-Employee Relations Act), for example, require good faith discussion and define "meet and confer" to mean that school boards and teacher organizations "shall have the mutual obligation to exchange . . . proposals; and to make and consider recommendations under orderly procedures in a conscientious effort to reach agreement by written resolution, regulation, or policy of the governing board effectuating such recommendations." The scope of representation includes "all matters relating to employment conditions and employer-employee relations," and the amendments also provide for fact-finding—advisory with recommendations—as an impasse procedure.

3. Joseph P. Goldberg, "Public Employee Developments in 1971," 95 Monthly Labor Review (U.S. Department of Labor) 56, at 63 (Jan. 1972).

4. N.H. Rev. Stat. Ann. §98-C:7 (Supp. 1969).

5. Joel Seidman, "State Legislation on Collective Bargaining by Public Employees," 22 Labor Law Journal 13, at 16 (1971).

6. See Smigel v. Southgate Community Schools, 81 LRRM 2944 (1972), reversing and remanding 23 Mich. App. 179, 74 LRRM 3080 (1970).

7. See In the Matter of Monroe-Woodbury Teachers Association and Monroe-Woodbury Board of Education, 3 PERB 3632 (1970); Farrigan v. Helsby, 346 N.Y.S.2d 39 (1973).

8. Seidman, loc. cit.

9. See also Magenheim v. Board of Education of the District of Riverview Gardens, 347 S.W.2d 407 (1961), wherein the Supreme Court of Missouri held that a school board could insist that teachers join professional associations (NEA and affiliates) in order to receive the benefits provided in the salary schedule, and Tremblay v. Berlin Police Station, 237 A.2d 668, 69 LRRM 2070 (1968), wherein the Supreme Court of New Hampshire, in a case involving a city and a policemen's union, held that a union shop clause in a bargaining agreement was "invalid as an unlawful delegation of municipal power."

10. Howard S. Block and C. Frederick Totten, "Scope of Negotiations vs. the Role of Civil Service Commissions," in Scope of Bargaining in the Public Sector—Concepts and Problems, Report, U.S. Labor Management Services Administration (Washington: U.S. Government Printing Office, 1972).

11. Ibid.

4

STATE ADVISORY COMMITTEE REPORTS: A COMPARATIVE ANALYSIS ON THE SCOPE OF BARGAINING

In recent years various advisory committees have been active in recommending policy and legislation to govern public sector labor relations.[1] These expert committees, which have been appointed by state and local governmental bodies, reflect the growing public concern with labor-management relations in government employment; and their reports have been influential in bringing about the enactment of new or revised statutes to formalize bargaining in the public sector.

Because the appropriate scope of bargaining is a crucial problem in public sector negotiations, several of these advisory commissions have commented extensively on this issue in their reports. Two major problems have had to be confronted: How can bargaining be implemented when many government employers lack the authority to enter into binding contracts with respect to issues governed by civil service codes, education laws, and municipal charters? Given the public interest and the unique responsibilities with which elected officials are entrusted, are there certain items that should be excluded from the scope of bargaining in public employment?

The recommendations of the study commissions regarding the scope of bargaining have differed significantly. This chapter will discuss the highlights of the commission reports and illustrate the similarities and differences among them. The report of New York's Taylor Committee is intentionally omitted from this chapter because it will be analyzed in detail in Chapter 6.

CONNECTICUT

The Connecticut Commission on Collective Bargaining by Municipalities issued its report in February 1965.* It recommended comprehensive legislation to govern collective bargaining in municipalities. Teachers, however, were excluded from the proposed legislation because in the opinion of the Commission, teacher-school board relations deserved "separate considerations by the General Assembly in view of the special nature and role of education in municipal government."[2]

The Commission suggested a relatively broad definition of collective bargaining: wages, hours, and other conditions of employment. Moreover, it added that "conditions of employment" was intended to include

> . . . the entire spectrum of conditions and benefits which apply to public employment, in addition to the commonly understood basic provisions relating to pay and hours of work, including but not limited to: seniority, grievance procedures, holiday and vacation pay, shift premiums, sick leave, jury duty, pensions and severance pay, insurance coverage of various kinds, seniority in promotions, transfers and layoffs, discipline and discharge, and grievance arbitration provisions.

The Commission's proposed legislation specified the action to be taken if conflicts arose between negotiated agreement provisions and existing municipal laws or regulations. It recommended, simply, that the results achieved through collective bargaining should prevail over any preexisting statutory restrictions on the authority of the employing agency.[3] The Commission did not recommend the repeal or nullification of any law, but merely the nonapplication of any rule or ordinance covering the subject matter already covered by a negotiated contract provision.

The Commission did, however, place certain restrictions on the scope of bargaining. It sought to protect the authority of the Civil Service Commission by excluding from negotiations the conduct of civil service examinations and the establishment of lists from which appointments were to be made. Second, it recommended that any negotiated agreement requiring legislative action or appropriation

---

* The 11-member Connecticut commission was composed of government officials, employer organization representatives, academicians, and state legislators, and was chaired by Professor Robert Stutz of the University of Connecticut.

of funds be approved by the legislative body with authority over the employing agency before such agreement was implemented. If the appropriate legislative body rejected an agreement, the parties would be forced to resume bargaining. The Commission believed this system would provide checks and balances to protect the public interest inasmuch as financial control of agreements would rest with the legislative body of the municipality, which, in many instances, would also be the budget authority.

In June 1965 the Connecticut legislature adopted, with few changes, the statute proposed by the advisory commission. Despite the two qualifications on the scope of bargaining, Connecticut's law embodies a relatively open-ended approach to negotiations and specifically gives weight to the provisions of collective bargaining agreements that, as is often the case, overlap with preexisting rules or legislation. During the same month, a law governing teacher collective bargaining was also enacted. This statute similarly authorizes bargaining with respect to salaries and conditions of employment.

ILLINOIS

Governor Otto Kerner of Illinois in 1966 appointed a special commission to recommend policy on labor-management relations in public employment. In March 1967 the Commission released its report.*

"The 'scope' of permissible negotiations was a complex and troublesome problem throughout the inquiry and was never fully resolved."[4] The Illinois Commission faced the same problems that other advisory commissions have attempted to tackle: (1) the fact that on most money items a public agency must secure approval of some superior administrative or legislative body; (2) the overlapping of collective bargaining subject matter with civil service codes already governing public employees; and (3) the problem of protecting the managerial function against employee encroachment while simultaneously encouraging meaningful negotiations.

In its final report the Commission recommended a scope of bargaining that extended to wages, hours, and working conditions but excluded regulations of the civil service merit-rating system.[5] It also stated that collective negotiations should not result in final

---

*The Commission included representatives of labor, management, government, and universities. Professors Martin Wagner and Milton Derber of the University of Illinois served as chairman and vice-chairman, respectively.

and binding agreements with respect to those matters that, by law, depend for their implementation on the action of a legislative or administrative body. The Commission did add that although the civil service law or rules provided a grievance procedure, an employing agency and an employee organization could negotiate a procedure for handling grievances under their agreement. This recommendation was an implicit recognition of the negotiability of arbitration provisions in public sector agreements.

During the course of its study the Illinois Advisory Commission heard the testimony of many organizations operating in the public sector. With respect to scope of bargaining, some employee groups, especially the professionals, "felt that their professional interests necessitated major involvement in shaping the mission of the agency and the standards of public service."[6] Although the Commission agreed that it was desirable for such employees to discuss matters of policy and standards with their employing agencies, it was not persuaded to include these items within the scope of formal negotiations. Collective bargaining, although a legitimate vehicle for employees to gain a voice in determining their working conditions, could not, according to the Commission, interfere with efficient management and operation of government service. It recommended, therefore:

> It should be the exclusive function of each public employing agency to determine the mission of the agency, set standards of services to be offered to the public, and exercise control and discretion over its organization and operations.
>
> It should be the right of each public employing agency to direct its employees, take disciplinary action, relieve its employees from duty because of lack of work or for other legitimate reasons, and determine the methods, means, and personnel by which the agency's operations are to be conducted. But this should not preclude employees from negotiating or raising grievances about the practical consequences that decisions on these matters may have on wages, hours, and working conditions.[7]

The inclusion of this strong management rights language significantly reduced the broadness of the Commission's recommendation that the scope of bargaining include "wages, hours, and working conditions." Also interesting was the recommendation that negotiations be permitted over the "practical consequences" of managerial decisions. Whereas the Commission apparently believed that the impact of management decisions should be negotiable, it did not recommend that the impact of civil service regulations also be negotiable. When discussing civil service, it merely recommended that employee organizations be allowed to voice complaints to the legislature and Civil Service Commission about the application of rules.

Although the governor endorsed the recommendations of the Advisory Commission, the Illinois legislature failed to pass the proposed legislation, largely because the Democrats, representing the labor vote, refused to endorse the no-strike provisions of the proposed law. Illinois still has not enacted a comprehensive statute for public sector bargaining. It has been suggested that Illinois' vigorous employee labor unions do not need a law to accomplish their goals and that, from their standpoint, it is better to do without any law than to suffer under an unsatisfactory one.[8]

MICHIGAN

In 1965 Michigan amended its 1947 law and granted public employees, including teachers but excluding those in the state classified civil service (constitutionally outside the legislative domain), the right to organize and bargain collectively over wages, hours, and other terms and conditions of employment. In 1966 Governor George Romney appointed a committee to review the law and to determine what changes, if any, were needed to encourage bargaining and, simultaneously, to protect the public against interruption of government services.*

In its report[9] the Committee stated that the Public Employment Relations Act had generated considerable employee organization and activity. In most cases agreements were consummated without interruption of public service. On the basis of its studies, the Committee concluded that the basic policy underlying the granting of "rights of unionization" was sound and should be continued. It insisted, however, that there were important differences between public and private employment that required continuing appraisal of the procedures and substantive aspects of collective bargaining in the public sector.

With respect to the scope of bargaining, the Committee reported that public management representatives had urged the enactment of a statutory "management rights" section to exclude certain managerial prerogatives from the realm of bargaining. These representatives also wanted the law amended to include a provision subordinating negotiated agreements to existing laws, resolutions, ordinances, rules, or regulations. Labor organizations, in contrast, encouraged

---

*Members of the committee were Gabriel N. Alexander, Edward L. Cushman, Ronald W. Haughton, and Charles C. Killingsworth. Russell A. Smith was chairman.

the rejection of any proposal to restrict the scope of bargaining.

The Advisory Committee recommended that any possible changes in the scope of bargaining, entailing either a statutory enumeration of the proper subjects for negotiation or a statutory listing of nonnegotiable "management rights," should be deferred and possibly considered at a later date after more experience under the Public Employment Relations Act.

The Committee did, however, recommend certain procedural changes that would affect the scope of bargaining. Specifically, it suggested that the duty to bargain collectively under the Act be broadened to include "the obligation to comply with the dispute settlement procedures stipulated by the statute and . . . to include a requirement that the parties shall be obligated to include, as a mandatory subject of bargaining, procedures for settling 'grievance' disputes." (Emphasis added.) With respect to this recommendation, the Advisory Committee specifically urged that it be stated public policy to encourage arbitration of unresolved grievances.

In conclusion the Committee viewed its most important recommendation as the establishment of a continuing Commission on Public Employee Relations whose members would include experts on industrial relations and whose function would be to make reports and recommendations to the governor and legislature.

> We think, finally, that the matter of public employee unionism, and the operation of the Act, should be made the subject of continuing examination by a commission of "public" members, with suitable budgetary support. This commission should be established by statute with appointment by the Governor.

Perhaps on the advice of the Advisory Committee, the Michigan legislature has not yet amended the scope of bargaining originally set forth in the Public Employment Relations Act. Public employment negotiations concern wages, hours, and other terms and conditions of employment; and the Act contains no statement of management rights. One positive act that the Michigan legislature took in response to an Advisory Committee recommendation concerns arbitration. The Committee had recommended the experimental adoption of compulsory arbitration to resolve collective bargaining disputes involving police and firefighters. The Committee thought it would be "in the public interest" to do this, "in order the better, ultimately, to be able to assess virtues and deficiencies" of this method of dispute settlement. Effective October 1, 1969, this recommendation was implemented by the enactment of legislation making arbitration available at the instance of either party. In 1972, the Michigan legislature amended this law to provide for "final offer" binding arbitration in police and fire disputes.

NEW JERSEY

The New Jersey Study Commission issued its report in January 1968.[*] Although the Commission's discussion of the scope of bargaining under its proposed law was succinct, it did state its belief that collective negotiations in public employment could be fruitful even though employing agencies frequently lack final authority to determine wages and working conditions, and must make recommendations to chief executives and legislatures. In the Commission's view, effective negotiation could be conducted on issues that fall within the discretion of the employer. In accordance with this view, it recommended that the scope of bargaining include wages, hours, and other terms and conditions of employment "within the power of the appointing authority to determine or recommend."[10] This recommendation was somewhat confusing, in that the range of items within the power of an agency to determine could be rather small while the scope of items on which it could make recommendations might be quite large. In any case the implication was that the scope of bargaining should be limited; furthermore, the Commission stated explicitly that civil service regulations affecting examinations, appointments, and promotions should be excluded from negotiations.

In 1969 the New Jersey legislature passed the New Jersey Employer-Employee Relations Act. It defines the scope of bargaining to be grievances and terms and conditions of employment, without making any references to employers' discretionary or recommending authority, as did the Commission. The Act does not reserve any specific rights to management, nor does it exclude civil service matters from the scope of negotiations.

MAINE

Maine's Legislative Research Committee published its Report on Collective Bargaining by Municipalities in January 1968.[11] Previous to that date the only public employee statute on the books in Maine was the Firefighters' Arbitration Law, enacted in 1965. According to the Committee, however, many municipal employers had been voluntarily entering into collective negotiations with employee organizations. In light of these informal developments, the

---

[*] The New Jersey Public and School Employees' Grievance Procedures Study Commission consisted of a dozen members, two from the Senate, two from the Assembly, and eight appointed by the governor. Marver H. Bernstein was the chairman.

60

Committee recommended that the state pass legislation clarifying and formalizing public policy and procedures regarding negotiations in public employment.

In its proposed legislation the Committee defined collective bargaining to mean the negotiation of "grievance procedures" and "personnel matters, including wages, hours, and working conditions. . . ."[12] The only limitation placed on bargaining was that the conduct and grading of merit examinations, as well as rating and appointment of candidates, were not to be negotiable.

In 1970 the Maine legislature enacted the Municipal Public Employees Labor Relations Law. The scope of bargaining extends to wages, hours, working conditions, and contract grievance arbitration. The law, however, specifies a restriction regarding teacher negotiations, in that "public employers of teachers shall meet and consult but not negotiate with respect to educational policies. . . ."

PENNSYLVANIA

The Governor's Commission to Revise the Public Employee Law of Pennsylvania issued its report in June 1968.* With respect to the scope of negotiations, it tersely commented that bargaining should cover wages, hours, and conditions of employment, "appropriately qualified by a recognition of existing laws dealing with aspects of the same subject matter and by a carefully defined reservation of managerial rights."[13] (These rights were not enumerated in the Commission's report.)

Pennsylvania's public employee bargaining law was enacted in 1970, and for the most part it embodies the recommendations of the Governor's Commission. While bargaining is allowed on wages, hours, and other terms and conditions of employment, public employers may not be required to bargain "over matters of inherent managerial policy." These include organizational structure and selection and direction of personnel. Employers are, however, required to meet and discuss policy matters affecting wages, hours, and terms and conditions of employment.

---

*Governor Raymond Shafer appointed the Commission, which consisted of Leon Hickman, chairman, eight citizen members, and two members of the legislature.

COLORADO

The Colorado Legislative Council presented its report on public sector bargaining in December 1968.[14] The report contains summaries of and excerpts from the many reports and recommendations that the Council received from various interest groups throughout the state. As was to be expected, most of the labor organizations favored as wide a bargaining scope as possible, whereas management representatives supported a statutory enumeration of management rights and protection of civil service codes from collective negotiations. Teacher organizations were most desirous of obtaining an unlimited scope of bargaining, so that they could participate directly in shaping school policies and objectives. The Colorado Association of School Boards and the Denver public schools objected to the inclusion of such items as curriculum, class size, and textbook selection within the scope of bargaining and endorsed negotiations only on working conditions and economic matters.

The Council proposed legislation that established collective bargaining rights for public employees and specified the procedures to be used by public agencies and employee organizations. Instead of creating a separate "public employment relations board" to administer the act (as do most public employee relations laws), the Council authorized the present State Industrial Commission to administer the proposed law.[15] This proposed role for the Industrial Commission was significant with respect to the recommended scope of bargaining. The Council determined that the scope of negotiations should include "terms and conditions of employment." "Terms and conditions of employment" was defined to mean those items that the Industrial Commission determined could be the subjects of bargaining between a particular public employer and the exclusive bargaining agent for his employees in a designated bargaining unit. These items could include, but not go beyond, "salaries, wages, hours, working conditions, and other personnel matters."[16]

The Council also recommended that if any provision of a negotiated agreement contravened an existing law or regulation beyond the power of the employer to alter, the employer could submit a proposed amendment of the law or regulation to the proper governmental body for action. The conflicting portion of the agreement was not to be implemented until action was taken on any necessary amendment. If no action were taken, the agreement provision which conflicted with the existing law or regulation would become void. The parties could then conduct further negotiations if they believed such action to be necessary. This procedure attempted to accommodate both collective bargaining and preexisting ordinances and civil service rules by allowing the employer to recommend to chief executives and legislative bodies the necessary legal or administrative changes to effectuate negotiated agreements. This procedure, however, would not have encouraged as wide a scope of bargaining as does the legislation adopted in Connecticut, which allows a negotiated agreement to prevail over conflicting laws or rules.

Although the Council issued its report almost six years ago, the Colorado legislature has not yet passed a collective bargaining law for public employees.

MARYLAND

In 1968 Maryland enacted a Professional Negotiation Statute, permitting teachers to organize and bargain collectively. Responding to increasing pressure to establish negotiating rights for all public employees, Maryland's Governor Spiro Agnew appointed a task force to study the feasibility of adopting new collective bargaining legislation governing all employees in the public sector. Early in 1969 the Task Force on Public Employee Labor Relations published its recommendations, which, with respect to the scope of bargaining, very closely resembled those of the Illinois Advisory Commission.[17]

The Maryland report stated that the scope of collective negotiations should extend to wages, hours, and other conditions of employment. While the Task Force sought to encourage meaningful negotiations, its members nevertheless believed that managers of government agencies should not be hindered from directing their operations efficiently and in the public interest. Therefore, the broad language of "wages, hours, and other conditions of employment" was somewhat restricted by the inclusion of the following management rights provision:

It should be the exclusive function of each public employing agency to determine the mission of the agency, set standards of services . . . and exercise control and discretion over its organization and operations.

It should also be the right of each public employing agency to direct its employees, take disciplinary action, relieve its employees from duty because of a lack of work or for other legitimate reasons and to determine the method, means, and personnel by which the agencies' operations are to be conducted.[18]

The Task Force did add, however, as did the Illinois Advisory Commission, that these reserved management prerogatives were not to preclude employees from negotiating or raising grievances about the "practical consequences" of managerial decisions on wages, hours, and working conditions.

Finally, the Task Force recommended that merit system principles be safeguarded. To accomplish this, civil service regulations concerning examinations, assignments, and promotions were excluded from collective bargaining.* Civil service regulations or preexisting grievance procedures instituted under the civil service system were not, however, to prevent an employing agency and an employee organization from negotiating their own procedure for handling grievances under their agreement.

Maryland's legislature has not yet adopted legislation as proposed by the 1969 Task Force report. The City of Baltimore and Prince Georges County, however, have adopted local bargaining ordinances covering their public employees.

OHIO

The Ohio Legislative Service Commission issued its report in February 1969.[19] It made a comprehensive study of labor relations in both public employment generally and in the state of Ohio, and it concluded that positive state legislation was necessary to formalize collective bargaining in Ohio's public sector. It did not, however, draft proposed legislation or make specific recommendations; rather, it considered, and offered for the legislature's study, several alternative proposals for legislative action.

Under its discussion of the scope of bargaining, the Commission sion stated:

> The scope of bargaining could be left undefined in the law, for each employer and employee representative to work out; could be defined in general terms, such as terms and conditions of employment; could be specifically defined in terms of what is to be included or excluded, such as an enumeration of items already covered by other laws or

---

*Two Task Force members dissented from this recommendation. Dr. Weinstein dissented to the extent that the merit system and civil service system "should be studied to suggest modifications" in order to avoid conflict between the proposed legislation and the existing systems. Mr. Heyman dissented on the basis that "the final determination of rules and regulations concerning recruitment, examination, promotion, and classification of employees should not be within the exclusive province of the Civil Service System. These are matters in which public employees have a vested interest and where the best interest of the public can be advanced by permitting employees to bargain over such matters."

ordinances; or could be generally defined (terms and conditions of employment) with a general exclusion (not otherwise provided by law).[20]

The Commission reported that it had conferred with several parties regarding the scope of bargaining. Many of those concerned with teacher negotiations favored legislation that would permit negotiations on "all areas of concern." Others, however, believed that school policies were management prerogatives that should be excluded from negotiations.

On the matter of scope of bargaining for all public employees, the suggestion most often made to the Commission was that collective bargaining be limited to wages, hours, and working conditions—with the retention of certain management rights, such as hiring, firing, transfer, and policy direction. The Commission noted, however, that wage negotiations could "complicate budget considerations and might encroach on the authority of the legislature or other bodies in the area of appropriations."[21] To alleviate this problem, it suggested that negotiations could be conducted on matters covered by law or requiring action by a legislative body, with the final result of the bargaining submitted to the appropriate body for its approval (the approach advocated by several other study commissions, including those of Connecticut and Colorado).

The Commission did not explore the problem of potential conflicts between civil service regulations and negotiated agreements other than to suggest that the legislature could preserve the existing civil service structure while it allowed bargaining on those items not covered by the regulations (the solution adopted in Wisconsin).

The final alternative proposed by the Commission was that negotiations be permitted on everything not specifically prohibited by legislation.

As stated above, the Commission did not endorse any of the approaches that it suggested for consideration. Ohio has not yet enacted legislation governing its public employees.

SOUTH DAKOTA

In 1969 South Dakota enacted Chapter 88, its first legislative attempt to define state policy on public employee labor relations. This law prohibits public employees from striking but allows them to form or join labor organizations, meet and confer with employing agencies with respect to grievances and conditions of employment, and submit such settlements as may be reached to the government bodies having authority to approve and act upon them.

After passing this law, the South Dakota legislature indicated to the State Legislative Research Council that the issues raised during the 1969 session deserved further study. The Council was charged with making a comprehensive study of the "feasibility of establishing a system of collective bargaining and arbitration of employment disputes of public employees . . ." in South Dakota.

The Council, like the Ohio Commission, did not draft a bill or offer specific recommendations. It reviewed significant issues in public employment and, in its own words, "attempted to set forth the basic concepts which have been accepted by the experts in this field."[22]

In discussing the scope of bargaining, the Council briefly noted the various approaches that have been used by other states "to appropriately limit the scope of collective negotiations." It did warn, however, that excessively severe limitations would jeopardize or destroy meaningful negotiations.

The Council suggested that certain restriction on collective negotiations should exist because some public officials are required by law to perform specified tasks:

> It would be a dereliction for a public officer to fail to perform a duty mandated by a state constitution or a city charter on the grounds he has not been able to negotiate successfully with an employee organization. Submission of a budget at a fixed date is an example of what such a duty might be.[23]

The Council added that in certain instances the way in which mandated duties were carried out could be subject to grievance procedures. It was silent, however, on whether they could also be subject to negotiations.

As a final alternative the Council suggested the adoption of a strong management rights clause. It referred, however, not to the adoption of such clauses in statutes but to their inclusion in negotiated contracts between employee organizations and employers. It was not clear, therefore, whether the Council was suggesting that the legislature include a management rights section in the law or whether this item should remain an issue for the parties to resolve through bargaining.

In February 1970 the South Dakota legislature modified the state's "meet and confer" law. The effect of the amendments was to liberalize Chapter 88, which had emphasized strike penalties, and to establish procedures to settle disputes. The significant, although indirect, change regarding scope of bargaining was the alteration of the "meet and confer" requirement to a "meet and negotiate" obligation with respect to grievances and conditions of employment.

TENNESSEE

The Legislative Council Committee of Tennessee adopted a far more cautious approach to public sector labor relations than did most of the other reports here analyzed. It had been authorized by the Tennessee legislature to "study the entire area of public employment relations, both as to state and local governments, and to report its findings. . . ." In January 1971 the Committee issued its study and recommendations.[24]

Most of the Committee's recommendations are directed toward changing and improving the civil service system in Tennessee rather than establishing a collective bargaining framework and dispute settlement procedures for public employees. The Committee advised passage of legislation providing for a grievance procedure through which employees could voice complaints; the adoption of regulations establishing criteria to be considered in developing work schedules; the adoption of regulations setting forth the grounds on which employees could file complaints; the enactment of a broad civil service system, empowered to establish binding rules regarding job security, seniority rights, working conditions, merit promotions, and grievance procedures; and the prohibition of any department head or agency from making, without the governor's approval, any binding decision concerning wages or hours with any employee or group of employees.

Toward the conclusion of its recommendations, the Committee offered the following remarks:

> In addition to providing for fair and workable civil service systems, we believe that we must recognize the fact that organized labor in the public sector does exist and that it is necessary and proper to establish guidelines to insure uniform practices and procedures. . . . [T]his is necessary in order to provide basic mechanics for orderly government, and it is desirable that both management and labor know specifically what is required of them in furthering responsible labor relations. . . .[25]

Thus, in what appears to be a spirit of resignation, the Committee recommended the passage of legislation that would establish "procedures and guidelines for recognition and negotiation with public employees' organizations. . . ."[26]

This was all that the Committee reported on the matter of public employee negotiations. It did add, however, that inasmuch as many governmental units "may not enter into agreements with employee organizations," the above recommendations take the form of enabling legislation, which would apply only to these government bodies actually making agreements with employee organizations.

CONCLUSION

Although the review of state commission reports presented in this chapter does not exhaust the list of study group recommendations, which have been made at all levels of government,[27] it has attempted to indicate the broad range of expert opinion on the appropriate scope of bargaining in public employment. An analysis of the advisory commission reports also explains, at least in part, why some state laws restrict the scope of bargaining while other statutes contain broad definitions of negotiable subjects.

While the advisory commissions of Connecticut, Illinois, Michigan, Maine, and Maryland endorsed a broad definition of the scope of bargaining (wages, hours, and conditions of employment), the Illinois and Maryland commissions severely restricted the meaning of this definition by recommending statutory enumeration of reserved management rights. The New Jersey and Pennsylvania commissions also narrowed their definitions of the bargaining scope: New Jersey recommended that bargaining subjects be within the power of the appointing authority to determine or recommend; and Pennsylvania stated that wages, hours, and terms and conditions of employment must be qualified by a recognition of existing laws covering the same subjects (as well as a statutory management rights clause). Five commission reports—Connecticut, Illinois, New Jersey, Maine, and Maryland—recommended the exclusion of the merit system or civil service codes from the scope of bargaining. Additionally, Connecticut, Illinois, and Colorado recommended some kind of legislative approval prior to implementation of negotiated agreements requiring legislative action or appropriation of funds.

On the other hand, several study commissions made efforts to loosen restrictions imposed by statutory management rights clauses and extensive civil service regulations by suggesting that the practical consequences of managerial decisions be subject to grievance procedures and negotiation (Illinois and Maryland), and by recommending that negotiating parties be permitted to negotiate their own grievance procedures (conceivably with binding arbitration as the last stage) regardless of the prior existence of any civil service grievance procedures (Illinois and Maryland).

The Ohio and South Dakota commissions apparently were overwhelmed by the complex problems and diverse approaches that characterize public employment labor relations and statutes. Declining to draft proposed legislation or make specific recommendations, they confined themselves to studying the experiences of other states and left it to their legislatures to consider the alternative courses of action and to enact a statute.

The state legislatures demonstrated a variety of reactions to their advisory commission reports. Connecticut adopted a statute

containing, with few changes, the recommendations of the Connecticut
State Commission. The Maine and Pennsylvania laws largely embody
their state commission recommendations, although the statutes
specify that educational policies (in Maine) and "inherent managerial
policy" (in Pennsylvania) may be conferred upon but not negotiated.
Michigan also followed the recommendations of its commission at
least with respect to the scope of bargaining, by not amending its
1965 public employee law. Several states, however, including Illinois,
Colorado, Maryland, and Ohio, have not taken any action on their
advisory commission reports; and in New Jersey, the legislature
virtually rejected the commission's recommendations on the scope
of bargaining by passing a law containing a broad definition of negotiable subjects and no restrictions on the scope of bargaining.

NOTES

1. Some of the better-known committee reports include the
Connecticut report of 1965, the New York (Taylor Committee) report
of March 1966, the Michigan report of February 1967, the Illinois
report of March 1967, the New Jersey report of January 1968, the
Pennsylvania (Hickman Commission) report of June 1968. It has
been reported, however, that recently legislative study groups have
been active in Florida, Georgia, Iowa, Kentucky, New Mexico, Texas,
and Utah. See Committee on Executive Management and Fiscal
Affairs, National Governors' Conference/1970 Supplement to Report
of Task Force on State and Local Government Labor Relations
(Chicago: Public Personnel Association, 1971).
2. Connecticut Commission on Collective Bargaining by Municipalities, Text of Report, 81 GERR D-1 (Mar. 29, 1965).
3. The Commission's draft law stated: "Where there is a conflict between any agreement reached by a municipal employer and
an employee organization and approved in accordance with the provisions of this Act any charter, special act, ordinance, or rules and
regulations adopted by a municipal employer or its agents . . . or
any general statute regulating the hours of work of policemen or
firemen, the terms of such agreement shall prevail." See ibid. at
D-9.
4. Milton Derber, "Labor-Management Policy for Public Employees in Illinois: The Experience of the Governor's Commission,
1966-67," Industrial and Labor Relations Review 21 (July 1968),
550.
5. 184 GERR at D-2 (Mar. 20, 1967).
6. Derber, op. cit., p. 551.
7. 184 GERR at D-2 (Mar. 20, 1967). Emphasis added.
8. Derber, op. cit., p. 558.

9. Michigan Advisory Committee on Public Employee Relations, Text of Report, 181 GERR F-1 (Feb. 28, 1967).

10. 229 GERR D-7 (Jan. 29, 1968).

11. Legislative Research Committee, Report on Collective Bargaining by Municipalities to Second Special Session of the One Hundred and Third Legislature, Publication 103-18 (Jan. 1968). The Committee was composed of six members, including Chairman Samuel A. Hinds.

12. Ibid., p. 6.

13. 251 GERR E-1 (July 1, 1968).

14. Colorado Legislative Council, Public Employee Negotiations, report to the Colorado General Assembly, Research Publication no. 142 (Dec. 1968).

15. The reason given was that machinery for labor-management relations in the private sector already existed within the Commission, which was experienced in labor-management relations. See ibid., p. xvii.

16. The Council authorized the Industrial Commission to distinguish between different employment situations in order to avoid problems concerning home-rule cities. The state constitution allows home-rule cities to enact laws overriding state statutes. By permitting the Industrial Commission to retain flexibility in establishing the scope of negotiations, the state hoped to avoid any conflict with home-rule city administrations that might disagree with a unitary approach. See Irving Sabghir, The Scope of Bargaining in Public Sector Collective Bargaining, report sponsored by New York State Public Employment Relations Board (Oct. 1970), p. 26.

17. For full text see 278 GERR AA3 (Jan. 6, 1969).

18. Ibid. at AA-6.

19. Ohio Legislative Service Commission, Public Employee Labor Relations, Report no. 96 (Feb. 1969).

20. Ibid., p. 69.

21. Ibid., p. 70.

22. State Legislative Research Council, Labor-Management Relations in Public Employment, staff memorandum (Dec. 1, 1969), p. 2.

23. Ibid., p. 25.

24. Legislative Council Committee, Study on Public Employer-Employee Relations 1970 (Nashville, Tenn., 1971).

25. Ibid., p. 76.

26. Ibid., pp. 79-80.

27. For other state commission reports, see Minnesota, A Report by the Governor's Committee on Public Employee Labor Relations Laws to Governor Karl F. Ralvaag (Mar. 1, 1965); Rhode Island, Report of the Commission to Study Mediation and Arbitration (Feb. 1966). At the federal level, see the Kappal Commission report

on the Post Office Department: Towards Postal Excellence, Report of the President's Commission on Postal Re-organization (Washington, D.C.: U.S. Government Printing Office, June 1968). (The Los Angeles County report of July 1968 is discussed in Chapter 5.)

THE SCOPE OF BARGAINING: SOME ALTERNATIVE APPROACHES BASED ON A REVIEW OF THE LITERATURE

The appropriate scope of bargaining in public employment has been a popular and controversial subject of discussion among labor relations experts. Many of these experts hold key government positions or have served on specially appointed committees similar to the state advisory study commissions, and their views have influenced the development of new statutes as well as current collective bargaining practices. This chapter presents the various approaches that have been advanced regarding the scope of public sector bargaining. Their variety reflects the complexity of the scope-of-bargaining problem and illumines the many factors that affect ''what is negotiable'' in public employment.

THE WILLIAM KILBERG VIEW: THE INAPPLICABILITY OF THE MANDATORY/PERMISSIVE DISTINCTION

In an incisive law review article, William J. Kilberg, then general counsel of the Federal Mediation and Conciliation Service, discusses what he believes should be the appropriate scope of bargaining in the public sector.[1] A major premise of Kilberg's article is that the mandatory/permissive delineation of the private sector is not useful in determining the scope of bargaining in public employment. In the private sector, under the Borg-Warner doctrine, mandatory subjects of bargaining may be negotiated to impasse; and economic weapons (for example, strike and lockout) may then be used to force agreement on the disputed subjects. Permissive subjects, however, may be negotiated only if the parties agree to discuss them. Moreover, a party is prohibited from insisting to the point of impasse on inclusion in the contract of a nonmandatory subject to which the other side is opposed. The use of the mandatory/

permissive classification in the private sector is, therefore, a useful means of limiting the number of issues that potentially could be the subjects of strikes or lockouts. Permissive subjects may be removed from the bargaining table by either party at any time during the negotiations, thereby minimizing the number of issues that may reach impasse and spark strong economic action.[2]

In the public sector, however, Kilberg observes, a distinction between mandatory and permissive subjects will not serve the same purpose, primarily because under most public employee bargaining statutes, the right to strike is prohibited. A bargaining impasse in public employment generally results in the implementation of such statutory procedures as mediation, fact-finding, and arbitration—all of which are substitutes for traditional economic weapons. Kilberg concludes, therefore, that inasmuch as the results of public sector impasses are not as disruptive as those in the private sphere, "there is a corresponding decrease in the need to minimize the number of subjects over which the parties could reach such impasse."[3]

Rejecting the mandatory/permissive distinction as unsuitable for the public sector, Kilberg argues that the state legislatures must assume the burden of clearly defining what is and what is not negotiable. In making this definition, the legislatures should pay close attention to the dissimilar economic and social contexts of the private and public sectors. Kilberg stresses, for example, that in the public, as opposed to the private, sphere, there is "no recognizable price structure or profit motive" (prices do not always reflect costs); it may be very difficult for local governments to expand their tax bases; the public stake often is very great in many areas of decision-making; the public employee union is less apt to bow to management's decisions in crucial policy matters because it does not believe in the possibility of bankruptcy of its employer; and the unions representing professional employees tend to encroach upon traditional managerial prerogatives.

Because of these unique aspects of public employment, as well as management's accountability to the public and responsibility for the maintenance of uninterrupted government services, Kilberg believes the legislatures should exclude from the scope of bargaining those subjects that must, for the good of the polity, be determined unilaterally by public management. These proscribed subjects, according to Kilberg, fall into three categories. The first category includes those items that would require noncompliance with superior statutory law or administrative regulation. Thus teachers, for example, should not be allowed to negotiate for the right to strike disruptive students, inasmuch as this would "arguably conflict with constitutional standards of equal protection and due process."[4] Because a civil service system, however, can be a "stumbling block" to free collective bargaining, Kilberg suggests that all non-merit functions should be transferred from the civil service commission to a personnel department under the chief executive officer of each local unit. If this were done, bargaining could cover many terms and conditions of employment presently excluded from negotiations while the civil service commission retained exclusive control over such areas as recruiting, examination, hiring, and training.

A second category of subjects that should be excluded, in Kilberg's view, includes those matters that vitally protect the public from harm. Kilberg argues that if a union representing policemen or firemen, for example, were permitted to negotiate and persuade a municipality to agree to certain demands, the public welfare might be placed in jeopardy. He suggests, therefore, that an arbitration panel be established that could determine "whether any particular union demand would be adverse to public safety if accepted by the city. If so, the local government would not be permitted to negotiate over the matter in question."[5]

A third area of nonnegotiable subjects covers demands proposed by many "social welfare" unions, including those of teachers, hospital employees, and welfare workers. In this area, says Kilberg, the legislature should set forth a comprehensive listing of negotiable and nonnegotiable subjects, "in each case balancing the public interest with the right of public employees to be heard on matters which directly affect their working conditions." He suggests that teachers, for instance, be consulted regarding matters of educational policy, curriculum planning, and textbook selection, but that they be denied the right to negotiate on these subjects, which should be determined "solely by individuals whose job it is to serve the long-run public good."[6]

THE VIEW OF THE U.S. ADVISORY COMMISSION ON INTER-GOVERNMENTAL RELATIONS: A NARROW SCOPE OF BARGAINING

The U.S. Advisory Commission on Intergovernmental Relations was appointed by President Nixon to study and make recommendations concerning public sector collective bargaining. In its 1970 report[7] the Commission recommended that the states enact "meet and confer" rather than collective bargaining legislation.* It defended this recommendation, stating:

> . . . the crying need . . . is for a general statute that
> balances management rights against employee needs,

*Maine Senator Edmund Muskie, Pennsylvania Governor Raymond Shafer, Wisconsin State Senator Robert Knowles, Westchester (N.Y.) County Executive Edwin Michaelian, and New York Governor Nelson Rockefeller dissented, believing that collective bargaining legislation should have been recommended.

recognizes the crucial and undeniable differences
between public and private employment, and establishes labor-management relationships in which
the public-at-large and their elected representatives have confidence.[8]

Under the recommended "meet and confer" legislation, the parties
would be obligated to meet at reasonable times, exchange information
and proposals, and attempt to reach agreement on matters concerning
wages, hours, and conditions of employment. The resulting memorandum of understanding would be submitted to a jurisdiction's
governing body, and would become effective if and when the implementary actions were agreed to and acted upon by the executive and
legislative officials. This kind of statute is preferable to a collective
bargaining law, according to the Commission because, to a greater
extent, (1) it protects management's discretion; (2) it seeks a reconciliation with the merit system; (3) it recognizes that a governmental
representative cannot commit his jurisdiction to a binding agreement,
and that only through ratifying and implementary legislation or executive orders can such agreement be effected; (4) it avoids detailed,
legally prohibited procedures applicable to all situations and, thereby,
permits greater "flexibility" and "adaptability" in actual implementation; and (5) it recognizes the differences between public and private
employment.[9]
  In line with this cautious approach to public sector labor relations
was the Commission's recommendation for a circumscribed scope of
bilateral discussion. First, it recommended that state laws specify
that agreements resulting from public employer-employee discussions
be governed by the provisions of any pertinent existing or future
statutes or regulations, including any applicable merit system laws
and rules.[10] Additionally, the Commission stated that labor relations
statutes should provide for employers to retain the unrestricted right
(a) to direct the work of their employees; (b) to hire, promote, demote
transfer, assign, and retain employees; (c) to suspend or discharge
employees; (d) to maintain the efficiency of governmental operations;
(e) to relieve employees because of lack of work or other legitimate
reasons; (f) to take actions necessary to carry out the mission of the
agency in emergencies; and (g) to determine the methods, means,
and personnel by which operations are to be carried on.[11]
  The recommendation for "something less" than collective
bargaining in public employment and the statutory enunciation of
management rights were significant features of the Commission's
recommendations. Although organized labor was very critical of its
report,[12] the Commission vigorously defended "meet and confer"
legislation and, with respect to management rights, stated that in a
democratic society, dealings between public employers and unions
must be restricted by legislatively determined policies and goals.

Listing management rights in law "eliminates many of the headaches of administrative elaboration and . . . the cross pressures generated by ambiguities.[13]

The Commission summarized its recommendation for a restricted scope of discussion by noting that experience in several "meet and confer" states indicates that as employee organizations grow strong, discussion can escalate to the level of collective negotiations. In light of this de facto development:

> It is likely that any concession made at the conference
> table by the employer's representative in connection with
> management rights or civil service procedures would
> lead to memoranda of understanding which subsequently
> could be repudiated by higher authority. This would create
> tension between the parties and possibly would lead to
> work disruptions.[14]

Hence, the need for incorporation in the statute of a specific provision prohibiting even discussion of management rights.

THE VIEW OF ROBERT HOWLETT: A BROAD SCOPE OF BARGAINING IN PUBLIC EMPLOYMENT

Contrasting with the views expressed in the Report of the Advisory Commission on Intergovernmental Relations are those favoring a broad scope of bargaining. The advocates of a wide scope of public sector negotiations include Robert G. Howlett, chairman of the Michigan Public Employment Relations Commission, who expressed his views at a 1970 conference on the newly enacted Hawaii Public Employment Relations Act.[15]

Disagreeing with the Advisory Commission on Intergovernmental Relations and other state commissions, Howlett said that the inclusion of management rights clauses in public employment statutes was "a mistake." Such statutory provisions, he said, have been enacted because legislators and government executives wish to retain their traditional unilateral powers, and they fear increasing employee influence on the determination of policy. As Howlett noted:

> In the private sector, subjects which twenty or ten years
> ago were not bargainable, are now the subjects of collec-
> tive bargaining. I question the wisdom of placing either
> government or employees in a statutory straitjacket.
> The concept of a public employment relations act, like a
> private sector act, is that the parties must sit around
> the table and bargain. The private sector statutes do not

76

attempt to specify the issues which are bargainable. Including a management rights clause in the statute limits
the subjects over which the parties may bargain. If the
statute excludes these certain issues from bargaining,
the parties may not legally bargain over them at all,
even though [they are] willing to do so.[16]

Moreover, Howlett pointed out, were the parties to include in a contract a subject that was prohibited by a management rights clause in
the statute, a taxpayer could successfully challenge the contract in
court. Alternatively, an employer, after agreeing to a contract clause
governing a prohibited item, could refuse to adhere to the contract
and would be upheld in court. Statutory management rights clauses
unnecessarily rigidify public labor relations because only the legislature can relax the restrictions on excluded subjects. The best
approach, therefore, is to make management rights clauses a subject
of bargaining between the parties, as is done in the private sector.*
    Howlett is particularly critical of the breadth of the statutory
management rights provisions that are being adopted in many public
employment relations statutes. He pointed out, for example, that the
openended provision giving management the right to "determine the
methods, means, and personnel by which operations are to be carried
out" cuts across many negotiable (or properly negotiable) issues
that affect employees' working conditions. Under the Hawaii law the
public employer has the right to "determine the qualifications, standards for work; the nature and content of examinations; hire, promote,
transfer, assign and retain employees in positions. . . ." Under this
restrictive language, Howlett comments, a union could not insist upon
negotiating work standards, a bidding procedure for promotion, or
the transfer and assignment of employees to various types of jobs.
With respect to schools:

If a school board has the absolute right to determine the
personnel by which operations are to be carried on, there
can be no bargaining over class size, a working condition
affecting teachers. If a school board has the complete

---

*Howlett also was critical of existing management functions
clauses because they do not contain the provision (found in all private sector contracts) stating that the powers retained by management
in the management rights provision are subject to the other terms of
the collective bargaining agreement. The omission of this proviso
in the state laws means that it is illegal to bargain over and include
in a contract any of the statutorily enumerated retained management
powers.

power to determine methods, means and personnel, there would seem to be no right to bargain on the school calendar. It would not be possible for teachers to bargain over preparation periods or transfers from one school to another. Clearly, the question of teachers performing lunchroom duty or patrolling the halls would not be bargainable.[17]

These examples indicate that statutory management rights clauses can restrict bargaining over issues that affect employee working conditions and that traditionally have been negotiated in the private sector. If bargaining is to be meaningful, said Howlett, there must be some accommodation of the conflict between statutory management functions provisions and the realities of collective bargaining, especially because if "public employees feel strongly enough about an issue, even though prohibited by statute, they will bargain about it."[18]

Howlett also is concerned about the limitations placed on collective bargaining by state tenure acts (education laws) and civil service codes. He stressed that the civil service system removes from bargaining items over which employees in private employment normally bargain, and again suggested that public employees "will insist on a voice in their significant working conditions," regardless of contrary statutes. He urged the transfer of certain items from the jurisdiction of the civil service to the realm of collective bargaining:

Civil service commissions are generally considered by employees, and by many public officials, to be part of public management. Generally, they are. For this reason, it is advisable that the disciplinary and discharge functions of civil service commissions be transferred to collective bargaining. Statutory changes may be required.[19]

Howlett also implied that public employees, or at least teachers, should not be statutorily prohibited from bargaining on policy matters. Expressing skepticism about the "practical aspects" of the Hawaii law's provision allowing consultation but not collective bargaining on policy matters, he stated that, contrary to the expectations of many, the Michigan Employment Relations Commission had had to adjudicate very few disputes centering on teachers' attempts to bargain on school policy. He admitted that teachers are discussing policy matters in negotiations, but school boards and superintendents are accommodating to it: "They are talking and reaching decisions. And as near as we can see, there has been no trauma because of it."

Robert Howlett believes in an "expanded" scope of bargaining. He thinks that many commentators overstate both the differences between the private and public sectors and the need to regulate public employment negotiations. He advocates a private sector approach

... with limitations spelled out in the collective bargaining agreement, not in the statute. The pre-collective bargaining method used by public employers to secure that which they believe of benefit to them or to the public was formerly, and continues to be in many places, by political action, including lobbying. Is it not better that working conditions, including some matters of policy (perhaps, particularly in the area of education) be discussed around the bargaining table rather than in the halls and cloakrooms of the State Capital?[20]

CONSULTATION VERSUS NEGOTIATION: THE REPORTS OF THE AARON COMMITTEE AND THE TWENTIETH CENTURY FUND TASK FORCE

The Aaron Committee, whose report of July 1968 formed the basis of a public labor relations ordinance for Los Angeles County,* adopted a "middle of the road" approach to the scope of bargaining.

Stating that attempts to model public collective bargaining statutes after private sector laws were "misguided and dangerous," the Committee's proposed ordinance reserved certain "exclusive rights" for management:

Managers of governmental agencies must insure that the functions intrusted to them are carried out promptly and without interruption. We think they should have the right initially to determine the manner in which these functions are to be performed. Accordingly, the provision we recommend explicitly sets forth those rights that County management may exercise unilaterally and without prior negotiation with employees or their organizations.[21]

Specifically, these management rights were (1) the right to "determine the mission of each of its constituent departments, boards, and commissions, set standards of services . . . and exercise control and discretion over its organization and operations"; and (2) the right "to direct its employees, take disciplinary action for proper cause, relieve its employees from duty because of lack of work or

---

*The Board of Supervisors of Los Angeles County appointed a consultants' committee to recommend an employee relations ordinance. It consisted of Benjamin Aaron, chairman, Lloyd H. Bailer, and Howard Block. Ordinance no. 9646, based on the committee's report, was adopted by the Board of Supervisors on September 3, 1968.

for other legitimate reasons, and determine the methods, means, and personnel by which [its] operation are to be conducted."

The Committee's report defined the scope of bargaining to include "wages, hours, and other terms and conditions of employment." Although the county's "exclusive rights" were not negotiable, all "matters affecting employee relations" were made subject to "consultation."* Additionally, the Commission recognized that managerial actions

> ... purportedly "in the public interest," sometimes are unnecessary or arbitrary. We have therefore provided that nothing in the section on employer rights shall preclude employees from raising grievances about the practical consequences that decisions on matters reserved for management may have on wages, hours, and other terms and conditions of employment.[22]

The Aaron Committee declined to give specific examples of what subjects should be considered mandatory and nonmandatory issues for bargaining. It argued that subjects proposed in collective bargaining, "like words in a sentence, take on color and meaning from their surrounding context." This is especially true of those items that, while affecting the level of service to be provided by government, also relate directly to conditions of employment. The Commission concluded, therefore, that since the line between bargainable issues and nonnegotiable management rights will not always be "clearly discernible," it would not be "wise to try to draw it, once and for all and for all subjects, in the ordinance. Rather, we recommend that in close and doubtful cases the [proposed enforcement] commission be empowered to draw the line on an ad hoc basis."[23]

In 1970 the Twentieth Century Fund Task Force on Labor Disputes in Public Employment published its report and recommendations, based on a one-year study of issues in public sector labor relations.[24] With respect to the duty to bargain, the Task Force stated that unions and employers should "meet and negotiate in 'good faith,' as the labor statute in the private sector requires."[25] In discussing the scope of bargaining, however, the Task Force said that the differences between private and public employment must affect what is negotiable. One major difference is that in the public sector, frequently it is not clear "who is the employer," that is, who has the authority to make an effective agreement on behalf of

---

*
Thus, the Committee's proposal stated that "every reasonable effort shall be made by management to consult with employees or their representatives prior to initiating basic changes in any rule or procedure affecting employee relations."

government. It is not unusual for employer negotiators in the public sector to lack the authority to implement the agreements they reach with unions because "a legislature, board, council, or budget director not represented in negotiations may have sole authority" to provide the necessary funds. The Task Force concluded that for negotiations to be meaningful, there must be a "clear line of communication between the actual participants and that body or official with final authority to accept and implement agreements reached in negotiations."[26]

In line with this conclusion, the Task Force stated that negotiations should not extend beyond the limits of an employer's authority to make binding agreements. It is, therefore, "impossible" to fashion a general definition of the subjects appropriate for bargaining in public employment because the degrees of autonomy granted to government agencies vary.

The Task Force concluded its discussion of the scope of bargaining by adding that no subject should be barred from consultation and discussion—as opposed to collective bargaining—regardless of the limitations on an employer agency's authority.

> It may be useful to hear the views of an organization representing employees even on employment matters beyond the administrator's ability to alter. . . . It is a meaningful extension of participatory rights to employees to consult and try to arrive at a common understanding on what may be recommended to the ultimate decision-making body with joint support.[27]

ORGANIZATIONAL POSITIONS ON THE SCOPE OF BARGAINING IN PUBLIC EDUCATION

The scope of bargaining in public education will be considered later. Appropriately included in this section, however, are the approaches that have been adopted by several educational organizations regarding the scope of teacher negotiations.

American Association of School Administrators

The American Association of School Administrators (AASA) expressed its views on the scope of bargaining in public education in two documents published in the late 1960s.[28] In both publications the AASA stated its preference for a "broadly construed concept of negotiations." However, in The School Administrator and Negotiation it appeared to have retreated somewhat from the broad approach it earlier espoused by distinguishing sharply between subjects appropriate for negotiations and those appropriate for "advisory consultation."

Expressing its belief in a wide scope of bargaining in School Administrators View Professional Negotiation, the AASA wrote, "If education is truly a profession, all professional personnel have a legitimate interest in the decisions that affect their pupil clientele, the effectiveness of their own work, and the quality of the educational program." Although the Association suggested that it might be "nonsensical" to bargain about the curricular sequence or educational material to be bought for third grade social studies, it emphasized that the process by which such decisions were made could be subject to formal negotiations. In its words, "The principle of including in decision-making those most directly responsible for carrying out the decisions is quite pertinent here."[29] Although the AASA added that not all aspects of public education were negotiable, it presented a list of subject areas, stating that, in its view, negotiations could "encompass all or some aspects of policy governing these areas: curriculum, in-service education, personnel policies, teaching assignments, transfers and promotions, recruitment of teachers, discharge and discipline of teachers, provisions of physical facilities for teachers, grievance procedures, recognition of the negotiating team, lunch and rest periods, salaries and wages, welfare benefits, class size, leaves of absence, expiration date of negotiation agreement, and other mutually agreed-upon matters that directly affect the quality of the educational program."[30] In its 1966 publication the AASA did not specifically exclude many subjects from negotiation. It suggested that school boards "not negotiate any items which would violate existing state laws"; and it mentioned that the selection of the school board's legal counsel, the determination of the board's financial and pupil accounting system, and the selection of the school superintendent should remain nonnegotiable.

Although not significantly different with respect to the scope of bargaining, AASA's 1968 publication presents a different tone. The section on bargaining scope begins with a comment on how teacher organizations "tend to press for broadening the scope of negotiation" and for "more teacher involvement in decision-making—not less." Shortly thereafter the Association comments that "teachers are insisting that they have a share in determining many other educational decisions concerning policies and procedures in carrying on the instructional program of the school system, matters relating to staff or pupil personnel service. . . ."

In order to solve the scope-of-bargaining problem, the AASA suggests that there be a distinction between negotiations and advisory consultation. The goal of teacher participation could be accomplished through a standing committee of teachers, supervisors, and administrators who would meet regularly and make "advisory recommendations" to the superintendent and board of education. The AASA suggests that the jurisdiction of this committee could be negotiable, although it offers, for example, lists of those items that it believes are negotiable and those that should be discussed in advisory consultation. Negotiable items include salary schedule, hospitalization benefits, reduced class size, compensation for committee work, duty-free lunch periods, and terminal leave pay. Advisory consultation issues include revision of policies and procedures on teacher assignment and transfer (in 1966 the AASA listed teaching assignments, transfers, and promotions as negotiable), review of leave-of-absence policies (in 1966 leaves of absence were listed as negotiable), teacher involvement in textbook selection and curriculum development (in 1966 curriculum was listed as bargainable), procedures for handling pupil discipline, establishment of an advisory committee on staff personnel administration, teacher involvement in planning of federally sponsored programs, and revision of policies governing attendance at professional meetings.

In conclusion the AASA, using its 1966 language, states that "a 'broadly construed concept of negotiation' makes sense." However, here the phrase "broadly construed" refers not to a wide scope of collective bargaining but to a broad approach to public school labor relations, involving "one stress for formalized negotiation and another for advisory consultation."

National Association of Secondary School Principals

The National Association of Secondary School Principals (NASSP) has expressed similar views of the scope of bargaining in public education. Robert L. Ackerly and W. Stanfield Johnson, writing for the NASSP, stated:

> It is a matter of major importance to principals that proper limitations be imposed upon subjects of negotiation. . . . Principals should enthusiastically endorse bargaining rights on issues involving the economic and physical welfare of employees and conditions which affect that welfare. Issues not related to employee welfare but involving school and educational policies are not proper subjects for bargaining.[31]

Ackerly and Johnson find fault with most state laws because they permit "the broadest interpretation of what is negotiable." Phrases such as "wages, hours, and conditions of employment" are, according to these authors, too loosely interpreted by teacher organizations, so that principals' prerogatives become bargaining issues.

They point out that even those statutes that limit the scope of bargaining by specifically excluding educational policy from negotiations are ambiguous because "educational policy" is subject to diverse interpretations. They suggest, therefore, that statutes should list certain subjects that "typify what is not subject to negotiation, such as curriculum, textbook selection, school discipline, hiring and assignment practices."[32]

In his pamphlet What Is Negotiable?, Benjamin Epstein, chairman of NASSP's Committee on Status and Welfare of Secondary School Administrators, presents a more incisive analysis of the scope of teacher bargaining.[33] Although he reaches conclusions similar to those of Ackerly and Johnson, Epstein appears more sensitive to the larger issues related to the scope of negotiations in education: the changing role of administrators, teachers' aspirations for increased professionalism, and the public interest in collective bargaining.

After discussing these issues, Epstein refers to NASSP's 1965 statement, The Principal's Role in Collective Negotiations Between Teachers and School Boards, wherein it was stated that the NASSP believed that teacher organizations should be involved in developing policy for dealing with such matters as types of school organization, curriculum, textbook selection, extracurricular activities, academic freedom, in-service training, and student discipline. "On the other hand," the statement continued,

> . . . NASSP emphasizes that discussions and decisions on purely professional problems cannot be considered in an atmosphere characteristic of the bargaining table. It proposes instead that such considerations take place in an atmosphere of colleagues working together as a professional team. It welcomes the establishment of formal councils made up of representatives chosen by teachers, principals, and supervisors.[34]

Epstein writes that the NASSP still believes that professional councils working under the leadership of the superintendent are "the most desirable vehicle" for guaranteeing teachers the right to participate in formulating policy. The NASSP agrees with the AASA that the structure and rights of these councils should be subject to negotiations.

Even after professional councils are formed, Epstein asserts that administrators will need guidelines for dealing with demands for the negotiation of what they consider "professional problems" rather than conditions of employment. NASSP therefore proposes the following criteria regarding the scope of teacher negotiations:[35]

> 1. No item should be considered negotiable which could be decided on the basis of the results of scientific

investigation, evaluations of experimental efforts, or other devices used by professional expertise to determine what is best for the education of pupils.*

2. No assignments of professional personnel should ever be made on the basis of automatic rotation or of any so-called "equitable" distribution of classes grouped according to levels of public ability or disciplinary difficulty, nor should assignments, transfer, or promotions . . . be determined on the basis of seniority.

3. The principle of accountability is one which should never be overlooked in determining the negotiability of any item. Who must face the responsibility of accounting for a judgment or decision?

4. Whenever in any negotiations there is a possible conflict between the interests and needs of the child and the organizational demands of teachers, the resolution of any differences must in every case be in favor of the child.

5. No educational policy-making is sound which involves school board members and teacher organization negotiators exclusively and omits administrators.

6. It will be to the interest of teachers' organizations to avoid negotiating petty items which in the eyes of school boards, administrators, the general public, and a great many of their own teacher members raise doubts about their professional zeal.

7. . . . there is no point in seeking to negotiate items that are beyond the power of a school board or administration to grant.

National Education Association and American Federation of Teachers

The views of the National Education Association (NEA) and American Federation of Teachers (AFT) are and have been, over the past few years, strikingly similar regarding the scope of bargaining. Using teacher professionalism as the rallying cry, both

---

*Epstein explains this guideline by stating that a teacher's daily work load, for example, would be negotiable. However, the size of a class "should be no less and no greater than that which produces maximum learning." Therefore, this item should not be negotiable. Similarly, the length of a class period should not be bargainable; it should be determined by such factors as student attention span and instructional efficiency.

organizations have endorsed an expansive scope of negotiations—one that includes wages, hours, and terms and conditions of employment—broadly interpreted.

Both the NEA and AFT have held that the welfare of teachers and the welfare of education are inextricably intertwined. As trained educators, teachers should have the right to shape and evaluate school policies—as well as conditions of employment—because such policies directly affect their professional roles and functions and, moreover, frequently are inseparable from working conditions. The following excerpt from a speech given by NEA's Allan West epitomizes teachers' views toward collective bargaining:

> A professional group should be permitted to negotiate with the board of education on matters which affect the quality of education other than those covered by the narrow definitions in labor law. This philosophy is based on the belief that the case for improved teacher welfare rests on the necessity for improving the quality of public education generally. Teachers have an interest in the conditions which attract and retain a better teaching force. They are concerned with in-service training programs, class size, selection of textbooks, the kinds of programs available for emotionally disturbed, physically handicapped children, and other matters which go beyond the limited industrial definition. . . . Professional associations are uniquely equipped . . . to bring to bear on negotiations the expert services necessary to make good decisions.[36]

The NEA Guidelines for Professional Negotiation, expressing the official NEA position on the scope of bargaining, states that all matters of joint concern to a local teachers' organization and school board should be subjects of negotiation. These issues include, "but are not limited to, setting standards in employing professional personnel, community support for the school system, inservice training of personnel, class size, teacher turn-over, personnel policies, salaries, working conditions, and communication within the school system."[37]

Donald Wollett, a former consultant to the NEA, stressed that the broad scope of bargaining advocated by the NEA rejects the "industrial relations" concept of distinguishing between conditions of employment and management prerogatives:

> The fact is that "professionalism" in public education means that teachers have an interest in every decision that affects their pupil clientele and the effectiveness of their work which reaches far beyond their narrow self-interest in "bread and butter." . . . [P]rofessional

associations with their expertise and special competence can give maximum assistance to the overworked and under-appreciated members of a lay school board.[38]

The AFT has expressed a similar view toward the scope of negotiations. It believes teacher involvement in school policy-making is not only inevitable, but constructive and beneficial to education. Because teachers are closest to the teaching/learning situation, they can effectively implement and judge new teaching techniques and provide vital information regarding curriculum, use of teaching materials, innovative devices, and staffing needs. Furthermore, "a significant factor in the introduction and success of change processes will be the extent to which organized teachers are included in the discussions of proposed innovations and in their evaluation."[39] According to the AFT, collective negotiation is the appropriate forum for teachers to gain the recognition and right to share in decision-making regarding these professional areas. As a former AFT president, Charles Cogen, stated:

> We would place no limit on the scope of negotiations. . . . Anything on which the two parties can agree should become a part of the agreement. . . .
> I look for a great expansion in the effective scope of negotiations. . . . Obviously, class sizes, number of classes taught, curriculum, hiring standards, textbooks and supplies, extra-curricular activities—in fact anything having to do with the operation of the school is a matter for professional concern and should thus be subject to collective bargaining.[40]

In 1969 the NEA drafted a proposed National Negotiations Act that was introduced in Congress. This bill, if passed, would mandate and govern collective bargaining between teachers and school boards, except in those states where comparable statutes already have been passed. This bill was published in the Educators Negotiating Service.[41] It is interesting to note, with respect to the scope-of-bargaining issue, that under "Definitions" the term "professional negotiation" means

> . . . meeting, conferring, consulting, discussing, and negotiating in a good faith effort to reach agreement with respect to the terms and conditions of professional service and other matters of mutual concern, and the execution, if requested by either party, of a written document incorporating any agreement reached.

Clearly, such a definition envisions a very wide range of negotiable issues.

On March 14, 1972, Donald E. Morrison, president of the NEA, addressed a Special Subcommittee on labor of the House Education and Labor Committee. He spoke concerning H.R. 9324, an NEA bill similar to S. 1951, the proposed National Negotiations Act presented here. His remarks highlight the concepts underlying the broad scope of bargaining that teachers have persistently advocated:

> In the private sector, the mandatory area of collective bargaining is defined as "rates of pay, wages, hours of employment, or other conditions of employment." Such a definition is unduly restrictive when applied to negotiation by many categories of public employees. A teacher, for example, having committed himself to a career of socially valuable service . . . has a special identification with the standards of his "practice" and the quality of the service provided to his "clientele." As a result of this identification, teachers characteristically seek to participate in decision-making in . . . matters designed to change the nature or improve the quality of the educational service . . . and they see negotiations as the vehicle for such participation. The statute should contain a broad definition of scope—a public employer should be obligated to negotiate in regard to "the terms and conditions of employment and other matters of mutual concern relating thereto."
>
> Proposals of this type invariably are resisted by employers who contend that employee demands in respect to the nature of the product produced or the quality of the service provided should be non-negotiable on the ground that they exceed the scope of legitimate employee concern and intrude into the area of management prerogatives. We believe that it is in regard to precisely these matters that teachers and other public employees with their special knowledge and competence can make their most valuable contribution.[42]

NOTES

1. William J. Kilberg, "Appropriate Subjects for Bargaining in Local Government Relations," 30 Maryland Law Review 179 (1970).
2. Ibid. at 188.
3. Ibid. at 189.
4. Ibid. at 195.
5. Ibid. at 196.
6. Ibid. at 197.

7. Advisory Commission on Intergovernmental Relations, Labor-Management Policies for State and Local Government, 51 GERR Reference File 101 (Mar. 1970).

8. Ibid. at 111.

9. Ibid.

10. Ibid. at 112.

11. Ibid.

12. American Federation of State, County, and Municipal Employees Union (AFSCME) President Jerry Wurf referred to the Commission recommendations as "a big step backwards." Service Employees International Union (SEIU) President David Sullivan said the Commission "missed the opportunity to make a meaningful and important contribution to stabilizing the sometimes chaotic conditions in the public sector." See "AFL-CIO Criticizes ACIR Report as 'Backward Step' in Bargaining," 343 GERR B-12 (Apr. 6, 1970).

13. Advisory Commission on Intergovernmental Relations, loc. cit.

14. Ibid.

15. Robert G. Howlett, "Scope of Bargaining in Public Employment," in John B. Ferguson and Joyce M. Najita, eds., Government Employees and Collective Bargaining, Hawaii PERB: Year One, proceedings of conference, December 19, 1970 (Honolulu: Industrial Relations Center, University of Hawaii, April 1971).

16. Ibid., p. 28.

17. Ibid., p. 29.

18. Ibid., p. 30. Howlett believes that much of this "accommodation" may occur through the mediation process, "with the mediator moving the item being discussed away from one of the statutory limitations and placing it under a subject which is bargainable."

19. Ibid., p. 35.

20. Ibid., p. 40. Emphasis added.

21. L.A. Report, at 8-9.

22. Ibid. Emphasis added.

23. Ibid. at 11-12.

24. Twentieth Century Fund, Pickets at City Hall—Report and Recommendations of the Twentieth Century Fund Task Force on Labor Disputes in Public Employment, 51 GERR Reference File 151 (1970).

25. Ibid. at 151-53.

26. Ibid. at 154.

27. Ibid.

28. American Association of School Administrators, School Administrators View Professional Negotiation (Washington, D.C.: the Association, 1966), pp. 38-40; and The School Administrator and Negotiation (Washington, D.C.: the Association, 1968), pp. 12-13.

29. AASA, "School Administrators View Professional Negotiation," in D.H. Wollett and R.H. Chanin, The Law and Practice of Teacher Negotiations (Washington, D.C.: Bureau of National Affairs, 1970),at 6:511.

30. Ibid.

31. Ackerly and Johnson, Critical Issues in Negotiations Legislation (Washington, D.C.: NASSP, 1969), p. 9.

32. Ibid., p. 11.

33. Benjamin Epstein, What Is Negotiable? (Washington, D.C.: NASSP, 1969).

34. Ibid., p. 20.

35. Ibid., pp. 21-28.

36. Allan West, "The NEA and Collective Negotiations," paper presented on April 2, 1965, at the Midwest Administration Center, University of Chicago, reprinted in S.M. Elam, Myron Lieberman, and M.H. Moskow, eds., Readings on Collective Negotiations in Public Education (Chicago: Rand McNally, 1967), pp. 147-61, at 158-59.

37. National Education Association, Guidelines for Professional Negotiation (Washington, D.C.: NEA, 1965), p. 2.

38. Donald Wollett, "Professional Negotiations: What Is This Thing?" quoted in M.H. Moskow, Teachers and Unions (Philadelphia: Wharton School, University of Pennsylvania, 1966), pp. 215-16.

39. Charles Cogen, "Changing Patterns of Employment Relations," in R.E. Doherty, J.R. Egner, and W.T. Lowe, eds., The Changing Employment Relationship in Schools (Ithaca: New York State School of Industrial and Labor Relations, Cornell University, 1966), p. 17.

40. Charles Cogen, "Collective Bargaining: The AFT Way," address to National Institute on Collective Negotiations in Public Education, July 8, 1965, at pp. 2, 7.

41. S. 1951, Proposed National Negotiations Act, published in Educators Negotiating Service (Feb. 15, 1972).

42. Donald E. Morrison, statement on labor bills, before House Education and Labor Committee, March 14, 1972, quoted in Educators Negotiating Service (Apr. 15, 1972).

LEGISLATIVE BACKGROUND

In 1938 the New York legislature adopted a constitutional provision that provided that "employees shall have the right to organize and bargain collectively through representatives of their own choosing."[1] This was a broad declaration of policy that "presumably applied to public as well as private employees."[2] However, in the absence of legislation specifying the procedures by which public employees might organize, gain recognition, and negotiate the terms and conditions of employment, the development of public sector bargaining, until recently, progressed very slowly.

The courts were especially reluctant to authorize collective negotiations in the absence of specific enabling legislation. In Quill et al. v. Eisenhower,[3] for example, the New York Supreme Court (New York County) held that the constitutional provision guaranteeing employees the right to organize and bargain collectively protected employees against legislation and acts that would prevent or interfere with their organization and selection of bargaining representatives, but it did not impose on Columbia University, which as an educational institution was excluded from coverage under the New York Labor Relations Law, a correlative duty to bargain collectively with its employees. Justice Bernard Botein wrote:

> It is evident that the constitutional provision guaranteeing employees the right to organize and bargain collectively . . . does not cast upon all employers a correlative obligation. The constitutional provision was shaped as a shield; the union seeks to use it as a sword. The duty of the employer to bargain collectively must be found in the . . . Labor Law, and does not extend to those who are expressly excepted from the scope of that article.[4]

Another factor contributing to the uncertainty of public sector labor relations in New York was the punitive and sketchily enforced Condon-Wadlin Act.[5] Passed in 1947 following labor unrest among public employees in New York City, Buffalo, and Rochester, the Condon-Wadlin Act prohibited strikes in public employment and established harsh penalties for public employees engaging in work stoppages.

In light of mounting criticism against the Act (and a New York City teachers' strike in April 1962), the staff of the Joint Legislative Commission on Industrial and Labor Conditions proposed a bill repealing the Condon-Wadlin Act and replacing it with a comprehensive negotiations law for public employees.[6] The proposed law provided for employees' rights to form and join labor organizations, the negotiation of terms and conditions of employment, exclusive representation, binding arbitration of grievances arising under a contract, and impasse procedures (mediation and advisory arbitration) for the resolution of disputes concerning contract terms. The bill banned strikes among public employees and stated that work stoppages were to be considered as misconduct under the Civil Service Law.

The legislature, however, did not pass the proposed law; instead, in 1963 it moderated the Condon-Wadlin penalties on a temporary basis for two years. In 1965, in order to prevent the statute from reverting to its original form, several bills were proposed to replace the Condon-Wadlin Act.[7]

Governor Nelson Rockefeller supported the 1963 modification of the Act and, in his annual message to the legislature, recommended that the temporary amendments to the Condon-Wadlin Act be made permanent provisions of the law. Legislation embodying this recommendation was introduced but not passed by the legislature.[8]

After considering several bills, in 1965 the legislature passed the Lentol-Rossetti bill, which provided for public employee organizational and bargaining rights, exclusive recognition, binding arbitration of grievances, and fact-finding concerning bargaining disputes over contract terms. The bill also authorized public employers to establish local labor relations agencies to assist parties in resolving representation and contract disputes.

The governor, however, vetoed the Lentol-Rossetti bill in a memorandum, stating that it would establish "an involved and ineffective procedure which would (1) undermine the deterrent to strike by public employees; (2) be unworkable and probably unconstitutional in certain aspects; and (3) impair vital functions of state and local government."[9] Rockefeller was especially concerned about the strike provision of the Lentol-Rossetti bill, which continued to treat the strike as misconduct within Section 75 of the Civil Service Law. Disturbed that in place of automatic dismissal, the bill would have allowed a range of penalties from reprimand to discharge, the governor stated:

In the light of experience in some areas of the state, the
effect of such flexibility would be to guarantee that if a
strike did occur, the foremost and most intransigent union
demand would be that government waive these penalties.
The consequence would be that no strike could be settled
without public officials foregoing the very sanctions the
bill purports to provide.[10]

The governor's veto resulted in the restoration of the original Condon-
Wadlin Act.

New York City Transit Authority employees initiated 1966 with
a crippling 12-day strike. This work stoppage, as well as other dis-
ruptions in public employment, made it clear to both Democratic and
Republican legislators that a replacement for Condon-Wadlin was
urgently needed. The self-defeating results of the Act's penalties
became most apparent when, after returning to work, the Transit
Authority employees threatened to strike again if the statutory penalties were imposed upon them. The legislature therefore speedily
passed a law granting amnesty to them.[11] (New York City Welfare
Department employees and ferryboat workers, who had previously
struck in violation of the Condon-Wadlin Act, also were exempted
from statutory penalties.)

During this winter of discontent, Governor Rockefeller appointed
a "blue ribbon" committee "to make legislative proposals for protecting the public against the disruption of vital public services by
illegal strikes, while at the same time protecting the rights of public
employees." The committee was chaired by George W. Taylor of the
University of Pennsylvania and included E. Wright Bakke of Yale
University; John T. Dunlop of Harvard University; Frederick Harbison
of Princeton University; and David L. Cole, noted labor relations
expert.

On March 31, 1966, the Taylor Committee published its Final
Report, acknowledging that although ". . . considerable time could
well have been used in the preparation of this Report," prompt proposals were necessary "because immediate changes in the Condon-
Wadlin Act are so urgently necessary and so widely demanded. . . ."[12]

The Taylor Committee recommended that the Condon-Wadlin Act
be repealed and replaced by a law that would:

. . . (a) grant to public employees the right of organization
and representation, (b) empower the state, local governments and other political subdivisions to recognize, negotiate with and enter into written agreements with employee
organizations representing public employees, (c) create a
Public Employment Relations Board to assist in resolving
disputes . . ., and (d) continue the prohibition against

strikes by public employees and provide remedies for violations of such prohibition.[13]

From the Taylor Committee Report emerged proposed legislation that became known as the Taylor bill. This bill was endorsed by Governor Rockefeller and passed by the Senate on June 7, 1966.[14] On the same day the Assembly passed a bill sponsored by Assemblyman Frank Rossetti, which differed significantly from the Taylor bill with respect to strike sanctions, the use of binding arbitration in grievance disputes, the type of agency to be established to administer the law, and the emphasis on local versus state control of administrative machinery. These differences between the two bills, "despite amendments ameliorating the strike sanctions of the Senate Bill, proved impossible to reconcile"[15] during the legislative session. Thus, at the end of 1966 the Condon-Wadlin Act remained intact.

During the 1967 session of the legislature, compromises were reached and on April 4, 1967, Governor Rockefeller signed into law the Public Employees' Fair Employment Act, or Taylor Law, effective September 1, 1967. Subsequently the Taylor Committee reconvened to consider possible amendments to the original statute. It issued an Interim Report with recommendations in 1968 and a Final Report in 1969.[16] The amendments made to the Taylor Law in 1969 (several of which will be discussed below) were basically consistent with the original report of 1966, the interim report of 1968, and the final report of 1969. Several significant additional amendments made in 1971 were based largely on experience, but they implemented rather than altered the basic approach inherent in the recommendations of the Taylor Committee.[17]

THE TAYLOR COMMITTEE AND THE SCOPE OF BARGAINING

The Taylor Law, as enacted by the legislature, follows closely along the lines of the original Taylor bill and reflects the conclusion of the Taylor Committee that "protection of the public from strikes in the public services requires the designation of other ways and means [besides harsh Condon-Wadlin-type penalties] for dealing with the claims of public employees for equitable treatment."[18] The Committee therefore recommended legislation that, although banning strikes, granted public employees full organizational and negotiating rights and provided for special governmental machinery for the resolution of disputes involving the negotiating unit, for the determination of the negotiating representative, and for the facilitation of impasse settlement.

The Taylor Committee emphasized that a sound labor relations program in public employment could not be achieved by transferring collective bargaining as practiced in private industry into the governmental sector. The "political" nature of collective negotiations in government (the fact that budget-making and tax-levying responsibilities rest ultimately with a legislature accountable to many public groups and interests), as opposed to the "economic" nature of private enterprise bargaining (the legal use of economic weapons and the reliance on marketplace constraints) made the strike inappropriate in public employment, the Committee concluded. Additionally, the unique role of government as sole provider of certain essential services constrained it from fashioning a collective negotiations scheme that, if strikes were permitted, potentially could victimize the public. In place of strikes, and necessary to the conduct of meaningful public sector negotiations, was the creation of new "procedures" to resolve employer-employee disputes as equitably as possible. This, then, was the basic philosophy underlying the Taylor Committee recommendations: the need to develop a law giving public employees the right to participate in establishing their employment conditions while, at the same time, preserving the precepts of a democratic government responsive to the electorate.

How was this philosophy reflected in the Taylor Committee's recommendations regarding the scope of bargaining?

Throughout its report the Taylor Committee alluded to the difficulties of determining the proper subjects for negotiations in public employment. A major constraint in public sector bargaining, it noted, is that government agencies, covered by civil service codes, education laws, municipal charters, and other controlling statutes, may lack the authority to enter into binding agreements concerning certain subjects. In addition to this legal problem is a crucial "policy" issue: To what extent should government, in light of its responsibilities to the public, retain certain nonnegotiable prerogatives?

Although the Taylor bill, which grew out of the Committee's Final Report, defined the scope of bargaining to include grievances, wages, hours, and conditions of employment, the Report itself indicates that the Committee may have wanted to circumscribe this definition with other—less expansive—statutory language. One indication of the Committee's reservations about broad statutory language was its reluctance to use the term "collective bargaining." The system of employee participation envisioned by the Committee was to be called "collective negotiations," inasmuch as "collective bargaining" implied the use of the strike and "has come to connote a type of joint-determination by unions and management which . . . cannot be transferred literally"[19] from the private to the public sector. The Taylor Committee preferred "the term 'collective negotiations' to signify the participation of public employees in the determination of at least some of their conditions for employment on an occupational or functional basis."[20]

The Taylor Committee was sympathetic to the needs of public employees. It believed, however, that the bargaining aspirations of employee organizations must be limited by the fact that "certain terms of employment are mandated by legislative enactment. . . . This circumstance reduces for those employees in State and local governments who are classified under Civil Service Law, the range and aspects of subjects about which negotiations can take place freely and without reference to other executives or legislative decision-makers."[21]

The Committee concluded that, in a "practical" sense, public sector collective bargaining could not entail more than "the negotiation of terms on the assumption of the necessity for a joint commitment of the negotiating parties to the terms, but with the necessity to seek approval and the appropriations to implement any agreement from a legislative body."[22] These constraints arise from the fact that monetary terms of a negotiated agreement cannot be implemented without legislative appropriations, and Civil Service Commission approval must be obtained for negotiated terms related to or overlapping with those legislatively mandated.[23] Traditional private sector collective bargaining could be conducted in the public sector

> . . . only if the public, through the action of its legislatures, is ready to delegate to a bargaining "team" composed of the executives of government agencies and the negotiators for employee organizations the virtual determination of its budget, the allocation of public revenues . . ., and the setting of the tax rate necessary to balance that budget. The delegation of those powers is not likely in the foreseeable future.[24]

As noted in Chapter 4, several state study commissions dealt directly with the question of whether the legislature should preserve for management certain nonnegotiable prerogatives through the enactment of a statutory management rights clause. Influenced by the Goldberg Task Force report at the federal level, the Illinois, Maryland, New Jersey, and Pennsylvania study commissions, for example, explicitly recommended the statutory enumeration of management rights outside the scope of bargaining.

The Taylor Committee also wrestled with this question, commenting that "the issue of the 'retained rights' of the employer (related in public service to the proper performance of both the legislative and executive functions) is more difficult to deal with in the public sector than in the private sector."[25] Despite this recognition of the problem, the Committee did not focus sharply on the question of management rights. The flavor of its discussion indicated, however, that it did not intend that government agencies negotiate away their mandated functions and responsibilities. Furthermore, because government employers at the negotiating table frequently have not been empowered to negotiate on particular issues, certain management rights or functions are automatically withheld from the scope of negotiations. As the Taylor Committee reasoned:

> Governmental employing agencies secure their authority from legislative bodies representing the various public interests and they may have to secure a validation of agreed upon terms from that body. In other words, the retained rights of government are defined, in the last analysis, by actions of the legislative body and executive officials who are subject to the restraints of the electorate.[26]

Generally, the inclusion in a collective bargaining law of a provision specifying negotiable and nonnegotiable subjects is recommended as a means of narrowing the scope of bargaining. By specifically categorizing issues, such a statutory provision prevents collective bargaining from encroaching upon areas reserved for exclusive managerial control. Interestingly enough, however, the Taylor Committee recommended this kind of statutory provision as a protection for public employees whose employers might improperly refuse to negotiate on the ground that the subjects proposed were within the exclusive control of management or the legislative body. "To discourage this practice," suggested the Taylor Committee, "there [should] be clarification by statute as to which subjects are open to negotiation in whole or in part, which require legislative approval of modifications agreed upon by the parties, and which are for determination solely by the legislative body."[27]

THE TAYLOR LAW AND THE SCOPE OF NEGOTIATIONS

Although during its first five years the Taylor Law has periodically suffered the criticisms of both labor and management, many observers, practitioners, and legislators have praised it for bringing greater stability and equity into public sector labor relations and for replacing the unworkable Condon-Wadlin Act. The legislative history of the Taylor Law indicates that it was neither easily conceived nor handily enacted; and it was probably with considerable trepidation, as well as excitement, that the 1967 legislature ultimately enacted the Taylor bill into law. As the product of both expert study and political compromising, the Taylor Law was less than perfect when enacted, and it still suffers flaws despite several legislative amendments. With respect to the scope of negotiations, the original statutory language still exists, for the most part, although several important amendments were adopted in 1969.

Section 203 of the Law entitles public employees to be represented by organizations "to negotiate collectively with their public employers in the determination of their terms and conditions of employment, and the administration of grievances arising thereunder."

Section 204.2 strengthens this right of representation by stating that where an employee organization has been certified or recognized, the employer is

> . . . required to negotiate collectively with such employee organization in the determination of, and administration of grievances arising under, the terms and conditions of employment of the public employees . . ., and to negotiate and enter into written agreements with such employee organizations in determining such terms and conditions of employment.

In line with the Taylor Committee's views that collective bargaining in the public sector must be distinguished from that of the private sector (particularly with respect to the right to strike), the Taylor Law mandates "collective negotiations" as opposed to "collective bargaining." It does not, however, define the duty to "negotiate." Walter Oberer, Kurt Hanslowe, and Robert Doherty point out, therefore, that it is likely, and indeed correct, that the development of the concept of the duty to "bargain" in the private sector is consulted for guidance in interpreting the duty to negotiate under the Taylor Law.[28] As was discussed in Chapter 1, the essence of the duty to bargain is a good faith effort on the part of both parties to reach an agreement. There is no reason to assume that the framers of the Taylor Law intended the statute to require any different behavior under the Law's obligation to negotiate.

A more complex problem arises in regard to the question of what the parties must negotiate. Section 204.2 mandates collective negotiations over terms and conditions of employment. Section 201.5, in National Labor Relations Act fashion, redundantly defines "terms and conditions of employment" to mean "salaries, wages, hours, and other terms and conditions of employment."

Aside from this expansive language regarding the scope of negotiations, the only reference in the original Taylor Act to subjects of negotiations is found in Section 205.5(g), which orders the Public Employment Relations Board (PERB)

> To conduct studies of problems involved in representation and negotiations, including . . . (iii) those subjects which are open to negotiation in whole or in part, (iv) those subjects which require administrative or legislative approval of

modifications agreed upon by the parties, and (v) those subjects which are for determination solely by the appropriate legislative body, and make recommendations from time to time for legislation based upon the results of such studies.*

The legislature's reluctance to define more narrowly "terms and conditions of employment," or to spell out management prerogatives in the Law, indicates its realization that the Taylor Law would be a successful experiment only if it were flexible enough to govern the dynamic labor relations of a vast array of public employees and employing agencies in New York State. After extending the Law's coverage to public employees, both professional and nonprofessional, at every level of government, the legislature wisely adopted language that allows each employee organization and public employer reasonable latitude in fashioning a scope of negotiations that best reflects the problems and needs of their governmental operation and that harmonizes with other laws applicable to their negotiating situation. This broad definition will also permit, as it has in the private sector under the NLRA, the gradual enlargement of the scope of negotiations as changes in the economy create new subjects for negotiations.

Curiously, the original Taylor Law, unlike the NLRA, contained no unfair labor practice provisions. This omission left unanswered the question of how employee rights granted by Sections 202, 203, and 204 were to be enforced. Several critics, notably Oberer, Hanslowe, and Doherty, argued that inasmuch as the Law expressly declared the organizing and negotiating rights of public employees, these rights carried with them implied duties on the part of the public employer not to interfere with or negate these rights.[29] But even if the Taylor Law did imply these employer duties, it provided no procedures to enforce either these implicit duties or the express obligation to negotiate collectively and enter into written agreements.[30] The state courts undoubtedly were a potential forum in which employee rights could have been enforced and meaningful remedies devised. Moreover, although the PERB did not possess specific authority to enforce employee (and employer) rights, it was argued that it could, under Section 205.5(i), (j), and (k), denote certain unfair practices and devise means of enforcing statutory rights. Under this section (since 1969 renumbered as Sec. 205.5(j), (k) and (l)), PERB was empowered (i) to "hold such hearings and make such inquiries as it deems necessary for it properly to carry

_____

*This authorization for the Public Employment Relations Board to conduct such studies differs from the original Taylor Committee recommendation that the statute specifically define the subjects falling into each of the above three categories.

out its functions and powers," (j) to "administer oaths and affirmations, examine witnesses and documents, take testimony and receive evidence, compel the attendance of witnesses and the production of documents by the issuance of subpoenas," and (k) "to make such rules and regulations . . . and to exercise such other powers, as may be appropriate to effectuate the purposes and provisions" of the Act.

As one critic commented with respect to the meaning of Section 205.5(k):

> This broad grant of authority would sanction the Board's enforcement of organization rights as well as the public employer's duty to negotiate. Under Section 205(5)(k) the Board would seem to have the power, if it chooses to exercise it, to issue cease and desist orders and to reinstate employees with back pay.[31]

In issuing its original rules of procedure, PERB did, in fact, recognize three types of unfair practices—reprisal, interference with representation procedures, and refusal to negotiate—and it used the authority granted to it under Section 205 to fashion remedies for violations of statutory rights granted under Sections 202 and 203 of the Law. An employer's refusal to negotiate with a recognized or certified employee organization, in violation of Section 204, was considered by the Board to be an act giving rise to a negotiating impasse, and thus initiating the procedures of Section 209 governing the resolution of negotiations disputes.

In attempting to deal with "unfair labor practices" under its own rules and regulations, PERB was acting in a manner consistent with the role that many legislators had envisioned for it as an impartial administrative agency. As Senator Thomas Laverne, member of the Joint Legislative Committee on Industrial and Labor Relations, remarked in January 1967:

> There was a fear that while giving persons the right to organize we should not create any problems or any right or any unfair labor or management practices. We didn't make a list of them as is customary in some areas. It was deliberately kept vague, not because they were trying to give powers that were meaningless, but because they felt it would develop in time and would be filled in. My answer to some of the vague language is that, that is what the Public Employment Relations Board is there for. I am convinced that while the Act (PEFEA) gives rights, it is the Public Employment Relations Board that is going to put responsibilities on public employers to deal fairly within the intention of the Act.[32]

But as Oberer, Hanslowe, and Doherty note in their review of the 1969 Taylor Act amendments:

> PERB was criticized from both sides of the table for its . . . handling of unfair practices, not expressly authorized by the original act. On the one hand, it was accused of having legislated in the guise of rule making. On the other, it was accused of having provided inadequate remedies and procedures for handling interferences with representation rights, not amounting to reprisals, and refusals to negotiate in good faith over terms and conditions of employment.[33]

The result was the enactment in 1969 of Section 209-a, which codifies improper employer and employee organization practices. Paraphrasing Sections 8(a) and 8(b) of the NLRA, Section 209-a(1) and (2) of the Taylor Law reads:

> 1. Improper employer practices. It shall be an improper practice for a public employer or its agents deliberately (a) to interfere with, restrain or coerce public employees in the exercise of their rights guaranteed in section two hundred two for the purpose of depriving them of such right; (b) to dominate or interfere with the formation or administration of any employee organization for the purpose of depriving them of such rights; (c) to discriminate against any employee for the purpose of encouraging or discouraging membership in, or participation in the activities of, any employee organization; or (d) to refuse to negotiate in good faith with the duly recognized or certified representatives of its public employees.
>
> 2. Improper employee organization practices. It shall be an improper practice for an employee organization or its agents deliberately (a) to interfere with, restrain or coerce public employees in the exercise of the rights granted in section two hundred two, or to cause, or attempt to cause, a public employer to do so; or (b) to refuse to negotiate collectively in good faith with a public employer, provided it is the duly recognized or certified representative of the employees of such employer.

Section 209-a(3) enjoins PERB from viewing as controlling precedent any body of state or federal law that governs the private sector:

> 3. Application. In applying this section, fundamental distinctions between private and public employment shall

be recognized, and no body of federal or state law applicable wholly or in part to private employment, shall be regarded as binding or controlling precedent.

PERB has not interpreted this provision to mean that it cannot look to private sector decisions for guidance or that it cannot apply private sector precedents to public employment labor relations. In many cases, public sector improper practices may not differ qualitatively or quantitatively from unfair labor practices in the private sector.[34] Undoubtedly what the legislature intended was for PERB to consider, in each instance, whether elements unique to public employment require a different interpretation or application of improper practices from those applied in the private sector.[35]

PERB is authorized in Section 205.5(d) to establish procedures for the prevention of the improper practices prohibited in Section 209-a. The Board's remedial powers regarding improper practices are limited in two respects, however, by Section 205.5(d). PERB is limited to issuing a cease and desist order in cases where an employer or employee organization has negotiated in bad faith. Apparently the legislature, in imposing this restriction, was seeking to preclude PERB from dictating the terms of the ultimate settlement or from assessing monetary sanctions upon a public employer guilty of refusing to negotiate in good faith. The second limitation is that the Board may not delay the processing of representation proceedings or seek to enjoin negotiations on the ground that an improper practice charge pertinent to the matter is being processed. This restriction would appear to indicate the legislature's intent to prevent the interruption of representation proceedings and negotiations upon a suspicion of wrongdoing or impropriety generated by the filing of an improper practice charge.[36]

Except for these restrictions the Board is arguably free to experiment in devising effective deterrents to the commission of future improper practices and in applying equitable remedies for established violations. And perhaps most significant, with respect to the issue of the appropriate scope of negotiations, is PERB's authority, under the 1969 amendments, to enforce the duty to negotiate in good faith by determining which issues are negotiable and which are not, within the meaning of the Act. Inasmuch as Section 209-a expressly declares it an improper practice for a public employer or employee representative to refuse to negotiate in good faith over terms and conditions of employment, the Board must, regardless of Section 2055(d)'s circumscription of its remedial power, determine which subjects are, in fact, "terms and conditions of employment," and therefore negotiable, under the Law.*

---
* If an employee organization believes that a certain issue is a proper subject of negotiations, and the public employer disagrees,

The 1969 legislature passed several other amendments that affect the scope of negotiations and are, therefore, deserving of comment. A new subdivision 13 was added to Section 201, which states:

201.13. The term "agreement" means the result of the exchange of mutual promises between the chief executive officer of a public employer and an employee organization which becomes a binding contract, for the period set forth therein, except as to any provisions therein which require approval by a legislative body, and as to those provisions, shall become binding when the appropriate legislative body gives its approval.

Section 204 was amended by the addition of the following subsections:

204-a. Agreements between public employers and employee organizations.
    1. Any written agreement between the public employer and employee organization determining the terms and conditions of employment of public employees shall contain the following notice in type not smaller than the largest type used elsewhere in such agreement:
        "It is agreed by and between the parties that any provision of this agreement requiring legislative action to permit its implementation by amendment of law or by providing the additional funds therefor, shall not become effective until the appropriate legislative body has given approval."
    2. Every employee organization submitting such a written agreement to its members for ratification shall publish such notice, include such notice in the documents accompanying such submission and shall read it aloud at any membership meeting called to consider such ratification.

---

the organization may file a charge alleging the employer's violation of Section 209-a(d) and seek a negotiating order for PERB. Formerly the Board appointed a hearing officer to conduct an initial hearing and make recommendations. But because of the necessity for a more prompt means of resolving scope-of-negotiations questions, PERB recently amended its rules to provide, upon the request of one of the parties, expedited determinations in disputes involving "primarily a disagreement as to scope of negotiations under the Act." The director will initially determine if it presents a true scope-of-negotiations issue. If so, he will inquire further into the matter and will transmit the papers to the Board for action.

Simply put, the thrust of these amendments is to make clear that the question of what can be negotiated has to be considered in concert with the authority of the public official or employer engaged in the negotiations to make binding commitments. Regardless of what may be "agreed" to at the negotiating table, before such agreements can be effectively implemented, reference must be made to key executive or legislative decision-makers who hold the purse strings and the power to amend existing law if necessary. As the Taylor Committee emphasized in its 1966 Final Report, negotiations in public employment must rest on the assumption that after the parties reach a joint commitment on the negotiated terms, it will be necessary to seek approval and financial appropriations from the legislative body in order to implement the agreement.[37] The Taylor Law's insistence that a notice to this effect actually appear in the negotiated agreement emphasizes to public employees that the agreements reached between their representatives and employers are only tentative until the appropriate legislative body takes necessary implementing action.[38]

Section 204-a, for obvious reasons, is not popular among public employee organizations. To date it has not presented a major problem to meaningful negotiations, however, because in many cases, especially teacher negotiations in independent districts, the legislative body is keenly aware of the progress of negotiations throughout the entire process. If, for example, the chief school officer agrees to a 6 percent salary increase, it most often is with the knowledge and authorization of the board of education. In such situations the school board's ultimate approval of the negotiated agreement, in accordance with Section 204-a, is a pro forma action- were it otherwise, public employees might lose all faith in the collective negotiation process, regardless of the Taylor Committee's assumptions about public sector negotiations.

Recently the New York State Teachers Association (NYSTA) and the New York State School Boards Association (NYSSBA) have expressed conflicting opinions on the role of the chief school officer (versus that of the board of education) in negotiations and on the meaning of Section 204-a of the Taylor Law. Because this issue relates directly to the meaning and scope of the duty to negotiate, it may be instructive to digress briefly and review the opposing positions adopted by NYSTA and NYSSBA.

According to NYSSBA, a negotiated agreement is a contract solely between a chief school administrator and an employee organization. Bernard T. McGivern, NYSSBA attorney, expressed its position as follows:

The addition of subdivision 13 to 201 of the Law makes it clear that the chief school administrator negotiates with employee organizations; and any agreements reached are binding only upon him and the organization. Under various

104

provisions of the Education Law, the chief school administrator has certain responsibilities and authority which he exercises, with or without the approval of the Board of Education; and in respect to those responsibilities and authorities, the agreement is binding. The Education Law gives certain other authority to Boards of Education in order that they may carry out their duties under the Law. No agreement between the chief school administrator and an employee organization can bind the school board to a particular course of action. . . . In order that it would be clear to everyone that the Board of Education was not bound by an agreement between an organization and the chief school administrator, the Legislature added 204-a to the Taylor Law.[39]

In a June 1972 memorandum to staff members, Daniel C. McKillip, assistant director of NYSTA field services, replied to McGivern's statement and expressed NYSTA's position on this subject.

NYSTA also agrees that proper implementation of the Law requires that the chief school administrator, or his designee, have authority to negotiate and reach agreement. Under Section 201.13, states McKillip:

. . . the school board must grant authority to the chief school officer to reach agreement on matters that have budgetary impact in that it is essential that "the officials of government at the level of the unit shall have the power to agree or to make effective recommendations to other administrative authority or legislative body with respect to the terms and conditions of employment upon which the employees desire to negotiate," (207.1(b) of the Taylor Law).

It is incorrect, however, asserts McKillip, to say that an agreement is binding only upon the chief school officer and the employee representative. The public employer must negotiate and execute written agreements with employee organizations, and "the public employer is defined in the case of school district negotiations as the school district (Sec. 201.7). The chief school officer is the agent of the public employer. . . . Therefore, he must have the authority to enter into binding contracts with the employee organization."

McKillip also asserts that McGivern has misinterpreted Section 204-a of the Taylor Act. NYSTA acknowledges that there are certain procedures established by the legislature, within the constitutional framework, that must be adhered to regarding expenditure of public funds and the operation of government. For example, notes McKillip, in order for public employees to receive a negotiated salary increase, the appropriate legislative body must approve the expenditures and levy the taxes

> . . . because only the legislative body of government has
> that authority as established by law. Thus, Section 204-a
> makes reference to a technical (not literal) procedure
> that must be adhered to in the operation of a local govern-
> ment. That section was not intended to provide the oppor-
> tunity for a school board to "pick and choose" what parts
> of an agreement they would approve or disapprove. In fact,
> failure on the part of the school board to take the technical
> "legislative action" to implement an agreement, or by
> refusing to provide the necessary funds for implementation
> would, in our opinion, be an Improper Practice.

The conflicting opinions of McGivern and McKillip highlight a problem at the crux of the public sector negotiations: public officials often lack the discretion to negotiate (and agree) on certain subjects because they depend for their authority and resources on elected, legislative bodies. On a theoretical level, therefore, NYSTA is incorrect in assuming that the legislature intended that local govern- ments have merely a "technical" or procedural role in approving agreements. Certainly the Taylor Committee was too concerned with the policy-making and fiscal responsibilities of government to have envisioned local legislative bodies as simply "rubber stamping" authorities. In a practical sense, however, the negotiations process would be rendered meaningless and chaotic were local governments to feel free to reject negotiated agreements that had been arduously hammered out by their subordinate public officials and employee representatives. In the eyes of NYSTA, and probably many public employee organizations, a local government that disapproved or refused to implement an agreement would be undermining the entire negotiations process by attempting to unilaterally determine employ- ees' wages, hours, and terms and conditions of employment. Perhaps the only way to resolve the problem is to narrow the separation of executive and legislative powers when it comes to collective nego- tiations. As noted above, local school boards frequently negotiate "behind the scenes"; although this often raises questions regarding the negotiating authority of the chief school officer, it practically guarantees approval and implementation of the parties' final agreement.

THE LEGISLATIVE ENVIRONMENT, 1969-72

In discussing the development of the scope of bargaining under the Taylor Law, it is interesting to note that there have been several legislative attempts to alter significantly the statutory language concerning the scope of negotiations.

On January 27, 1969, the Select Joint Legislative Committee on Public Employee Relations was appointed to study the Taylor Law and its impact on public sector labor relations during its first two years in effect.*

One of the issues that concerned the Select Joint Committee was the scope of collective negotiations. Although the Committee recognized that the appropriate scope of negotiations differs among employers, depending on the nature of the services performed and geographical area of the state, it nevertheless believed that the scope of negotiations should have been more clearly delimited by the Taylor Law. Inasmuch as public employers generally do not have a profit motive, public enterprise frequently continues on, regardless of how poorly it is managed or what has been agreed to at the bargaining table. "Moreover," concluded the Committee, "the consequences of some negotiated provisions are not always apparent at the time they are negotiated. Weak or inept employers seem to be particularly vulnerable to employee pressure to include all sorts of extraneous matter into the agreement."[40]

For these reasons, the Joint Legislative Committee determined that public labor relations laws required a clearer definition of the scope of bargaining than did those statutes governing employee relations in private employment. The Committee introduced a bill (S. 5540) that set forth general guidelines for employers and employee organizations, outlining those management prerogatives about which a government employer could not be forced to negotiate, while permitting negotiations at the option of the employer:

> The bill would have provided guidelines for PERB in the exercise of its new powers to compel negotiations. Essentially, the employer was to be protected in his right to determine the standards of his services, the standards for selection of his employees, direct his employees, determine the content of job classifications, and determine his facilities and the numbers of his personnel.[41]

S. 5540 would have amended Section 204.2 to read as follows:

> 2. Where an employee organization has been certified or recognized pursuant to the provisions of this article, the appropriate public employer shall be, and hereby is,

---

*This committee was chaired by Senator Thomas Laverne and had as members Senators John E. Flynn and Basil A. Patterson and Assemblymen John E. Kingston, Alfred D. Lerner, and Frank G. Rossetti.

required to negotiate collectively with such employee organization in the determination of, and administration of grievances arising under, the terms and conditions of employment of the public employees . . ., and to negotiate and enter into written agreements with such employee organizations. . . . Notwithstanding the foregoing, it is the right of every government to determine the standards of its services; determine the standards of selection of its employees; direct its employees; take disciplinary action; relieve its employees from duty because of lack of work or other legitimate reasons; maintain the efficiency of governmental operations; determine the content of job classifications; take all necessary action to carry out its mission in emergencies; and exercise control and discretion over its organization and methods by determining the facilities, limitations, means and number of its personnel. Such rights of government are subject to the conditions, rights and limitations as may be applicable under law and must be exercised consistant [sic] with the provisions of the written agreement.[42]

S. 5540 was not passed by the legislature in 1969. It was reserved for examination during the 1970 session, but was not enacted.

Assembly Bill 5476

In 1970 Assemblyman Daniel Becker introduced a bill to add a new section (213) to the Taylor Act. This section, governing only teacher negotiations, would have enumerated those powers of boards of educations that were management prerogatives and, therefore, nonnegotiable. In a memorandum accompanying the bill, Becker presented his reasons for sponsoring it:

There has been a constant eroding of the historical powers of boards of education so that these boards are compelled to negotiate items which are strictly school board responsibilities, and which should be determined by boards of education who are elected to run the school facilities. . . . By retaining in the boards of education the powers which are strictly theirs, and taking the same from the negotiating table, the bill will promote . . . harmonious and cooperative relationships. This bill is a step forward and [sic] putting responsibilities for the conduct of boards of education within the board where it properly belongs.[43]

108

A. 5476 would have provided for Section 213 to read as follows:

213. Certain powers of boards of education which are deemed to be non-negotiable regarding teachers. The following is a list of several of the historical powers of boards of education which are considered non-negotiable. In no event shall the following be considered the sole non-negotiable powers of such boards:
1. Teacher selection and certification;
2. Teacher assignment within a district;
3. Classroom selection regarding pupils with different abilities;
4. School facilities planning;
5. Selection and approval of textbooks, instructional materials and curricula;
6. Fiscal planning and implementation;
7. Class size and teaching load.
Notwithstanding any provision of law, rule or regulation to the contrary, any contract containing provisions relevant to the non-negotiable items enumerated herein shall be null and void.

This bill was not passed by the legislature.

Assembly Bill 7796

Assembly Bill 7796, commonly known as the Kingston-Jerabek bill, was introduced in early May 1971. Among other provisions it would have amended the Taylor Act's definition of "terms and conditions of employment" to read as follows:

The term, "terms and conditions of employment" means "salaries, wages, hours, and other terms and conditions of employment," provided, however, such terms shall not include, and the public employer shall have the sole right to determine, its mission, purposes, objectives and policies, including but not limited to the standards of admission to its facilities and the nature and content of curriculum or programs offered; the facilities, methods, means and number of personnel required for conduct of its programs, including but not limited to the ratios and standards of staffing of its facilities; the standards of examination, selection, recruitment, hiring, appraisal, training, retention, discipline, promotion, assignment, and transfer of its employees; the direction, deployment, and utilization of its work force; the establishment of specifications for each class of positions; and the classification and reclassification and allocation and reallocation of new or existing positions.[44]

In his June 1971 report to the Fleischmann Commission, Myron Lieberman stated that A. 7796 "came as a complete surprise and was not supported by any systematic evidence pertaining to schools."[45]

Interestingly, the 1969 Select Joint Legislative Committee on Public Employee Relations had suggested, in its report, that a sample of collective agreements negotiated during the first two years of the Taylor Law "be scrutinized to determine how broad an interpretation the parties have placed on the expression 'other conditions of employment.'"[46] Recommendations based on this survey could subsequently be made, said the Committee, with respect to whether the scope of negotiations defined in the Taylor Law should be spelled out, narrowed, or even broadened, at least for professional employees. In response to the Joint Legislative Committee report, Irving Sabghir conducted a study in 1970 on the scope of bargaining under the Taylor Law. Although the findings of this study will be discussed in a later chapter, it is important to note here that Professor Sabghir's report was the only known study prepared in direct response to the Joint Legislative Committee report; and the major recommendation of his report was that bargaining experience under the Taylor Law did not warrant a change in the statutory definition of the scope of negotiations. Thus the empirical basis for the conclusions in the Kingston-Jerabek bill was, at best, questionable.

Commenting on the inconsistencies between the Kingston-Jerabek bill and Sabghir's report, Myron Lieberman suggested that perhaps

> . . . the rhetoric of professionalism rather than the actual scope of teacher contracts (as distinguished from the scope of what may have been discussed during teacher negotiations) is what has fanned the fears over management prerogatives. As long as teachers assert the right to negotiate about everything, they tend to evoke counter-measures to limit the scope of negotiations. This analysis is consistent with the conclusions of the Sabghir report, which . . . had not been widely distributed to the legislature . . . until the Kingston-Jerabek bill was introduced. Nevertheless, the Legislators may have been responding to the rhetoric instead of to the realities of teacher negotiation.[47]

A. 7796 was not passed by the legislature.

1972 REPORT OF THE JOINT LEGISLATIVE COMMITTEE
ON THE TAYLOR LAW

The Joint Legislative Committee on the Taylor Law was created
by joint resolution of the New York State Senate and Assembly on
April 20, 1970. Its charge was to make a comprehensive study of the
Taylor Law and to offer recommendations for its continued improvement. Senator Theodore D. Day was named chairman of the Committee
and former Industrial Commissioner and Dean of the New York State
School of Industrial and Labor Relations, M.P. Catherwood, was
appointed executive director.*
    In its report the Joint Legislative Committee devoted consider-
able attention to the problem of the scope of negotiations.[48] For this
reason, and to do justice to the Committee's discussion of the issue,
several passages from the 1972 report are quoted verbatim here.
    The Committee noted that the absence of a "substantial definition"
of "terms and conditions of employment" in the Taylor Law had
occasionally led to confusion and controversy as to what topics are
subject to mandatory negotiations. One of the problems in determining what items fall under "terms and conditions of employment" is
often due to the impact of other laws, such as those relating to
civil service, education, and finance. When the legislature passed
the Taylor Law, it did not repeal or specifically amend any of the
other statutes.

    Consequently, without the guidance which would have been
    provided by a somewhat more specific definition of the
    scope of negotiations, it has been necessary to make
    assumptions as to how far the Legislature intended to go
    in superseding other provisions of law with the provisions
    of the Taylor Law relating to "terms and conditions of
    employment." Disputes over such assumptions have in
    some instances been carried to court. Decisions in such
    cases are gradually having an impact on the definition of
    scope.[49]

    Still other problems occur, explained the Committee, with
respect to items that, although clearly negotiable terms and conditions of employment, require legislative approval before they are
implemented. Although the separation of legislative and executive

_____

    *Committee members included Senators John E. Flynn, Leon E.
Giuffreda, Thomas Laverne, and Waldaba Stewart, and Assemblymen
Stanley Fink, Benjamin A. Gilman, Lawrence Herbert, Charles A.
Jerabek, and Chester J. Straub.

powers is a laudable feature of democratic government, it produces
great frustration in the area of collective bargaining:

> ... the different roles of the executive and legislative
> branches of government, in relation to collective negotia-
> tion, have not always been clearly defined and accepted.
> To try to meet the problem by delegation of powers from
> the legislative branch to the executive branch would raise
> issues of policy and form of government going beyond what
> were contemplated when a system of collective negotiations
> was adopted.[50]

The Committee also grappled with the problem of the collective
bargaining process versus the political process. Even in the absence
of the Taylor Law, public employees historically have had many pro-
tections provided by other laws. Although today labor may criticize
these other statutes for precluding from negotiations issues that
should be negotiable, many legislators and public employers criticize
these same statutes for providing benefits that, in their views, are
excessive when combined with those gained through negotiations.
"One aspect of this issue," notes the Committee, "is not whether
we should abandon the Taylor Law and depend on other legislation,
but rather on the degree to which dependence is to be placed on negotiations under the Taylor Law versus the political processes as
reflected in 'other legislation.'"[51]

Theoretically, posits the Committee, one way to resolve some
of these scope-of-bargaining problems would be by listing in the Law
either all the issues that are negotiable or, alternatively, all the
issues that are not negotiable. However, it quickly concedes that
"in the absence of uniformity in terminology and in definition, and
with the infinite relationships involving legislation other than the
Taylor Law,"[52] it would be impossible to provide a complete enumeration of all subjects that either are or are not negotiable. Moreover, such statutory listings might become too limiting or rigid as
political and economic changes gradually occur, making it necessary
to recategorize items that are subject to mandatory negotiations,
those that are permissible bargaining subjects, and those that are
illegal topics for bargaining.

What does impress the Joint Legislative Committee as a reasonable means of clarifying the proper scope of negotiations is a management rights clause. Although nowhere in its report does the Committee
either specifically propose a management rights clause for inclusion
in the Law or endorse previously proposed amendments to this effect,
it states that "a reasonable management rights clause would be
helpful, quite possibly to both employees and employers."[53] It also
would "provide guidelines without which negotiations sometimes get
far afield."[54] The Committee refers to and defines both contractual

and statutory management rights clauses but is somewhat vague in not clarifying which type of clause it favors. The flavor of the text, however, leads one to conclude that the Committee most probably would support a statutory management rights clause as a means of more uniformly insuring that certain management prerogatives remain outside the scope of negotiations.

In addition to protecting the employer against "inappropriate encroachments" by employee organizations, a management rights clause in legislation

> . . . provides some guidelines for mediators, fact-finders and arbitrators in the interpretation of the various provisions of the contract without encroachment on rights reserved to the employer. Likewise a management rights clause in legislation provides some guidelines for public agencies and for the courts in the resolution of charges that one of the parties is refusing to negotiate on negotiable issues.[55]

In support of its position, the Committee notes that a management rights clause has existed for some time in the local procedures providing for the public employee relations system in New York City. Although neither labor nor management is entirely satisfied with this management rights clause, according to the Committee, "both have learned to live with it."[56] The Committee therefore suggests that "if a management rights clause is to receive serious consideration at the State level, experience with the clause in New York City should be critically examined."[57]

At several points the Joint Legislative Committee suggests, perhaps naively, that labor, as well as management, would find a management rights clause "helpful" and "facilitative" to negotiations. Referring to the controversial Kingston-Jerabek bill, the Committee states:

> It is difficult to know to what degree the very strong labor opposition to the scope of negotiations proposal during the 1971 legislative session was based on the subject matter of the proposal or on the absence of advance knowledge and consultation or on both. Although public employee representatives naturally prefer a broad rather than a narrow scope of bargaining and a limited rather than a broad management rights clause, it is not clear that they would be unwilling to accept reasonable definitions.[58]

Unfortunately the Committee gives no indication of what it might consider a "reasonable definition." And until public employee organizations see a management rights clause that, to their thinking, is

113

more "reasonable" than the Kingston-Jerabek bill, or the similar bills preceding it, they will continue to insist that the present Taylor Law definition of the scope of negotiations remain intact.

DECISIONAL HISTORY OF THE SCOPE OF BARGAINING IN NEW YORK

Monroe-Woodbury

In the Matter of Monroe-Woodbury Teachers' Association and Monroe-Woodbury Board of Education[59] was the first case presented to PERB that raised the issue of the scope of negotiations, that is, whether specific items were negotiable.

In this case cross-charges of failure to negotiate in good faith were filed by the school board and teachers' association. The board of education alleged that the association had violated Section 209-a.2(b) (Taylor Law) in not withdrawing from negotiations two proposals that the board believed were not negotiable, and the association claimed that the employer's refusal to negotiate on these two proposals constituted a violation of Section 209-a.1(d). The contested proposals concerned the association's demand for the establishment of an evaluation and dismissal procedure for probationary teachers and the establishment of an agency shop.

The school board did not argue that the disputed subjects were not "terms and conditions of employment." Rather, it contended that its bargaining duty under the Taylor Law did not extend to subjects that, although terms and conditions of employment, involved vested management rights as granted in the Education Law or that were unlawful. With respect to both the evaluation procedure and agency shop clauses, the school board argued that Sections 3012 and 3013 of the Education Law conferred on chief school officers exclusive control of procedures concerning the evaluation and dismissal of probationary teachers. Any diminution of the chief school officer's authority regarding these subjects, argued the employer, would have to come from the legislature and not the collective negotiations process. Moreover, an agency shop was illegal in that it violated Section 202 of the Taylor Law, which gives public employees the right to refrain from forming, joining, or participating in employee organizations.

The teachers' association defended the legality of its proposals, maintaining that the absence from the Taylor Law of any restrictions on the scope of negotiations authorized the parties to construe their negotiating duty as broadly as possible.

114

In its decision PERB upheld the hearing officer, Janet Axelrod, in concluding that the Education Law does not preclude a school board from voluntarily establishing an evaluation and dismissal procedure that goes beyond what is required by the Education Law. PERB held that the association's proposed procedure, ". . . if included in a negotiated agreement, would require the Employer to follow procedures in the denial of tenure that absent an agreement the Employer would not be required to follow." The Board concluded that the teachers' association's proposed evaluation and dismissal procedure was a term and condition of employment that did not contravene existing law and was, therefore, a mandatory subject of negotiations.*

With respect to the agency shop proposal, PERB again upheld the hearing officer's decision that the agency shop (1) is inconsistent with the statutory grant of right under the Taylor Law that employees may refrain from "participating in" an employee organization; (2) is prohibited under Section 3012.2 of the Education Law, dealing with the dismissal of tenured teachers on only certain specified grounds; and (3) is barred by Section 93-b of the General Municipal Law, providing that dues may be deducted from an employee's salary only upon his authorization, which may be withdrawn at any time.

There were, however, certain subtle differences between the discussions of the hearing officer and PERB regarding this issue. In discussing the meaning of the duty to negotiate, Mrs. Axelrod stated that a party could not reasonably be held to have violated its negotiating obligation by refusing to negotiate on a matter "which was constitutionally barred, prohibited by existing statutes, or removed from the negotiating arena by judicial fiat."[60] Nevertheless, she explained,

> . . . it is desirous that parties be free to discuss and consider such matters as long as they are not unconstitutional, and for this reason no onus should fall upon a party submitting such a matter to negotiations, provided that the progress of negotiations on mandated matters is not linked to the resolution of such a "permissive" item.[61]

Although the hearing officer ultimately concluded that the agency shop was unlawful, she stated that the subject had neither been constitutionally barred nor "otherwise expressly removed from the purview of negotiations." Thus, the parties, had they both desired, could have discussed and negotiated this "permissive" subject, although

---

*PERB issued an order directing the Monroe-Woodbury board of education to negotiate on this proposal.

"the Association had an obligation not to insist on [its] negotiation as a precondition to reaching agreement."62

Mrs. Axelrod's conclusion was interesting in that despite her reliance, in part, on the private sector's mandatory/permissive/illegal terminology, she altered the meaning of this delineation with respect to permissive and illegal subjects. Under the NLRA, subjects that are illegal or inconsistent with the basic policy of the Act may not lawfully be included in a bargaining contract, regardless of the parties' intent or wishes to waive any legal proscriptions.63 Mrs. Axelrod's conclusion apparently supports the proposition that only expressly prohibited subjects may never be negotiated and included in an agreement. Other subjects, although "unlawful" or unauthorized by statute, may be negotiated as long as both parties voluntarily agree to discuss them and neither party insists to the point of impasse upon their inclusion in an agreement.

PERB, in contrast with the hearing officer, did not explicitly confer "permissive" status upon the issue of an agency shop. Approaching the subject more cautiously, the Board stated: "We agree with the conclusion of the Hearing Officer that the agency shop proposed by the Association is unlawful and is, therefore, not a mandatory subject of negotiations."64

The Board agreed with the hearing officer that although the teachers' association in Monroe-Woodbury refused to withdraw its agency shop proposal during negotiations, it did not insist upon the school board's negotiation of the proposal as a precondition to reaching an agreement. It therefore was not found guilty of violating its obligation to negotiate in good faith. By implication the teachers' association would have violated Section 209-a.2(b) had it insisted upon the school board's negotiation of the agency shop proposal as a condition precedent to a final settlement. Whether or not either or both parties would have violated the Taylor Law had they voluntarily negotiated and reached written agreement on the "unlawful" agency shop is a question that the Board's decision did not broach. It is possible that PERB intentionally left the agency shop proposal unlabeled (as either a permissive or illegal subject of negotiations) because at that time it, rather than the courts, was declaring it unlawful. Until the legality of this controversial issue was judicially determined, the Board may have wished to leave the question open while at least protecting the right of an employer to refuse to negotiate the subject.65

Farrigan v. Helsby

PERB's Monroe-Woodbury decision regarding the agency shop was upheld by the New York Supreme Court in an Article 78 proceeding.66 On appeal the Appellate Division affirmed the lower court.67

Petitioner Farrigan, president of the Monroe-Woodbury teachers' association, contended that PERB acted arbitrarily when it held that the Monroe-Woodbury board of education did not violate Section 209-a.1(a) of the Taylor Law by refusing to negotiate over the association's agency shop proposal. Farrigan alleged that PERB lacked the power to determine whether the agency shop proposal was legal, or if it had such power, its characterization of the agency shop as unlawful was arbitrary.*

Writing for a unanimous appellate court, Justice Robert Main agreed with PERB that Section 202 of the Taylor Law makes illegal a contract demand compelling forced payment of association dues or their equivalent. Moreover, the legislature made the intent of Section 202 "crystal clear" with the enactment of Sections 209-a.1(c) and 209-a.2(a), which prohibit an employer from discriminating against any employee for the purpose of encouraging or discouraging membership or participation in labor organizations and prohibit an employer from interfering with, restraining, or coercing an employee in the exercise of Section 202 rights. Finding the agency shop illegal, the court concluded that the Monroe-Woodbury board of education had no obligation to bargain on the teachers' association proposal.[68]

As to whether PERB had the authority to determine the illegality of the agency shop proposal, the court held:

> It is unquestioned that [PERB] has the power to determine whether the contending parties have failed to negotiate in good faith and, upon such a finding, to order the public employer or employee organization to bargain in good faith. . . . We hold that the Public Employment Relations Board, in order to carry out these responsibilities and in order to conform to the above statutory and case law, must necessarily have the authority to rule upon the legality of the subject matter of the negotiations.[69]

Central Office Administrators v. Rochester Board of Education

PERB continued the process of defining the scope of negotiations in In the Matter of Association of Central Office Administrators and Board of Education, City School District of Rochester.[70] In its brief

---

*According to the petitioner, PERB is restricted to deciding whether an agency shop is a term and condition of employment within the ambit of the Taylor Law; and if PERB finds that it falls within that ambit, the parties must negotiate over that item.

decision upholding the hearing officer, Janet Axelrod, PERB dismissed an improper practice charge brought by the City School District of Rochester against the Association of Central Office Administrators for its refusal to negotiate the employer's proposal to include a residency requirement in the collective agreement.*

The Association refused to negotiate the employer's proposal primarily on the ground that a residency requirement was not a mandatory subject of negotiations because it was too "remote" from the Taylor Law's definition of "terms and conditions of employment." Moreover, negotiations on the residency requirement would be illegal, argued the Association, because the proposal violated provisions of the Education Law regarding the grounds on which tenured administrators could be dismissed and the equal protection clause of the Constitution.†

The employer contended that a residency requirement did constitute a "term and condition of employment" within the meaning of the Taylor Law.‡

In determining the case, the hearing officer offered several incisive remarks regarding the criteria to be used in defining terms and conditions of employment under the Taylor Law. Because Section 201.5 tautologically defines terms and conditions of employment to mean "salaries, wages, hours, and other terms and conditions of employment," PERB must assume the responsibility for determining

---

*The Association represented a unit of central office administrators and supervisors, comprising civil service personnel and certificated personnel. The residency requirement in question would have applied to the certificated personnel only.

†The residency requirement proposal stated that a noncomplying administrator might be permitted to continue living outside the City School District only at the discretion of the board of education. The proposal and subsequent brief filed by the school board implied that a noncomplying administrator was subject to dismissal or denial of promotion.

The Association alleged denial of equal protection in that the imposition of a residency requirement upon only one class of employees—certified administrators—had no reasonable justification and was, therefore, an act of arbitrary discrimination.

‡The school board based its contention on rather questionable reasoning. Compliance or noncompliance with the residency requirements, if implemented, was to have direct influence on whether an employee received a promotion, or, alternatively, became subject to disciplinary measures. What the board of education was arguing, therefore, was that since compliance or noncompliance would affect employees' terms and conditions of employment, the residency requirement per se was a condition of employment.

the range of subjects that properly fall within this broad definition. To perform this task, PERB must look to the private sector for guidance:

> The lesson of the private sector is that no litmus paper test can be devised to automatically identify a "term and condition of employment." In general, however, the phrase is considered to cover any subject which has a "significant or material relationship" to conditions of employment, unless it involves decisions concerning the basic goals and direction—the mission—of an employing enterprise.[71]

The hearing officer concluded that this approach should be followed in the public sector, too, because management's right to make basic policy decisions is, "if anything, more compelling in the public sector where the employer . . . has the added responsibility of fulfilling a public trust."[72]

Applying this reasoning to the present case, the hearing officer (and PERB) determined that the decision to impose a residency requirement was not a mandatory subject of negotiations:

> A residency requirement is not a condition of, but a qualification for, employment. Like other employment qualifications, it defines a level of achievement or a special status deemed necessary for optimum on-the-job performance. Traditionally, qualifications for employment have been matters of managerial prerogative, and no cogent reason appears to justify a departure from this rule.[73]

Although her decision did not reach the question of whether the impact of an established residency requirement would be a mandatory subject of negotiations, the hearing officer cautioned the parties that a residency requirement, as proposed by the employer, would have "a direct and significant impact upon the working lives of . . . employees. Accordingly, it would seem that the circumstances under which a residency requirement would be implemented are mandatory subjects for negotiation."[74]

As a sidelight it is interesting to note that Mrs. Axelrod apparently still espoused the position she adopted in Monroe-Woodbury regarding permissive subjects of negotiations. In a footnote to her Rochester Administrators decision, she stated that the Administrators' Association was correct in asserting that the dismissal of a tenured employee who refused to comply with the residency requirement would conflict with Section 3020-a of the Education Law, which permits the dismissal of such employees only on certain grounds. The Association, therefore, could legally refuse to negotiate any proposal that sought, unlawfully, to enforce the residency requirement. Nevertheless, one may infer from Mrs. Axelrod's conclusion that this unlawful proposal could have been negotiated and included in a contract, had both parties so agreed. Apparently Mrs. Axelrod is unwilling to label an unlawful or statutorily unauthorized subject as an illegal subject for negotiations, in the private sector sense.

School District No. 3, Town of Hempstead
v. East Meadow Teachers

In In the Matter of Board of Education, Union Free School District No. 3, Town of Hempstead, and East Meadow Teachers' Association,[75] PERB agreed with earlier findings of hearing officer Harvey Milowe in declaring that the board of education engaged in an improper practice when it unilaterally imposed a condition, apart from those contained in the collective agreement, requiring unit employees,

> . . . as a condition for the granting of . . . sabbatical leave, to . . . return to employment . . . over a period of not less than two years.[*]

The hearing officer determined, and PERB agreed, that the issue of sabbatical leave was a term and condition of employment and, therefore, a mandatory subject of negotiations. PERB supported the hearing officer and held that Section 1709, subdivision 16, of the Education Law, empowering the school board to adopt rules or regulations for the granting of leaves of absence, did not negate the conclusion that sabbatical leave was a term and condition of employment that must be negotiated, if the employee representative so requests. As a result of the school board's action, "employees were deprived of their statutory right to have the employee organization of their choice negotiate with regard to a significant change in a condition of employment."[76]

One of the affirmative defenses raised by the respondent school board was that it could not be found guilty of refusing to negotiate in

---

[*]The agreement had provided: "The existing practices, policies, and procedures respecting sabbatical leaves to teaching personnel are confirmed and shall remain in effect except that (a) a teacher eligible for sabbatical pay may select a half-year sabbatical at full pay for full-time study or its equivalent upon approval of the Superintendent . . . and (b) in selecting among applicants for sabbatical leave, length of service in the District shall be one of the prime considerations."

good faith where the probative act occurred after the implementation of a collective agreement. To this argument the hearing officer responded:

> . . . it is clear that by signing an agreement a public employer indicates its acquiescence in those enumerated terms and conditions of employment which have been negotiated with the statutory representative of its employees. Clearly, the purposes of the Act would be aborted if an employer was then to be granted a franchise to unilaterally enact additional provisions. It follows that the statutory obligation to negotiate in good faith does not cease subsequent to the execution of a collective agreement.[77]

Although PERB's decision was not as explicit regarding this point, it stated:

> The act mandates that a public employer negotiate terms and conditions of employment with the certified or recognized representative of its employees. This obviously precludes the unilateral imposition of terms and conditions of employment.[78]

The East Meadow board of education had also contended that its action should have been relegated to the parties' agreed-upon grievance procedure. The hearing officer reasoned, and PERB quoted him, in part, in its decision:

> The claim here does not relate to the interpretation of any clause of the collective agreement; rather, it is directed at the respondent's deliberate refusal to negotiate an additional provision which is both a mandatory subject of negotiations and one not expressly covered by the existing collective agreement.[79]

The hearing officer concluded that the dispute was one of statutory obligation, and not of contract interpretation. Therefore, the Teachers' Association could properly invoke the improper practice section of the Taylor Law rather than the grievance procedure of its collective agreement.

Perhaps more troubled by this question than was the hearing officer, PERB stated that the issue was one of first impression before the Board and "it raises some basic questions," the first of which was: Does PERB have the jurisdiction to police and enforce collective agreements negotiated by public employers and employee organizations? Looking to the private sector for guidance, PERB concluded that it did not have this jurisdiction, particularly because the New York legislature did not provide that a breach of a collective agreement is per se an improper practice. But, PERB continued, certain conduct in breach of contract "may also" constitute an improper practice, and in such cases PERB may lawfully exercise its jurisdiction. In the present case the board of education agreed to maintain existing policies and practices concerning sabbatical leaves. By unilaterally changing these without negotiations, the school board violated its duty to negotiate in good faith. PERB declined even to reach the question of whether it should, in such circumstances, defer to the grievance and arbitration procedures in a collective agreement, because the contract in the East Meadow district did not provide for binding arbitration. To have left the dispute for resolution through the grievance procedure would, therefore, have provided no guarantee that the employer could have been persuaded either to refrain from enforcing the new post-sabbatical leave provisions or to negotiate concerning the proposed changes.

The East Meadow case is significant not merely because it established that sabbatical leave is a term and condition of employment, which is a mandatory subject of negotiations, but, more importantly, because it held that an employer's unilateral action on a mandatory negotiations subject, whether taken in the first instance or during the life of an agreement, is "the antithesis of good faith negotiations."[80] Finally, in the East Meadow case PERB reinforced the strength of the Taylor Law's improper practices section by insisting that conduct in violation of a collective agreement may also be an improper practice under Section 209-a and, therefore, subject to the Board's jurisdiction, at least in cases where a contractual grievance procedure does not provide for binding arbitration as the last stage.

City of New Rochelle v. New Rochelle Federation
of Teachers

In a very significant case concerning the scope of negotiations, In the Matter of the City School District of New Rochelle and New Rochelle Federation of Teachers,[81] PERB held that an employer's approval of budgetary cuts and reallocation of funds terminating the services of a substantial number of employees, without prior notification to or negotiation with the employee organization, was not a mandatory subject of negotiation. However, the impact of the employer's decision on employees' terms and conditions of employment was held to be a mandatory subject of negotiations.

Bypassing the intermediate step of hearing officer, PERB stated that it considered the issue of the negotiability of budget reductions one of "such immediacy" as to warrant a direct hearing by the Board.*

In developing its decision PERB referred to the bargaining duties imposed upon employers in the private sector under the NLRA. Although mindful of the Taylor Law's provision that no body of federal law applicable to the private sector shall be considered binding or controlling precedent in the public sector, PERB stated that the experience of the private sector could provide useful guidelines in the consideration of the present case. In the private sector the NLRA does not compel employers and employee organizations to bargain "upon every subject which interests either of them; rather, the specification of wages, hours, and other terms and conditions of employment defines a limited category of subjects that are mandatory subjects of bargaining."[82] This construction of the bargaining obligation under the NLRA, said PERB, is equally applicable to public sector negotiations because the terms used by the NLRA and the Taylor Law are similar.

According to PERB, the proposed budgetary cuts, resulting in job eliminations, "clearly involve a managerial decision. The employer contends that the budgetary cuts are predicated on available resources and a determination as to how such resources are to be allocated in carrying out the mission of the City School District." Although the district's decision, if implemented, would affect conditions of employment, PERB concluded:

> . . . it does not follow that every decision of a public employer which may affect job security is a mandatory subject of negotiations. We conclude . . . that the decision to curtail services and eliminate jobs is not a mandatory subject of negotiations, although the employer is obligated to negotiate on the impact of such decision. . . .[83]

PERB pointed out that a public employer exists to provide certain essential services to its constituents. Acting through its executive or legislative body, it must determine the extent of its services and the means by which such services shall be rendered, "subject to the approval or disapproval of the public . . ., as manifested in the electoral process." A public employer's decisions regarding the

---

*Another charge (U-0240), concerning the negotiability of the school calendar, also was raised in the New Rochelle case. In a supplemental decision and order, PERB held that the employer could not unilaterally promulgate elements of a school calendar that are negotiable, and the parties were ordered to negotiate with respect to those aspects of the school calendar.

carrying out of its mission, "such as a decision to eliminate or curtail a service, are matters that a public employer should not be compelled to negotiate with its employees."[84]

At the same time PERB noted that an employee organization may seek negotiations concerning such decisions on a permissive basis and, in fact, recommended that "it would seem most desirable for a public employer to meet and discuss with the representative of its employees concerning such decisions, particularly where, as here, the employees are professionals. . . ."[85]

West Irondequoit

Shortly after it rendered its New Rochelle decision, PERB was confronted with another scope-of-negotiations dispute in In the Matter of Mrs. Lloyd Herdle, et al. Constituting the West Irondequoit Board of Education and West Irondequoit Teachers Association.[86] Inasmuch as this case centers on class size, which is the focus of the third part of this study, the West Irondequoit decision will be analyzed in detail in a subsequent chapter. For purposes of continuity, however, the holding in West Irondequoit will be discussed here briefly.

The negotiability of several subjects was resolved in this case. The hearing officer, Janet Axelrod, had held that promotional policy for job titles outside the negotiating unit and employment qualifications for job titles within the unit were not mandatory subjects of negotiation. Promotional procedures for unit employees and numerical class size, however, were ruled by Mrs. Axelrod to be mandatory subjects.

In a controversial decision, with one Board member dissenting, the PERB upheld the hearing officer's ruling except with respect to class size, which it determined was a policy decision of government and, therefore, not a mandatory subject of negotiations. Referring to its New Rochelle decision, PERB declared that the school board may make class size decisions unilaterally, but must negotiate the impact of these decisions on the terms and conditions of employment of its personnel.

PERB also added, as it did in New Rochelle, that nothing in its decision was intended to prohibit permissive negotiations on the subject of class size. In fact, consultation with teachers' organizations on educational policy was to "be encouraged so as to take advantage of the teachers' professional expertise."

The third case to be decided in what might be called the New Rochelle trilogy was In the Matter of the City of White Plains and Professional Fire Fighters Association of White Plains, Inc., Local 274, International Association of Fire Fighters, AFL-CIO.[87] In that case the Fire Fighters alleged that the city of White Plains had committed an improper practice by refusing to negotiate on six demands, which fell into three categories: reduction in work force; tours of duty; and manpower. Hearing the case under its new expedited procedure (wherein cases are brought directly to the Board), PERB determined that two issues, reduction of work force and titles and levels of supervision, were not mandatory subjects of negotiation. Tours of duty and minimum number of on-duty firemen per truck and engine, however, were found to be mandatory. In a brief opinion the New York Supreme Court (Albany County) enforced PERB's order directing the city of White Plains to comply with the Board's decision.[88] It is to this PERB decision that we now turn for an analysis of the complex issues involved in the case.

With respect to the work force reduction issue,* PERB quoted extensively from its New Rochelle decision, which it held to dispose of the reduction issue. Having decided that a public employer may unilaterally choose to eliminate or curtail a service, the Board concluded:

> . . . it necessarily follows that a public employer may abolish positions which had been necessary for the provision of that service and that it may not be required to negotiate with respect to that decision. Of course, consistent with our decision in New Rochelle, the employer is required to negotiate with respect to the impact of its decision to curtail services and abolish positions.[89]

Thus, PERB reiterated in White Plains the conclusion it reached in New Rochelle: not every managerial decision that affects terms and conditions of employment (such as job security) is a mandatory subject of negotiations. But the impact of such decisions—for example the work loads of retained employees, order of layoffs, and severance pay—are mandatory subjects of negotiations.

---

*The union had demanded the following contract provision: "The City agrees that there shall be no reduction in the number of employees . . . during the term of this agreement, by any means other than attrition or discharge for cause."

With respect to the union's demand concerning tours of duty,[*] the employer contended that under New Rochelle a public employer may unilaterally make decisions regarding the deployment, as well as employment, of its personnel. Moreover, it is the sole responsibility of the city to decide the extent of the fire protection it needs at different hours. The union referred to Sections 204.2 and 201.4 of the Taylor Law, mandating negotiation of wages, hours, terms and conditions of employment, and argued that the demand regarding tours of duty was a demand concerning hours.

PERB agreed with the city that it alone could determine how many fire fighters to have on duty at any given time. But, it added, there are many ways in which the schedules of fire fighters could be arranged in order to meet the city's requirement for adequate fire protection:

> It is this manipulation of the schedules of individuals and groups of firemen which is involved in the Fire Fighters' demand. Within the framework which the City may impose unilaterally that a specified number of Fire Fighters must be on duty at specified times, the City is obligated to negotiate over the tours of duty of the Fire Fighters within its employ.[90]

Four of the union's demands pertained to manpower,[†] and it is with respect to this issue that the Board rendered its most provocative decision.

---

[*]The union's demand regarding tours of duty was as follows:

> . . . .Association members who regularly perform fire fighting or dispatching duties shall work . . . a 24 hours tour of duty starting at 6 PM and continuing for a period of 24 consecutive hours ending at 6 PM the following day.
> . . . Association members who regularly perform "day work" duty . . . shall work . . . a 7 hour tour of duty starting at either 8 AM or 9 AM and continuing for a period of 7 consecutive hours ending at 3 PM or 4 PM respectively.

[†]Briefly summarized, the union's demands regarding manpower were the following:

> It is agreed between the parties that a minimum of 5 fire fighters be on duty at all times with each engine and with each truck.
> Furthermore, it is agreed . . . the Department membership be increased so that a minimum of 7 paid fire

The city, in defending its refusal to negotiate over these man-power proposals, relied on the West Irondequoit decision, in which PERB held that the maximum class size was a matter of educational policy—even though it affected teachers' work loads—and therefore was not a mandatory subject of negotiations.

Responding to the city's argument, PERB distinguished the circumstance in West Irondequoit from that in the present case, inasmuch as in West Irondequoit, teachers' interest was limited to work load, whereas the interest of the Fire Fighters also involved safety. ". . . [It] is clear that there is a relationship between the numbers of Fire Fighters who man a piece of equipment and their safety. We believe that the demand that a minimum number of Fire Fighters be on duty at all times with each engine and each truck constitutes a mandatory subject of negotiations."[91]

The union's last three demands, however, which would have required the city to provide supervisors of specified rank, did not achieve equal status. PERB made it clear that the union's demand to negotiate supervisory assignments and titles exceeded the meaning of "terms and conditions of employment" under the Taylor Law:

The Fire Fighters have a legitimate interest in adequate supervision because it is directly related to their safety while fighting fires, but it is not for them to determine the rank of the persons assigned to supervise them. The rank assigned to supervisors is a management prerogative.[92]

The Board concluded its decision with an interesting comment:

We find that, although fire fighters' demands for adequate supervision would constitute a mandatory subject for negotiation, the specifics of their demands . . . that supervisors of specified rank be provided, does not.[93]

---

fighters be on duty at all times with each high-value engine and ladder company, and 6 paid fire fighters be on duty at all times with all other engine companies. . . .

A paid Fire Lieutenant shall be assigned to each and every Engine Company for each and every tour.

The City shall restore the rank of captain for ladder companies.

A paid Deputy Chief shall be on duty at all times for each and every tour. This Deputy Chief shall be assigned to "line duty" and shall be in addition to any other Department Deputy Chief(s). . . .

When the PERB News published a summary of the White Plains Fire Fighters decision in February 1972, it stated that the Board "issued a decision in which . . . the numbers, titles, and levels of supervision were determined not to be mandatory subjects of negotiation."[94] Was this, however, exactly what the Board held? PERB stated that "adequate supervision" was directly related to job safety and went so far as to call it a mandatory subject of negotiation. Although the Board did not attempt to define what it meant by "adequate supervision," it is difficult to think of this concept in other than numerical terms. Despite the PERB News summary, it seems that PERB intentionally left the door open for negotiations on the numbers of supervisors assigned to a particular unit or job task and on the breadth of their supervision.

Interesting, too, is the way in which the White Plains decision may relate to West Irondequoit. As noted above, in West Irondequoit, the Board determined that the element of educational policy so outweighed the element of work load in the issue of class size as to make the teachers' demand a nonmandatory subject of negotiations. In White Plains, however, the Board concluded that at least one of the fire fighters' demands was a mandatory subject of negotiations because it reflected employees' concern for safety as well as work load. Job safety, held PERB, is a condition of employment, within the meaning of the Taylor Law, which is directly related to the number of men manning equipment. At the risk of reading too much into the White Plains decision, it seems that the safety issue with respect to work load may be one avenue by which public employee unions—especially teachers—may try to limit, if not erode, the effects of the West Irondequoit decision. Teachers, for example, could probably make a good case for the mandatory negotiation of limitations on class size in industrial arts courses and special subject areas where class size is directly related to safety. Of course PERB might respond by holding that (1) children's safety in school is, like class size, an educational policy matter and (2) teachers' safety while instructing in these special subjects is not jeopardized—as was the case in White Plains. These arguments, however, are not conclusive, and effective counterarguments could be developed. The point here is not to resolve the issue but simply to suggest that the meaning and scope of the White Plains decision are not as obvious as they may at first appear.

The Significance of New Rochelle

Having reviewed PERB's determinations in New Rochelle, West Irondequoit, and White Plains, one can appreciate the significance of the New Rochelle decision. In that precedent-setting case

PERB laid down the ground rules regarding the way in which it would thereafter define "terms and conditions of employment" and, hence, mandatory subjects of negotiation. The case was significant not only because it settled the nonnegotiability of budget and job reductions, but also because it distinguished between a managerial decision and the impact of such a decision on employees' conditions of employment—a distinction that became crucial in West Irondequoit and White Plains.

In New Rochelle the teachers' federation argued that the "legislative intent" was not to restrict the scope of negotiations under the Taylor Law. It based its argument, in part, on the 1971 legislature's failure to enact A. 7796, which, as discussed earlier, would have limited the scope of negotiations.

PERB was not persuaded by this argument. It concluded that the proposed amendments to the Taylor Law were highly restrictive and, for this reason, were not enacted:

> . . . the proposed limitation on the scope of negotiations
> went beyond the limitation we now find to have been inherent
> in the original law. Thus, the fact that the bill did not pass
> could be attributed to objections to some of the other
> limitations on the scope of negotiations which the bill
> articulated and the recognition that a limitation on the right
> to negotiate a management decision to lay off employees
> was redundant.[95]

Thus, in New Rochelle, PERB established the fact that there are limitations on the scope of negotiations that are "inherent" in the Taylor Law despite its broad definition of "wages, salaries, hours, and other terms and conditions of employment." The Board has determined that a public employer may retain certain managerial prerogatives and that amendments to the Taylor Law are not necessary in order to protect these prerogatives. This point was emphasized at a February 1972 meeting of PERB panel members during which New Rochelle and West Irondequoit were discussed.[96] Apparently PERB was apprehensive about the enactment of amendments that would have limited the scope of negotiations, and it advised the legislature against such action. The New Rochelle decision, therefore, was crucial politically, because in holding that the present Taylor Law language does not permit an unrestricted scope of negotiations, PERB hoped to quell the fears of those legislators and representatives of public management who were clamoring for restrictive legislation.

Additionally, under the present statutory language PERB has the authority and responsibility, as does the NLRB under the NLRA, to use its discretion in gradually defining the scope of negotiations on a case-by-case basis. This is how it should be. The passage of amendments to restrict the statutory definition of the scope of negotiations would not have clarified all the issues and probably would have led to increased frustration at the negotiating table as the parties struggled to understand the meaning and extent of the management rights enumerated in the Law. Under the present procedure one may hope that a consistent body of decisional law will emerge from the scope-of-negotiations cases heard by PERB and, with the Board's decisions always subject to judicial review, the collective negotiations process will be given maximum opportunity to succeed and the public interest will be protected.

The Test for Mandatory Subjects of Negotiations

The May 1971 issue of PERB News was devoted to a review of the Taylor Law and the progress of public employment labor relations during 1970. Under a discussion of "good faith bargaining," it was stated:

> While the Taylor Law is silent on what is or is not negotiable, the statutory duty to negotiate in good faith requires an employer to negotiate all terms and conditions of employment not constitutionally barred, prohibited by statute or judicially removed from the negotiating arena.[97]

This familiar language was first used by Janet Axelrod in her Monroe-Woodbury decision of July 1970.

Interestingly, by August 1971 (and immediately after PERB rendered its New Rochelle decision) the Board apparently had modified its position concerning the scope of the duty to negotiate. Paul Klein, director of public employment practices and representation, writing in PERB News about recent developments in improper practices, noted the new trend in PERB decisions:

> The test used as to negotiability is that a party will be required to negotiate an item that constitutes a term or condition of employment unless (a) it is deemed to be a matter of managerial prerogative in that it involves a primary policy goal or the basic direction of the employer, or (b) the negotiability of the item has been constitutionally barred, prohibited by existing statute, or removed from the negotiating arena by judicial fiat.[98]

Thus New Rochelle signaled a change in PERB's "test for negotiability," the ramifications of which, as was soon borne out in West Irondequoit, even the experienced Janet Axelrod did not fully understand.

130

As will be discussed subsequently, the decis of New Rochelle is difficult to implement in many situations. It requires, first, that a distinction be made between decisions and the impact of these decisions on employee terms and conditions of employment. Is it always possible to make such a distinction? Is class size, for instance, easily separated from work load? Second, under New Rochelle, in order to determine a subject's negotiability, one must first be able to identify it as either a term or condition of employment or as a policy issue merely affecting terms and conditions of employment. Is this identification easily made? Do the elements of "policy," for example, outweigh the elements of work load with respect to the issue of class size? The differences of opinion in West Irondequoit between Janet Axelrod and dissenting PERB member George Fowler, on the one hand, and Board members Robert Helsby and Joseph Crowley, on the other, indicate that the answers to these questions posed here are by no means clear.

The Huntington Decision

Superimposed on all of the above decisions is the recent landmark decision of the New York Court of Appeals in Board of Education of Union Free School District No. 3, Town of Huntington v. Associated Teachers of Huntington, Inc.[99] Handed down in March 1972, the Huntington decision has since been the subject of much discussion and controversy, as public employers and employee organizations have attempted to understand its holding and implications for collective negotiations.

The Court of Appeals was faced with two major questions: (1) Does a school board have the authority to enter into a collective agreement granting economic benefits to teachers, absent specific statutory authorization to do so? (2) Does such a board lack the power to enter into a collective agreement containing a provision providing for arbitration of disputes concerning disciplinary action taken against tenure teachers?

The Huntington school board and teachers' association had entered into a written agreement for the 1969-70 school year. This agreement contained provisions granting: (1) reimbursement to teachers for personal articles lost or damaged during the performance of duty, (2) tuition reimbursement for graduate courses, (3) a salary increase in the last year preceding retirement, and (4) grievance arbitration of disputes concerning dismissal of tenure teachers. During the negotiations on the 1969-70 contract, the Huntington school board questioned the legality of the above provisions and its own authority to bind itself to them; and shortly after the execution of the agreement, it brought action for a judgment (1) declaring those provisions illegal and (2) staying arbitration proceedings that the teachers' association had initiated under the grievance provision. The Supreme Court held illegal the provisions concerning tuition reimbursement and the grievance procedure, but validated the remaining clauses. On appeal the Appellate Division agreed that the grievance arbitration provision was illegal, but validated the tuition reimbursement clause along with the others (36 A.D.2d 753).

The Court of Appeals, however, held all the contract provisions to be valid and legal. Reviewing Section 204 of the Taylor Law, and its mandate that parties negotiate with respect to terms and conditions of employment, Chief Judge Stanley Fuld stated that the validity of a negotiated contract provision turns upon whether it constitutes a term or condition of employment. If it does,

> . . . the employer must negotiate as to such item and, upon reaching an understanding, must incorporate it into the collective agreement unless some statutory provision circumscribes its power to do so. . . . It is manifest that each of the provisions here challenged constitutes a term or condition of employment.[100]

Judge Fuld did not offer much explanation as to why the contested provisions actually were terms or conditions of employment. He argued the merits of two of the provisions—those pertaining to personal property reimbursement and grievance arbitration—and noted that they were "commonly" found in collective bargaining agreements in both the private and the public sectors. He said that the tuition reimbursement provision "clearly relates" to a term and condition of employment because teachers are paid salary differentials for completing specified numbers of graduate credit hours. Stating that the retirement benefit "also involves a term and condition of employment," Judge Fuld held:

> Employers . . . have traditionally paid higher salaries based upon length of service and training. In addition to the fact that the payment was to be for services actually rendered during their last year of employment, the benefit provided for served the legitimate purpose of inducing experienced teachers to remain in the employ of the school district. It is not, therefore, a constitutionally prohibited "gift." . . .[101]

Having determined that all of the disputed items were terms and conditions of employment, Judge Fuld dealt with the Huntington school board's premise that absent a statutory provision expressly authorizing a school board to provide a certain term or condition of employment, it is legally prohibited from doing so. Using strong language, Judge Fuld disposed of the school board's argument:

> . . . the Board's premise is fallacious. Under the Taylor Law, the obligation to bargain as to all terms and conditions of employment is a broad and unqualified one, and there is no reason why the mandatory provision of that act should be limited, in any way, except in cases where some other applicable statutory provision explicitly and definitively prohibits the public employer from making an agreement as to a particular term or condition. . . .
> Were it otherwise, a school board would have a hard time bargaining effectively with its teachers concerning terms of employment, since it would frequently be difficult, if not impossible, to find an express grant of power with respect to any particular subject.
> Public employers must be presumed to possess the broad powers needed to negotiate with employees as to all terms and conditions of employment.
> It is hardly necessary to say that, if the Board asserts a lack of power to agree to any particular term or condition of employment, it has the burden of demonstrating the existence of a specific statutory provision which circumscribes the exercise of such power.[102]

Judge Fuld went on to state that the Huntington board of education cited no statutes that expressly "or even impliedly" prevented it from incorporating into the agreement the tuition or damage reimbursement provisions. The court also found the board's contentions that the retirement and grievance arbitration provisions violated the Retirement and Social Security Law (Sec. 113a) and Education Law (Sec. 3030-a) to be "without substance."[*]

---

[*]The Court's analysis of the arbitration issue was incisive. Under the so-called Tenure Law (Ed. Law Sec. 3020-a), before a teacher can be disciplined, he must be granted a hearing before an impartial panel, which then makes recommendations to the school board. The board, however, is not bound by these recommendations. Since a decision by the board itself to discipline a teacher is a prerequisite to arbitration, the grievance provision in dispute did not supplant this aspect of the Tenure Law. Additionally, noted Judge Fuld, under the Education Law a teacher "feeling himself aggrieved" may voluntarily appeal to the commission of education or initiate an Article 78 proceeding. "In other words," concluded Judge Fuld, "the Legislature has given a tenure teacher a choice of

In regard to the arbitration issue, Judge Fuld stressed, "It is of more than passing significance" that the Taylor Law expressly vests employee organizations with the right to represent public employees not only in the negotiation of terms and conditions of employment, "but also as to 'the administration of grievances arising thereunder.'" Furthermore, it is the declared policy of the state, under Section 200(c), "to encourage public employers and . . . employee organizations to agree upon procedures for resolving disputes." And arbitration is, "of course, part and parcel of the administration of grievances." The legislature, concluded Judge Fuld, did not intend for the Tenure Law, by implication, either to deprive employee organizations of the right to represent public employees in the administration of disciplinary grievances or to deny public employees the opportunity to have unresolved grievances determined by a qualified practitioner of labor relations.*

The Significance of the Huntington Decision

Most public employee organizations were understandably jubilant over the Court of Appeals' Huntington decision. As one NYSTA staff member commented, the Huntington decision "puts to rest completely the argument of non-negotiability."[103] A close reading of Judge Fuld's opinion, however, indicates that although the court's language was both strong and expansive, there are still limitations on the scope of negotiations that the Huntington decision may not have erased.

In Huntington the court specifically held four issues to be negotiable. It also set forth what can be considered a guideline or test concerning the negotiability of certain subjects: all terms and conditions of employment are mandatory subjects of negotiation unless

----

two methods of statutory appeal if he desires to challenge an adverse decision of the school board. But it does not follow from this that the Board is inhibited from agreeing that the teacher may choose arbitration as a third method of reviewing its determination."

*The court added that its opinion would not entitle an employee to appeal, under Sec. 3020-a of the Education Law, to the commissioner of education or the Supreme Court after he has submitted to arbitration and lost or, conversely, to the arbitrator after he has lost before the commissioner or court. The court's decision merely held that a collective bargaining agreement could provide an employee with a possible third means of reviewing a board determination. Once a decision is reached by any one of these means—arbitrator, commissioner, or judge—the matter is closed.

they are "explicitly and definitively" prohibited by law. However, the phrase "terms and conditions of employment" has not been concisely or uniformly defined by the NLRB, PERB, or the courts. There has been a general recognition that the phrase is not conducive to concise, general definition because of the great variety of industry customs, employer-employee relationships, possibilities for future technological change, and so on. The most concise definition was used by the Fourth Circuit Court in Westinghouse Electric Corp. v. NLRB,[104] and again by Janet Axelrod in her Rochester Administrators decision: "Any subject with a significant or material relationship to conditions of employment constitutes a term and condition of employment unless it involves decisions concerning basic goals and directions of employers." But even this definition is difficult to apply with certainty, especially since the parties often have very divergent views as to which issues are central to the basic mission and direction of the employer. As more scope-of-negotiations cases in the public sector are resolved, precedents will emerge and it will become clearer just what constitutes a term and condition of employment. But in the meantime, even under Huntington's broad standard of negotiability, parties to negotiation probably will still disagree over what is a term and condition of employment within the meaning of the Taylor Law. And the Board and courts in the public, as in the private, sector will resort to existing precedent and analogy to precedents in order to resolve the disputes.

One additional point warrants comment. Although it is doubtful that the Court of Appeals decision supersedes PERB's previous decisions regarding scope of negotiations, Huntington indicates that PERB and the court may not agree on the same standards to test a subject's negotiability.

Most of PERB's scope-of-negotiations decisions turned on the question of whether or not an item constituted a term and condition of employment. The issues generally were resolved by applying the above-noted definition that any subject with a "significant and material relationship to conditions of employment constitutes a term and condition of employment unless it involves decisions concerning the basic goals and directions of the employer." PERB also developed a negotiability "test" that requires a party "to negotiate an item that constitutes a term or condition of employment unless (a) it is deemed to be a matter of managerial prerogative . . . or (b) the negotiability of the item has been" prohibited by the constitution, law, or judicial fiat. PERB's standard for negotiability is somewhat rigorous, especially because under its "test" not all terms and conditions of employment are mandatory subjects of negotiation, regardless of the Taylor Law's broad language. Consistent with the "inherent" limitations that, in New Rochelle, PERB stated exist in the Taylor Law, only those terms and conditions that are legal and not basic to an employer's mission may be considered mandatory subjects of negotiation.

The Court of Appeals in Huntington, on the other hand, applied a far less rigorous standard in determining whether the provisions in question were mandatory subjects of negotiation. The court merely said that, in the case of the four contested clauses, it was obvious that they were terms and conditions of employment because each one was "commonly found" in collective bargaining agreements in both the public and private sectors and because each clearly "related" to a term or condition of employment. In upholding the validity of the challenged provisions, Judge Fuld emphasized that a public employer must, pursuant to Section 204, negotiate all terms and conditions of employment unless a specific statutory provision limits its power to do so. Unlike PERB, Judge Fuld did not exclude from the scope of mandatory negotiations those terms and conditions that are "deemed to be matters of managerial prerogative" or basic to the goals of the employer.

A labor attorney recently wrote that the Huntington decision "can be cited for the proposition that whenever an item is commonly found in collective bargaining agreements in the public and private sectors, it must be a term and condition of employment."[105] This author, however, finds it hard to believe that the court intended the application of such a loose standard for defining terms and conditions of employment. But even if it did, it is not clear that any of the items that PERB has determined not to be within the scope of negotiations are commonly found in collective negotiations agreements. And, even if they were, the question of how often a clause must appear to be "commonly found" still must be answered and is subject to disagreement. Finally, this decision does not mean that where an item is not common, it is not a term and condition of employment. It may still be a term and condition of employment because a court decision has rendered it so or because it satisfies the definition PERB has previously used. How PERB responds to the Court of Appeals decision will be seen only in time. It will not be surprising, however, to see public employee organizations urging the Board to pay closer attention to the "commonness" of certain contract provisions in making its scope-of-negotiations determinations.

NOTES

1. New York State Constitution, Art. I, Sec. 17.
2. Joint Legislative Committee on the Taylor Law (Public Employees' Fair Employment Act), 1971-72 Report, Legislative Document (1972) no. 25, at 10.
3. 113 N.Y.S.2d 887 (1952).

4. Ibid. at 889.

5. New York State Civil Service Law, Sec. 108.

6. Staff report to the New York State Joint Legislative Committee on Industrial and Labor Conditions, Proposed Bill and Supporting Report on Employee-Management Relations in the Public Service (Dec. 1962).

7. For an excellent discussion of the provisions of these bills, see Kurt L. Hanslowe, The Emerging Law of Labor Relations in Public Employment (Ithaca: New York State School of Industrial and Labor Relations, Cornell University, 1967), pp. 79-82.

8. Ibid., p. 83.

9. New York State Legislative Annual, 1965, p. 556.

10. Ibid.

11. Hanslowe, op. cit., p. 84.

12. Governor's Committee on Public Employee Relations, State of New York, Final Report (March 31, 1966), p. 9.

13. Ibid., p. 6.

14. S. Int. no. 4784, Pr. no. 5895 (1966).

15. Hanslowe, op. cit., p. 90.

16. Governor's Committee on Public Employee Relations, State of New York, Interim Report (June 17, 1968); and Report of January 23, 1969.

17. Joint Legislative Committee on the Taylor Law, op. cit., at 19.

18. Governor's Committee on Public Employee Relations, State of New York, Final Report (1966), loc. cit.

19. Ibid., p. 11.

20. Ibid.

21. Mandated terms "include hire and tenure procedures, trial period, promotions, seniority in layoffs, discipline, general standards of compensation, minimum and maximum salaries and increment schedules, process for changes in individual salaries and wages, hours and overtime, fringes such as insurance, pensions, vacations, holidays, sick leave, etc. These terms are mandated for all State and many municipal employees by the State and/or municipal Civil Service Commissions." Ibid., pp. 57-58.

22. Ibid.

23. Ibid., p. 59.

24. Ibid., pp. 60-61.

25. Ibid., p. 17.

26. Ibid., p. 18.

27. Ibid., p. 46.

28. Walter E. Oberer, Kurt L. Hanslowe, Robert E. Doherty, The Taylor Act: A Primer for School Personnel, Bulletin 59, New York State School of Industrial and Labor Relations, Cornell University (May 1968), p. 24.

29. William F. McHugh, "New York's Experiment in Public Employee Relations: The Public Employees' Fair Employment Act," 32 Albany Law Review 58, at 63 (1967-68); Oberer, Hanslowe, and Doherty, op. cit., p. 5.

30. Oberer, Hanslowe, and Doherty, loc. cit.

31. William B. Gould, "The New York Taylor Law: A Preliminary Assessment," 18 Labor Law Journal 323, at 330 (1967).

32. Albany District Chapter, Public Personnel Association, Institute of Labor Relations in the New York State Public Service 52 (Jan. 16, 1967).

33. Walter E. Oberer, Kurt L. Hanslowe, and Robert E. Doherty, The Taylor Act Amendments of 1969: A Primer for School Personnel, Bulletin 62, New York State School of Industrial and Labor Relations, Cornell University (June 1970), p. 10.

34. In discussing Section 209-a(3), Oberer, Hanslowe, and Doherty comment that "there is a somewhat amusing and plaintive quality to paragraph 3," in that Section 209-a is itself merely a paraphrasing of Sections 8(a) and 8(b) of the NLRA. Apparently the differences between private and public employment were not so great as to discourage the legislature from using the NLRA's "unfair labor practices" as a model for the Taylor Law's "improper practices." And it is doubtful, they note, that the cautioning words of Section 209-a(3) will dissuade PERB from looking to the private sector for guidance. Ibid., p. 12.

35. Joint Legislative Committee on the Taylor Law, loc. cit.

36. Paul E. Klein and Janet Axelrod, "The Taylor Law and Public Schools: A Look at the Areas of Representation and Improper Practices," 21 Labor Law Journal 420, at 431 (1970).

37. Governor's Committee on Public Employee Relations, State of New York, Final Report (1966), pp. 33-34, 57-60.

38. Oberer, Hanslowe, and Doherty, The Taylor Act Amendments of 1969, p. 17.

39. Bernard T. McGivern, New York State School Boards Association, Inc., Position Statement (Negotiations and Management Institute, Jan. 7, 1971). Emphasis added.

40. Select Joint Legislative Committee on Public Employee Relations, 1969 Report, Legislative Document (1969) no. 14, at 36.

41. Ibid. at 25.

42. Ibid. at 70.

43. Memorandum by Daniel Becker accompanying A. 5476, February 17, 1970, quoted in Philip E. Garber, "The Scope of Negotiations in the Public Sector" (unpublished manuscript, 1971), p. 56.

44. Assembly Bill 7796, quoted in Joint Legislative Committee on the Taylor Law, 1972 Report, at 110.

45. Myron Lieberman, The Impact of the Taylor Act upon the Governance and Administration of Elementary and Secondary Education, report to the Fleischmann Commission (June 1971), p. 47.

46. Select Joint Legislative Committee on Public Employee Relations, op. cit. at 36.

47. Lieberman, op. cit., p. 49. Emphasis added.

48. Joint Legislative Committee on the Taylor Law, op. cit.

49. Ibid. at 35.

50. Ibid. at 43.

51. Ibid.

52. Ibid. at 33.

53. Ibid. at 42.

54. Ibid. at 34.

55. Ibid.

56. Ibid.

57. Ibid.

58. Ibid.

59. 3 PERB 3104, at 3632 (1970).

60. 3 PERB 4510, at 4550.

61. Ibid.

62. Ibid.

63. Charles J. Morris, ed., The Developing Labor Law (Washington, D.C.: American Bar Association, 1971), p. 388.

64. 3 PERB 3104, at 3634.

65. Garber, op. cit., p. 62.

66. 327 N.Y.S.2d 909 (1971).

67. 346 N.Y.S.2d 39 (1973).

68. The Appellate Division relied on Board of Education, Union Free School District No. 3, Town of Huntington v. Associated Teachers of Huntington (30 N.Y.2d 122 [1972]) and Matter of Teachers Association, Central High School District No. 3 (34 A.D.2d 351 [1970]). Both of these cases are discussed below and in subsequent chapters.

69. 346 N.Y.S.2d 39, at 42.

70. 4 PERB 3058, at 3703 (1971).

71. 4 PERB 4509, at 4599 (1971).

72. Ibid.

73. Ibid.

74. Ibid. at 4600.

75. 4 PERB 3018, at 3659 (1971).

76. 3 PERB 8021, at 8219 (1970).

77. Ibid. at 8221.

78. 4 PERB 3018, at 3662.

79. Ibid.

80. Hearing officer's decision, 3 PERB 8021 (1970).

81. 4 PERB 3060, at 3704 (1971).

82. 4 PERB 3060, at 3706 (1971).

83. Ibid.

84. Ibid.

85. Ibid. at 3707.

86. 4 PERB 3070, at 3725; aff'd on rehearing, 4 PERB 3089 (1971), at 3753.

87. 5 PERB 3008, at 3013 (1972).
88. 5 PERB 7019, at 7025 (N.Y.S. Ct. 1972).
89. 5 PERB 3008, at 301 (1972).
90. Ibid. at 3.
91. Ibid. at 5.
92. Ibid.
93. Ibid. at 6. Emphasis added.
94. Public Employment Relations Board, PERB News 5, no. 2 (Feb. 1972): 1.
95. 4 PERB 3060, at 3707 (1971).
96. Address by a PERB staff member to PERB panel members, Albany, New York, Feb. 15, 1972. The author was permitted to listen to this speech.
97. Public Employment Relations Board, PERB News 4, no. 5 (May 1971).
98. Paul Klein, "Recent Developments in Representation and Improper Practices," PERB News 4, no. 8 (Aug. 1971). Emphasis added.
99. 331 N.Y.S.2d 17, 79 LRRM 2881 (1972).
100. 331 N.Y.S.2d 17, at 21.
101. Ibid. at 22.
102. Ibid. at 23.
103. Confidential letter to author, from NYSTA staff member, Mar. 20, 1972.
104. 387 F.2d 542, 66 LRRM 2634, at 2638 (4th Cir., 1967).
105. Bernard Ashe, Memorandum on the Huntington Case, Albany, July 7, 1972 (prepared for NYSTA staff).

PART

II

LEGAL AND CONCEPTUAL
PROBLEMS AFFECTING
THE SCOPE OF PUBLIC
SECTOR BARGAINING

In Part I of this study I laid the groundwork, so to speak, for an analysis of sophisticated scope-of-bargaining problems and for the presentation of original, empirical research. In reviewing the evolution of the scope of bargaining in the private sector, the development of state legislation for public sector bargaining, the views of expert committees and practitioners as to how laws should be fashioned, and especially the legislative and decisional history of public employee negotiations under New York's Taylor Act, I hoped to construct a foundation of knowledge on which to build an analysis of research findings and draw final conclusions as to how the scope of bargaining should be structured in public employment.

One significant question studied in Part II is the conflict between the Taylor Law and preexisting statutes. I alluded to this conflict at several points, and certainly the Huntington decision raises questions regarding the relationship between the Taylor Law and other legislation and the degree to which collective negotiations under the Taylor Law supersedes other statutory provisions. As Robert Helsby commented in an address to the New York State Commission on the Quality, Cost, and Financing of Elementary and Secondary Education:

> A whole series of problems . . . arise from the fact that the Taylor Law was, in effect, imposed upon a whole super-structure of laws, some permissive and others restrictive. For example, civil service is, in effect, a personnel system operated by the employer. The Taylor Law provides that the terms and conditions of employment will be determined bilaterally—that is, through negotiations. Thus, there appears to be some conflict between the traditional concept of civil service and the objectives of the Taylor Law.
> . . . . . .
> Of course, civil service is not the only area in which [public employers] may be faced with employee demands for a benefit which they are precluded from providing by State law.[1]

The resolution of the conflict between laws is no simple matter, and the cases discussed in Chapter 7 illustrate the problems that arise when a legislature mandates public sector collective negotiations and simultaneously continues to legislate, through existing statutes, the terms and conditions of employment of public employees.

Some of the most heated controversy regarding bargaining in public employment concerns professional employee negotiations and the question of the extent to which professional organizations should be allowed to bargain over institutional policies and professional standards.

The contention of these professional employee organizations that professional standards and the quality of services provided be negotiable is an interesting and ironic development of their history.[2] Originally professionalism was offered by these organizations as an alternative concept to collective bargaining. "The labor movement predictably derided such programs as anemic substitutes for collective bargaining, as sterile expressions of middle class snobbery, involving the sacrifice of the bona fide interests of professional groups for a personal key to the wash room." [3] Many believed that the concern of these organizations with professional issues reflected, to a large extent, the interests and influence of management.

In recent years, however, it has become clear that the involvement of professional public employees in matters of enterprise policies and operations and professional standards is no longer a substitute for "real" collective bargaining—this involvement is merely a new dimension added to the process. Professionals insist that the nature of their training and on-the-job responsibilities necessitates their participation in professional and policy matters; but many employers, practitioners, and legislators see these employee demands as encroachments on vested management rights. Arvid Anderson, chairman of the Office of Collective Bargaining in New York City, voiced his concern over this new bargaining dimension

> The impact of collective bargaining on our society is also evidenced by the fact that a number of public employee organizations look upon collective bargaining as a means for effectuating social change, as well as a procedure for improving wages, hours and fringe benefits. I refer to the demand of teachers who want to bargain about the school curriculum or class size; welfare workers who want to bargain about the level of benefits to welfare recipients; . . . nurses who wish to bargain about the number of duty stations; policemen who want to regulate the number of men on a patrol or their authority to make arrests. . . . While I consider all of such topics as proper subjects of discussion between the public employer and employee organizations, I do not agree that the collective bargaining process is the appropriate means of resolving all major public policy questions. In some jurisdictions, there are laws and procedures for resolving disputes over the scope of bargaining, while in others, ad hoc decisions are being made.[4]

In many jurisdictions the legislatures have delegated to the courts the task of distinguishing between working conditions and policy matters and the problem of apportioning power between government and unions representing public employees. Legislative guidance is frequently lacking; and, as Harry Wellington and Ralph Winter observe, the clarification of the "seemingly innocuous phrase" of terms and conditions of employment "will require agencies and courts to resolve issues that are politically, socially, and ideologically among the more explosive in our society; ones that adjudicating tribunals are institutionally ill suited to resolve."[5]

The determination of the scope of bargaining is further complicated by the employment in government of professionals whose demands for autonomy often run counter to society's demands for accountability. In light of judicial uncertainty about the meaning of professionalism in public employment and the validity of distinguishing between professional and nonprofessional public employees, it is not surprising that sharply divergent opinions on the scope of bargaining have been handed down by the boards and courts of various states.

The following chapters will explore the conceptual and legal problems underlying the determination of appropriate bargaining subjects in public employment. Chapter 9 reflects on both private and public sector experience to date and offers this author's concept of a sound approach to the determination of bargaining subjects in government negotiations.

NOTES

1. Robert D. Helsby, "Impact of the Taylor Law on Public Schools 1968-1970," remarks before the New York State Commission on the Quality, Cost, and Financing of Elementary and Secondary Education, Syracuse, April 2, 1971.

2. Paul Prasow and Edward Peters, "A Theoretical Framework for Scope of Negotiation," in Scope of Bargaining in the Public Sector—Concept and Problems (Los Angeles: Institute of Industrial Relations, University of California, 1971), p. 19.

3. Ibid.

4. Arvid Anderson, an address to United States Conference of Mayors, Denver, Colorado, June 14, 1970, pp. 5-6.

5. Harry H. Wellington and Ralph K. Winter, Jr., The Unions and the Cities (Washington, D.C.: Brookings Institution, 1971), p. 148.

THE CONFLICT AMONG
LAWS AFFECTING THE
SCOPE OF BARGAINING
IN PUBLIC EMPLOYMENT

INTRODUCTION

Interpretation is often spoken of as if it were nothing but the
search and the discovery of a meaning which, however ob-
scure and latent, had none the less a real and ascertainable
pre-existence in the legislator's mind. The process is, indeed, that at times, but it is often something more. The
ascertainment of intention may be the least of a judge's
troubles in ascribing meaning to a statute. "The fact is,"
says Gray in his lectures on the "Nature and Sources of
the Law," "that the difficulties of so-called interpretation
arise when the legislature has had no meaning at all; when
the question which is raised on the statute never occurred
to it; when what the judges have to do is, not to determine
what the legislature did mean on a point which was present
to its mind, but to guess what it would have intended on a
point not present to its mind, if the point had been present.[1]

Justice Benjamin Cardozo first referred to this problem of
ascertaining legislative intent in The Nature of the Judicial Process,
published in 1921. The issue, however, has much relevance today
with respect to determining the scope of bargaining in public employment.
    The scope of bargaining is shaped not only by public employee
bargaining laws but also by constitutional provisions, court decisions,
state comptroller opinions, civil service codes, and especially by
other statutes, such as municipal, finance, and education laws. A
problem has frequently arisen, however, because state legislatures
have rarely given sufficient consideration to the problems that may
result from imposing a collective bargaining requirement covering

"terms and conditions of employment" upon this preexisting statutory and decisional structure.

In New York, for instance, the chairman of the Public Employment Relations Board has stated that the Taylor Law was, "in effect, imposed upon a whole superstructure of laws, some permissive and others restrictive."[2] The civil service, for example, has traditionally been a personnel system unilaterally administered by the public employer. The Taylor Law mandates that employees' terms and conditions of employment be determined bilaterally through collective negotiations. There is, therefore, a potential conflict between the civil service system and the mandates of the Taylor Law. "An attempt could have been made to resolve these apparent conflicts in advance by attempting to determine and define by statute what is negotiable and what is not. The Taylor Law makes no such attempt."[3]

Potential reallocations of governmental power can occur when employees, under bargaining laws, seek to negotiate over subjects encompassed by the definition of "wages, hours, and terms and conditions of employment," but traditionally regulated by other statutes or by the legislature through its exercise of undelegated powers. A court faced with this problem must grapple with a two-horned dilemma: it could determine that issues within a bargaining law's broad definition of negotiable subjects, but traditionally regulated by other statutes or by the legislature through the exercise of undelegated powers, are outside the scope of bargaining. Alternatively, it could decide that the statutory definition of negotiable subjects represents an implied delegation of broad bargaining power to a public official whom the statute defines as a public employer.[4] The first approach might exclude important items from the scope of bargaining, while the latter conclusion might result in an unintended reallocation of legislative power.[5]

In discussing the regulation of the scope of bargaining, Harry Wellington and Ralph Winter suggest that the perpetuation of "anachronistic" civil service systems often interferes with appropriate collective negotiations:

Mindful of a spoils system with its corrupting influence on the public service and of the need for impartiality . . . in the recruitment, promotion and discharge of government employees, advocates of civil service have been extremely successful in obtaining legislation at [all] levels. Not infrequently, however, the civil service has become encrusted with bureaucratic barnacles, and frequently its administration complicates the achievement of a rational regime of collective bargaining.[6]

Additionally, in recent years civil service systems have expanded to encompass many aspects of employment conditions other than

147

recruitment, classification, and promotion. New areas of regulation have included grievance handling, employee training, salary administration, and safety—the very issues that most employee representatives view as appropriate for negotiations.

The reconciliation of the civil service concept with the notion of bilateral determination of terms and conditions of employment relates to a unique governmental labor problem: defining who the employer is. Frequently civil service commissions urge that they, alone or in concert with other agencies, are the public employer for collective bargaining purposes. In most jurisdictions, however, bargaining authority rests with the chief executive officer of the local governmental unit. If he has the statutory duty to negotiate over terms and conditions of employment, but the civil service commission insists on regulating personnel matters ordinarily negotiable, the scope of bargaining will be unduly restricted.

One scholar suggests that in order to effectuate the collective bargaining principle, "all nonmerit functions should be transferred from the civil service commission to a personnel department under the chief executive officer of each local unit."[7]

Many states, however, are reluctant to tamper with the authority of the civil service. In Wisconsin, for example, the public employee bargaining law excludes from the mandatory scope of bargaining an extensive range of matters regulated by law or by civil service.[8] Connecticut, Kansas, and Maine exclude from negotiations the conduct and grading of merit examinations and the appointment of candidates from lists based on such examinations.[9] The Hawaii statute stipulates that the parties "shall not agree to any proposal which would be inconsistent with merit principles."[10] In Massachusetts the public employee bargaining law expressly stipulates that it shall not "diminish the authority and power of the civil service commission. . . ."[11] And in California, the law states:

> Nothing contained herein shall be deemed to supersede the provisions of existing state law and the charters, ordinances and rules of local public agencies which establish and regulate a merit or civil service system. . . . This chapter is intended, instead, to strengthen merit, civil service and other methods of administering employer-employee relations through the establishment of uniform and orderly methods of communication. . . .[12]

The Connecticut Municipal Employee Bargaining Law, on the other hand, imposes restrictions on the authority of civil service commissions. As noted in Chapter 3, the statute provides that the conduct and grading of merit examinations, the rating of candidates, establishment of lists from such examinations, and appointments from such lists are not subjects of collective bargaining. The law also states, however:

> Where there is a conflict between any agreement reached by a municipal employer and an employee organization and approved in accordance with the provisions of this act on matters appropriate to collective bargaining, as defined in this act, and any charter, special act, ordinance, rules or regulations adopted by the municipal employer or its agents, such as a personnel board or civil service commission . . . the terms of such agreement shall prevail.[13]

Thus the Connecticut law makes nonnegotiable only the recruitment, testing, and promotion responsibilities of the civil service.

Because many state legislatures, in enacting bargaining laws, considered neither the potential competition among tribunals traditionally authorized to determine conditions of employment nor possible conflicts among statutes regarding the scope of bargaining, the various state courts and public employee relations boards have had to resolve the following questions:

1. Which public official or agency is, for collective bargaining purposes, the "public employer" authorized to negotiate with employee representatives?

2. Do newly enacted bargaining laws in any way expand the preexisting authority of public employers to confer benefits on employees, within the meaning of the term "wages, hours, and terms and conditions of employment"?

3. Are regulations and statutes enacted prior to the passage of bargaining laws superseded by the later legislation mandating bargaining over wages, hours, and terms and conditions of employment?

4. Which tribunal or government officer—the state comptroller, commissioner of education, civil service commission, or public employment relations board—is empowered to make decisions concerning appropriate subjects for bargaining?

Although boards and courts in several states have handed down decisions concerning these and related questions,[14] Michigan and New York stand out as the two jurisdictions in which there has been extensive litigation regarding these "conflicts" issues. Indeed, one commentator has noted that during recent years, with respect to public employment, "By far, the most significant work of the courts has concerned the reconciliation of [Michigan] PERA with other laws."[15]

Although this chapter is concerned primarily with the ways in which the New York courts are resolving the uncertain relationship between the Taylor Law and other statutes, the decisions rendered by the Michigan courts provide a richly colored backdrop against which to paint the New York experience.

149

THE MICHIGAN CASES

Mt. Morris

In Charles Rayburn, Byron S. Reetz, David Larson and the Mt. Morris Education Association and Board of Education of Mt. Morris Consolidated School District, No. 3,[16] Circuit Judge Elliott reversed a 1968 attorney general's opinion that had declared illegal school board agreements providing terminal leave, payment for accumulated sick leave, and reimbursement of tuition credits for graduate study.*

The attorney general's opinion had held that such specific laws as the School Code of 1955 and the Teachers Retirement Act took precedence over the general Public Employment Relations Act (PERA), enacted in 1965. Judge Elliott, however, decided that the attorney general's "fundamental premise was erroneous," that his "conclusions missed the point" of PERA and, therefore, "would defeat its purpose."[17]

The PERA, according to Judge Elliott, was intended to grant teachers and other public employees many of the rights and kinds of benefits enjoyed by workers in the private sector

> . . . except as the same would be repugnant to existing laws or an abuse of the authority of the public employer—considering the nature of public service involved and laws affecting it. . . . [PERA] creates a monumental change in this State, from a public policy that a school board could not contract with its employees except as the legislature had specifically or impliedly permitted, to a public policy authorizing and requiring a school board to bargain with its teachers' representative about any subject that would be a lawful objective of a union of private employees . . . unless because of the nature of the public employment or existing . . . laws, agreement on such subject is prohibited. . . .[18]

In reaching this conclusion Judge Elliott relied heavily on the NLRA as a "model" for PERA. He noted that the disputed contract provisions in the present case were "clearly within the well-established meaning of 'Wages'" as developed under the NLRA.

---

* The negotiated agreement between the Mt. Morris Education Association and the board of education contained specific provisions concerning all of these benefits prohibited by the attorney general's opinion. The Association sued the school board for noncompliance in order to obtain a court determination.

150

The Mt. Morris decision emphasized that a basic rule of statutory construction is to discover and, if possible, "give effect to the intention or purpose of the legislature." Thus, a significant conclusion was reached:

It appears that the legislature's purpose is to make the provisions of [PERA] controlling on the subject of the authorized scope of public collective bargaining. . . . Reading that act with all other statutes . . ., we find no necessary repugnancy between them. On the contrary, none of the other statutes pertains to the permissible scope of public employment collective bargaining agreements nor irreconcilably limit [sic] the negotiable subjects.[19]

City of Detroit, Civil Service Commission

In City of Detroit, Civil Service Commission and AFSCME, District Council 77, the Detroit Civil Service Commission had sought a court ruling affirming the following proposition:

(A) That the Charter of the City of Detroit vests exclusively in the Detroit Civil Service Commission the authority to make classification and position allocations in the classified service of the City,
(B) That the provisions of [PERA] do not upset the local structure of municipal government that places certain powers, including the classification and position allocation authority beyond the reach of executive and legislative officials,
(C) That the Mayor and the Common Council . . . have no power or authority to bind the Civil Service Commission on matters of classification or position allocation in collective bargaining agreements . . .;
(D) That classification and position allocation determinations are within the exclusive jurisdiction of the Civil Service . . . and the Commission is the proper forum for decisions on classification.[20]

Approving the developing doctrine that PERA must prevail in instances of conflict with the Civil Service Act, the Wayne County Circuit Court held that the charter of the city of Detroit no longer vested in the Civil Service Commission the exclusive authority to make classification and position allocations in the classified service of the city. Under the provisions of PERA, the Mayor and Common Council now had the authority, on matters of classification or position

151

allocation, to bind the Civil Service Commission through their approval of collectively bargained contracts. Moreover, the Civil Service Commission's determinations were, according to the court, made legally subject to the "process and restrictions" negotiated by the American Federation of State, County, and Municipal Employees (AFSCME) and the city in their master agreement. One of the fundamental "process and restrictions" involved in the contract concerned the authority of an arbitrator to hear and dispose of grievances on classification and position allocations.

The crux of the Civil Service Commission's case concerned Article 26 in AFSCME's master agreement with the city, which provided for provisional changes in classification status so that an employee could be compensated at the appropriate higher level when, during an emergency, he had to assume the duties of a higher classification for more than four hours. The Commission argued that the agreement did not specifically authorize an arbitrator to dispose of grievances pertaining to classification and position allocation, especially in light of Article 7 of the agreement, which stated that "the arbitrator shall be without authority to require the City to delegate, alienate, or relinquish any powers, duties, responsibilities, obligations or discretions which by state law or city charter the City cannot delegate, alienate, or relinquish."[21]

The court disagreed with the Civil Service Commission that Article 7 prohibited arbitration concerning grievances based on Article 26, citing a Michigan Employment Relations Commission (MERC) decision as the correct "modern view":

We can conceive of no valid reasons for excepting disputes in the employer-employee relationship from the general power of a public employer to arbitrate disputes between the public employer and other contracting party.[22]

The court granted AFSCME's motion for an accelerated judgment, dismissing the Commission's complaint for a declaratory judgment.

Loose v. City of Dearborn Heights

The Michigan Court of Appeals considered the conflict between civil service law and the PERA in Loose v. City of Dearborn Heights.[23] In this case the city had promoted an individual to the position of chief of police without conducting a competitive examination. A state civil service law, however, required competitive examinations prior to promotions in all municipal police departments.* On a petition for mandamus, the trial court upheld the legality of the challenged promotion and ruled that the civil service law establishing the requirements for promotion in municipal police departments was impliedly repealed by the enactment of the PERA, directing employers to bargain over "wages, hours, and other terms and conditions of employment."

Stating that "the repeal of a statute by implication is not permitted if it can be avoided by any reasonable construction of the statute," the Court of Appeals rejected the trial court's conclusion of implied repeal.[24] It decided, however, that a negotiated contract between a union and appropriate municipal employer—here, the city of Dearborn Heights—could change the terms of existing state law. The Court succinctly concluded:

> In our opinion there is no conflict between these provisions of the civil service act and the public employees' labor relations act. The civil service act in the instant case provides day-to-day procedural rules to be followed by the employer. The public employees' act provides the mechanism for changing those procedural rules.[25]

As a result of this decision, when a conflict arises between the conditions of employment established in a negotiated contract and state law, the contract will prevail over those employees covered by the agreement; but the provisions of the law will govern those public employees not covered by the agreement.

<h2 style="text-align:center">Wayne County Civil Service Commission
v. Board of Supervisors</h2>

A three-sided contest between the Wayne County Civil Service Commission, the Wayne County Board of Supervisors, and the Wayne County Road Commission was resolved in Wayne County Civil Service

---

*MCLA §38.512 (Stat. Ann. 1969 Rev. §5.3362) states:

(b) Vacancies in positions in the fire and police department above the ranks of fireman or patrolman shall be competitive and filled by promotions from among persons holding positions in the next lower rank in the departments. . . . Promotions shall be based upon merit to be ascertained by tests to be provided by the civil service commission and upon the superior qualifications of the persons promoted as shown by his previous service and experience.

Commission v. Board of Supervisors[26] by the Michigan Supreme Court's per curiam holding that the Road Commission was a public employer under PERA and the sole employer of its employees.

This landmark decision of Michigan's highest court stemmed from a dispute that originated in March 1966, when the Board of Supervisors adopted a resolution establishing a three-member Labor Relations Board to represent the county in employee bargaining. This Board, which was composed of representatives of the Board of Supervisors, Wayne County Civil Service Commission, and the Road Commission, in effect displaced the Civil Service Commission in bargaining for rates of pay and terms and conditions of employment.

Basing its claim upon the 1941 County Civil Service Act,[27] the Wayne County Civil Service Commission had brought a complaint against the Board of Supervisors, the Labor Relations Board, and the Board of Road Commissioners for a declaratory judgment for determination of the collective bargaining rights of the parties. The Civil Service Commission contended that the 1941 Act, no. 370, had made it "the exclusive body to represent the county . . . and all bodies within the county in matters dealing with terms and conditions of employment, salaries, and wages . . .,"[28] subject only to the concurrence of the Board of Supervisors on salaries and wages. It sought a judicial declaration that bargaining was to be conducted "in accordance with the requirements of Act 370."[29]

Under Act 370, the Civil Service Commission was authorized to:

> Provide by regulation for the hours and conditions of service, for the length and periods of vacations, and for the regulation of sick leaves in the county service, and for such other matters pertaining to the carrying out of the provisions of this act . . . .[30]

It also was authorized to conduct competitive examinations for purposes of selection and appointment, to classify positions, and to submit uniform pay plans for standardizing salaries.

The Board of Supervisors was authorized to represent the county and to have "care and management of the property and business of the county in all cases where no other provisions shall be made."[31] It also was empowered to approve all decisions made by the County Civil Service Commission. On appeal to the Supreme Court, it argued that the PERA (Act 379),[32] to the extent that it placed wages, hours, and terms and conditions of employment into the area of collective bargaining, superseded "pro tanto those provisions or parts of Act 370 dealing with the same subject matters."[33]

Finally, the Board of Road Commissioners, relying in part upon a separate constitutional provision and statute, contended that it was the "public employer" of its own employees for collective bargaining purposes. Essentially, the Board of Road Commissioners had the power to hire, fire, demote, promote, discipline, and pay its employees performing road work, subject to P.A. 1941, no. 370.[34]

The issue in Wayne County was the conflict between two statutes for jurisdiction over the process of collective bargaining. Reviewing the purposes of both acts, the Supreme Court pointed out that Civil Service Act 370 was intended to guarantee fair and equal opportunity in the public service, to establish working conditions that would attract individuals of ability and character, and to improve the efficiency of government service through improved methods of personnel administration. The 1965 PERA was intended to prohibit strikes, provide review of disciplinary action, allow mediation of grievances and the holding of elections, declare and protect the rights of public employees, and prescribe means of enforcement of the Act's provisions. But the real crux of the problem was the legislature's failure, in drafting PERA, to define specifically the term "employer" for purposes of collective bargaining or to denote the relationship that was to exist between Acts 370 and 379.

A three-judge circuit court panel ruled that the Board of Supervisors alone had the power to act as the representative of the county in collective bargaining matters. The circuit court stated, ". . . the Wayne County Road Commission is not an employer separate and distinct from the County of Wayne . . ., the public employer is the County of Wayne, acting through and by the Board of Supervisors."[35] It held, moreover, that provisions of P.A. 370, which were inconsistent with P.A. 379, were impliedly repealed.

This judgment was reversed in part by the Court of Appeals, which concluded that the Civil Service Act and PERA were reconcilable and that bargaining authority was split among the Civil Service Commission, the Road Commission, and the Board of Supervisors: "There is no single body or individual in county government who has the right or responsibility, exclusively, to represent the County in matters dealing with the establishment of salaries, wages, terms and conditions of employment of employees in the classified service."[36]

Entering what it termed the "chaos of legislation," the Supreme Court first noted that when the Civil Service Act was passed in 1941, collective bargaining by public employees could not "have been in the minds of the people" or of the legislature:

The right of collective bargaining, applicable at the time to private employment, was then in comparative infancy and portended no suggestion that it ever might enter the realm of public employment.[37]

In the Court's view, Acts 370 and 379 could not be harmonized. It concluded that the 1965 legislature did not realize that the provisions of PERA would both encroach on and, to an extent, impair the previously assigned authority of the Civil Service Commission operating under Act 370. Thus, the legislature did not include the needed exclusory clause, which would have evidenced its intent. "We are left to guess," concluded the Court, "what the 1965 legislature would have done had the point come to attention."[38]

Emphasizing its long-standing view that repeals by implication are not favored, the Court determined that this was a striking case in which two laws were so incompatible that both could not fully stand. The PERA, therefore, operated "to the extent of the repugnancy," as a partial repeal of Act 370, "but no more than that."

> In short shrift this means that the purposed thrust of the act of 1965, that of prohibiting strikes . . . and providing collective bargaining, negotiation and enforced mediation of labor disputes . . . must be implemented and administered exclusively as provided therein. Hence, the original authority and duty of the plaintiff civil service commission was diminished pro tanto, by the act of 1965, to the extent of free administration of the latter according to its tenor.[39]

Noting that the status of specific divisions or classes of Wayne County employees under Act 379 had not yet been considered, the Court recalled that the circuit court had determined that the Road Commission was not a distinct employer from the county and that the Court of Appeals had reversed this ruling. Upholding the appellate court, the Supreme Court asserted:

> From as far back as 1909 . . . county road law has authorized . . . county road commissioners to "employ" necessary "servants and laborers." The section leaves no doubt of original and present intent that each board of county road commissioners shall be the employer of its employees. . . . Such are our reasons for . . . agreement with the defendant road commission that it is, within the act of 1965, the "public employer" . . . .[40]

Thus, in this case the Supreme Court reversed the Court of Appeals in part and held that the Road Commission alone was empowered to bargain under Section 15 of the PERA.

City of Detroit v. Detroit Police Officers Association

Some bargaining laws, unlike that of Michigan, specifically define the term "public employer," often including within that definition every governmental body, agency, or officer having control over employees' terms and conditions of employment. Sometimes, however, individuals not falling within the statutory definition may establish working conditions. For instance, some local government charter provisions that are adopted under a broad delegation of state legislative power require the electorate to define certain municipal working conditions through referendum.[41] In these cases, when the state legislature mandates that city employers bargain in good faith on working conditions, the courts and administrative agencies must decide either that conditions of employment established by referendum are implied exceptions to the statutory scope of collective bargaining, or that the bargaining statute requires even electorally determined working conditions to be negotiated by a city official on the demand of employee representatives.[42]

MERC recently confronted this situation in City of Detroit v. Detroit Police Officers Association,[43] and held that the PERA's mandate to bargain over wages, hours, and terms and conditions of employment was in "irreconcilable conflict" with a city charter provision requiring a referendum to approve certain working conditions.

Citing a trial examiner's decision, which was rendered in a case analogous to the instant one,[44] MERC concluded:

> . . . it was the legislative intent that PERA should prevail over any City Charter, to the extent that they may conflict. This conflict may arise whenever a Home Rule City has a charter containing provisions that relate to the rates of pay, wages, hours or employment or other conditions of employment of the city employees, and there is a legally recognized bargaining agent of employees. . . . At the time of recognition of such a bargaining representative, the City is obligated to bargain in respect to rates of pay, wages, hours of employment or other conditions of employment without regard to any provisions of the City Charter. . . . It is obvious that this is in keeping with the legislative intent, for to hold otherwise would result in the collective bargaining obligation varying from community to community throughout the State . . ., depending upon the City and Charter provisions involved.[45]

In light of this conclusion, a contract negotiated between the city and union would be valid and binding regardless of any contrary charter provision.

THE IMPLICATIONS OF THE MICHIGAN DECISIONS

The thrust of these recent Michigan decisions has been to create a hospitable climate in which the provisions of the 1965 PERA can be fully effectuated. But the attitude of the judiciary and MERC, which, in essence, has favored broad interpretation of the bargaining statute and narrow interpretation of laws restricting the scope of negotiations, has not been unanimously applauded. The doctrine of repeal by implication, as applied by the Supreme Court in Wayne County, has been viewed as "unsound" and "extreme."[46] If the full implementation of PERA requires the repeal of the County Civil Service Act to the extent of its repugnancy, then, says one critic:

> . . . little is left of the Civil Service system that will not be
> replaced by the collective bargaining contract. If this
> rationale applies to the County Civil Service Act, it would
> equally apply to the Firemen and Policemen Civil Service
> Act. Since disputes as to what is to be included in a collec-
> tive bargaining contract covering firemen and policemen
> are subject to binding arbitration under Public Act 312,
> the typical areas of Civil Service may well be left to the
> arbitrator's compromise. . . . The conclusion that PERA
> and the County Civil Service Act are not reconcilable leads
> to this harsh result.[47]

But is the result so "harsh"? And does it truly stem from the Court's holding that PERA impliedly repeals inconsistent provisions of the Civil Service Act? To this writer's way of thinking, the doctrine of pro tanto repeal is simply another way of bringing about a reconciliation between two laws. MERC and courts have adopted the position that the 1965 PERA was intended to inject into the public employment scheme a new concept of bilateralism with respect to the determination of wages, hours, and terms and conditions of employment. This concept reflected the recent, yet growing, belief that all employees, whether private or public, have a legitimate interest in establishing reasonable working conditions and fair grievance procedures. But, as the Supreme Court pointed out in Wayne County, at the time P.A. 370 was enacted, the idea of introducing collective bargaining into the public service had not yet been born.

Under PERA public employees have been denied the right to strike, but in return have been given organization and representation rights as well as statutory procedures for meaningful negotiations. What the courts have realized, however, is that the right to bargain ceases to be the quid pro quo for the prohibition of strikes if the scope of bargaining is unduly restricted.

In Loose v. Dearborn Heights the doctrine of pro tanto repeal was rejected, whereas the Supreme Court decision in Wayne County held that aspects of P.A. 370 and P.A. 379 could not be harmonized. The practical results of these determinations, however, were not different. By authorizing municipal public employers to negotiate contracts that supersede, or at least bypass, preexisting state laws and municipal charters, the Michigan courts have used the general PERA definition of negotiable subjects as the basis for reallocating legislative power over employee working conditions and for giving effect to the legislature's intent to permit employees to participate meaningfully in establishing terms of their employment. What ultimately emerges from these Michigan cases is the tacit conclusion on the part of the courts that PERA is preemptive because it provides the broadest scope of bargaining and that the employer to be recognized under PERA is the governmental entity most directly concerned with the employment function. And whether or not one goes so far as to say that PERA impliedly repeals contrary provisions of the Civil Service Act, in terms of the ultimate effect on governmental power, any difference between construing PERA as an implied delegation of power, which the Court of Appeals held in Loose, and construing it as an implied repeal of preexisting limitations, which the Supreme Court decided in Wayne County, is illusory.

THE NEW YORK EXPERIENCE

Public employer-employee relations in New York have traditionally been governed by Civil Service Law, General Municipal Law, Education Law, and the state constitution. Additionally, local public employers generally have been attentive to comptroller's opinions interpreting state laws and constitutional provisions, while school boards, in particular, have also relied on decisions and opinions of the commissioner of education and the counsel for the Education Department.

The enactment of the Taylor Law has provoked many questions, as did Michigan's PERA, concerning inconsistencies between the objectives of the Law and previous legislation and administrative rulings regarding labor-management relations in public employment. Although the Taylor Committee had expressed concern about preserving the civil service system,[48] the Taylor Law, as enacted, does not expressly exclude any aspects of civil service from the scope of bargaining. Questions have arisen, therefore, regarding the relationship between the Taylor Law and the civil service system.

In contrast with the Michigan PERA, however, the Taylor Law does contain a definition of the "public employer."* But, interestingly, controversies have still occurred in New York because of the "eschelonning [sic] and fragmentation of managerial authority."[49] Because of the structure of government, management at the unit level frequently lacks sufficient authority to negotiate—or, stated differently, authority to bargain is shared by several sources (such as the school board, city council, mayor, governor, and state legislature). Questions concerning the identity of the public employer and its authority to negotiate terms and conditions of employment significantly affect the scope of bargaining. The remainder of this chapter is devoted to an analysis of the problems that have arisen and the judicial opinions that have been rendered concerning the reconciliation of the Taylor law with other statutes.

In 1970 Robert Helsby, chairman of the Public Employment Relations Board (PERB) and Thomas Joyner, PERB's director of research, prepared a report on the three-year impact of the Taylor Law on local governments.[50] In this report they stated:

> ... there has been almost no conflict with respect to civil service—the major area in which many thought there would be a head-on collision. Instead, local government employees have sought, through bargaining demands, the most effective implementation of the civil service system. Thus, among other things, they have demanded that civil service exams be given more often, that classification system be updated, and that the Civil Service Law be strictly followed at the local level.[51]

The dearth of recorded cases concerning conflicts between employee demands and civil service requirements indicates that these conclusions were essentially correct. Even Helsby and Joyner admit, however, that "local civil service classification systems may well

---

*Section 201 of the Taylor Law defines the "public employer" to mean

(a) the state of New York, (b) a county, city, town, village or any other political subdivision of civil division of the state, (c) a school district or any governmental entity operating a public school, college or university, (d) a public improvement or special district, (e) a public authority, commission, or public benefit corporation, or (f) any other public corporation, agency or instrumentality or unit of government which exercises governmental powers under the laws of the state.

be in the process of being submerged by negotiated rates which are more sharply defined or more reflective of actual market conditions."[52]

In areas other than civil service, local governments have been confronted with union demands for benefits that, employers have argued, are nonnegotiable under state law. For example, Helsby and Joyner reported that certain unions have demanded that public employers establish a unilaterally administered welfare fund. Employer response outside New York City has been that since such plans are not authorized by law, they are illegal. The unions have argued that these plans exist in New York City and have been held legal by the New York City corporation counsel.[53] Another example lies in union demands that retiring employees be given a retirement benefit, usually in the form of compensation for unused sick leave. Local governments generally have argued that such a benefit is illegal, citing a comptroller's opinion holding that this kind of payment constituted a violation of the gift provision of the state constitution.[54] The negotiability of issues such as these is ultimately being resolved by the courts.

The next question, therefore, is how the courts are resolving these problems. Is the scope of negotiations under the Taylor Law to be restricted by other legislation or administrative decisions affecting employee working conditions? Is express statutory authorization necessary for each subject over which a public employer may bargain?

LAWS AFFECTING PUBLIC EMPLOYEE RELATIONS

For purposes of the forthcoming analysis, it will be helpful first to understand the pertinent, sometimes conflicting, provisions of the New York statutes often at issue in disputes concerning the supremacy of laws and the public employers' authority to enter into collective agreements. The section that appears below highlights these relevant statutory provisions.[55]

General Municipal Law

Sections 92, 93-b, and 681-685 of the General Municipal Law are particularly relevant to the scope of bargaining. Section 92 permits cities to establish vacation and sick leave plans and to pay employees the unused portion of any vacation upon termination of employment. (The law is silent with respect to compensation of unused, accumulated sick leave at termination or retirement.)

Section 93-b allows employees to authorize dues deductions. Such authorization may be withdrawn by the employee at any time. Sections 681-685 establish a grievance procedure for municipal employees, including those of school districts. Grievance boards develop advisory recommendations for public employers upon a review of employee appeals. Under this procedure, grievances are defined as

> Any claimed violation, misrepresentation or inequitable application of the existing laws, rules, procedures, regulations, administrative orders or work rules, of a government or a department or agency thereof, which relate to or involve employee health or safety, physical facilities, material or equipment . . ., or supervision of employees; provided, however, that such term shall not include any matter involving . . . rate of compensation, retirement benefits, disciplinary proceeding or any matter which is otherwise reviewable pursuant to law or any rule or regulation having the force and effect of law.

Education Law

In New York there are six types of school districts: common school, union free school, central school, central high school, city districts of less than 125,000 inhabitants, and city districts with more than 125,000 inhabitants. Although the powers and duties of each type of school board are set forth in separate articles in the Education Law, the common school district may serve as a guide, since the provisions applicable to other school districts are largely repetitive of those pertaining to the common school district. With respect to teacher employee relations, powers and duties of school board trustees are listed below:

Article 33, section 1604:
Subsection 8. to contract with and employ as many legally qualified teachers as the schools in the district require . . .; to determine the rate of compensation and the term of the employment of each teacher and to determine the terms of school to be held during each year . . . the regular teachers . . . may be employed at an increased compensation or otherwise and by separate agreement, written or oral, for one or more of such additional duties.
Subsection 10. to prescribe the course of studies to be prescribed in such schools. . . .

162

Subsection 27. to reimburse members of the teaching and
supervising staff for expenses actually and necessarily
incurred in the performance of their official duties and
to make such rules and regulations in relation thereto as
they shall deem necessary and proper. . . .
Subsection 29. to prescribe the text-books to be used in
the schools, and to compel a uniformity in the use of the
same. . . .
Subsection 30. to have in all respects the superintendence, management and control of the educational offices
of the district, and, therefore, shall have all the powers
reasonably necessary to exercise power granted
expressly or by implication and to discharge duties imposed expressly or by implication by this chapter or
other statutes.
Subsection 31-a. At its discretion, to provide under a
group insurance policy . . . life insurance or accident
and health insurance benefits or medical and surgical
benefits or hospital service benefits or any two or more
of such kinds of benefits to teachers. . . . Such board of
education is authorized to pay from such monies as may
be available for the purpose, a share of the cost . . .
including the whole thereof.

In addition to these provisions dealing with powers and duties of
school boards are other sections of the Education Law that potentially
affect teacher employee relations:

School Year—Section 1704
This section specifies that "except as otherwise provided by law," a school year must be no less than 180
days.
Leaves of Absence—Sections 3005, 3005-a, 3005-b
These sections deal with leaves for teaching in other
schools or in foreign countries and leaves for personal
illnesses.
Tenure—Sections 1954, 2509, 2573, 3012, 3013, 3014
These provisions give the school board the right to
establish probationary periods of five years. Probationary teachers may be terminated upon a minimum
of 60 days' notice without a hearing.
Procedures for Appeals by Tenure Teachers—Sections
310, 2573, 3020-a
These sections specify procedures for hearings and
appeals involving charges against tenure teachers,
including review by the commissioner of education
and judicial review.

Hours of Duty for Full-Time Teachers—Section 3029
This section provides that teachers shall not be assigned more than 5 hours of continuous duty, and that they shall have at least 30 minutes of duty-free time if their daily total of hours of duty exceeds 5.

Teacher Salaries—Sections 3102, 3103, 3105
These sections authorize school boards to give discretionary grants of transfer credit to teachers for service in other districts, but mandates that such transfer credit count as service in the district. They also specify certain minimum salary levels, credit for graduate hours, and minimum compensation for substitute teachers. (Recent legislation, however, repealed mandated 10-step increments of $250 each.)

The Comptroller, Finance Law, and the Constitution

With respect to state finance, the comptroller derives authority directly from Article V, Section 1, of the state constitution, which states:

The comptroller shall be required: (1) To audit all vouchers before payment and all official accounts; (2) to audit the accrual and collection of all revenues and receipts; and (3) to prescribe such methods of accounting as are necessary for the performance of the foregoing duties. The payment of any money of the state, or of any money under its control, or the refund of any money paid to the state, except upon audit by the comptroller, shall be void. . . . In such respect the legislature shall define his powers and duties and may also assign to him: (1) supervision of the accounts of any political subdivision of the state; and (2) powers and duties pertaining to or connected with the assessment and taxation of real estate. . . .

Additionally, Article 2, Section 8, of the State Finance Law specifically lists the duties of the comptroller:

The comptroller shall: 1. Superintend the fiscal concerns of the state.
2. Keep, audit and state all accounts in which the state is interested, and keep accurate and proper books. . . .
3. Examine, audit and settle the accounts of all public officers and other persons indebted to the state. . . .

7. Audit all vouchers of any person, corporation, association, state or other public officer, department or institution, to whom or which moneys appropriated are payable, or are authorized or directed to be paid pursuant to law, before issuing his warrant for the payment thereof. . . .

8. Draw warrants on the treasury for the payment of the moneys directed by law to be paid out of the treasury, but no such warrant shall be drawn unless authorized by law, and every such warrant shall refer to the law under which it is drawn.

The comptroller therefore plays a primary role with respect to the superintendence and expenditure of state funds. This role is to decide "in the first instance the lawfulness of any proposed expenditure. This is not a final power, however. The action of the Comptroller in refusing any expenditure is subject to judicial review."[56]

The comptroller frequently issues opinions with respect to local as well as state expenditures, even though there is no specific or clearly implied general power granted to him in either the constitution or laws to pass on the substantive propriety of local expenditures. Hanslowe and Oberer note:

The assumption of authority by the Comptroller in cases presenting questions of substantive propriety is an interesting and instructive example of an institution expanding to fill the need of municipalities and other local governments for "authoritative" legal advice. . . .[57]

With respect to state and local expenditures, one other constitutional provision is particularly important. Section 1 of Article VIII provides that, subject to certain exceptions not material here, "[n]o county, city, town, village or school district shall give . . . any money or property to or in aid of any individual, or private corporation or association." This provision, like the prohibition directed toward the state itself in Section 8 of Article VII of the constitution, was intended to curb raids on the public purse for the benefit of favored individuals or groups furnishing no corresponding benefit or consideration to the state. As the cases below will demonstrate, the constitution's "gift provision" is frequently cited as a legal prohibition against granting certain economic benefits demanded by employee organizations.

The Taylor Law and PERB

The provisions of the Taylor Law relevant to the scope of bargaining were thoroughly analyzed in Chapter 6. For purposes of this section, however, it is instructive to consider the legislature's statement of policy. Section 200 of the Act provides:

. . . it is the public policy of the state and the purpose of this act to promote harmonious and cooperative relationships between government and its employees and to protect the public by assuring, at all times, the orderly and uninterrupted operations and functions of government. These policies are best effectuated by (a) granting to public employees the right of organization and representation, (b) requiring the state, local governments and other political subdivisions to negotiate with, and enter into written agreements with employee organizations . . ., (c) encouraging such public employers and employee organizations to agree upon procedures for resolving disputes, (d) creating a public employment relations board to assist in resolving disputes between public employees and public employers, and (e) continuing the prohibition against strikes. . . .

The Taylor Law thus establishes a mechanism for the recognition of employee negotiating representatives (Sections 204, 205, 206, 207) and specifies (Section 204.2) that ''. . . the appropriate public employer shall be, and hereby is, required to negotiate collectively with such employee organization in the determination of, and the administration of grievances arising under, the terms and conditions of employment of the public employees as provided in the article, and to negotiate and enter into written agreements. . . .'' The Law defines negotiable subjects as ''salaries, wages, hours and other terms and conditions of employment'' (Section 201.5). The 1969 amendments defined improper employer and employee practices, similar to those listed in the National Labor Relations Act. Furthermore, PERB was given ''exclusive nondelegable jurisdiction'' over matters involving improper practices as well as the power to fashion remedies that would effectuate the purposes of the Taylor Law, that is, encourage collective bargaining and protect public employees in the exercise of their rights under the Law.

COMPTROLLER'S OPINIONS AND THE
SCOPE OF BARGAINING

The comptroller has issued a number of advisory opinions dealing with the negotiability of certain issues. For the most part he has held that the proposed contract provisions either would be violative of Article VIII, Section 1 of the constitution, as illegal gifts for services not rendered, or would be invalid because they

166

are not expressly authorized by statute. The following summaries of several comptroller opinions indicate the way in which he has viewed the relationship between the Taylor Law and other statutes affecting the terms of public employment and the right of local employers to negotiate agreements.

In a 1967 opinion[58] the comptroller held that a central school board's proposed retirement benefit plan, providing for salary increases of teachers during their last one or two years of employment, was (1) beyond the statutory powers of the board of education and (2) an unconstitutional gift of public monies.

In considering the question the comptroller emphasized that boards of education are solely creatures of the Education Law, and they "must look to the statute for all of their powers and duties."[59] The Education Law contains no express provision authorizing the establishment of a retirement system by a board of education of a central school district. Moreover, continued the opinion, a locally developed retirement benefit system would contravene provisions of the Retirement and Social Security Law, Section 113, and Education Law, Section 526, which indicate that the state has preempted the field of retirement and pensions and that all local teachers' retirement systems, other than that of New York City, have been merged with the state teachers' system. Even if the retirement benefit were to be viewed as a "salary increase" rather than a "retirement system," the proposed plan, stated the comptroller, would arbitrarily discriminate among teachers (by benefiting only those teachers evincing an intent to retire) and would violate the constitution because bonuses or rewards for past services amount to unauthorized gifts.

In another situation a city school board sought the comptroller's advice concerning the bargainability of several demands that had been presented by AFSCME, representing the district's nonteaching personnel.[60] Two of the union's proposals pertained to terminal leave cash payments: 30 days for each 10 years of service and balance of accumulated sick leave allowance.

Referring to the Taylor Law, the comptroller made the following significant statement:

> The new statutory provisions do not in any way enlarge the legal benefits which public employers may confer on their employees nor has there been any expansion of the authority of such public employers in regard to these benefits. Therefore, it will be necessary for us to consider . . . the employee demands herein to determine whether, irrespective of collective bargaining, this school district may legally comply with the same.[61]

Finding no language in the Municipal or Education Laws specifically allowing payments of the first type proposed by the union, the comptroller held: "Since it would be straight terminal leave pay, not based on any accrued . . . vacation or overtime accumulations, we have no alternative but to view the proposed arrangement as unauthorized"[62] and prohibited by the gift provision of the constitution. The provisions of the General Municipal Law would also militate against paying employees for unused accumulated sick leave, concluded the comptroller in a frequently cited passage:

> Where a sick leave plan has been adopted, the principle supporting it is that, should the employee become sick, he is entitled to a prescribed number of days off with pay. Where he does not become sick, however, the condition upon which the plan is based and which activates his entitlement—namely, his becoming sick—never occurs. To pay him for these accumulations upon his separation from service . . . would be in direct contravention of the aforesaid principle, would be a payment without consideration and . . . in conflict with the gift prohibition in the State Constitution.[63]

In another 1967 opinion,[64] the comptroller held invalid a contract provision requiring the payment of all accrued sick leave to the estate of a deceased employee. The reasons were the same as those discussed in the preceding opinions: payment of accumulated sick leave would be a constitutionally prohibited gift. Also, since Section 92(1) of the General Municipal Law makes no mention of payments for unused sick leave, such compensation cannot be part of a collective bargaining agreement under the Taylor Law, "because this Act does not broaden powers of this type already granted to municipalities."[65]

The comptroller's opinions followed a similar trend during 1968. One inquiry concerned the authority of a village, as part of a labor agreement, to provide policemen with a life insurance policy paid for entirely by the village.[66] Although the comptroller answered affirmatively, provided there were to be at least 25 policemen in the covered group, he reiterated that the scope of negotiations under the Taylor Law was no greater than the scope of the unilateral power held by public employers under preexisting laws:

> The question of whether the village may purchase such life insurance . . . is determined not by the provisions of . . . the "Taylor Act," but rather by pertinent provisions of the General Municipal Law and the Insurance Law. The "Taylor Act" does not determine what may be the subject of collective bargaining, but rather sets forth a procedure for such bargaining. The authority to comply with the demands of the municipality's employees must be found in other statutes.[67]

168

Although public employers have sought new legal ways to negotiate benefits for retiring employees, the comptroller has consistently held invalid all plans not expressly authorized by law. When asked whether a central school district could grant teachers paid leaves of absence immediately prior to retirement (the number of days' absence to be computed according to a formula based on accumulated sick leave credits), the comptroller again answered negatively.[68] Although school boards may legally grant paid leaves, the comptroller said that in this case "leave of absence" was "a mere subterfuge" to convert unused sick leave into cash, contrary to law.

Many of the provisions held invalid or nonnegotiable by the comptroller arguably fall within the Taylor Law's "wages, hours, and other terms and conditions of employment." For example, in one opinion the comptroller held that unless a teacher suffered an accident compensable under the Workmen's Compensation Law, except in certain city school districts he could not be compensated for loss of personal property.[69]

In another case a proposed contract between a school district and employee organization contained a provision under which the school board would have paid, as a refund, half of the tuition for approved graduate courses taken by the district's teachers.[70] The comptroller stated that boards of education have no legal authority to offer such refunds. The Education Law encourages teachers to continue their studies, and Section 3103(3) authorizes boards of education to provide increased salaries for teachers satisfactorily completing graduate courses. Nevertheless, according to the comptroller:

> Graduate courses taken by a teacher actually inure to
> his personal and private benefit, and payment for his tui-
> tion costs should be properly considered his own personal
> obligation. Such training is clearly not within the scope of
> General Municipal Law Section 77-b, which authorizes
> attendance by municipal officers at schools conducted for
> the benefit of a municipal government. . . . Thus, a refund
> of a portion of the cost of the course taken by a teacher is
> in violation of New York State Constitution Article 8
> Section 1.[71]

Although PERB has determined that sabbatical leaves are clearly terms and conditions of employment,[72] the comptroller has issued opinions restricting the authority of school boards to agree to certain contract terms on sabbaticals. In one case a school board desired to grant sabbatical leaves and to pay teachers in advance for such leaves.[73] The comptroller recognized that both the Education Law and the Municipal Law provide authority for school districts to adopt rules and regulations concerning paid sabbatical leaves. "There is no authority," however,

. . . to pay such compensation at the beginning of the leave. The teacher is deemed to be in the service of the school district during the leave. If this were not so, he could not be paid at all (State Const. Art. VIII, Sec. 1). He should, therefore, be paid at such intervals and in such proportion on his full compensation for the period of leave as he would be paid if he were teaching during that time.[74]

In an unpublished opinion concerning a sick leave bank plan, which this writer proposed to a school board during teacher negotiations, the comptroller concluded that a collective agreement could not authorize the transfer or assignment of sick leave credits from one employee to another.[75]

The proposed plan provided for a sick leave program under which unused sick leave credits of each teacher would be deposited into a bank, from which the association could direct the allocation of additional emergency sick leave to any teacher whose sick leave days had been exhausted.

The comptroller held that a school board lacks "statutory power" to agree to a sick leave bank. Boards of education

. . . have only such powers as are reasonably necessary for the discharge of their functions, and these powers must be granted either expressly or by necessary implication (Ed. Law, Sec. 2503(3)). . . . There is nothing in the cited statute or elsewhere which could, by any stretch of the imagination, be said to imply an authorization to assign or transfer from one teacher . . . to another a benefit which is, by its very nature, personal and unassignable.

THE STATE EDUCATION DEPARTMENT

The Education Department has issued far fewer opinions than has the comptroller with respect to the scope of negotiations. The counsel for the Education Department has, however, written at least two opinions to school boards that, although not published, have become available because they were used in connection with court cases:

1. A May 1969 opinion to the Huntington board of education concluded that the board could not legally agree to a contract provision making certain actions affecting tenure teachers subject to the grievance procedure.
2. In an opinion to Mepham Central School District, No. 3, it was determined that a school district could not pay employees for unused sick leave.

170

In another unpublished opinion[76] the associate counsel to the Education Department held invalid the sick leave bank provision alluded to above. The opinion stated that "there would be no legal authorization" for a board of education to agree to such a contract provision. By allowing the teachers' association to administer a sick leave bank consisting of the unused sick leave days of staff members, the board would "abdicate its governmental functions to a private association" in violation of the Education Law.[77]

SUGGESTED SOLUTION FOR RESOLVING CONFLICTS: HANSLOWE AND OBERER MEMORANDUM TO PERB

Professors Kurt Hanslowe and Walter Oberer of Cornell University were commissioned by PERB to study the relationship between the Taylor Law and other New York statutes and the consequent impact of this relationship upon the scope of negotiations. In their memorandum these consultants discuss (1) the weight to be given by PERB to the opinions of other agencies and the courts in determining the scope of bargaining, (2) the problems raised when an employer lacks authority at the unit level to negotiate on items that are conditions of employment, and (3) the impact of the Taylor Law on the pre-Taylor scope of employer authority to confer employee benefits. Their conclusions as to what course of action PERB should follow concerning these issues provide a sharp analysis of the problems discussed in this chapter. The following summary of their paper is offered as a prelude to the last part of this chapter, which reviews court decisions concerning statutory conflicts over the scope of bargaining.

The Relationship of PERB to Other Administrative Agencies

Hanslowe and Oberer conclude that it is PERB's responsibility in the first instance to determine the negotiability of each issue challenged under Section 209-a of the Taylor Law. In so doing PERB must decide whether the subject "should be deemed, as a matter of sound public employment relations, to be within 'terms and conditions of employment'" and, if so, whether the subject is beyond the scope of negotiations because of "the operation of some competing provision of law."[78]

In discharging its function PERB should consider not only the Taylor Law but also other pertinent statutory and constitutional provisions, including the interpretation of these provisions by other administrative and judicial bodies. With respect to subjects that

171

constitutional and statutory provisions and Court of Appeals decisions have unambiguously excluded from the scope of "terms and conditions of employment" under the Taylor Act, PERB should issue no bargaining orders. But in considering constitutional and statutory provisions and Court of Appeals decisions of questionable relevance to the issue before PERB, and enactments and decisions of sources of law lower than the constitutional convention, state legislature, and Court of Appeals (lower courts, local legislative bodies, other administrative agencies and executive officials), "PERB should make its own fresh analysis of the issue of pre-emption and decide it on the basis of the soundest public employment policy permitted by the competing law. . . ."[79]

Employer Authority to Negotiate at the Unit Level

Hanslowe and Oberer note the problems that can arise when the subject sought to be negotiated is clearly a "term or condition of employment" within the Taylor Law's definition but is not within the authority of management at the unit level.

According to the Retirement and Social Security Law, for example, the state comptroller is the administrative head of the retirement system and has the authority to formulate rules regarding "the administration and transaction of the business of the retirement system. . . ." Yet at the state level the Office of Employee Relations, not the state comptroller, represents the public employer in negotiations with state employees. With whom do these employees have a right to negotiate over pensions? Should PERB require bargaining where a subject is clearly within the scope of "terms and conditions of employment" but is not within the authority of the public employer?

Hanslowe and Oberer have considered three possible alternatives. Pension plans might be nonnegotiable except with the comptroller; negotiable only if the comptroller chooses to negotiate concerning the exercise of his discretionary authority; or negotiable only to the extent that the Office of Employee Relations and the employee organization may agree upon joint recommendations to be made to the comptroller or the legislature.[80]

The professors recommend that issues such as this be divided into two categories: mandatory and permissive subjects. Those subjects over which the employer has the ability to make "effective recommendations" would be mandatory bargaining items; those upon which it can make only "ineffective recommendations" would be considered permissive. Although they do not explain what they mean by "effective" and "ineffective," the terms most probably relate to the degree of force or influence that an employer's recommendation

172

might have on the government body ultimately responsible for approving or financing the costs of a negotiated agreement.

Impact of Taylor Law on Employer Authority to Determine Terms and Conditions of Public Employment

Hanslowe and Oberer conclude that the scope of bargaining under the Taylor Law "may well be broader" than the scope formerly exercised unilaterally by employers. First, a new agency, PERB, has been statutorily established to decide issues never before authoritatively resolved, with respect to employer authority to confer employee benefits. Second, the passage of the Taylor Law represents the introduction of bilateralism into the determination of employees' terms and conditions of employment. In this sense "strong reason exists for concluding that the legislative intent was to have such gray-area problems resolved through the process of collective negotiations."[81]

DECISIONS OF THE NEW YORK COURTS

As the cases discussed in Chapter 6 indicate,[82] PERB has, with little exception, adopted the approach suggested by Hanslowe and Oberer. It has exercised its responsibility under Section 209-a of determining appropriate subjects of bargaining by deciding whether issues are terms and conditions of employment. It also has given due consideration to the impact of relevant statutory and constitutional provisions, orienting its interpretations toward sound public employment relations.

The state courts, as well as PERB, have been playing an important role in shaping the scope of bargaining. Frequently parties have sought declaratory judgments regarding their bargaining rights and have avoided the improper practice route by going directly into state court. Thus the courts have resolved disputes concerning the jurisdiction of competing agencies to preside over public employee relations and have determined the applicability of conflicting laws to particular bargaining situations. As litigation on the scope of bargaining has increased, a discernible trend has emerged. In contrast with the judicial attitude in the early years following the Taylor Law's enactment, since 1970 the courts have exhibited greater inclination to interpret the Taylor Law "liberally," in order to effectuate "public policy" and "legislative intent." Additionally, lower court decisions, which often have taken a more restrictive view of the

Taylor Law's impact on employers' authority to confer benefits,[*]
have been reversed at the appellate levels by judges who emphasize
the discretion granted to public employers to negotiate on terms and
conditions of employment.[83] The discussion that follows highlights
this trend and indicates how statutory "conflicts questions," as they
affect the scope of bargaining, will ultimately be resolved.

Since 1967, school districts and teachers frequently have locked
horns in attempting to reconcile the Taylor Law with the Education
Law. A significant problem stems from teachers' efforts to establish
procedures dealing with the evaluation of probationary teachers and
grievance procedures covering the discipline or discharge of tenure
teachers. Additionally, PERB has fought vigorously to assert its
jurisdiction pursuant to Section 209-a of the Taylor Law in cases
where it has determined that probationary teachers were discharged
solely in reprisal for their union activities.

Town of Claverack

Matter of Helsby v. Board of Education, Central School District
No. 2, Town of Claverack,[84] was an early case involving the dismissal of a probationary teacher, allegedly for union activities. In
December 1968 PERB determined that Mrs. Faith Gagnier had been
denied tenure by the board of education, despite a positive recommendation by the superintendent, in reprisal for her participation in
the teachers' union. PERB ordered the school board to reinstate
Mrs. Gagnier. Under the Education Law tenure provisions, sections
3012 and 3013, such reinstatement would have resulted in automatic
tenure. The school board appealed PERB's decision, and the Supreme
Court held that PERB was without jurisdiction to determine the case,

_____

[*]In two unreported cases, for example, Kenmore Club, Police
Benevolent Association, Inc. v. Civil Service Commission and Local
1333, and International Association of Fire Fighters, AFL-CIO v.
Civil Service Commission, City of North Tonawanda, the disputes
involved conflict between the Taylor Law and civil service laws. The
civil service codes were upheld by the supreme courts hearing the
cases. As the court stated in North Tonawanda:

> No agreement between a municipal corporation and its em-
> ployees although sanctioned by the Taylor Act has any pre-
> cedence and makes no claim to any precedence over the
> Civil Service Law. . . . It does not lie within the City's
> power to dilute rights given the North Tonawanda Civil
> Service Commission by the Civil Service Law. . . .

in light of the exclusive provisions of the Education Law.[85] The court rejected PERB's contention that it had implicit authority under the Taylor Law to effectuate the latter's purposes. In 1970 the Appellate Division upheld the lower court.[86]

The court affirmed that the Taylor Law "was not so designed to imply that PERB would have the responsibility and duty of regulating and securing all of the rights of public employees expressly or inherently granted therein.[87] If a board of education determined to dispense with a teacher's services in violation of his Taylor Law rights, his only remedies were under the Education Law. This case developed, however, before the passage of the 1969 improper practices amendments to the Taylor Law. Realizing that the absence of these statutory provisions was likely to prove fatal to further litigation, PERB did not appeal the Gagnier case.

Grand Island

In 1970 a similar case developed involving the Grand Island School District.[88] An improper practice charge was filed with PERB by the Grand Island Teachers' Association, alleging that five probationary teachers were denied tenure because of their union activity. The school board tried to prevent PERB even from holding a hearing, arguing that PERB lacked jurisdiction to consider the dismissals because, under the tenure provisions of the Education Law, a school board has sole authority in this area. On October 22, 1970, the Supreme Court of Erie County dismissed PERB's contention that the 1969 amendments to the Taylor Law gave PERB jurisdiction and enjoined the agency from proceeding with the improper practice charge. Judge Michael Catalano held: "In the absence of a clear power delegated to PERB to enforce rights of teachers, the statutory rule of construction expressio unius est exclusio alterius . . . makes the remedies in Education Law exclusive."[89] Moreover, he added, the Taylor Law did not grant PERB the jurisdiction to enforce a public employee's right to participate in a labor organization.

Judge Catalano's decision was confusing in that he rested a substantial part of his holding on Section 3020-a of the Education Law. He emphasized that in enacting this provision in 1970, the legislature expressly provided the remedies and penalties applicable to probationary teachers. Apparently the judge misinterpreted Section 3020-a, which covers only tenure—not probationary—teachers.

Judge Catalano also reached this questionable conclusion:

When a probationary teacher joins or participates in an employee organization, he is not immune from discharge before his period has expired. Otherwise, such employee

175

could secure tenure during his probation by merely joining
an employee organization, thereby defeating the entire probationary program. Such a reductio ad absurdum was not
intended by the legislature. PERB lacks jurisdiction
herein.[90]

This reasoning lacked logic. PERB never contended that a probationary teacher who joined an employee organization could not be discharged. Rather, the Board, in trying to administer the Taylor Law,
was attempting to assure that a probationary teacher would not be
dismissed because he joined or participated in the organization.

PERB appealed the adverse judgment,[91] confronting the appellate
court with this central question: Could PERB proceed to hear an
improper practice charge based on a claimed deprivation of certain
statutory and constitutional rights enjoyed by all teachers? Writing
for a unanimous court, Judge Domenick Gabrielli held that PERB
had jurisdiction to hear and act upon the charge filed by the Teachers'
Association.

The school board challenged PERB's jurisdiction on the ground
that the traditional authority to review teacher dismissals rested in
Article 78 proceedings or with the commissioner of education under
the Education Law.

After noting that the lower court mistakenly relied on Section
3020-a, which applies only to tenure teachers, the court discussed
the meaning of the Taylor Law. In enacting Section 209-a, the legislature specifically prohibited public employers from interfering with,
restraining, or coercing employees in the exercise of their Section
202 rights and from discriminating against an employee for the purpose of encouraging or discouraging membership or participation in
a labor organization. At the same time the legislature authorized
PERB to establish procedures for the prevention of such employer
practices and mandated that it "shall exercise exclusive nondelegable
jurisdiction" of the powers therein conferred upon it.

Judge Gabrielli stated that although the Education Law grants
school boards discretion concerning probationary teachers, "there
is no reason to believe that this discretion is boundless, particularly
when the protection of constitutional and statutory rights is involved.
Neither does it follow that PERB is without jurisdiction simply because the Commissioner is cloaked with power of review."[92] Because
the legislature granted public employees the right to participate in
labor organizations, and prohibited school boards from discriminating
against employees on account of such participation:

. . . it is reasonable to conclude that it was the intendment
of the Taylor Law to provide that PERB should exercise
State-wide jurisdiction over improper labor practices in
all sectors of public employment.[93]

Judge Gabrielli noted the conflicting opinion reached in the Gagnier case, but observed that the court there nevertheless stated:

It should be noted that pursuant to the case law governing the dismissal of probationary teachers for the purpose of denying tenure, it would appear that unless such dismissal was solely occasioned by the denial of a constitutional or statutory right, a school district cannot be directed to reinstate a teacher when such direction would necessarily result in a grant of tenure.[94]

Thus, concluded Judge Gabrielli, the Gagnier court by implication agreed that if the dismissal of a probationary teacher "resulted solely from the denial of a constitutional or statutory right, a school board could be compelled to reinstate the teacher."

The Grand Island case involved a crucial relationship between the Education Law and the Taylor Law. Had the school board prevailed, boards of education thereafter would have been left free to discriminate against and deny tenure to employees active in their unions. The result would have been the effective denial of rights guaranteed by the Taylor Law (as well as First Amendment rights of freedom of speech and association). In upholding PERB the court has held that in certain situations, PERB will have the power of tenure.

The Grand Island decision should not be interpreted to mean that membership in a labor organization precludes dismissal of a probationary teacher for otherwise legitimate reasons. A board of education must retain discretion to insure a qualified faculty. The court's decision simply holds that PERB is empowered to determine factually whether a school board's action in dismissing a teacher was a retaliatory measure taken in violation of his or her statutory rights to participate in an employee organization.

Associated Teachers of Huntington v. Board of Education

In Associated Teachers of Huntington v. Board of Education, UFSD No. 3,[95] the dispute concerned procedures to be followed in determining tenure. Here the teachers' association protested because the school board had violated a contractual procedure requiring that probationary teachers be notified of tenure decisions by March 1, which was sooner than the 60-day minimum required under the Education Law. The contract also contained a grievance procedure ending in binding arbitration. The association filed a demand for arbitration and contended that by not giving timely notice that tenure would not be granted, the school board had forfeited its right to dismiss a probationary teacher. The school board argued that the issue was outside the scope of the grievance procedure, since terminations of nontenure teachers were expressly made nongrievable in the contract; furthermore, the issue was nonarbitrable because tenure matters were governed exclusively by the Education Law.

The Suffolk County Supreme Court held that since this case involved merely the procedural aspects relating to tenure and not the substance of the matter, it was not outside the scope of the contract. The Court also found that the 60-day period for notification of a tenure decision, as provided for in the Education Law, was a minimum and not maximum period:

> The statute, by requiring notice of termination "not later than sixty days" before termination, impliedly permits notice before that day. Certainly, this statutory provision does not bar earlier notice. The respondent school board seems to imply that any provision which is broader than the statutory benefits is invalid. . . . The position of the respondent is without legal foundation or rational basis.[96]

The court also stated that the grievance procedure set forth in the General Municipal Law, Sections 681-685, was not intended to be exclusive and therefore did not prohibit the parties from negotiating a different procedure.

Referring to the well-established doctrines pertaining to grievance arbitration, the court held that the instant issue was arbitrable:

> An order to arbitrate, the particular grievance should not be denied unless it can be said with positive assurance that the arbitration clause is not susceptible to an interpretation that covers the asserted dispute. Doubts should be resolved in favor of coverage. United Steel Workers of America v. Warrior and Gulf Navigation Co.[97]

The Huntington school board did not appeal the decision and the grievance was arbitrated. The arbitrator held that although the time limits stipulated in the collective agreement were not observed by the board, the contract did not establish this as a basis for granting tenure.

The cases discussed in this section (and PERB's Monroe-Woodbury decision, which upheld the negotiability of a contractual procedure dealing with evaluation and dismissal of probationary teachers) carefully distinguish between procedure and substance—between the steps to be followed in reaching a decision and the decision itself. The Court of Appeals to date has not resolved a dispute involving the relationship between the Education Law and the Taylor Law with respect to rights of probationary teachers. The issue therefore has not been authoritatively decided; and it is likely that many school boards, unlike those of Monroe-Woodbury and Huntington, will continue to argue that procedures concerning the granting of tenure are nonnegotiable.

This writer agrees with those who argue that contract provisions establishing tenure procedures neither encroach upon school board powers conferred by the Education Law nor reduce a school board's ability to staff its schools with qualified personnel. The right to negotiate such procedures is consistent with the Taylor Law and is a step toward greater "due process" for teachers.

In an article in the Saturday Review, Myron Lieberman effectively argues in favor of negotiated contract provisions dealing with dismissal procedures. Discussing the act of the 1971 New York legislature extending a teacher's probationary period from three to five years, Lieberman explains:

> The only statutory obligation placed on an administration not reappointing a probationary teacher is to notify the teacher "not later than sixty days immediately preceding the expiration of this probationary period." Thus . . . a teacher who has taught for five years and had an outstanding record would be entitled only to a notice of nonreappointment sixty days before the expiration of the five year probationary period. This is outrageous personnel policy, and it is likely to backfire both legally and practically.
>
> . . . . . .
>
> Teachers not re-employed have an interest in improving their skills, correcting inaccurate impressions about their work, exposing improper reprisals or infringements upon academic freedom, and overcoming the reasons for nonreemployment. . . . Tenure laws, such as that in New York, make it easier to understand why the federal courts have adopted a more activist role in protecting the rights of probationary teachers. In doing so, the courts are achieving a result that should have been achieved by competent educational administration in the first place.[98]

Irving Sabghir also advocates the negotiability of tenure procedures and even criteria that school boards could adhere to in making tenure decisions. In his comments to the Fleischmann Commission, he stated:

> . . . it also follows that probationary teachers should have the right to negotiate a method of challenging an adverse tenure decision possibly to impartial arbitration. . . .
> [A]ccountability in no way diminishes . . . the ability of a school board to maintain educational excellence. . . . [A]

board should stand ready and able to justify its decisions on matters of tenure.[99]

THE COMPTROLLER AND THE COURTS

Several court decisions have overruled opinions issued by the comptroller concerning the negotiability of certain items.

Lecci v. Nickerson

Lecci v. Nickerson[100] concerned the legality of a provision in a collective agreement between the Nassau County Patrolmen's Benevolent Association (PBA) and the Nassau County Police Department. The disputed provision, paragraph 7k, related to termination pay; it provided for increments to be paid to a police officer (or his legal representative) upon his retirement or separation from the force after twenty years of service.*

Although the County Board of Supervisors approved the contract, County Executive Nickerson argued that paragraph 7k was illegal, since it represented a retirement bonus, which was prohibited by the Retirement and Social Security Law, and because it violated Article VII, Section 1 of the state constitution.

Petitioner Lecci, on behalf of the PBA, contended that the termination pay was earned compensation for actual services rendered, which was merely deferred until retirement. Furthermore, the termination pay was not a gift, since a gift connotes something for nothing, with a lack of consideration on the part of the recipient.

The Supreme Court, Nassau County, had to determine whether termination pay, as described in paragraph 7k, was a gratuity (a voluntary transfer of money without any consideration) or a form of earned compensation (an allowance or pension made by a government to an individual for past services performed by him). Clearly, the former would be in conflict with the constitution's gift provision.

The court determined that the termination pay was legal. "That the police officer must perform his duties satisfactorily for twenty years before he becomes eligible to the accumulated pay negates the idea of a reward or gift upon retirement."[101] The termination pay was "but an additional mode of earned compensation in the form of

---

*The increment was to be calculated on an entitlement basis of three days for each year of completed service.

180

a pension . . . benefits are based on actual services . . . but the compensation is deferred until retirement."102

Article V, Section 7 of the state constitution, noted the court, makes membership in any retirement system of the state "a contractual relationship, the benefits of which shall not be diminished or impaired." The parties themselves determine the terms of the contract through assent and the law of contracts.

Being a contractual relationship, this Court [sic] will favor those terms agreed to by the parties unless sufficient statutory objection is shown. . . . [H]ere the defendants seek to be relieved of their contractual promise to pay the increased pension benefits through a strict interpretation of Art. VIII, Sec. 1 of the New York State Constitution. . . . [But] the inducement to enter and remain in public service, which pensions and other benefits promote, is valid consideration to the state and not within the constitutional ban.103

The court emphasized that Article VII, Section 8 of the constitution empowers the legislature to legislate on pensions. The constitution states:

(2) . . . nothing in this constitution contained shall prevent the legislature from providing . . . for the increase in the amount of pensions of any member of a retirement system. . . . The enumeration of legislative powers in this paragraph shall not be taken to diminish any power of the legislature hitherto existing.

Since this language in the constitution empowers the legislature to increase benefits, "under the Taylor Law," stated the court,

This power can be delegated to the "public employer," or in this case, the County. . . . The public employer under the Taylor Law is empowered to enter into binding collective negotiation as to the terms and conditions of employment in the form of employee rights and benefits not otherwise authorized by law.104

In order to effectuate the legislature's intention in enacting the Taylor Law, the court concluded that the Taylor Law must be interpreted "liberally." Furthermore, because the Taylor Law delegates to local governments the power to bargain collectively in the name of the state, the 1967 Act "supersedes any inconsistent provision of the earlier Retirement and Social Security Law which does not coincide with the stated purposes of this new Civil Service Law. . . ."105

Matter of Teachers Association v. Board of Education, Central High School District No. 3[106] was similar to Lecci v. Nickerson in that it involved a negotiated agreement allegedly contravening Article VIII, Section 1, of the constitution; and it concerned a type of earned compensation, deferred to retirement and calculated on prior years of service.

The agreement between the school district and the association provided that in the event of the death of an employee, the employee's estate would be entitled to payment for the employee's accumulated unused sick leave, on the basis of the same increase in salary as the employee would have been entitled to receive. The contract also provided for arbitration of disputes concerning the interpretation and application of its terms. The teachers' association sought arbitration of a claim on behalf of the estate of a deceased teacher.

The question presented to the arbitrator was whether the death benefit provision of the contract was valid. The arbitrator decided that it was enforceable. The Supreme Court held to the contrary, finding that payment of the award would violate the gift provision of the constitution. On appeal the Appellate Division reversed the Supreme Court in a 4 to 1 decision and confirmed the arbitration award.

Citing several cases, the opinion noted that the courts have recognized that the state and its municipalities, in granting pensions, vacations, or military leave, are not conferring gifts; essentially, the promised rewards are conditions of employment—a form of deferred compensation. Sick leave, as a condition of employment, enjoys the same protection from the constitutional ban on gifts. It induces competent individuals to enter public service, and the right to accumulated sick leave encourages employees to remain in government service and to avoid unnecessary absences for trifling illnesses.

In addition to the issue of constitutional validity, the school district, relying on opinions of the comptroller and State Education Department, contended that as a creature of legislatively endowed power, it lacked the authority to contract for the payment of unused sick leave. In response to this contention, the court emphasized that a board of education possesses ''broad authority to make contracts for the employment of teachers.'' This broad power is granted under both the Education Law and the Taylor Law. The following passage contains the crux of the court's decision:

In the absence of an express legislative restriction against bargaining for that term of an employment contract between

a public employer and its employees, the authority to provide for such payment resides in the [employer] under the
broad powers and duties delegated by the statutes. Were it
otherwise, a board of education would not be able to . . .
make agreements concerning terms of employment with its
teachers unless specific statutory authority for each provision of the agreement existed. . . . [S]uch a narrow and
inflexible construction would virtually destroy the bargaining powers which public policy has installed in the field of
public employment. . . .[107]

Local 456, International Brotherhood of Teamsters
v. Town of Cortlandt

In Local 456, International Brotherhood of Teamsters v. Town of
Cortlandt,[108] the issue was whether, pursuant to a collective agreement, a municipal corporation could make payments to a Teamster
Union health and welfare fund that, in turn, purchased various insurance plans for the municipal employees. Although the state comptroller's opinions indicated otherwise, the Supreme Court (Westchester County) answered affirmatively, deciding that insurance
benefits, as forms of compensation, were negotiable terms of
employment for inclusion in a contract.
   Specifically, the agreement provided that the town was to make
payments to the Local 456 welfare fund for the purchase by the
fund's trustees of insurance plans providing medical, dental, hospital, eyeglass, and life insurance benefits.* After receiving the
comptroller's opinions advising that there was no authority to
establish a trusteed welfare plan for municipal employees, the town
refused to make its payments.†

---

*The fund was a trust fund established and administered by em-
ployer and union trustees under the trust plan pursuant to the provisions of the Taft-Hartley Law and Article 3-A of the Insurance
Law.
†The comptroller's opinion had stated:

We find nothing in either section of the General Municipal
Law . . . which would authorize the payment of moneys for
the prescribed purposes. . . . Further, we do not believe
that any such arrangement . . . could be deemed a ''contract'' or ''plan'' within the intended meaning of the General
Municipal Law, Section 92-a and 93(2).
              • • • • • •

Judge John Marbach, writing for the court, disagreed with the comptroller. The comptroller's conclusions that the payments were not a "contract" or "plan" within the meaning of the General Municipal Law and that they would be tantamount to treating the union as an insurance company "ignores the stated public policy behind Article 3-A of Insurance Law which specifically authorizes payments by employers to a union welfare fund."[109] Moreover, the comptroller overlooked the public policy provisions "stated and inherent in the Taylor Law."

After reviewing the decision in Matter of Teachers Association v. Board of Education, Central High School District No. 3, Judge Marbach stated:

> This court finds that there are equal, if not greater, reasons for finding that medical, dental, and life insurance premiums constitute terms or conditions of employment, are in fact a form of present compensation . . . and are even a more recognizable form of compensation than payment for accumulated sick leave benefits.
>
> . . . . . .
>
> Such payments are for a public purpose and are not an attempt to give or lend public money to aid a private enterprise.[110]

Judge Marbach offered an incisive analysis of the public policy considerations underlying this case. The state public policy behind the Taylor Law, he emphasized, was to encourage collective agreements between public employers and employees. It also has been the recognized policy of the state that Article 3-A employee welfare funds are of great benefit to employees and their families; ". . . the Legislature has specifically found that they are in the public interest."

Pursuant to the Taylor Law, the parties bargained in good faith and entered into an agreement on insurance benefits, which are terms and conditions of employment. Citing Lecci v. Nickerson, the court affirmed that contractual agreements between a municipality and a union are looked upon with favor by the courts unless sufficient constitutional or statutory objection is shown. "This is particularly so when the policy provisions inherent in the Taylor Law are interpreted in conjunction with the stated public benefit purpose of

---

In effect, the proposal . . . would be tantamount to . . . treating the union as an insurance company and paying over district moneys to such a union for the latter to hold, invest, or use in whatever way it chooses. We find absolutely no authority for this.

Article 3-A. The end result of interpretation must be to sanction an agreement such as this."[111]

In his opinions the comptroller maintained that a municipality lacked authority to contract to make payments to a union welfare fund. But, held the court, "analogous precedent" indicated otherwise, in light of public policy favoring employer assumption of such authority. Article IX, Section 2, of the constitution provides that under home rule power to enact local laws, a town may pass a law regulating the powers, duties, qualification, number, mode of selection and removal, compensation, hours of work, protection, welfare, and safety of its officers and employees. Insurance benefits are a form of compensation and are closely related to the welfare of employees. Thus, concluded Judge Marbach, although there was no indication that any local laws were adopted for this purpose,

. . . if the Town has the power to adopt a local law to provide for it, it should also be able to contract for it. What such a constitutional provision does indicate is that the power to provide for its employees does reside in the municipality.[112]

In Local 456 Judge Marbach relied on analogous precedent, public policy, and statutory authority to reach the conclusion that the disputed contract provision was valid. The major thrust of his opinion is toward effectuating what he called the "public benefit purpose" of the Taylor Law and its mandate concerning negotiations on wages, hours, and terms and conditions of employment. Advocating a liberal interpretation of the Taylor Law, he concluded: "It is well settled that all statutes must be construed to further the purpose of their enactment."

Board of Education, Union Free School District No. 7, Town of North Hempstead v. Great Neck Teachers Association

Board of Education, UFSD No. 7, Town of North Hempstead v. Great Neck Teachers Association[113] represents still another example of the way in which the courts have reconciled the Taylor Law with preexisting laws.

In this case a teacher claimed back pay on the grounds that she was not given appropriate service credit for two previous years' substitute teaching experience when hired full-time in September 1967. The school board sought here to stay the arbitration of that claim, demanded under the collective agreement of July 1, 1971.

The board recognized the validity of the agreement to arbitrate, but contended that as a matter of interpretation, the agreement to arbitrate did not apply retroactively to a 1967 hiring; and since under

185

Section 3813 of the Education Law, three months' notice is required from the time of accrual of a claim against a board of education, the claim sought to be arbitrated was barred by such a "limitation of time" as provided by N.Y. Civil Practice Laws and Rules (CPLR) 7501.

Whether a 1967 hiring was arbitrable, said Judge Bertram Harnett, writing for the Supreme Court, Nassau County, Special Term, depended on an interpretation of the agreement and the intention of the parties as to disputed hirings predating that agreement. In cases where the settlement of a dispute depends "primarily on a reading and construction of the agreement . . . it is for the arbitrators to decide what the agreement means and to enforce it. . . ."[114] In this case, because the agreement in "carefully drafted words" did not clearly exclude arbitration over this particular issue, the court left the question of arbitrability ultimately to the arbitrator.

With respect to the timeliness of the teacher's claim, it was undisputed that the teacher and association, while following the prescribed steps of the grievance procedure, did not simultaneously file a verified claim pursuant to Section 3813 of the Education Law. The school board therefore attempted to take advantage of that failure to file, despite its binding agreement to use the negotiated grievance procedure without any requirement that a Section 3813 claim be submitted.

Not persuaded by the school board's arguments, the court reviewed the purposes of the Taylor Act and concluded that the legislature "attached great importance" to the process of collective bargaining and to "adherence to negotiated agreements." Section 3813, the court explained, was intended to give a school district the chance to investigate claims in order to obtain evidence quickly, while still available, and to adjust or make payments before litigation was begun. The collective agreement in this case, however, by its time limit provisions, including the waiver of grievances not timely raised, served the same purposes, although by substitution of different time limits, procedures, and written notice requirements.

"Under the critical power conferred under Article 14 of the Civil Service Law, the board has by agreement substituted certain grievance procedures for those otherwise imposed by statute . . . the bargaining process . . . would be undermined by holding otherwise."[115]

The court concluded that the legislature's emphasis on collective bargaining as the proper means for resolving disputes compelled it to honor the negotiated grievance procedure. The Great Neck school board had the obligation to enter into a contract regarding the administration of grievances. The section of the contract providing for such administration of grievances was "whole and exclusive" and was "not limited by the operation of Section 3813 of the Education Law."[116]

THE COURT OF APPEALS DECISION IN HUNTINGTON

After considering all of these New York State Supreme Court and Appellate Division cases concerning the relationship between laws and governmental authorities as they affect the scope of bargaining, one might well ask: What impact does the Court of Appeals' Huntington[117] decision have on this growing body of decisional history? Huntington, having been decided by the highest court in the state, is now binding precedent. The two major issues in that case were whether a school board was authorized to enter into a collective agreement granting economic benefits to teachers, absent specific statutory authority to do so, and whether such a board lacked the power to agree to a contract provision providing for arbitration of disputes concerning disciplinary action taken against tenure teachers.* Overruling the lower courts and comptroller opinions that held to the contrary, the Court of Appeals found that all of the contested contract provisions were legal and enforceable.

An extensive analysis of the Huntington decision was presented in Chapter 6. However, since the discussion there did not focus directly on the conflicts issues as considered in this chapter, several aspects of this landmark decision warrant further exploration.

The basic question, suggested Judge Stanley Fuld in his opinion, was whether there was "any fundamental conflict between the provisions of the Taylor Law and the provisions of any other statute dealing with the powers and duties of school boards."[118] Reviewing Section 204 of the Taylor Law, and its mandate that parties negotiate with respect to terms and conditions of employment, he stated that the validity of a negotiated contract provision turns upon whether it constitutes a term or condition of employment. If it does,

> . . . the employer must negotiate as to such item and upon reaching an understanding, must incorporate it into the collective agreement unless some statutory provision circumscribes its powers to do so. . . .[119]

After determining that all of the disputed provisions were terms and conditions of employment, Judge Fuld turned to the school board's major contention—that, absent a statutory provision specifically

---

*The specific contract provisions in dispute concerned reimbursement to teachers for personal articles lost or damaged during the performance of duty, tuition reimbursement for graduate courses, a salary increase in the last year preceding retirement, and grievance arbitration of disputes concerning dismissal of tenure teachers.

authorizing a board of education to provide a particular term or condition of employment, it is legally prohibited from doing so. Holding that the school board's premise was "fallacious" and that the Education Law confers on boards of education "a broad grant of powers," Judge Fuld reached this significant conclusion, which, although quoted in Chapter 6, bears repeating:

> Under the Taylor Law, the obligation to bargain as to all terms and conditions of employment is a broad and unqualified one, and there is no reason why the mandatory provisions of that act should be limited, in any way, except in cases where some other applicable statutory provision explicitly and definitively prohibits the public employer from making an agreement as to a particular term or condition. . . .
>
> Were it otherwise, a school board would have a hard time bargaining effectively with its teachers, since it would frequently be difficult, if not impossible, to find an express grant of power with respect to any particular subject. . . .120

In Huntington, concluded Judge Fuld, the school board cited no legislation "which expressly or even impliedly" prevented it from agreeing to the disputed contract terms. The Court found without substance the school board's arguments that Section 113-a of the Retirement and Social Security Law, Section 3020-a of the Education Law, and Article VIII, Section 1, of the constitution circumscribed its power to include in a collective bargaining agreement provisions concerning retirement awards, reimbursement for damaged property, tuition reimbursement, and grievance procedures for tenure teacher dismissals.

In Chapter 6 this writer suggested that despite Judge Fuld's expansive language, the Huntington decision may not have erased all limitations on the scope of negotiations.

Huntington was a pragmatic decision that, without substantial theoretical or legal analysis, held four issues to be negotiable. The decision also set forth what can be considered a guideline concerning the negotiability of proposed items: all terms and conditions of employment are mandatory subjects of negotiation unless they are "explicitly and definitively" prohibited by law. The problem emphasized in Chapter 6, however, was that the phrase "terms and conditions of employment" has never been consistently and finally defined by the NLRB, PERB, or the courts. Although PERB has held that "any subject with a significant or material relationship to conditions of employment constitutes a term and condition of employment unless it involves decisions concerning basic goals and directions of employers," this definition is difficult to apply with certainty because parties often disagree as to what issues are central to the basic mission and direction of the employer. Compounding the problem, this writer suggested, was the difference between the negotiability test that PERB had been applying in its cases and the test announced by Judge Fuld in Huntington. The Court's test appeared to be less rigorous and more conducive to broadening the scope of bargaining.*

Aside from the potential restriction of the scope of bargaining due to what PERB calls the "inherent limitations" in the Taylor Law's definition of terms and conditions of employment, the Huntington decision itself suggests a limitation by excluding from bargaining subjects prohibited by law.† Certainly the thrust of the decision is toward a broad scope of bargaining, in that the excluded items must be specifically proscribed and the employer has the burden of demonstrating such express prohibition. It can be seen, however, that the Court of Appeals, unlike the Michigan Supreme Court in Wayne County, was not willing to say that the Taylor Law impliedly

---

*PERB's test required a party "to negotiate an item that constitutes a term or condition of employment unless (a) it is deemed to be a matter of managerial prerogative . . . or (b) the negotiability of the item has been prohibited by the constitution, law, or judicial fiat." In Huntington, with respect to the four contested clauses, the Court merely said it was obvious that they were terms and conditions of employment because each one was "commonly found" in negotiated contracts and because each clearly "related" to a term or condition of employment. Judge Fuld emphasized that all terms and conditions of employment must be negotiated, absent a statutory prohibition. Unlike PERB, he did not exclude from the scope of mandatory bargaining those terms and conditions deemed to be matters of managerial prerogative or basic to the employer's goals.

†Moreover, noted Bernard Ashe, counsel to the New York State United Federation of Teachers:

> The danger is, that in the face of considerable statutory support for an implication contrary to what the standards of Huntington would require, namely an explicit and definitive prohibition, courts may strain to find an explicit and definitive prohibition where none in fact exists or may even retreat to the language of the Court of Appeals that "the Board cites no legislation which expressly or even impliedly prevented it from including the tuition and damage reimbursement provision." Weak as that language may be, considering the holding and thrust of the bulk of the decision, it, nevertheless, leaves room for a possible argument that the door was left open given the proper circumstances. (Confidential memorandum, Mar. 23, 1972)

repeals all prior inconsistent legislation. It is arguable that the Court of Appeals did not have to go so far as to endorse repeal by implication, because the effect of its decision was to uphold the Taylor Law anyway. It will be interesting to see, over the next few years, how liberally the Huntington decision is applied. If this writer's hunch is correct, the differences between the Wayne County and Huntington decisions, in terms of their impact on the scope of bargaining in their respective states, may ultimately be quite minimal.

CIVIL SERVICE AND COLLECTIVE BARGAINING: IS RECONCILIATION POSSIBLE?

This chapter has focused on the problem of accommodating conflicting statutes that affect the scope of negotiations. One major issue, especially in Michigan, concerned the clash between civil service laws and collective bargaining statutes. It is now appropriate to ask: Is reconciliation possible between the two?

In discussing the compatibility of collective negotiations with the merit system, one civil service administrator commented:

> I know that the average public employee does not look to those of us who are civil service commissioners [or] merit system directors . . . as being wholly their chosen representatives. Instead, we should recognize that it is membership in a union that provides for some employees, at least in their eyes, the possibility of choosing a representative who will bravely, intelligently, and articulately speak up for him to management in government.[121]

No doubt, collective bargaining laws have had a tremendous impact on traditionally administered civil service systems. Although civil service historically has promoted political neutrality in government service, equal opportunity, and advancement based on merit, many public employees now believe that unions "will get more for them—more pay, more benefits, more aggressive protection against possible arbitrary management actions."[122]

The disenchantment of public employees with civil service is not without justification. Many merit systems embody unilateral decision-making by management and paternalism; they deny public employees any effective role in their own governance. As Jerry Wurf, AFSCME's president, has stated:

> . . . civil service commissions are not genuine "third-party organizations." They are management-oriented, because they are appointed by the "boss," the chief executive; true,

councilmanic confirmation of the appointments may be required, but the legislature is also management . . . we think that conditions of employment are best handled by bilateral negotiation rather than unilaterally by an allegedly neutral civil service commission.[123]

There also is widespread feeling among public employees that civil service personnel boards, no matter how impartial their members profess to be, are a part of management. Because civil service unilaterally determines the work rules and procedures that are to govern public employees, the unions contend that civil service commissions cannot serve as impartial judges to determine whether such rules have been fairly administered with respect to discipline, discharge, promotion, and other employee grievances.[124] Thus, public employee organizations have urged the amendment of civil service appeal procedures in favor of grievance and arbitration machinery similar to that existing in private employment.

As the cases discussed in this chapter illustrate, civil service officials are reluctant to give up their jurisdiction over public employment matters. Felix Nigro expresses well their concern over collective bargaining in public service:

Merit system officials are worried . . . by what to them appears to be the unions' desire to replace the civil service law and regulations with collective agreements. They fear that the unions believe in personnel administration by contract, rather than by law. As they analyze the unions' intentions, the civil service commission would be stripped of all functions except recruitment. . . . These fears mount if a union argues that the contract should prevail when a clause in it conflicts with existing provisions of law and regulation.[125]

Public officials also are concerned that unions do not accept the principle of competitive ranking of candidates. They believe unions want to entirely substitute seniority for merit in the promotion of employees. They also think that collective bargaining inevitably means the end of equal pay for equal work, since different unions representing different bargaining units may bargain separately for employees often doing the same kind of work. "A clerk fortunate to be represented by a strong union will be paid at a higher rate than the one represented by a weaker union"[126]—even though both employees may have similar responsibilities. Administrators fear that unions will strive to negotiate into contracts the use and selection of examinations, service plans and individual ratings, and most "technical" personnel processes. The result will, in effect, make arbitrators personnel experts because they will have to interpret contract language on tests, ratings, and other traditional merit system matters.

Both public employee unions and civil service administrators have legitimate concerns. The question, therefore, is: Can both the merit system and collective bargaining survive?

First, it should be noted that many public employee unions do not advocate the elimination of civil service. In an unpublished letter to the New York Times, Victor Gotbaum, president of District Council 37 of AFSCME in New York City, stated:

> The alternatives to civil service, however, are political patronage, large-scale corruption, and less merit, fairness and personal initiative. . . . It is no accident that the very worst personnel systems are those where the civil service is either minimal or absent altogether. . . . This is not to say that the civil service . . . does not require greater flexibility, and programs of career development to improve morale and service. It is a fact, however, that these goals can be accomplished within the guidelines and standards of a good civil service system.[127]

Jerry Wurf also indicated that ways should be found to make collective bargaining and civil service compatible: "We are not opposed to merit systems as such, but the imposition of such systems . . . should carry with it a corollary right and duty to enter into collective bargaining relationships."[128]

This writer believes, however, that to a considerable extent existing merit systems and collective bargaining cannot be harmonized. Many civil service commissions are an arm of management. Their codes and regulations encompass not only recruitment, classification, and promotion but also grievance processing, salary administration, safety, and employee training—traditional concerns of unions. Thus the effectuation of collective bargaining statutes, requiring negotiation on wages, hours, and terms and conditions of employment, necessarily involves the incorporation into the bargaining process of subjects hitherto under the unilateral control of civil service commissions.

Collective bargaining need not, however, spell the doom of the merit principle, which is distinct from the merit system. As one commentator writes:

> We should distinguish [merit systems] from the merit principle under which public employees are recruited, selected, and advanced under conditions of political neutrality, equal opportunity, and competition on the basis of merit and competence. Public employee unions do not question this principle in general and have done

little to weaken it, as yet. When we say merit systems, however, this has come to mean a broad program of personnel management activities. Some are essential to carrying out the merit principle: recruiting, selecting, policing of anti-political and anti-discrimination rules. . . . Others are closely related and desirable: position classification, pay administration, employee benefits, and training. Unions are of course interested in both categories.[129]

To make collective bargaining meaningful, nonmerit functions should be removed from civil service commissions and placed within the responsibility of labor relations departments in the executive branch of government. Recruitment, testing, hiring, and development of standards for promotion—the original functions of the civil service system—should remain within its jurisdiction to assure equal opportunity in employment and to protect government service from the spoils system. But subjects commonly considered terms and conditions of employment, especially grievance procedures, belong within the purview of collective negotiations.

The most desirable way to bring about these changes is through legislation rather than judicial action. As the Michigan Supreme Court lamented in Wayne County, too often new bargaining laws reflect no evidence of legislative intent concerning what their impact is to be on preexisting legislation. The courts are left to "guess" at what relationship the legislature intended to exist between old and new statutes. Hence, civil service functions should be statutorily redefined to reflect legislative endorsement of the doctrine of bilateralism in public employer-employee relations. In this way the essentials of the merit system can be expressly preserved while meaningful collective bargaining is allowed to develop.

CONCLUSION: THE IMPACT OF BARGAINING LAWS ON EMPLOYER AUTHORITY

The second major issue brought to light in this chapter concerns the effect of bargaining laws on the power of public employers to determine terms and conditions of employment. The Michigan Supreme Court courageously determined that the PERA impliedly repeals prior inconsistent legislation. Although the New York courts have not adopted as radical an approach, they have held that public employers have a broad grant of power to bargain on wages, hours, and terms and conditions of employment.

This writer would add only that the subjection of public employers to bargaining laws does not derogate their basic administrative authority over government operations but, rather, requires only that they use their statutory authority to its fullest extent. Chief Judge DeBruler of the Indiana Supreme Court wrote persuasively on this point in the context of teacher negotiations:

It must be kept in mind that the local governing boards of school corporations have a great deal of discretion over the terms and conditions of employment of teachers. Any decision within this discretionary area is authorized by the government and, therefore, obviously does not deny the authority of government. The teachers seek to compel choice within that discretionary area. They do not seek to destroy the body politic or pressure employers into violating their statutory duties.[130]

The cases analyzed in this chapter also indicate that whether or not one concludes that bargaining laws impliedly supersede prior legislation or, alternatively, grant to public employers new powers to bargain on terms and conditions of employment, the practical effect may well be the same.

The Michigan and New York Courts have held that bargaining laws must be interpreted liberally to achieve their public benefit purpose. More importantly, their decisions emphasize that the enactment of bargaining laws represents the introduction of bilateralism into public sector labor relations. As David Stanley comments, collective bargaining means a "weakening of what might be called management-by-itself. The era of unilateralism, of unquestioned sovereignty, is over."[131] Under bargaining laws public employers do have an expanded scope of authority to confer employee benefits because the legislature has sanctioned a new process—good faith collective bargaining—to be used in resolving disputes and determining terms and conditions of employment. In the final analysis, therefore, the only real difference between the Michigan Supreme Court and New York Court of Appeals decisions lies in the semantic approach used by each court to achieve a symbiotic relationship between a bargaining law and preexisting legislation.

NOTES

1. Benjamin Nathan Cardozo, The Nature of the Judicial Process (New Haven: Yale University Press, 1921).
2. Robert D. Helsby, "Impact of the Taylor Law on Public Schools, 1968-1970," remarks before the New York State Commission on the Quality, Cost, and Financing of Elementary and Secondary Education, Syracuse, April 2, 1971, p. 10.
3. Ibid.

4. Patricia N. Blair, "State Legislative Control over the Conditions of Public Employment: Defining the Scope of Collective Bargaining for State and Municipal Employees," 26 Vanderbilt Law Review 1, at 12 (1973).

5. Ibid.

6. Harry H. Wellington and Ralph K. Winter, "Structuring Collective Bargaining in Public Employment," 79 Yale Law Journal 805, at 861 (1970).

7. Charles M. Rehmus, "Constraints on Local Governments in Public Employee Bargaining," 67 Michigan Law Review 919, at 927 (1969).

8. Wis. Stat., §111.91 (1970).

9. Conn. Gen. Stat. Ann. §7-474(f) (Supp. 1969); Kansas S.B. 333, L. 1971, §10(a); Me. Rev. Stat. Ann. tit. 26, §969.

10. Ch. 89, HRS, as enacted by Act 171, L. 1970, §9(d).

11. Mass. Ann. Laws ch. 149, §1781 (Supp. 1972).

12. Ann. Cal. Code, Government, §3500 (Supp. 1969).

13. Conn. Gen. Stat. Ann. §7-474(f) (Supp. 1969).

14. See, for example, Typographical, Pressman's and Bindery Unions v. Personnel Division, decision of Oregon Public Employee Relations Board, 400 GERR B-6 (Mar. 31, 1971).

15. Jack R. Clary, "Labor Law," 18 Wayne Law Review 371 (1972).

16. Case no. 13414, Genessee Circuit Court, Michigan, Apr. 22, 1969, in 296 GERR B-5 (May 12, 1969).

17. Ibid.

18. Ibid.

19. Ibid. at B-6.

20. Case no. 124936, Michigan Circuit Court, Wayne County, Apr. 18, 1969, in 295 GERR B-2 (May 5, 1969).

21. Ibid. at B-4.

22. Oakland County Sheriff's Department, 1968 MERC Lab. Ops. 1(a), 21-22; 227 GERR F-1 (1969).

23. 64 CCH Lab. Cas. 67,853 (Mich. At. App., 1970).

24. Ibid. at 67,854.

25. Ibid.

26. 384 Mich. 363, 184 N.W.2d 201 (1971).

27. P.A. 1941, no. 370 [Mich. Comp. Laws Ann. (MCLA) §38.401 et seq.; Stat. Ann. 1961 Rev. §5.1191(1) et seq.].

28. 22 Mich. App. 287, at 294.

29. 384 Mich. 363, at 371-372.

30. MCLA §38.409 [Stat. Ann. 1961 Rev. §5.1191(9)].

31. MCLA §46.11 [Stat. Ann. 1969 Cum. Sup. §5.331].

32. P.A. 1965, no. 379 [MCLA §423.201 et seq.; Stat. Ann. 1968 Rev. §17.455(1) et seq.].

33. 384 Mich. 363, at 371.

34. MCLA §224.9 [Stat. Ann. 1958 Rev. §9.100].

35. Civil no. 85,654 (Cir. Ct., Wayne County, Mar. 12, 1968).
36. 22 Mich. App. 287, at 300.
37. 384 Mich. 363, at 372.
38. Ibid. at 373.
39. Ibid. at 374.
40. Ibid. at 375-376.
41. Blair, op. cit. at 11.
42. Ibid.
43. 1971 MERC Lab. Ops. 237.
44. City of Flint and Council 29, AFSCME, 1970 MERC Lab. Ops. 348.
45. 1971 MERC Lab. Ops. 237, at 247. Emphasis added.
46. Clary, op. cit. at 372; Kurt L. Hanslowe and Walter E. Oberer, "Determining the Scope of Negotiations Under Public Employment Relations Statutes," 24 Industrial and Labor Relations Review 432, at 441 (1971).
47. Clary, op. cit. at 373.
48. In its 1966 report the Taylor Committee stated:

Phrasing the problem in terms of collective negotiations, as previously defined, provides a constructive way . . . of getting at the heart of the matter, i.e., protecting the rights of public employees to representatives of their own choosing . . . without an unacceptable infringement upon the stability and viability of the Civil Service System. In our considered judgment, occupational representation should not be denied and can be provided without undermining the Civil Service System . . . public employees have an obligation to recognize that collective negotiations must be conducted within the framework of our democratic political structure out of which the civil service idea has evolved.

Governor's Committee on Public Employee Relations, State of New York, Final Report, Mar. 31, 1966, p. 12.
49. Walter E. Oberer and Kurt L. Hanslowe, Cases and Materials on Labor Law: Collective Bargaining in a Free Society (St. Paul, Minn.: West Publishing Company, 1972), p. 938.
50. Robert Helsby and Thomas Joyner, "Impact of the Taylor Law on Local Governments," in R.H. Connery and W.V. Farr, eds., Unionization of Municipal Employees, which is Proceedings of the Academy of Political Science 30, n. 2 (1971): 29.
51. Ibid., p. 36.
52. Ibid.
53. Ibid.
54. Ibid.
55. This summary was taken, in part, from a report prepared by Irving Sabghir for the Fleischmann Commission and quoted in

Myron Lieberman, The Impact of the Taylor Act upon the Governance and Administration of Elementary and Secondary Education, report to Fleischmann Commission, June 1971, pp. 73-77.

56. Hanslowe and Oberer, "Determining the Scope of Negotiations Under Public Employment Relations Statutes," at 435.
57. Ibid.
58. 23 Op. State Compt. 291 (1967, #67-355).
59. Ibid. at 292.
60. 23 Op. State Compt. 316 (1967, #67-378).
61. Ibid. at 318-319.
62. Ibid. at 319.
63. Ibid.
64. 23 Op. State Compt. 649 (1967, #67-735).
65. Ibid. at 650.
66. 24 Op. State Compt. 253 (1968, #68-244). Emphasis added.
67. Ibid. at 253-254.
68. 24 Op. State Compt. 370 (1968, #68-357).
69. 25 Op. State Compt. 11 (1969, #69-15).
70. 25 Op. State Compt. 109 (1969, #69-196).
71. Ibid. at 110.
72. 4 PERB 3018, at 3659 (1971).
73. 25 Op. State Compt. 388 (1969, #69-991).
74. Ibid. at 390.
75. Unpublished comptroller's opinion #69-195.
76. Letter to district principal, Lansing Central School District, from John P. Jehu, associate counsel, State Education Department, Feb. 18, 1972.
77. Ibid.
78. Hanslowe and Oberer, op. cit., at 439.
79. Ibid. at 441.
80. Ibid. at 437.
81. Ibid. at 439.
82. See, for example, PERB's decision in Monroe Woodbury, 3 PERB 3104, at 3632 (1970).
83. See, for instance, Teachers Association, Central High School District No. 3 v. Board of Education, 34 A.D.2d 351 (1970), reversing 61 Misc.2d 492; Board of Education of Union Free School District No. 3, Town of Huntington v. Associated Teachers of Huntington, 331 N.Y.S.2d 17 (1972), reversing 36 A.D.2d 753 and 62 Misc.2d 906; Board of Education, Central High School District No. 1, Town of Grand Island v. Helsby, 326 N.Y.S.2d 452 (1971), reversing 64 Misc. 2d 473.
84. 1 PERB 3241 (1968).
85. 2 PERB 7027, 59 Misc.2d 943 (1969).
86. 3 PERB 7055, 34 A.D.2d 361, 312 N.Y.S.2d 355 (1970).
87. 34 A.D.2d 361, at 363; 312 N.Y.S.2d 355, at 358.

88. 3 PERB 7011, at 7065, 64 Misc.2d 473 (1970).
89. 3 PERB 7011, at 7067.
90. Ibid. at 7068.
91. 326 N.Y.S.2d 452 (1971).
92. Ibid. at 456.
93. Ibid.
94. 326 N.Y.S.2d 452, at 457, quoting 34 A.D.2d 361, at 363. Emphasis added by Judge Gabrielli.
95. 2 PERB 8009, at 8102, 60 Misc.2d 443 (1969).
96. 2 PERB 8009, at 8105.
97. Ibid. at 8104.
98. Myron Lieberman, "Why Teachers Will Oppose Tenure Laws," Saturday Review, Mar. 4, 1972, pp. 55-56.
99. Sabghir, op. cit., p. 85.
100. 313 N.Y.S.2d 474 (1970).
101. Ibid. at 477.
102. Ibid.
103. Ibid. at 479.
104. Ibid. at 480. Emphasis added.
105. Ibid. at 481. Emphasis added.
106. 34 A.D.2d 351, 312 N.Y.S.2d 252 (1970).
107. 312 N.Y.S.2d 252, at 256 (1970).
108. 4 PERB 8021, at 8300.
109. Ibid. at 8302.
110. Ibid. at 8303.
111. Ibid. at 8304.
112. Ibid. at 8305.
113. 69 Misc.2d 1061 (1972), 5 PERB 7509, at 7517.
114. 5 PERB 7509, at 7518.
115. Ibid. at 7520.
116. Ibid. at 7521.
117. 331 N.Y.S.2d 17, 79 LRRM 2881 (1972).
118. 331 N.Y.S.2d 17, at 21.
119. Ibid.
120. Ibid. at 23.
121. Raymond F. Male, "Labor Crises and the Role of Management," Developments in Public Employee Relations (Chicago: Public Personnel Association, 1965).
122. David T. Stanley, "What Are Unions Doing to Merit Systems?" 31 Public Personnel Review 108, at 109 (1970).
123. Jerry Wurf, quoted in Felix Nigro, "Collective Bargaining and the Merit System," in Connery and Farr, eds., op. cit., p. 57.
124. Arvid Anderson, "Personnel Opinions," 27 Public Personnel Review 52, at 56 (1966).
125. Nigro, op. cit., p. 58.
126. Ibid., p. 59.

127. Victor Gotbaum, letter to the New York Times, Public Employee Press (District Council 37's journal), Dec. 12, 1969.

128. Jerry Wurf, statement to Senate Subcommittee on Intergovernmental Relations, quoted in Nigro, op. cit., p. 63.

129. Stanley, op. cit. at 109.

130. Chief Justice DeBruler, dissenting opinion in Anderson Federation of Teachers v. School City of Anderson, 252 Ind. 558, 251 N.E.2d 15 (1969), certiorari denied, 399 U.S. 928 (1970).

131. Stanley, loc. cit.

CHAPTER

8

DEFINING THE SCOPE
OF BARGAINING FOR
PROFESSIONAL EMPLOYEES

Who's in charge, anyway?
Should teachers set policy for the schools? Should
social workers help set welfare standards? Should policemen have a voice in determining the size and deployment
of the police force?
. . . [T]hose are the questions that state, county, and
local governments and their employes are wrestling with.
. . . For as the wages, hours and working conditions of
these organized public employes greatly improve, their
unions, particularly those of professionals, are attempting
to broaden the scope of negotiations to include policy questions that used to be the exclusive province of elected
officials.[1]

Professional employees are not content to bargain on traditional
subjects of wages, hours, and working conditions.[2] They want to
negotiate on issues of educational policy, "or the number of duty
stations which a nurse must serve, or the level of benefits for relief
recipients. Some of these bargaining requests involve what is called
the mission of the agency and would utilize the collective bargaining
rather than the legislative process for effectuating change in social
and economic policy."[3]
Public management has maintained that many of these employee
demands are managerial prerogatives or public policy issues and,
therefore, nonnegotiable.[4] But professional employee spokesmen
argue that, by virtue of their training and functions, professional
employees should negotiate on policy decisions. As professionals,
they have an interest and expertise concerning many policy matters
that nonprofessional employees do not have. As Michael Moskow
writes:

200

One of the most valuable resources of the school board is the teaching staff. They are experienced and knowledgeable in the . . . operations of the school system. As professional personnel, they are theoretically concerned more with the public interest than their own private interests. In addition, they have been professionally trained and probably have some ideas on how the school system could be improved. Obviously, not all of their ideas will be acceptable, but it nevertheless would be foolish not to take advantage of their expertise. It is possible that collective bargaining may be the mechanism which could be used by the school board to receive the benefits of the teachers' experience.[5]

There are several reasons why the professional employee seeks an expanded scope of bargaining. First, the subjects traditionally considered within the definition of ''terms and conditions of employment'' do not embrace the kinds of issues that form the professional's working conditions. As AFSCME's Victor Gotbaum comments, ''To the professional—the teacher or the case worker—things like class size and case load become as important as the number of hours in a shift is to the blue-collar worker.''[6] Second, many decisions that would not affect the terms and conditions of employment of nonprofessional employees do have a significant impact on the working conditions of professionals. For instance, notes one commentator, a clerical worker in a typical government agency works from 9 A.M. to 5 P.M. ''If there are fewer fellow clerks working with him, this simply means that work is turned out more slowly; it does not result in more burdensome working conditions for the clerk. On the other hand, fewer teachers means that each teacher has a greater load of students and this does affect the conditions of his employment.''[7] Teachers therefore want to bargain on such issues as class size; the number of special teachers for such subjects as art, music, and remedial reading; and the availability of teachers' aides. Third, the effectiveness and satisfaction of many professionals depend, to a large extent, on the ability of fellow colleagues, who share the responsibility of serving ''clients,'' and on the competence of superiors, who administer the government enterprise. Thus it is not uncommon for teacher representatives to seek to negotiate over hiring standards for new teachers, peer evaluation procedures, the granting of tenure, and even selection procedures for school administrators.

SOME CONCEPTS ABOUT PROFESSIONALISM AND
COLLECTIVE BARGAINING

It has been suggested that collective bargaining will have a profound and unique impact on the decision-making processes of those enterprises involving salaried professionals.[8] A major reason for this distinctive impact lies in the aspirations and self-conceptions of professionals generally. As Archie Kleingartner suggests, the concept of professionalism embodies a logic that imposes on those occupations aspiring to or characterized by professional standards certain imperatives in bargaining and in the employee-management relationships. These imperatives "encourage a broad approach to defining scope of bargaining."[9]

Sociologists have discussed at length the concepts of "profession" and "professionalism." Many definitions of the term "profession" have been suggested, but none has been universally accepted. Yet it is clear that recognition of an occupation as a profession has significant legal, social, and economic consequences for the members of the occupation and for society. To be recognized as—or to claim the status of—professional carries certain privileges that distinguish a professional from other workers and implies certain responsibilities to the recipients of professional services.[10]

In an essay this writer attempted to identify the distinguishing attributes of a profession.[11] Although that essay is not entirely relevant to the present discussion, a review of some of the elements that characterize a profession helps to explain the kinds of concerns expressed by professionals at the bargaining table.

The Professional Exercises Authority, Based on Competence, Which Is Recognized by the Public

The intellectual preparation of the professional imparts to him a special competence and the right to make professional judgments. This fact is the basis for the professional's authority. Since a professional's work demands a high degree of intelligence and training, he requires authority, that is, freedom to exercise skill and judgment in the field within which he has been educated. Because the layman is relatively ignorant in professional matters, he accedes to the professional's judgment, confident that the professional will act in his best interests.

Professions Possess a Broad Range of Autonomy

Autonomy and authority are similar. As used here, however, authority refers to the professional's recognized right to make decisions in the best interests of his client, whereas autonomy refers to a profession's freedom to govern itself. If a community sanctions the autonomy of a profession, it generally grants it the privilege of setting its own standards and regulating the activities of its members. Among the powers exercised autonomously by a profession are the right to control entry and exit from the profession, and the right to set standards for licensing practitioners. A large measure of autonomy also implies a correspondingly large measure of responsibility. As Abraham Flexner wrote, "This quality of responsibility follows from the fact that the professions are intellectual in character; for in all intellectual operations, the thinker takes upon himself a risk."[12]

A Profession Possesses a Code of Ethics

Because the unregulated exercise of broad powers of authority and autonomy would present hazards to the public, a profession formulates a code of ethics, interpreted and enforced by its members, to foster high standards of professional conduct. "Through its ethical code, the profession's commitment to the social welfare becomes a matter of public record, thereby insuring for itself the continued confidence of the community."[13] In addition, a code governs colleague relationships. It emphasizes cooperation and the mutual support professionals must give each other vis-a-vis clientele and community.

A Profession Is Dedicated to the Performance of an Essential Social Service That Is Delegated to It

"The social values of a professional group are its basic and fundamental beliefs, the unquestioned premises upon which its very existence rests."[14] Outstanding among these values are the essential worth of the service that the profession renders and its devotion to it. A profession believes its work is unique and socially beneficial. A profession also exhibits a unique attitude toward its work; a professional's career is his "calling." The true professional places greater emphasis on the service he renders than on the rewards he receives. It is this dedication to the work, not as a means but as an end itself, that characterizes the service orientation of a profession.

Professional authority suggests a practitioner's right, even duty, to act in accordance with his best professional judgment. He expects to be trusted, and not commanded, by those to whom he renders service. Although the salaried professional theoretically values authority just as highly as the independent practitioner, he is subjected to special strains as a result of his employment in bureaucratic organizations.[15] There is an inevitable tension between the exercise of professional authority and the need for administrative control. Amitai Etzioni notes this conflict:

> Only if immune from ordinary social pressures and free to innovate, to experiment, to take risks without the usual social repercussions of failure, can a professional carry out his work. It is this highly individualized principle which is diametrically opposed to the very essence of the organizational principle of control and coordination by supervisors—i.e., the principle of administrative authority.[16]

Salaried professionals in public employment are similar to other professionals in that they seek to assume a large degree of personal responsibility for their work, and they desire to maintain high standards of professional practice. The difficulty lies in trying to achieve these broad professional objectives within the context of public employment relationships.

In another sense, many of the goals that professionals in public employment try to realize in their work lives do not differ from those that all employees seek to satisfy. But

> . . . the intensity with which the former seek certain goals, the particular "mix" of work-related values that will provide optimum satisfaction and the hierarchy of these goals, tends to distinguish professionals from other groups. . . . Clearly, for most professionals, work is more than "just a job." They expect to give a good deal of effort to their work . . ., and they expect to obtain a high level of reward. . . .[17]

With respect to the scope of negotiations, professional workers in government, like all public employees, have basic "bread and butter" goals. They are concerned about adequate compensation, satisfactory working conditions, good fringe benefits, job security, and equitable treatment on the job. These "bread and butter" demands, although frequently not agreed to by management, are accepted as falling within the meaning of "wages, hours, and terms and conditions of employment."

In addition to these short-run goals, however, professionals have equally compelling, long-run career aspirations. Often these aspirations pertain to the mission and content of the work performed by members of the profession.[18] In collective negotiations, although the bread and butter demands often are more expensive to the public employer, they frequently are less contested as inappropriate subjects for bargaining. The professional goals certainly have economic ramifications, but are particularly troublesome to management because they represent a basic challenge to managerial authority. Thus, collective bargaining in the public sector often reflects the unique tensions between salaried workers with professional aspirations and career commitments and government employers who are accountable to the public and are traditionally entrusted with nondelegable powers to administer government operations in accordance with their best judgment and the dictates of public policy. This tension pervades the scope-of-bargaining conflicts that characterize negotiations between professional unions and public employers.

BARGAINING DEMANDS AFFECTING THE NATURE AND QUALITY OF GOVERNMENT SERVICES

In light of these concepts about professionalism, the attempt of salaried employees to influence decisions affecting the nature and quality of services provided by the public employer is not surprising.[19] For example, in 1971 the curators of New York's Museum of Modern Art struck because, among other things, they objected to a trustees' decision, made for economic reasons, to reduce the number of exhibits from 40 to 10 a year.[20] In January 1967 the New York City Social Service Employees Union included in its bargaining demands proposals for a 25 percent increase in welfare benefits and semiannual clothing grants to welfare recipients.[21] Teacher-school board agreements often contain provisions requiring the school administration to hire a certain number of specialists, such as psychologists, speech therapists, and other personnel specially trained to improve the quality of educational services available to "exceptional" children—those either gifted or disadvantaged. Some contracts provide for the formation of a joint faculty-administration committee to develop plans for designing and equipping new and remodeled school facilities. It is not uncommon for contracts to establish joint educational development committees, which are charged with the development of new curricula, the setting of priorities, and the evaluation of new and existing programs.

Occasionally the courts have had to resolve the conflicts concerning the negotiability of noneconomic, professionally rooted demands. In Nickels v. Board of Education of Imlay City Community

Schools,[22] an AFT local sued the school board to enforce a contract provision requiring the school district to take advantage of federal funds available for special and remedial programs. The circuit court found that the school board had indeed contractually agreed to apply for federal benefits to be provided for a Head Start program for the school year in question. The court, in ruling that the decision as to whether or not to develop a Head Start program was a policy matter over which the school board had the duty to maintain continuing discretion, and on which it could not bind itself by contract for the future, stated:

> An agreement which controls or restricts . . . the free exercise of discretion for the public good vested in a public officer or board is illegal, so that no redress can be given to a party who sues for himself in respect of it.
>   Enforcing this rule in 1971, the Michigan Supreme Court said, "Indeed it is impossible to predicate reasonableness of any contract by which the governing authority abdicates any of its legislative powers, and precludes itself from meeting in a proper way the emergencies that may arise. Those powers are conferred in order to be exercised again and again, as may be found needful . . . and those who hold them in trust today are vested with no discretion to circumscribe their limits or diminish their efficiency, but must transfer them unimpaired to their successors."

The court was not persuaded that the enactment of the Public Employment Relations Act was intended to modify this principle.

> The contract with which we are concerned goes full range. It . . . requires participation in all Federal Programs within certain categories without regard to cost or local need. I am unable to find from the language of the statute, or otherwise, a legislative intent to make such a sweeping alteration in the structure of government. Rather it is my opinion that the legislature intended to authorize collective bargaining with public employees with respect to working conditions within the framework of policies and projects selected, from time to time, by duly elected officials.

Some of the most difficult scope-of-bargaining problems stem from the fact that certain issues, while clearly working conditions, also affect or relate to policy matters generally considered non-negotiable. Or, alternatively, certain policy decisions have substantial impact on conditions of employment, and employees therefore want to bargain over them. Albert Shanker, co-president of the New York

State United Federation of Teachers, has commented on this ticklish problem: ". . . what we're primarily interested in is improving the teachers' working conditions." The difficulty is, he adds, that "there is hardly anything which cannot simultaneously be viewed as a working condition and a matter of educational policy."[23]

The Wisconsin Supreme Court was faced with this kind of issue in City of Madison v. Wisconsin Employment Relations Board,[24] a case involving the negotiability of the school calendar. Although the school superintendent had argued that the school calendar was a matter for consultation (as opposed to negotiation) with the union, the Court disagreed and affirmed an order of the Wisconsin Employment Relations Board upholding the negotiability of the calendar. In the Court's view, the calendar had a "direct and intimate relationship" to the salaries and working conditions of school employees because it set the number of days to be worked and the dates of the beginning and end of the school year. Referring to private sector experience under the National Labor Relations Act, the Court cited Local Union No. 189, Amalgamated Meat Cutters v. Jewel Tea Co,[25] wherein the United States Supreme Court stated:

> . . . we think that the particular hours of the day and the particular days of the week during which employees shall be required to work are subjects well within the realm of "wages, hours, and other terms and conditions of employment" about which employers and unions must bargain.[26]

In response to the school board's contention that negotiating on the school calendar would require it to illegally delegate its authority on a matter of basic educational policy, the Court stated that negotiating on the calendar would neither take away nor impede any of the duties or powers conferred on the board by law or constitution. Although many items in the school calendar are fixed by state law and therefore cannot be regulated through collective bargaining, "what is left to the school boards in respect to the school calendar is subject to compulsory discussion and negotiation."[27] In a provocative statement the Court did suggest, however, that "the contents of the curriculum would be a different matter. Subjects of study are within the scope of basic educational policy and additionally are not related to wages, hours, and conditions of employment."[28]

ARGUMENTS FOR AND AGAINST AN EXPANDED SCOPE OF BARGAINING

School administrators and board of education members probably were somewhat relieved by the Wisconsin Supreme Court's comment that curriculum would not be a negotiable subject. At least one commentator has suggested, however, that the Court's conclusion concerning the nonnegotiability of curriculum may have been too restrictive: ". . . if the decision to change the curriculum results in the elimination of certain job positions, the union should be permitted to bargain over this decision because the traditional labor interests of its members are at stake."[29]

But suppose teachers seek to bargain on school curricula in instances where their job security is not in jeopardy? Or, to put the question more abstractly, should professionals have bargaining rights commensurate with their job responsibilities?

The discussion up to this point has attempted to make more understandable the professional employee's response to these questions. He would contend that he should participate in determining the policies of his employing organization because he is in closest touch with the actual product and work performed by the enterprise. He would insist that his education has instilled in him a concern for the public interest that enables him to transcend his own private interests. He also would emphasize that the essence of professional work is personal responsibility—that this responsibility demands his participation in establishing the standards that will guide and measure his work. David Selden, president of the American Federation of Teachers, expressed the essence of the professional's attitude when he stated: "No doctor would let a hospital board tell him what kind of knife to use when he's in the operating room. It's the same thing with many public employees. There are questions of professional integrity involved."[30]

Other commentators have sympathized with this position. Chief Justice DeBruler of the Supreme Court of Indiana, in his dissenting opinion in Anderson Federation of Teachers,[31] urged negotiations on matters of mutual interest to professionals and their employers, even if these matters touched upon policy issues. His remarks were lengthy but worth quoting in their totality:

> Teachers especially, as professionals, have a wide range of concerns other than purely monetary. They do and ought to have a strong interest in the establishment of the priorities in the allocation of the total school budget; they are interested in the details of the teacher transfer programs designed to promote integrated faculties; they are interested in the emphasis and techniques to be used in furnishing special services to underprivileged and ghetto children; they have an interest in controlling how much of their time must be given to patrolling rest rooms searching out smokers, or collecting tickets at basketball games; they have an interest in the quality of texts and audio-visual materials to be used; they have an

interest in the whole question of the substitute teacher system. The local governing [school] boards do have discretion in these areas in addition to wide discretion with reference to salaries, job classification, job requirements, etc. The existence of this discretion means that there is something for teachers and local school boards to bargain about. It also means that there is a wide scope for arbitrary and unfair actions by those boards which can be avoided only if the teachers have the effective means to pressure the boards into good faith bargaining on the issue.[32]

It also has been suggested that professional employee interest in the quality of public services is relevant with respect to averting and settling bargaining disputes. Third-party neutrals may err if they assume that proposals reflecting this interest are "mere 'window-dressing' for public beguilement. This is not to say that all proposals . . . will be altruistic. But there will usually be a blend of self-concern and 'professional' concern which is not characteristic of collective bargaining in many other fields."[33] It is urged, therefore, that neutrals encourage employer consideration of bargaining proposals manifesting professional employees' concern with the quality and effectiveness of their work.

Certainly a wide scope of bargaining will be beneficial to the public professions themselves. Employee involvement in decision-making is likely to improve salary levels, fringe benefits, and working conditions; these improvements, in turn, may be expected to attract more highly qualified professionals into public service. The right to meaningful participation in decision-making also raises the professional's self-image. In education, "the disillusioned teacher is offered an alternative to passive resistance; the dissident teacher is offered an alternative to carping, destructive criticism; and the professionally ambitious teacher is offered a means to influence educational policy without having to leave the classroom and become an administrator."[34]

Professional workers "develop fewer institutional loyalties than other workers, probably because the character of their training creates a relatively greater feeling of community among them. As a result, they often have more commitment to profession than to place of work."[35] With respect to labor-management relations, this means that job satisfaction frequently is considered a condition of employment by professional employees. The demands, for example, of the curators of the New York City Museum of Modern Art that the level of services offered by the museum should not be curtailed were, at least partially, motivated by this consideration.[36]

Participation in policy matters also may provide a "psychic salary" for some professional employees. Thus, one observer has speculated that it may be "expedient" to allow professional public employees a stronger role in policy decisions; their participation in decision-making may lower their demands on economic matters.[37] "As the 'job action' by the police in New York City in October 1968 indicates, the worker who feels frustrated with a lack of recognition is likely to take out his frustration in demands for higher pay, when no other means are available."[38]

On the other hand, as public employee salaries and fringe benefits continue to inch upward, it is hard to find evidence indicating that collective bargaining gains on noneconomic issues have stimulated substantial concessions on economic demands. The very sincerity of employees in making demands that seek to improve the quality of their public service convinces them that what they want is for the good of their employer and for the citizenry in general, as well as for themselves. Therefore, they should not be compelled to make sacrifices in order to effect these improvements. The now familiar slogan "Teachers Want What Children Need" exemplifies this attitude. It is not realistic, however, to assume that employees, even professionals, can be entirely objective in resolving policy issues that affect their personal interests. Most positions adopted by a union necessarily reflect what its members believe is sound policy consistent with their own self-interest. As George Taylor wrote:

> Even granting that satisfied teachers are an essential requirement for quality teaching, there are limitations to the proposition that what is good for the teachers is good for the students and, hence, for the public.[39]

Some observers fear increased professional participation on the grounds that experimentation and innovation will be difficult to implement once employees are entrenched in decision-making. In education, for example, the unified salary schedule has increasingly fallen under fire as a rigid, inefficient system for paying teachers. "The educational work force is extremely variegated," writes Robert Doherty, "and the problem with the unified salary schedule is that it does not accommodate to this kind of heterogeneity."[40] Doherty, as well as other critics, suggests that salary schedules should be made more responsive to the job market; they should allow for differentials for those teaching positions that are difficult to fill and require lengthy training. Additionally, merit pay is urged to make financial rewards more reflective of actual individual teaching performance.

> If teaching is indeed a profession, then teachers should learn to accept the risks of professionalism. Incompetent doctors, lawyers, architects don't get the financial rewards

that the good ones do, and we all agree that's the way it should be. When it comes to public school teaching, we seem to have succumbed to the fiction that competence is somehow synonomous with formal training and longevity.[41]

Teacher organizations, however, have been most reluctant to experiment with nonschedule compensation systems. The NEA believes merit pay systems have a "deleterious effect on the educational process."[42] The AFT considers them "misnamed and impractical."[43]
There is no doubt that merit pay plans are difficult to administer fairly and can be very damaging to staff morale. But teacher organizations also object to this innovation because the internal politics of labor unions and the dynamics of collective bargaining tend toward egalitarianism.[44] For a teacher spokesman to accept the notion that some teachers are more skilled than others, and therefore entitled to higher pay, or that high school science teachers are in greater demand and thus more deserving of salary increases than kindergarten teachers, could lead to political suicide. To agree to these innovative management proposals—regardless of their professional tone or educational value—probably would result in internal union dissension and ultimately would debilitate the bargaining position of the organization.
An expanded scope of bargaining for professional employees also raises questions concerning the extent to which collective negotiations will change the distribution of lay and professional authority over fundamental policies. As the scope of bargaining enlarges to include basic policies for financing and operating the public enterprise, public employers must take a Hobson's choice. If they engage in full collective bargaining on policy matters, the taxpayers whom they represent are effectively excluded from many significant decisions. But to the extent that public employers weaken the bargaining process by involving the community in matters that vitally affect employees' terms and conditions of employment, they will embitter relations with their employees' unions. Where the line is drawn between negotiable and nonnegotiable subjects will, therefore, importantly affect the relative influence on decision-making of labor organizations as against the influence of taxpayers and community groups.
In education, while it may be true that teachers want what children need, it is not always true that what teachers want, the taxpayers either want or need. New York City exemplifies the acute problems that can develop as a result of the conflicting interests between professional and client groups. As one commentator noted during the 1968 teachers' strike:

The public school system of New York City is on the brink of collapse. No compromise between the teachers' union and the school board is likely to resolve the fundamental conflicts between the school staff and the advocates of black community control.[45]

It has been said that the major issue in the politics of American education "has always" been the conflict between laymen and professionals for control over the schools: "Conflict . . . has taken a hundred forms. Professionals always want more money for the schools, while laymen almost always want to trim the budget. . . . Professionals almost never want anyone fired . . ., while laymen are inclined to fire . . . people, for both good and bad reasons."[46] Under collective bargaining this conflict has increased in intensity. One militant union leader states the teachers' position:

> The coming of age of the teaching profession, through collective bargaining, forces us to meet, head-on, the critical problem of the respective roles of teachers and civic and parent groups in the system of public education. . . . It is inconceivable that laymen will insist on keeping the educational process out of the control of educators. . . . Lay groups will have to recognize and accept the realities of the new world of collective bargaining. . . . By definition, bargaining means co-determination, together with Boards of Education, and not unilateral decisions.[47]

On the other hand, school boards insist that a teacher's authority rests with the local community—not with his profession—and that his role cannot encroach upon areas of managerial discretion. A former president of the National Association of School Boards expresses this point of view:

> Just as war is too important to be left to the generals, education is too important to be left to the educators . . . early Americans delegated this responsibility to boards of education, who for the most part are elected by all of the people in the school district, are directly responsible to them, and can be replaced by them. . . . The school board which shares or gives up its statutory decision-making authority limits or gives up its ability to respond to the wishes of the citizens of the school district.[48]

The questions of lay versus professional control and, more broadly, of the public interest in collective bargaining is a vital one that will be discussed more fully in a later chapter. But, simply put, the public interest means that various community groups have different views about the operation of public services and ought to have an opportunity to "make [themselves] heard at some crucial stage in the process of decision."[49] To the extent that the scope of bargaining is expanded to include the mission and policies of public agencies, collective negotiations disenfranchise groups of citizens whose interests are competitive with those of employee unions. Jerome Lefkowitz, deputy chairman of the New York State Public Employment Relations Board, has stated that as decision-making is "shifted from bodies representative of a broad range of interests, such as legislative bodies, to the limited number of parties—two—which can be accommodated by the process of collective bargaining, there is a major change in our political structure. It is a change which must be accepted with caution."[50]

One other point should be made regarding the wisdom of enlarging the scope of bargaining to include policy matters. Collective negotiation has been called an exercise in power politics[51]—an adversary system for the articulation and resolution of group conflict on the basis of power. There is considerable skepticism that the give-and-take of the bargaining table—the political compromising and strategic maneuvering—is conducive to the resolution of policy issues. Certainly a heated bargaining session is not the proper forum for determining whether welfare recipients should receive higher benefits or whether fifth grade math should be taught by closed-circuit television. The justification for introducing certain programs or making changes in existing policies should be their necessity and measurable effectiveness—not the amount of power wielded by parties at the bargaining table. Wellington and Winter crystallize this point:

> The issue is not a threshold one of whether professional
> public employees should participate in decisions about the
> nature of the services they provide. We take it as given
> that any properly run governmental agency should be
> interested in, and heavily reliant upon, the judgment of
> its professional staff. The issue rather is the method
> [and extent] of that participation.[52]

THE EXPERIENCE OF THE UFT AND NEW YORK CITY
BOARD OF EDUCATION: DEVELOPING A PROPER
SCOPE OF BARGAINING FOR TEACHERS

A vivid account of the evolving relationship between the New York City board of education and the UFT was presented by Ida Klaus in an incisive essay[53] that illustrates the difficulty of defining the appropriate scope of bargaining for professional employees.

Ms. Klaus described this relationship as it developed in four stages between 1962 and 1969, and her analysis of the New York City experience provides what may be a prognosis for the trend of school negotiations in other cities.

In the first stage, "exploration and experimentation," the school board and union had their initial bargaining encounters and negotiated their first collective agreement. This 38-page document covered various aspects of salaries, hours, and terms and conditions of employment, including a detailed grievance procedure ending with binding arbitration.

The second stage, which Klaus called "crisis and turning point," began in 1963, during the negotiations for a second contract. The major conflict during this stage focused on the appropriate scope of bargaining:

> Where is the line between what is primarily within the sphere of working conditions and hence subject to nego- tiation and bilateral discussion, and what is essentially within the realm of educational policy and hence within the exclusive authority of the Board or the Superintendent and not subject to negotiation and agreement? The Union sought to extend collective bargaining to new aspects of educational administration, and the Board rejoined that such matters were reserved exclusively to the discretionary professional judgment and policy-making authority of the Board and of the Superintendent.[54]

With the assistance of a mediation panel, an agreement was reached that included several compromise provisions on those union demands whose negotiability had been strongly contested. For instance, the board of education conceded that a class might be so large as to constitute an excessive teaching burden. In that sense, class size could be viewed as a "working condition" subject to negotiation to set the maximum number of students that a teacher could reasonably be expected to teach.

> Since class-size limitations became part of the working conditions section of the contract, any claimed departure from those limitations was subject to all phases of the grievance procedure. . . . On the other hand, teacher assignments and qualifications for assignments remained within the discretion of the school principals. Still, the parties devised special procedures to promote fair and objective selection of teachers for coveted non-teaching assignments. . . .[55]

The board of education also agreed to establish a system of joint consultation, away from the bargaining table, so that the superintendent and union could periodically discuss issues of mutual concern. In the preamble to their agreement, the board and union declared their "mutual intent to work together toward the achievement of common aims of educational excellence." They therefore agreed to meet once a month and confer on matters of educational policy and development. One of the specific subjects of consultation was the development of a program for the improvement of "difficult schools."

Additional scope-of-bargaining clashes resulted from the union's demands that the contract contain provisions concerning the length of the school year, the length of teacher vacations, and related matters, all of which the board of education had traditionally regulated by means of bylaw. The board admitted that these subjects had a "direct bearing on working conditions but insisted that they were essential to its discretionary authority to manage the school system and hence could not be bargained away."[56] The parties finally resolved the conflict by narrowing the subjects in dispute to sick leave, sabbatical leaves, vacations, and holidays. The board specifically agreed that it would continue its "present policy" as to these subjects, "except insofar as change is commanded by law."

By 1965, when the negotiations for a third contract began, collective bargaining had become the accepted method for determining salaries and terms and conditions of employment for New York City teachers. The bargaining relationship was now entering the stage of "maturity and union power." Additionally,

The process of regular joint consultation on a year-round basis added a new and broader dimension to the teacher-Board relationship. Through this process the Union became a truly powerful force in school administration. . . . It participated in planning the Board's internal procedures for administering the provisions of the collective bargaining agreement. . . . On several occasions, the Board withdrew items appearing on the calendar for action at a public meeting upon the Union's insistence that the matter was a proper subject for collective bargaining and that "prior consultation and negotiation" had not taken place.[57]

During the third round of negotiations, the union's demands were directed at enhancing its status in the school system and on gaining security for itself as a labor organization. It won many of these demands on the theory that favored treatment was "an accepted perquisite of exclusive representation" and that it would encourage a "stable and responsible collective bargaining relationship in the school system."[58]

Ms. Klaus called the fourth stage of the union-board relationship "the emergence of public-interest issues peculiar to the enterprise." This stage began in 1967 and was still in effect when Ms. Klaus wrote her article in 1969.

By the eve of the fourth round of contract talks, the board of education and several parent groups had become persuaded that the improved working conditions granted to teachers in past contracts had hampered efforts to provide better education where it was needed most. The school board, therefore, presented a set of demands that sought to change the "unrealistic" working conditions previously granted in teacher contracts and to recoup some of the authority it had agreed to share with the union. The union, on the other hand, sought additional improvements in working conditions and an extension of its role in school governance.

The clash of positions on these and other public-interest issues remained persistently intractable through three separate phases of mediation efforts. . . . Among the public-interest differences were two which proved to be particularly divisive: the problem of the so-called "disruptive" pupil and the controversy over the More Effective Schools program (MES). The conflict over these issues illustrated how difficult it is to separate the realm of collective bargaining from the domain of governmental policy-making, and how delicate the balance is between the pull of public-interest concerns and the force of special group demands.[59]

After extensive negotiations and a bitter strike, an agreement was concluded in which the UFT "achieved most of its final substantive demands directly affecting teacher working conditions." In return it did, however, make several concessions having the effect of limiting its role in what the board of education considered to be matters of educational policy.

In reviewing Klaus's analysis of the evolution of the bargaining relationship between the UFT and New York City board of education, this writer has not intended to suggest that employer-employee relations in all professional—or even all school—situations will pattern themselves after the New York City experience. What may well be duplicated, however, is the movement in professional employee collective bargaining from the assertion and achievement of "bread and butter" goals to the negotiation of demands focused on professional objectives.

The New York City experience demonstrates that, over time, the subjects introduced and negotiated by the parties increased in variety and in breadth. Many subjects that in the early 1960s were viewed as nonnegotiable, managerial prerogatives ultimately made their way into the bargaining process. Additionally, once the union succeeded in achieving its basic short-run demands for improved salaries and working conditions, it concentrated its efforts on injecting itself into the policy-making processes of the educational system. Thus the development of the bargaining relationship between the UFT and board of education brings into sharp focus the difficulties inherent in the task of defining the proper scope of bargaining for professional public employees. It also points to a dilemma that is significant to those concerned with shaping the boundaries and directions of public sector bargaining: How can the government employer preserve the crucial aspects of its public trust and mission to serve the community and, simultaneously, satisfy the demands presented by professional employee unions?

THE PROBLEM OF DEFINITION

Underlying the difficulty in defining the scope of bargaining for professional employees is the problem, alluded to earlier, of distinguishing between "policy matters" and "salaries and working conditions." No less difficult is the differentiation between "policy" matters and "professional" issues. In education, decisions about curriculum, textbook selection, and methodology are simultaneously "policy" issues for the school board and "professional" questions for the faculty. In urban schools the issue of teacher transfers raises particularly thorny problems because it involves working conditions, policy decisions, and the public interest. Although teachers regard transfer policies as working conditions, school boards may decide, as a matter of educational policy, that they want a high proportion of experienced teachers in ghetto schools. Experienced teachers, however, often are reluctant to leave upper middle class schools for a position in the "inner city." Since ghetto areas generally have a much higher proportion of inexperienced, substitute, and inferior teachers than middle class schools, the problem becomes acute, often involving pressures from civil rights and other community groups, as well as from the teachers' union. Teachers do not want transfer decisions made unilaterally under the guise of educational policy; but school boards frequently refuse to negotiate about transfer policies that are based on educational considerations.[60] Compounding the problem is the involvement of parent, often minority, groups, which want to improve their ghetto schools and participate in setting policies affecting the staffing and operation of such schools.

New York's laws do not expressly deal with the problem of community organizations whose interests diverge from those of public employees, although the Public Employment Relations Board has recognized the problem of the public interest and has determined that matters affecting the mission of a public enterprise are not mandatory subjects of negotiations.[61] As has been suggested, however, the line between matters of exclusive and traditional concern to employees and matters vital to the public interest is a fuzzy one. For example, in the White Plains Firefighters decision, PERB stated:

> It is the City alone which must determine the number of firemen it must have on duty at any given time. It cannot be compelled to negotiate with respect to this matter. However, there are many ways in which the schedules of individuals and groups of firemen may be manipulated in order to satisfy the City's requirement for fire protection. It is this manipulation of the schedules . . . which is involved in the Fire Fighters demand. Within the framework which the City may impose unilaterally that a specified number of Fire Fighters must be on duty at specified times, the City is obligated to negotiate over the tours of duty of the Fire Fighters within its employ.[62]

PERB's decision indicates how elusive the boundary is between negotiable and nonnegotiable subjects. And, as has been discussed, the problem of distinguishing between working conditions, professional issues, and policy matters is even more difficult in public services that traditionally have been characterized by a high degree of public participation and where the employees are now attempting to achieve fuller professional status through the collective bargaining process. The tension between professional employee aspirations and the constraints of the traditional employer-employee relationship doubtless will grow as professional services provided by government become generally considered a right rather than a privilege.

NOTES

1. Allan J. Mayer, "Who's in Charge?—Public Employe Unions Press for Policy Role; States and Cities Balk," Wall Street Journal, Sept. 7, 1972, p. 1.
2. In September 1967 the New York Times reported that the United Federation of Teachers was seeking not only "a large money package" but also "insisting on a voice in policy matters, such as a contract clause that would bring smaller classes." New York Times, Sept. 7, 1967, p. 30 col. 2. Three days later the Times noted that the major demands raised by the UFT in its negotiations

with the Board of Education, in addition to pay increases, were
reduced teaching loads, expansion of the More Effective Schools program (developed by the UFT and aimed at improving the education
of children in ghetto area schools), and authorization for teachers
to remove disruptive students from their classrooms. New York
Times, Sept. 10, 1967, p. 79, col. 1.

    3. Arvid Anderson, "Public Employees and Collective Bargain-
ing: Comparative and Local Experience," in Thomas Christensen,
ed., Proceedings of New York University Twenty-First Annual Conference on Labor, May 1968 (New York: Matthew Bender, 1969),
p. 465.

    4. On Jan. 11, 1967 Herbert Haber, director of the New York
City Office of Labor Relations, stated that negotiations with the
Social Service Employees Union were continuing but that difficulties
had developed around the union's demands to bargain over what the
city considered to be policy matters. New York Times, Jan. 12,
1967, p. 43, col. 8. One of the major problems was ". . . whether
certain union demands were negotiable. The city has taken the view
that the union is trying to bargain on policy matters that should
rest strictly with the administration," reported the Times. The
Times quoted Mitchell Ginsberg, then head of the Welfare Department, as saying, "We feel strongly that labor management contracts
cannot be the vehicle by which reform in public welfare is accomplished." New York Times, Jan. 14, 1967, p. 17, col. 4. Shortly
after the signing of the 1963 contract between the UFT and New York
City Board of Education, conflict developed over the interpretation
of certain provisions in the agreement. Charles Cogen, a union
spokesman, suggested that, according to the preamble of the contract,
teachers would play an active role in forming school policy. Nation's
Schools, Oct. 1963. Calvin E. Gross, superintendent of schools, disputed this statement, stating that although the contract called for
monthly meetings between his staff and union representatives, this
did not mean that teachers would share any administrative responsibility. Nation's Schools, Nov. 1963, p. 80. This point was emphasized in the concluding section of the 1967-69 contract, which stated:
"The Board has complete authority over the policies and administration of the school system which it exercises under the provisions
of the law. . . ." Agreement Between the UFT and Board of Education, 1967-69, at 75.

    5. Michael H. Moskow, Teachers and Unions (Philadelphia:
Wharton School, 1966), pp. 181-82.

    6. Victor Gotbaum, quoted in Mayer, op. cit.

    7. Frederick R. Livingston, "Collective Bargaining and the
School Board," in Sam Zagoria, ed., Public Workers and Public
Unions (Englewood Cliffs, N.J.: Prentice-Hall, 1972), p. 68.

    8. Donald H. Wollett, "The Coming Revolution in Public School
Management," 67 Michigan Law Review 1017, at 1022 (1969).

9. Archie Kleingartner, "Impact of Professionalism on Scope of Bargaining in the Public Sector," in Scope of Bargaining in the Public Sector—Concepts and Problems, Report, U.S. Labor Management Services Administration, Paul Prasow and others (Washington: U.S. Government Printing Office, 1972).

10. It is not important for the present discussion to determine whether or not the public employment professions—teaching, social work, nursing—are "true" professions, in terms of the various sociological standards that have been proposed. This writer agrees with those sociologists who suggest that a profession is not an "all or nothing" status. Rather, as Ernest Greenwood suggests, occupations may be placed along a continuum; at one end are those characterized by little professionalism, and at the other pole are those recognized as full professions. In this way occupations may be viewed as more or less "professionalized." It is maintained here that the public sector "professions" may be placed near the full professional end of the continuum, and that many of the collective bargaining activities of these occupational groups are aimed at gaining greater recognition as professions and at increasing the professionalization of the occupation. See Ernest Greenwood, "Attributes of a Profession," Social Work 2, no. 3 (July 1957): 44-55; also in Howard H. Vollmer and Donald L. Mills, eds., Professionalization (Englewood Cliffs, N.J.: Prentice-Hall, 1966).

11. Joan Weitzman, "The Professional Test: Can Teachers Pass?" Industrial and Labor Relations Forum 7, no. 4 (Dec. 1971): 1-40. In preparation of this chapter, the author has made use of portions of her essay, with the kind permission of the editor of Forum.

12. Abraham Flexner, "Is Social Work a Profession?" quoted in Myron Lieberman, Education as a Profession (1956), p. 4.

13. Ernest Greenwood, "Attributes of a Profession," in Vollmer and Mills, op. cit., p. 14.

14. Ibid., p. 16.

15. Archie Kleingartner, Professionalism and the Salaried Worker Organization (Madison: Industrial Relations Research Institution, University of Wisconsin, 1967), p. 83.

16. Amitai Etzioni, Modern Organizations (Englewood Cliffs, N.J.: Prentice-Hall, 1964), pp. 76-77.

17. Kleingartner, "Impact of Professionalism," p. 35.

18. Ibid., p. 40.

19. The NEA Guidelines for Professional Negotiation, expressing the official NEA position on scope of bargaining, states that all matters of joint concern to a local teachers' organization and school board should be subjects of negotiation. These issues include, "but are not limited to, setting standards in employing professional personnel, community support for the school system, inservice training of personnel, class size, teacher turn-over, personnel policies,

salaries, working conditions, and communication within the school system." National Education Association, Guidelines for Professional Negotiation (Washington, D.C.: NEA, 1965), p. 2. Charles Cogen, former president of the American Federation of Teachers, expressed a similar view about the scope of negotiations: "We would place no limit on the scope of negotiations. . . . Obviously, class sizes, number of classes taught, curriculum, hiring standards, textbooks and supplies, extra-curricular activities—in fact anything having to do with the operation of the school is a matter for professional concern and should thus be subject to collective bargaining." Charles Cogen, "Changing Patterns of Employment Relations," in Robert Doherty, Joan Egner, and William Lowe, eds., The Changing Employment Relationship in Schools (Ithaca: New York State School of Industrial and Labor Relations, Cornell University, 1966), p. 17.

20. New York Times, Aug. 21, 1971, p. 17, col. 3.

21. Ibid., Jan. 17, 1967, p. 20, col. 4.

22. Nickels v. Board of Education of Imlay City Community Schools, File no. 1546, Lapeer County Circuit Court, Jan. 3, 1967.

23. Albert Shanker, quoted in Mayer, op. cit.

24. Joint School Dist. #8, City of Madison v. Wisc. Employment Relations Board, 37 Wisc.2d 483, 155 N.W.2d 78 (1967).

25. 381 U.S. 676, 85 S. Ct. 1596 (1965).

26. Ibid. at 691, 85 S. Ct. at 1602.

27. 155 N.W.2d at 82.

28. Ibid. at 82-83.

29. Note, "Collective Bargaining and the Professional Employee," 69 Columbia Law Review 277, at 289 (1969).

30. David Selden, quoted in Mayer, op. cit.

31. Anderson Federation of Teachers v. School City of Anderson, 252 Ind. 558, 251 N.E.2d 15 (1969), certiorari denied, 399 U.S. 928 (1970).

32. Ibid. at 565.

33. Wollett, op. cit. at 1030.

34. Charles S. Benson, "Economic Problems of Education Associated with Collective Negotiations," in Robert Doherty, Joan Egner, and William Lowe, eds., The Changing Employment Relationship in Public Schools (Ithaca: New York State School of Industrial and Labor Relations, Cornell University, 1966), p. 2.

35. Ben-David, "Professionals and Unions in Israel," 5 Industrial Relations 48, at 63 (1965).

36. Jerome Lefkowitz, "Unionism in the Human Services Industries," 36 Albany Law Review 603, at 620 (1972).

37. "Collective Bargaining and the Professional Employee" at 291.

38. Ibid. at 291-92.

39. George Taylor, "The Public Interest in Collective Negotiations in Education," in Stanley Elam, Myron Lieberman, and

Michael Moskow, eds., Readings on Collective Negotiations in Public
Education (Chicago: Rand McNally, 1967), p. 13.
40. Robert Doherty, "Teacher Bargaining, Resource Allocation
and Representative Rule," Industrial Relations Research Association
Proceedings (Winter 1969), p. 253.
41. Robert Doherty, "Letter to a School Board," Phi Delta
Kappan 48, no. 6 (Feb. 1967): 276; also reprinted as New York State
School of Industrial and Labor Relations, Reprint Series no. 208.
42. National Education Association, Addresses and Proceedings
of the 103rd Annual Meeting (Washington, D.C.: NEA, 1965), p. 413.
43. AFT Goals, 1966.
44. Doherty, "Teacher Bargaining," p. 254.
45. C. Jencks, "Private Schools for Black Children," New York
Times Magazine, Nov. 3, 1968, p. 30.
46. Ibid., pp. 132-33.
47. Quoted in Charles R. Perry and Wesley A. Wildman, The
Impact of Negotiations in Public Education (Worthington, Ohio: Jones,
1970), p. 166.
48. Mrs. Radke, quoted in E. Wright Bakke, "Teachers, School
Boards and the Employment Relationship," in Robert Doherty, ed.,
Employer-Employee Relations in the Public Schools (Ithaca: New
York State School of Industrial and Labor Relations, Cornell University, 1967), p. 43.
49. Robert Dahl, quoted in Harry H. Wellington and Ralph K.
Winter, "Structuring Collective Bargaining in Public Employment,"
79 Yale Law Journal 805, at 854-55 (1970).
50. Lefkowitz, op. cit. at 628.
51. John T. Dunlop and James J. Healy, Collective Bargaining
(1955), p. 53.
52. Wellington and Winter, op. cit. at 859.
53. Ida Klaus, "The Evolution of a Collective Bargaining Relationship in Public Education: New York City's Changing Seven-Year
History," 67 Michigan Law Review 1033 (1969).
54. Ibid. at 1043.
55. Ibid. at 1045.
56. Ibid. at 1046.
57. Ibid. at 1047-48.
58. Ibid. at 1051.
59. Ibid at 1058. The More Effective School program was a
plan essentially developed by the union that included

. . . reduced class size, an increased ratio of classroom
teachers and guidance counselors to pupils, additional
small-group instruction, increased funds for educational
materials and school supplies, and frequent consultation
between faculty and administrators on teaching and school
supervision goals and techniques. Moreover, each school

222

was to have on its staff a full-time team of experts in pupil-personnel services. . . . The Union regarded itself as the real architect of the fundamental design of the plan. It had looked upon the plan as the best "school-by-school approach to the problem of providing schools which can really educate children in spite of any environmental handicaps they may bring to school with them." Ibid. at 1060.

The second difficult issue was the union's demand for "a program to remove disruptive children from regular classrooms." The major goal was to give teachers substantial discretion in determining whether a student's behavior was so disruptive as to necessitate his removal from a regular classroom to other facilities more "appropriate" to his educational needs.

60. Myron Lieberman, "Collective Negotiations by Teachers," in Myron Lieberman and Thomas H. Patten, When School Districts Bargain, Public Personnel Association, PERL #5 (1968), p. 9.

61. See Matter of City School District of the City of New Rochelle, 4 PERB 3060 (1971).

62. Matter of City of White Plains, 4 PERB 3074 (1971).

The scope of bargaining does not embrace a finite collection of subjects; the bargaining area is constantly evolving and changing dimensions to accommodate new issues in need of negotiation.

In immature bargaining relationships the scope of negotiable subjects tends to be limited because (1) management generally resists bargaining on any but the most fundamental conditions of employment, and (2) unions are unable to develop a strong consensus on and commitment to issues other than those that will benefit all members.

There is evidence in both the public and private sectors that as bargaining relationships mature, the scope of negotiable subjects expands.[1] Charles Perry and Wesley Wildman write that in private employment, the scope of bargaining has widened to include an ever-increasing range of management policies and practices. Accompanying this expansion in scope has been change in the basic union emphasis in nonwage areas from individual grievances to organizational security and control over hiring, transfers, promotions, and layoffs to hours of work, worker effort, job security, and worker income maintenance.[2]

Similar tendencies can be traced in public sector bargaining. Initially union concerns are focused on "bread and butter" issues: improved wages, hours, basic working conditions, and fringe benefits. Public employers exhibit great concern for traditional managerial prerogatives and assert that the concepts of lay control, illegal delegation of authority, and government sovereignty should restrict the scope of bargaining. As public acceptance of collective bargaining increases, however, and court and public labor board decisions clarify the meaning of good faith bargaining, the range of negotiable items tends to widen. Additionally, the professional aspirations of many groups of public employees, coupled with the pressures they are able to exert as sole providers of "essential" services, lead to bilateral determination of an increasing number of economic and noneconomic issues.

It has been suggested herein that meaningful collective bargaining requires a wide scope of bargaining; that professional employees have legitimate concerns regarding not only the standards and development of their professions, but also the mission and quality of their employing agencies; and that government agencies, in many instances, would better serve the public interest were they to listen to and negotiate on the demands of their staffs.

It also has been recognized, however, that there are certain matters that should not be considered negotiable; these involve the very functions of government and the administrative power to determine how operations are to be conducted. The scope-of-bargaining problem thus boils down to the question of how to balance the interests of public employees, which include their right to influence policy and the conditions of their employment, with the interests of a society that today is relying on government more heavily than ever before to furnish necessary services and bring about broad social improvements.

A NEED FOR LEGAL RESTRICTIONS?

Efforts to limit the scope of bargaining stem primarily from an apprehension that institutionalizing private employment practices in the public sector may ultimately pervert the political process.[3] Inasmuch as decisions concerning allocation of resources in the public sector are political, and not merely economic, it has been contended that collective negotiations in government may give labor a way to impose its will on others less highly organized in the quest for government funds.[4]

This writer believes, however, that collective bargaining can be made compatible with the public interest. In fact, if public employees are viewed as one of the many constituencies to which government is responsible, collective bargaining can be considered simply as the means that this group uses to participate in the political process. In other words, if resource allocation in government is the result of a "tug-of-war" among many interest groups, which most agree it is, then collective bargaining in public employment is every bit as legitimate as lobbying, voting, and other political activities that are utilized to influence public policy and government functions. Of course society must stay on the alert, lest self-serving interests subordinate the general welfare. But this caveat does not negate modern political reality: that in our society competition among differing interest groups provides the fuel on which our political democracy operates.

With respect to the scope of bargaining, this writer believes that neither a statutory definition of bargainable matters (other than wages, hours, and terms and conditions of employment) nor a statutory description of nonnegotiable management rights is necessary. The collective bargaining agreement that has been negotiated by the parties at any one time should contain the appropriate definition of management rights and bargainable matters—even if the contract is silent on what constitutes management rights. If one assumes that management initially has all rights and is limited only by the provisions of the agreement, then it reserves all residual rights. In the future, however, it may qualify these residual rights by agreeing to the addition of other items to the agreement. Certainly management's goal will be to limit the bargaining area, while employee organizations will try to widen it. This is the very heart of collective bargaining, and it is doubtful that the issues can be statutorily determined for all time to come.[5] Thomas Plunkett writes:

> The desire for a clear-cut definition of the bargaining area and the rights of management stems, I suspect, from the traditional requirement of public management for clarity and definition. But we are dealing here with a highly volatile area of human relations, which in the social and economic change and flux of modern society cannot really be rigidly defined. Moreover, if collective bargaining is going to have any meaning, flexibility must be the keynote. There must be a good deal of free wheeling at the bargaining table if agreements are to be arrived at which have any potential for acceptability.[6]

Collective bargaining has been referred to as a therapeutic process,[7] one that should allow the parties to address fully all problems affecting the bargaining relationship. Furthermore, statutory management rights provisions unnecessarily rigidify public sector labor relations because only the legislature can relax the restrictions of excluded subjects. Public employers express a legitimate concern in trying to protect their right to manage government operations efficiently, but the best approach is to make management rights clauses a subject of bargaining between the parties, as is done in the private sector. This is preferable to permitting a public employer simply to refuse to discuss a subject on the ground that it is statutorily nonbargainable. As Justice John Harlan wrote in his dissenting opinion in Borg-Warner:

> The bargaining process should be left fluid, free from intervention . . . leading to premature crystallization of labor agreements into any one pattern of contract provisions, so that these agreements can be adapted through collective

bargaining to the changing needs of our society and to the changing concepts of the responsibilities of labor and management.[8]

It is true, as Sabghir reported in his study,[9] that "a substantial number of items have been included in contracts that in the past have undoubtedly been viewed as managerial prerogatives." This statement, however, applies to any item or condition of employment that becomes subject to negotiations. Whenever a negotiated contract replaces unilateral determination of working conditions, there is a limit on management's right to act independently.

Of course the practical impact of this limitation will be influenced by the range of subjects negotiated. Generally, the more comprehensive the agreement, in terms of the number of items covered, the more restricted management's right to act unilaterally. But the nature of the specific items also is significant. A contract may include a provision on class size, but the contract language may be merely exhortative or rhetorical—memorializing the status quo or requiring little affirmative action on the part of school management. Alternatively, an agreement may cover only a few subjects but severely restrict managerial discretion on those items.

After reviewing a representative sample of school agreements on file with the New York State Public Employment Relations Board, Myron Lieberman reported to the Fleischmann Commission that collective bargaining has resulted in certain limitations on managerial authority in school districts. But, he emphasized:

It seems equally clear . . . that the basic problem is not management agreement to items which are not terms and conditions of employment. It is management agreement to indefensible terms and conditions of employment. The best way to solve these problems is by upgrading the quality of school management at the negotiating table. Legislation that would have eliminated the ill-advised clauses [noted in the sample contracts studied] would also have ruled out meaningful negotiations on significant terms and conditions of employment.[10]

Lieberman concludes that, in general, managerial authority has not been irreparably weakened as a result of collective negotiations. Most of the contract items that excessively limit management discretion raise personnel rather than legislative issues. Moreover, any attempt through a statutory management rights clause to prevent public employers from ceding vital managerial prerogatives probably would so limit bargaining as to make it ineffective.

How, then, can public employers prevent the encroachment by unions upon their rights and responsibilities to direct government

227

enterprises in the public interest? A simple answer, and one not offered facetiously, is to bargain "hard." Public employers concerned about maintaining flexibility and authority should be able to reject unreasonable or unworkable union proposals—and give adequate reasons for doing so.

Public employers also should start using collective bargaining as a mechanism to gain concessions from employees regarding improved quality and quantity of services.[11] Robert Doherty emphasizes this point with respect to school negotiations, but it certainly is applicable to all government employers:

> . . . school boards can use the bargaining table to press their own demands. Increasingly, as has been shown in private bargaining . . ., employers are exploiting the bargaining situation to win concessions. Wage increases and improved job security, for example, can be traded off for adjustments in seniority provisions and work rules. And some employers are finding that through bargaining they are able to make changes in employment conditions they wouldn't have dared to propose unilaterally. Their workers, unionized or not, would have not stood still for them.[12]

Assuredly employment conditions in public employment do not exactly parallel those in heavy industry. Yet public and private employment are analogous at least with respect to employees' desires to achieve improvements in working conditions and employers' efforts to improve their enterprises through increased efficiency and reduced operating costs. Collective negotiations can help both sides of the bargaining table to reach their goals.

New York City's experience with productivity bargaining provides a noteworthy illustration of this point. In 1970 New York City became the first municipality to make productivity improvements a bargaining demand in labor negotiations. Basically the city adopted the position that pay increases would not be granted unless they were justified by commensurate increases in productivity. The city developed a comprehensive productivity program that strives to improve the quantity and quality of public service provided per dollar invested in the following ways:

- Where output is easily measurable—such as the number of tons of refuse collected per Sanitation truck shift—it aims to reduce unit costs and improve the responsiveness of city operations.
- Where output it very hard to measure, such as in providing police or fire protection—it aims to improve the deployment of resources so as to maximize the proba-

bility that our resources will be available at the time and place they are needed most.

- It aims to improve the organization and processing procedures of government, particularly through imaginative use of computers.
- And it aims to develop new technological devices and approaches . . . to make the best possible use of every increasingly expensive city employee.[13]

As might have been expected, the city's public employee unions initially found the concept of productivity bargaining a difficult one to swallow. The city, however, adopted a hard bargaining stance. It ultimately sought the unions' cooperation in implementing its productivity targets, and it agreed to substantial wage increases—in exchange for productivity gains. The city's real achievement, however, has been in forcing the municipal unions to recognize that collective bargaining is a "two-way street": the public is entitled to improved government service in exchange for its ever-increasing taxes, which are used, in part, to finance collective bargaining agreements.[14]

This writer is keenly aware that union pressures for bilateral determination of policy matters as well as working conditions often are enormous and that the scope of bargaining must have some limits lest unions usurp the managerial role. It has been argued herein, however, that remedies for these problems lie substantially within the bargaining process itself, especially if employer negotiators present their own bargaining demands and persist in rejecting union demands that are deemed inappropriate. The task is difficult and requires great perseverance, but that is what collective bargaining is all about—certainly public employee unions have exhibited a mastery of this art.

In urging hard bargaining and rejection of statutory restrictions of the scope of negotiations, Myron Lieberman offers a persuasive argument:

After all, every undesirable limitation on board authority in a collective agreement has been agreed to by school management somewhere; otherwise, the limitation would not exist. Finally, the fact that negotiations sometimes result in undesirable limitations on board prerogatives is not per se a valid reason for rejecting the process. We do not deprive citizens of the right to vote merely because they sometimes vote for incompetent public officials. Similarly, we should be careful not to deprive parties of the right to meaningful negotiations merely because they sometimes agree to undesirable limitations on board prerogatives.[15]

FIBREBOARD RE-EXAMINED

Suggestions to keep the bargaining process unencumbered by the imposition of statutory management rights clauses and exhortations directed at public employers to bargain hard do not, however, resolve the major scope-of-bargaining problem. Issues will still be raised at the bargaining table that one side or the other will absolutely refuse to negotiate on the ground that it does not fall within the phrase "wages, hours, and terms and conditions of employment." Hence the question remains: What is the fine line that separates working conditions from managerial policy? Must this line be drawn, and, if so, according to what criteria?

Having given considerable thought to this question and the various expert and legislative responses to it, this writer is drawn back to the U.S. Supreme Court's decision in Fibreboard Paper Products,[16] which points the way toward a sensible approach to the issue of negotiability in public employment.

Although Fibreboard was discussed in some detail in Chapter 2, it may be worthwhile to recall the highlights of the Court's decision. Stated most generally, the Court ruled that Fibreboard was obligated under Section 8(a)(5) of NLRA to bargain with the Steelworkers Union about the company's decision to subcontract on-premises maintenance work then being performed by members of the bargaining unit. Chief Justice Earl Warren, writing for the majority, first examined the statutory wording and determined that subcontracting fell "well within the literal meaning of the phrase 'terms and conditions of employment.'" Fibreboard's decision to subcontract led to the termination and replacement of employees who were capable of doing the subcontracted work. Thus, the company's decision to contract out the maintenance work substantially affected its employees' job security. Although the company considered subcontracting to be a means of achieving savings through a reduction of the work force, decreased fringe benefits, and lower wages, its unilateral decision was, in effect, a breach of the duty to bargain about such matters with the employees' representative.

In addition to this rationale, however, the Court relied on two very practical considerations. Its inquiry was basically two-pronged: First, was it likely that through collective negotiations the union could contribute to the solution of the particular problem faced by the employer? Second, did industrial experience indicate that the subject in question was, in fact, dealt with in negotiations?

With regard to the first question, the Court believed that the ability of collective bargaining to mitigate the adverse impact on union members of an employer's decision affecting their employment is adequate reason for subjecting that decision to the bargaining process. Justice Warren emphasized that because the company was concerned about lowering the costs of its maintenance operation and little else (there was no capital investment involved and no change in basic plant operations), collective bargaining might have led to a compromise that would have satisfied the company and, simultaneously, been acceptable to the union. One of the major purposes of the NLRA, stated Justice Warren, was to encourage peaceful settlement of disputes by subjecting labor-management controversies to the mediatory influence of negotiation. Moreover, "collective negotiation has been highly successful" in achieving peaceful accommodation of conflicting interests:

> To hold, as the Board has done, that contracting out is a mandatory subject of collective bargaining would promote the fundamental purpose of the Act by bringing a problem of vital concern to labor and management within the framework established by Congress as most conducive to industrial peace.[17]

As to the second aspect of its test, the Court concluded:

> Experience illustrates that contracting out in one form or another has been brought, widely and successfully, within the collective bargaining framework.[18]

Among the Court's citations in support of this conclusion was a Department of Labor survey of 1,687 collective bargaining agreements that indicated that "approximately one-fourth (378) contained some form of a limitation on subcontracting."[19] Conceding that although industrial bargaining practices are not determinative, the Court held that it is proper to consider such experience in judging the propriety of including a particular subject within the scope of mandatory bargaining.

In his often-quoted concurring opinion, Justice Potter Stewart expressed reservations about the broad implications of the Court's decision. His concurrence rested on the specific facts in the Fibreboard case. As to management decisions "which are fundamental to the basic direction of a corporate enterprise or which impinge only indirectly upon employment security," Justice Stewart believed they should be excluded from the bargaining area defined by Section 8(d) of the NLRA. Referring to the situation in Fibreboard, he stated:

> This kind of subcontracting falls short of such larger entrepreneurial questions as what shall be produced, how capital shall be invested . . . or what the basic scope of the enterprise shall be. In my view, the Court's decision in this case has nothing to do with whether any aspects of those larger issues could under any circumstances be considered subjects of collective bargaining.[20]

As was discussed in Chapter 2, the post-Fibreboard line of cases has sparked lively debate among practitioners of labor law, the NLRB, and the courts.[21] The Board has tended to rely on the literal wording of the NLRA, as did the majority in Fibreboard, while the courts have embraced the cautious dicta of Justice Stewart's opinion regarding the limitations of the decision.[22]

The actual meaning of the Fibreboard decision, however, emerges through a conjunctive reading of the Warren and Stewart opinions. Read together, the majority and concurring opinions suggest a pragmatic solution to the real question underlying the Fibreboard controversy: What kinds of issues can realistically be settled through collective negotiations? The practical lesson of Fibreboard has been partially submerged by the NLRB-circuit court rivalries concerning the proper interpretation of the Supreme Court's decision, particularly with respect to an employer's duty to bargain on plant closings.* Careful consideration of the case, however, suggests an approach to the problem of determining bargainable subjects that may be especially well suited to the public sector.

To reiterate, the Fibreboard decision did not turn merely on the fact that subcontracting of bargaining unit work fell within the definition of "wages, hours, and terms and conditions of employment," and was therefore a mandatory subject of bargaining. The decision

---

*
Essentially the Board has held that almost any decision that terminates bargaining unit work falls within the phrase "terms and conditions of employment." The duty to bargain over such decisions, argues the Board, does not interfere with management's right to operate its enterprise.

The judicial response to Fibreboard has been a narrow reading of the decision. Justice Stewart's opinion has been a major source of guidance, and the courts also have looked to the following language in Chief Justice Warren's majority opinion:

> The factors of the present case illustrate the propriety
> of submitting the dispute to collective negotiation. The
> Company's decision to contract out the maintenance work
> did not alter the Company's basic operation. . . . No
> capital investment was contemplated; the Company merely
> replaced existing employees with those of an independent
> contractor to do the same work under similar conditions
> of employment. 379 U.S. at 213.

The courts have seized upon this passage to support the view that management decisions affecting basic operations, plant closings, and capital investments are managerial prerogatives outside the scope of mandatory bargaining.

rested more firmly on the Court's consideration of the probability that collective negotiations could facilitate compromise between the employer and union and on the study of industrial practices to learn whether similar subcontracting decisions were being negotiated with employee representatives.[23] The suggestion this writer puts forward, therefore, is: Why not make a similar twofold inquiry in public sector disputes concerning the scope of bargaining? Public employment provides an excellent environment for such a case-by-case method of determining the appropriate scope of negotiations. Issues such as the number of firemen manning a fire truck, the case load assigned to social workers, class size, student discipline, and school calendar clearly relate to wages, hours, and working conditions. At the same time they touch upon managerial prerogatives and policy questions. These hybrid issues are not neatly dichotomized into mandatory or permissive categories; and the Fibreboard two-pronged approach therefore presents a sensible method of resolving questions that essentially boil down to a balancing of conflicting, yet legitimate, interests.

Bargaining Practices

Under the Fibreboard test, any subject whose negotiability is contested must be run through a two-step analysis, one step of which focuses on bargaining experience. As will be noted in Chapter 11, class size provisions, for example, have been included in over half the contracts throughout New York state. Although such provisions vary in comprehensiveness, a wide range of class size issues have been negotiated into agreements: average class sizes, maximum class sizes, subject area and grade level averages and limits, class size ranges, teacher-pupil ratios. Other researchers also have reported the appearance of class size in negotiated agreements: Perry and Wildman, for instance, in their nationwide study of school districts, found that "many" contracts contained provisions on this subject.[24]

The Sabghir findings also provide a source of information regarding public sector bargaining practices. Although Sabghir presents statistics covering various categories of public employees, for purposes of illustration only his findings with respect to teacher contracts are presented here. The list below ranks several subjects in terms of the absolute number and percentage of contracts in Sabghir's sample that included them.[25]

Length of school day	36	(65 percent)
School calendar	31	(65 percent)
Class size	31	(56 percent)

233

Teacher assignment procedures	30	(54 percent)
Teacher evaluation procedures	28	(50 percent)
Association use of school facilities	28	(50 percent)
Teacher work load	24	(43 percent)

Sabghir also refined these statistics by categorizing the same subjects on the basis of school district size.

	Enrollment under 3,000 (in percent)	Enrollment more than 3,000 (in percent)
School day	55	76
School calendar	42	72
Class size	39	76
Teacher assignment procedures	42	68
Teacher evaluation procedures	39	64
Association use of school facilities	32	72
Teacher work load	26	64

Thus, Sabghir's study indicates that overall 56 percent of the sample contracts contained class size provisions. When school districts were broken down by size, it became apparent that contracts in larger school districts were more apt to include class size clauses than were contracts in smaller districts. The same finding was reported with respect to the six other subjects on the list.

The purpose of referring to Sabghir's study was not primarily to review his precise findings but, rather, to demonstrate how bargaining parties, when involved in a dispute concerning the negotiability of particular subjects, might study the bargaining experience of other unions and employers in comparable government agencies. A review of bargaining practices may yield not only statistics as to how many contracts contain provisions on a particular subject, but also new ideas not considered previously by the parties as ways to resolve their dispute.

Probability of Settlement as a Result of Negotiations

The likelihood of resolving differences through bargaining of course involves a much more abstract inquiry. Undoubtedly it is less difficult to examine the bargaining practices of other parties than it is to predict the extent to which a public employer and union will be able to settle their particular problem through negotiations. The Supreme Court recognized that collective bargaining cannot guarantee settlement but nevertheless stated:

[Although] it is not possible to say whether a satisfactory solution could be reached, national labor policy is founded upon the congressional determination that the chances are good enough to warrant subjecting such issues to the process of collective negotiation.[26]

Thus the obligation to bargain should rest on whether the issue itself may be suitable for discussion at the bargaining table.

Again using class size as an example, one can make a strong argument that problems relating to or stemming from this issue might well be resolved through negotiations. Local teacher organizations often make class size bargaining demands in response to particular class size difficulties in their schools that, through earnest negotiating sessions, could be resolved to the satisfaction of both administration and faculty. Although school boards tend to reject collective bargaining on this subject because substantial class size improvements may ultimately mean large capital outlays for new classroom facilities, experience indicates that compromises can be worked out in the form of team teaching of larger classes, allowing more preparation time to compensate for larger classes, negotiating class size ranges instead of absolute limits for certain subjects and grade levels, providing extra compensation for teachers assigned to particularly large classes, using closed circuit television and other audio-visual devices to teach certain classes, and negotiating larger class sizes in subjects conducive to relatively high enrollment so that class sizes can be reduced in remedial areas or in subjects requiring very individualized instruction. In addition, as will be discussed in Chapter 11, the study of class size contract clauses indicated that in some districts, teachers are satisfied with merely rhetorical or procedural contract provisions. The psychological satisfaction of gaining even a flexible clause in the contract may be all the teachers seek—or at least what they are willing to accept.

The same arguments apply, of course, when the public employer is about to make unilateral changes involving issues arguably negotiable, as in Fibreboard. At the least, the union should be afforded the opportunity to offer alternative solutions to the employer's problem or demonstrate why the employer's proposed solution is ill-advised or unworkable. Furthermore, unions do on occasion make substantial concessions when fully apprised of an employer's difficulties and the reasons underlying management's proposed course of action. And even where the collective bargaining results only in the securing of impact benefits, those concessions are inextricably related to decision bargaining. If a city, for instance, is planning to curtail a particular operation, the union may insist that the operation not be phased out until all employees are relocated in other municipal jobs. These considerations pertain to the decision itself and cannot be raised if bargaining is restricted to impact questions.[27]

Most importantly, one must remember that the Fibreboard obligation to bargain does not require agreement. Once the employer has fulfilled his duty to negotiate, he still may proceed with whatever plans he has in mind. Additionally, the employer has the right to bargain in good faith for future unilateral control of the contested subject.

The application of the Fibreboard test discussed herein would give the public employer the same latitude as his private sector counterpart. Regardless of whether the employer or union initiates the proposal, once the bargaining obligation has been met, no further concession is required.

Robert Doherty and Walter Oberer suggest that "almost all" issues of sufficient concern to teachers to warrant their arising in negotiations should be discussed at the bargaining table. Although this position may go even a step beyond what is suggested here, their reasoning is equally applicable to the twofold Fibreboard approach and worth quoting fully. Elaborating on their suggestion, Doherty and Oberer state:

> This does not mean that school boards should relinquish the power of unilateral determination as to all such subjects broached by the teachers; it means rather that they should not adopt a "management rights" stance which precludes discussion, but should instead "demand" (i.e., bargain hard) for a retention of unilateral control over matters which, in their judgment, merit such. This approach . . . would achieve four desirable ends. (1) It would preclude the bitterness and strife resulting from refusal even to discuss an issue on its merits. (2) It would require the board representatives to attempt to justify on a basis of reason their desire for maintaining unilateral control over the particular matter, thus rendering less tenable a position of "power for the sake of power." (3) It would expose the board to the potential enlightenment resulting from a full hearing of the teachers' views. (4) It would, reciprocally, expose the teachers to the potential enlightenment resulting from a full hearing of the board's views.[28]

LIMITATIONS OF THE FIBREBOARD APPROACH

It was stated earlier that the true meaning of Fibreboard emerges only through a conjunctive reading of the majority and concurring opinions. The test that has been suggested for application in the public sector is drawn solely from Chief Justice Earl Warren's opinion, but it must be balanced by a recognition of the limitations suggested in Justice Potter Stewart's opinion.

1. The issue must vitally affect employees. In Fibreboard, Justice Stewart stated that decisions infringing only indirectly upon employee job security should not be mandatory bargaining subjects. This expression reflected his view that issues with merely a marginal or potential effect on employees should be excluded from the bargaining table, lest the employer be unduly hampered in running his business. This reasoning is applicable to the public sector as well. A public employer's decision, for instance, to purchase office equipment from one supplier as opposed to another has at best an indirect effect on employees and is not an issue to be negotiated. Thus, issues that do not materially or significantly affect employees' working conditions cannot be considered terms and conditions of employment.

2. The issue must be within the expertise of both parties. Although professional employees rarely will concede that any matter involving their employment or employing agency is beyond their expertise, there are technological and managerial problems that should be resolved away from the bargaining table. Although a union may be able to offer constructive ideas about the value of a new computer, or the disadvantages of a labor-saving machine, in most instances it will lack the scientific knowledge to insist in bargaining that an employer accede to its proposals. This does not excuse the employer from bargaining on the impact, if any, of the technical decision upon employees' working conditions. Nor does it imply that a public employer should refrain from meeting on and discussing, outside of negotiations, matters of managerial discretion.

3. If the reasons or circumstances underlying a public employer's refusal to bargain on a union's demand are so compelling or beyond its control that collective bargaining could not alter the employer's position, negotiations should not be mandatory on that specific demand. Because of the structure of government—the separation of powers, legislative possession of taxing and budget powers, public referenda on certain issues, need for legislative approval prior to implementation of certain contract provisions—a public employer cannot always agree unconditionally to union demands. Thus, in a school district where all classroom facilities were being used to capacity, and the teachers' organization proposed that the employer agree to build a new school wing so that class sizes could be reduced, even if the employer's negotiator earnestly wanted to accede to the demand, the matter would be beyond his control. The teachers' proposal could not be a required subject of bargaining. Only the taxpayers, through a referendum, could authorize such school construction. The most, therefore, that the employer could

237

agree to do would be to recommend to the voters that a new building program be enacted or a new school bond issue passed. To put this limitation in Hanslowe-Oberer terms, the teachers' demand to build a new school wing would be a proposal on which the employer could make only ineffective, as opposed to effective, recommendations; it would, therefore, constitute only a permissive subject of bargaining.[29]

Another example pertains to relevant constitutional and statutory provisions. Where law, constitutional provisions, and decisions of the highest state court have clearly removed items from the scope of bargaining, they cannot be negotiated. In negotiations the party refusing to bargain on an item on the basis of this reason has the burden of proving, however, that the item is judicially, constitutionally, or legally barred from negotiations.

These three limitations represent a realistic balance to the practical Fibreboard scope-of-bargaining test. They insure that decisions fundamental to the basic direction of a government agency will not be subject to compulsory bargaining, but they do not preclude a wide scope of bargaining. With the passage of time, the application of the two-pronged bargaining-practices and likelihood-of-resolution test probably will result in mandatory bargaining on an increased number of issues. But insisting that a subject directly affect employees, requiring mutual expertise on a bargainable subject, and recognizing a public employer's lack of full discretion to act on certain issues will protect the employer from unnecessary restrictions in directing government services. Moreover, these limitations will preserve the public interest by respecting the structure of government and acknowledging the legislature and body politic as the repositories of final authority.

WESTWOOD COMMUNITY SCHOOLS

In a significant scope-of-bargaining decision, the Michigan Employment Relations Commission (MERC) applied a two-part test similar to the Fibreboard test. Westwood Community Schools[30] could thus become a landmark decision representing a pioneering departure from the application of the Borg-Warner doctrine to public employment.

In Westwood, MERC was asked to determine whether the school calendar establishing the beginning and terminating dates of the school operating period was a mandatory subject of bargaining. The Commission noted that until then, disputes involving negotiable subjects had been determined on a case-by-case basis, using the traditional private sector distinctions between mandatory, permissive, and illegal subjects of bargaining. Under this approach, however, "the elusive question" still remained concerning the meaning of "other terms and conditions of employment" and "Borg-Warner provided little help."

The Commission therefore turned to Fibreboard and suggested that two tests flowed from the Supreme Court's decision: (1) Is the subject of such vital concern to both labor and management that it is likely to lead to controversy and industrial conflict? (2) Is collective bargaining appropriate for resolving such issues?

In Westwood the employer argued that establishment of the opening day of school was a management prerogative. The Education Association contended that the employer's unilateral act affected a vital employee interest: teachers' planning for summer activities. This conflict, said MERC, was a classic confrontation between management rights and employee interests—a conflict that could be reconciled by balancing the interests involved.

In determining that the matter was a mandatory subject of bargaining, the Commission stated that neither the Michigan statutes nor the regulations of the Michigan Department of Education interfered with a holding that the school calendar was mandatorily negotiable. The Commission also cited the Wisconsin Supreme Court decision in City of Madison v. WERB,[31] which held that the school calendar had a direct and intimate relationship to teachers' salaries and working conditions. Thus the "substantial interest" of teachers in planning their summer outweighed any claim of interference with the employer's right to manage the school district. Furthermore, added the Commission, the duty to bargain did not command agreement, only good faith negotiations on the subject.

The Westwood decision is provocative in that MERC not only developed a Fibreboard-type of test to determine the bargainability of a subject, but also suggested that the mandatory-permissive dichotomy was inappropriate for the public sector:

A balancing approach to bargaining may be more suited to the realities of the public sector than the dichotomized scheme . . . used in the private sector. [The private sector] scheme prohibits the use of economic weapons to compel agreement to discuss non-mandatory subjects of bargaining, but strikes are permissible once the point of impasse concerning mandatory subjects of bargaining is reached. Economic force is illegal in the public sector in Michigan. . . . [I]n the public sector, economic battle is to be replaced by invocation of the impasse resolution procedures of mediation and fact finding.

An expansion of the subjects about which the public employer ought to bargain, unlike the private sector, should not result in a corresponding increase in the use of economic force to resolve impasses. In the absence of legal public sector strikes, our only proper concern in the area of subjects of bargaining is whether the employer's management functions are being unduly restrained. All bargaining has some limiting effect on an employer.

Therefore, we will not order bargaining in those cases where the subjects are demonstrably within the core of entrepreneurial control. Although such subjects may affect interests of employees, we do not believe that such interests outweigh the right to manage.[32]

Thus the Westwood decision puts forth the interesting proposition that the duty and scope of bargaining in public employment should be wider—and not narrower—than in the private sector. Because, theoretically, public employees do not strike and there is, therefore, no legal use of economic weaponry to force a settlement, the necessity of limiting the scope of mandatory bargaining is greatly reduced. The public employer must simply negotiate in good faith and, where it believes a union's demand is unacceptable, remain steadfast in its refusal to agree.

This approach is relatively novel in the public sector. Derek Bok and John Dunlop, however, have also suggested that the method of settling bargaining disputes should affect the scope of negotiations:

In the end, the scope of bargaining will be influenced by the procedures adopted to resolve impasses in negotiations. If public employees are permitted to strike, the range of bargainable topics presumably should be closely confined. . . . If disputes are settled by the more reasoned process of fact finding and arbitration, on the other hand, the scope of negotiation may be somewhat broader, although there will still be many important matters excluded from bargaining on the ground either that they should be within the province of management or that they seem more suited to resolution through the political process.[33]

A caveat must be expressed, however, with respect to both the Westwood and Bok and Dunlop approaches. As Harry Edwards comments in his discussion of MERC's decision, the validity of the Westwood broadened scope depends not only on the existence but also on the effectiveness of the strike prohibition. In jurisdictions where strikes are legally permitted, Westwood may not be applicable. And in those states where strikes are banned but the prohibition is not enforced, adoption of the Westwood test may give public employee unions an unfair advantage at the bargaining table, enabling them to force negotiations on subjects that would not be mandatory bargaining items in the private sector.[34]

The Westwood decision also may raise other questions. MERC's two-part test involves a more speculative inquiry than does the literal Fibreboard test. Whereas one prong of both tests is almost identical (the likelihood of resolution at the bargaining table [Fibreboard] versus the appropriateness of collective bargaining to resolve a dispute [Westwood]), MERC apparently rejected the bargaining practices test in favor of the "vital concern" standard. Under the bargaining practices test, although the parties might initially have to resolve problems regarding what sources to use as indicators of bargaining practices, once this is accomplished, their investigation should yield relatively objective data on which they can rely. As noted above, the second part of the Fibreboard test is necessarily more subjective, although not impossible to apply.

Under the Westwood test neither inquiry can produce "hard" data; and difficult controversies may arise as to whether a disputed subject is of such vital concern as to produce conflict and whether collective bargaining is appropriate for resolving the dispute. In other words, both prongs of the Westwood test involve predictions that can be verified only after the fact. Other problems may develop because, again unlike the approach suggested here, Westwood was vague about how managerial items would be defined. The Commission simply stated that a balancing test would be used, and subjects "demonstrably within the core of entrepreneurial control" would not be mandatorily bargainable. No criteria were developed, however, that could be applied to determine if an item were such a "core" subject. The limitations spelled out in the test suggested earlier go further in specifying what standards will be applied to exclude an issue from the scope of bargaining.

Despite the questions that Westwood raises, the decision is exciting because it represents a relatively new and realistic approach to defining subjects of bargaining in the public sector. It is to be hoped that the weaknesses of the decision will not preclude its effective application to scope-of-bargaining disputes in Michigan. Certainly the bargaining experience under Westwood will be worth watching.

ADJUDICATING SCOPE-OF-BARGAINING DISPUTES

It frequently occurs that in the course of good faith negotiations, a dispute develops between the parties concerning the negotiability of one or more subjects. In many jurisdictions such disputes are resolved only through the filing, by one or both parties, of a refusal-to-bargain charge with the appropriate adjudicatory agency. This improper practice charge route to a determination of bargainability often is costly, lengthy, and psychologically upsetting to a bargaining relationship because the losing side may get its "wrists slapped," so to speak, although its bargaining conduct is not, in any other respect, characterized by bad faith.

A more sensible legal process for resolving scope-of-bargaining questions involves a declaratory judgment procedure. Wisconsin, for example, uses this kind of procedure to settle negotiability questions when there is a genuine difference of opinion between the parties as to whether subjects fall within the meaning of "terms and conditions of employment" or are nonnegotiable matters of policy. The New York City Collective Bargaining Law (NYCCBL) also separates disputes over the scope of bargaining from conduct that is subject to improper practice charges of refusal to bargain in good faith. Under 1173-5.0(2) of the NYCCBL, the Board of Collective Bargaining is empowered "on the request of a public employer or certified or designated employee organization to make a final determination as to whether a matter is within the scope of bargaining." This power is separate and apart from the Board's authority to prevent and remedy employer and employee improper practices that include the refusal to bargain in good faith.

SCOPE OF BARGAINING AND THE USE OF MEDIATION AND FACT-FINDING

Only the public employment relations boards, subject to review by the courts, can issue scope-of-bargaining decisions based on law. Neutrals involved in impasse resolution, however, can and should play a role in settling disputes concerning negotiability.

Mediators certainly should be free to grapple with scope-of-bargaining controversies. Their sole objective is to help the parties reach agreement; and assuming that they do not knowingly encourage negotiations on statutorily prohibited demands, their actions need not be controlled by legal theories on bargainability.

The role of the fact-finder is more problematical, but I believe that he should be empowered to make recommendations regarding the negotiability of subjects where neither party has already filed an improper practices charge. The approach of the fact-finder, however, should apply the bargainability test suggested above for public employment relations boards and the courts. Inasmuch as a fact-finder's recommendation may eventually reach a public employment relations board in an unfair labor practice case, consistency of approach or criteria used in determining an item's negotiability would be valuable. Also, even in cases not ultimately reaching an employment relations board, some degree of uniformity of approach among fact-finders would be important.[35]

There are several reasons for encouraging fact-finders to make recommendations on the bargainability of disputed subjects. The first has to do with the underlying purposes of most public employee bargaining laws, which are to establish the rights of public employees to bargain on their terms and conditions of employment and to develop peaceful methods of dispute settlement. Fact-finding in a scope-of-bargaining dispute may clarify questions regarding the good faith bargaining duty and facilitate a voluntary settlement by providing the parties with the well-reasoned, unbiased views of a neutral. Second, a persuasive fact-finding recommendation on an issue's negotiability may spare the parties from the expensive, lengthy, and irritating litigation that generally accompanies the filing of a formal improper practice charge. Sabghir points out that although fact-finders lack authority to hear or determine improper practice charges in the absence of such a charge, their recommendations on a subject's bargainability could serve three useful purposes:

(1) They may settle the matter by convincing the parties that the issue is or is not bargainable.

(2) They may settle the matter without the long delay inevitable in matters involving improper practice charges.

(3) They may prove helpful to a public employment relations board in the event that the matter is subsequently filed as a formal charge.[36]

There are, of course, potential difficulties in permitting fact-finders to participate in the resolution of negotiability disputes. The most obvious one concerns what prejudicial effect, if any, upon the negotiating relationship would be produced by a fact-finder's recommendations on a subject that a public employment relations board ultimately determined to be nonnegotiable.[37] Second, to what extent might the fact-finding process be undermined, if at all, by a subsequent board decision upholding a subject's negotiability whereas a fact-finder previously found it nonnegotiable?

The potential problems in allowing both fact-finders and employment relations boards to determine negotiability should not be overlooked. It is to be hoped, however, that application of the same criteria by both fact-finders and employment relations boards would encourage consistent findings. Public employment relations boards would also be expected to maintain close communications with their fact-finders engaged in this delicate type of dispute resolving. Finally, if it is frankly acknowledged that fact-finding on negotiability is an experiment, as are so many procedures in public sector labor relations, the technique could be tried, and eliminated in the event of administrative and policy difficulties resulting from its use.

George Taylor wrote that "some of the most critical labor-management conflicts" have arisen over the differentiation "between those subjects which can and should be co-determined in negotiations and those subjects which should remain subject to unilateral determination by the management. . . . The dilemma is sharp in the joint determination of conditions such as class size, contact hours with students, assignment to special classes and to difficult schools, . . . and a host of other similar matters."[38] The public interest, suggested Taylor, requires that public employers and employee organizations be ready to use fact-finding with recommendations in impasses

> . . . between school agencies responsible for educational standards and teacher organizations responsible for enhancing the rights of teachers. The public is entitled to an informed but outside judgment in such cases because this is public business.[39]

NOTES

1. Charles R. Perry and Wesley A. Wildman, The Impact of Negotiations in Public Education (Worthington, Ohio: Jones, 1970), p. 112.
2. Ibid.
3. Harry Edwards, "The Emerging Duty to Bargain in the Public Sector," 71 Michigan Law Review 885, at 916 (1973).
4. Harry H. Wellington and Ralph K. Winter, The Unions and the Cities (Washington, D.C.: Brookings Institution, 1971), pp. 29-32.
5. Thomas J. Plunkett, "The Seminar in Retrospect," in Kenneth O. Warner, ed., Collective Bargaining in the Public Service: Theory and Practice (Chicago: Public Personnel Association, 1967), p. 188.
6. Ibid., pp. 188-89.
7. Edwards, op. cit. at 916.
8. 356 U.S. 342, at 358-59 (1957).
9. Irving Sabghir, The Scope of Bargaining in Public Sector Collective Bargaining, report sponsored by PERB, Oct. 1970.
10. Myron Lieberman, The Impact of the Taylor Act upon the Governance and Administration of Elementary and Secondary Education. Report to the Fleischmann Commission, June 1971, p. 58. Emphasis added.
In a similar vein Robert Helsby, in his testimony before the Fleischmann Commission, stated:

> Three years of negotiating experience has demonstrated a distinct lack of labor relations skill on both sides of the table, but particularly on the part of school districts. While there is some evidence that such skills may be increasing, it cannot be said that the negotiating skills of the parties are increasing at a desirable rate.

Robert D. Helsby, "Impact of the Taylor Law on Public Schools, 1968-1970," remarks before the New York State Commission on the Quality, Cost, and Financing of Elementary and Secondary Education, Syracuse, Apr. 2, 1971.

11. See "Weinberg Advocates 'Hard Bargaining' Rather Than More Experiments to Solve Future Public Sector Labor Disputes," 486 GERR B-1 (Jan. 15, 1973).

12. Robert Doherty, "Letter to a School Board," Phi Delta Kappan 48, no. 6 (Feb. 1967): 275, also published as ILR Reprint Series no. 208 (Ithaca: New York State School of Industrial and Labor Relations, Cornell University).

13. See John V. Lindsay, "Overview of the New York City Productivity Program," address given at Productivity Conference: The New York City Approach to Improving Productivity in the Public Sector, New York City, Mar. 19, 1973.

14. For additional information on the scope of productivity bargaining in New York City, see Herbert L. Haber, "Productivity Bargaining," speech delivered at the Productivity Conference: The New York City Approach to Improving Productivity in the Public Sector, New York City, Mar. 19, 1973, also excerpted in LMRS Newsletter 4, no. 6 (June 1973). Also see Edward K. Hamilton, Productivity Program: Annual Summary Fiscal Year 1972-1973 (New York: Office of the Mayor, July 26, 1973); Damon Stetson, Productivity: More Work for a Day's Pay, report published by Labor-Management Relations Service, November 1972; Barry Newman, "The Vice Squad: New York City Seeks 'More Bang for Buck,' Pushes for Efficiency," Wall Street Journal, Apr. 12, 1973, p. 1.

15. Lieberman, op. cit., p. 65.

16. 379 U.S. 203 (1964).

17. Ibid. at 211.

18. Ibid.

19. Ibid. at 212 n. 7.

20. Ibid. at 225.

21. See Robert J. Rabin, "Fibreboard and the Termination of Bargaining Unit Work: The Search for Standards in Defining the Scope of the Duty to Bargain," 71 Columbia Law Review 803 (1971); "The Development of the Fibreboard Doctrine: The Duty to Bargain over Economically Motivated Subcontracting Decisions," 33 University of Chicago Law Review 315 (1965); Elihu Platt, "The Duty to Bargain as Applied to Management Decisions," 19 Labor Law Journal 143 (1968); "The Scope of Collective Bargaining," 74 Yale Law Journal 1472 (1965); Harry H. Wellington, Labor and the Legal Process (New Haven: Yale University Press, 1968).

22. See, for example, NLRB v. Adams Dairy, 350 F.2d 108 (CA 8, 1965); Hawaii Meat Company v. NLRB, 321 F.2d 397 (CA 9,

1963); Royal Plating and Polishing Company, 350 F.2d 191 (CA 3, 1965); Ozark Trailers, Inc., 161 NLRB 561 (1966); NLRB v. Transmarine Navigation Corp., 380 F.2d 933 (CA 9, 1967); NLRB v. Thompson Tractor Co., 406 F.2d 698 (CA 10, 1969).
23. Rabin, op. cit. at 821.
24. Perry and Wildman, op. cit., p. 206.
25. Sabghir, op. cit., p. 64.
26. 379 U.S. at 214.
27. Rabin, op. cit. at 826.
28. Robert E. Doherty and Walter E. Oberer, Teachers, School Boards, and Collective Bargaining: A Changing of the Guard (Ithaca: New York State School of Industrial and Labor Relations, Cornell University, 1967), p. 92.
29. Kurt L. Hanslowe and Walter E. Oberer, "Determining the Scope of Negotiations Under Public Employment Relations Statutes," 24 Industrial and Labor Relations Review 432, at 438-39 (1971). For a discussion of this concept, see Chapter 7.
30. 7 MERC Lab. Ops. 313 (1972).
31. Joint School Dist. #8, City of Madison v. Wisconsin Employment Relations Board, 37 Wisc.2d 483, 155 N.W.2d 78 (1967).
32. 7 MERC Lab. Ops. 313, at 320-21.
33. Derek Bok and John Dunlop, Labor and the American Community (New York: Simon and Schuster, 1970), p. 327.
34. Edwards, op. cit. at 923.
35. Hanslowe and Oberer, op. cit. at 440.
36. Sabghir, op. cit., p. 121.
37. Hanslowe and Oberer, loc. cit.
38. George Taylor, "The Public Interest in Collective Negotiations in Education," in Stanley Elam, Myron Lieberman, and Michael Moskow, eds., Readings on Collective Negotiations in Public Education (Chicago: Rand McNally, 1967), pp. 19-20.
39. Ibid.

PART

III

THE ISSUE OF
CLASS SIZE:
APPLYING THEORY IN
THE PUBLIC SCHOOL
SETTING

In no other field does the controversy over scope of bargaining appear in sharper relief than in public education, where increased teacher demands for a stronger role in school management have led to heightened apprehension among school administrators and boards of education. The subject of class size has become particularly controversial because of its implications for both employers and employees.

It has been said that "few aspects of his professional life concern a teacher more than the size of the class he teaches, other than the size of his paycheck."[1] Yet class size is a class example of a subject that is difficult to define. Bernard Donovan, the former superintendent of schools in New York City, described the uncertainty about class size as a negotiable subject when he asked:

What is class size? Is it a working condition or is it a matter of educational policy? If you think it over, you will find it is a gray area. There are elements in it that have to do with a teacher's working conditions, in terms of load. But there are also elements in it that have to do with the proper number of children that can be handled for a specific type of subject under particular circumstances.[2]

Collective bargaining agreements containing class size provisions are not uncommon. But in the controversial West Irondequoit decision the New York Court of Appeals, affirming the Appellate Division and PERB, held that class size was a policy matter and, therefore, not a mandatory subject of bargaining. The court agreed with PERB that school boards may make class size decisions unilaterally and must negotiate only on the impact of such decisions.

West Irondequoit has raised many questions about the negotiability of "hybrid" items that are important not only to public employers and their employees, but also to the community. The chapters that follow provide an in-depth analysis of the widespread controversy concerning the negotiability of class size. Chapter 10 compares and contrasts several notable judicial and agency decisions dealing with the bargainability of class size. Chapter 11 reports the results of a survey that I conducted in several hundred school districts in New York regarding the issue of class size. I undertook this study because I wanted to understand how the parties are dealing with a controversial issue in the absence of clear statutory language defining its negotiability. It is only through an appreciation of the views and bargaining experience of the parties themselves that we can measure the success of the Taylor Law, the problems of professional employee negotiations, the meaning of PERB's decisions, and the need, if any, for changes in present public policy regarding the scope of bargaining in public employment.

Class size is significant not merely because it is frequently proposed as a bargaining demand or because several labor boards and courts have ruled on its negotiability. Rather, class size is just one of many similar "gray area" subjects that often attempt to make their way into the negotiations process but end up bringing the system to a standstill. Thus an understanding and resolution of the class size issue perhaps will point the way toward solving other scope-of-bargaining disputes.

NOTES

1. David Selden, "Class Size and the New York Contract," Phi Kappa Deltan, Mar. 1964, p. 283.
2. Bernard Donovan, "Speaking for Management," in Stanley Elam, Myron Lieberman, and Michael Moskow, ed., Readings on Collective Negotiations in Public Education (Chicago: Rand McNally, 1967), p. 288.

250

CHAPTER

10

THE ISSUE OF
CLASS SIZE AND ITS
DECISIONAL HISTORY

Class size can be approached and discussed on at least three different levels. To many school employers it is an issue involving educational policy. In contrast, many teachers view it primarily as a professional issue, which should be negotiable because it vitally affects teachers' functions, their job satisfaction, and the educational environment in their classrooms. David Selden writes:

A machine operator is paid by the hour to operate his machine and so long as he is not "sweated" and operates his machine under satisfactory working conditions, his only legitimate concern is with his wages and other benefits. In industry the nature and quality of the product are not the concern of the worker. . . . But a teacher is not merely a production worker. He is a professional. In addition to having a responsibility to maintain professional standards, the size of the class he teaches has a definitive effect on the amount of satisfaction he derives from practicing his profession.[1]

Class size also may be viewed primarily as a working condition, which is negotiable because of its effect on teachers' work loads. As will be illustrated later in this chapter, most of the administrative agency and court decisions upholding the negotiability of class size rely on this argument that class size is a condition of employment. Albert Shanker concedes that class size may be approached either as a professional question of "what's best for the children" or as a problem of resource allocation. "But, obviously, handling a lot of kids is more difficult than handling just a few. And in this way, it's most certainly a working condition,"[2] that should be subject to collective bargaining.

The basis on which class size is argued by teacher representatives is, indeed, often crucial to their success in negotiating it into a contract.* But, as Robert Doherty comments, whether teachers are "motivated by sound educational principles or the very human desire to avoid strain and irritation, they want classes to be of reasonable size."[3] And it is this basic objective that underlies most collective bargaining demands for class size contract provisions.

IS THERE AN OPTIMUM CLASS SIZE?

The question of class size is not new in education. In the fourth century B.C., Herodotus spoke of "classes of thirty." Two thousand years later Comenius stated that it was not only possible, but necessary for the benefit of both pupils and teachers, for one teacher to teach several hundred pupils at once.[4] In contrast, John Locke believed that a teacher with a class of 50 or more could not be expected to teach students properly in other than their books.[5]

Modern research findings indicate that there is not one best class size, nor one best teacher-pupil ratio. There is evidence sugfesting that the teacher's personal outlook and his teaching methods are significant factors that make a difference as class size varies. Additionally, the competence of the teacher, the nature of the learners, the subject taught, and the classroom space in which the learning takes place are important variables affecting what and how children learn. Research findings suggest that in order to produce optimal results—for both students and teachers—"the size of the class must be appropriate to the intellectual-emotional needs of the pupils, the skills of the teacher, the type of learning desired, and the nature of the subject matter."[6]

The 1968 report of the New York State Teachers Association (NYSTA) Special Committee on the Duty of Teachers stated, nevertheless, that certain factors "appear to have stood the tests of rigorous research analysis":

- Small classes generally offer opportunity for teachers to know their students better.
- Small classes are likely to encourage teachers to use a greater variety of instructional materials and methods.

---

*This writer believes that school boards may be more willing to agree to contract language on class size when the issue is presented as a working condition, for to bargain on it as a matter of professional concern represents a sharing of authority regarding educational policy decisions, which many school boards may find unacceptable.

- Small classes are likely to provide opportunities for experimentation, innovation, and invention.[7]

A report prepared by the British Columbia School Trustees Association also indicated that research findings support the hypothesis that reduced class size improves teacher morale.[8] The NEA concurred with this conclusion:

> . . . research studies have substantiated the argument that class size affects teacher morale. Teachers generally tend to prefer small classes. The majority of teachers also prefer small classes with no help to large classes with outside help. Slightly over four of every five teachers responding to a 1967 NEA Research Division nationwide poll thought they could teach more effectively in classes of 25 to 30 pupils with all the clerical and nonteaching duties to do themselves than in classes of 40 to 50 pupils with a full-time non-professional aide to do those tasks.[9]

There are numerous research studies on class size, and more should be undertaken if there is to be greater understanding of the relationship between class size, student learning, and teaching effectiveness. But because this chapter deals with class size as a labor relations issue, and not as a subject of educational science, the writer has not included in the text discussion on the various theories and studies concerning optimum class size. The appendixes, however, include questionnaires on class size and tables on mean class size in New York state.

For purposes of this study, it is important for the reader simply to know that the class size issue is of special interest today for several reasons. Reduced class size is being increasingly emphasized as a variable in the education of culturally disadvantaged children (such as Head Start). The experimentation with new methods of teaching and staff utilization also have implications for class size. Such experimentation has involved team teaching, flexible scheduling, independent study, use of teacher aides, and computer-assisted instruction. And perhaps most important, class size is an issue of current concern because teacher representatives are increasingly demanding to discuss and bargain about it. While the significance of class size may not yet have been scientifically determined, many teachers agree with David Selden that "nothing is a greater determinant of educational quality than the number of students assigned to a teacher."[10]

With this background in mind, the increasing appearance of class size in lists of teachers' bargaining demands and the significance of agency and court decisions concerning class size become more understandable. An analysis of these recent decisions follows.

WEST HARTFORD EDUCATION ASSOCIATION v. DECOURCY

In West Hartford Education Association v. DeCourcy,[11] the Connecticut Supreme Court determined, among other issues, the negotiability of teacher work load, length of school day, school calendar, extracurricular activities, binding arbitration of grievances, and class size.*

The West Hartford Education Association had sought a declaratory judgment, an injunction, and other relief, alleging that the West Hartford board of education had failed to bargain in good faith on these issues. The parties had reached an impasse over these topics in bargaining sessions for both their 1969-70 and 1970-71 contracts. After the Association began litigation in September 1970, the parties reached agreement on a 1970-71 contract, but not on the listed subjects, which the Association contended were conditions of employment and, therefore, mandatory subjects of bargaining.

The Court's decision, written by Judge Ryan, reviewed the conduct of the board of education during two years of negotiation with the Association. The school board was absolved of all charges of improper practices, mostly because of insufficient evidence to support the complaints. The Court did, however, determine the negotiability of the disputed subjects and outline a public employer's expected role in teacher bargaining.

The Court first noted that under law, local school boards were traditionally empowered to act as policy-makers on behalf of the state and for the local community on educational matters.[12] But in its 1951 landmark decision, Norwalk Teachers Association,[13] the Court held that under a school board's broad grant of authority, it could negotiate about wages and employees' working conditions, even in the absence of a specific bargaining statute. Contrary to what had been contended, the Court in Norwalk held that such bargaining did not represent an illegal delegation of authority. In 1965 the state legislature adopted the Teacher Negotiation Act, which provides that the parties shall negotiate with respect to "salaries and

---

*Other issues in the case were whether the school board failed to bargain in good faith by (1) not making counterproposals on the alleged working conditions; (2) asserting that the topics could be unilaterally settled by board action; and (3) stating that these issues should be included in the "board prerogatives" clauses of the collective bargaining agreement.

254

other conditions of employment." The Court noted that the duty to bargain encompassed an obligation to "confer in good faith with respect to salaries and other conditions of employment, or the negotiation of an agreement, or any question arising thereunder and the execution of a written contract. . . ." The duty did not, however, require the making of any concessions.

In contrast with the word "salaries," the statutory phrase "other conditions of employment," the Court noted, is unclear and in need of judicial interpretation. "To find the legislative intent we look at the wording of the statute, its legislative history and its policy."[14]

Traditionally Connecticut labor relations laws have closely followed the Taft-Hartley Act, under which parties bargain over "rates of pay, wages, hours of employment, or other conditions of employment." The Court noted that the Connecticut Labor Relations Act requires collective bargaining with respect to "rates of pay, wages, hours of employment or other conditions of employment," while the state's Municipal Employee Relations Act, which excludes teachers from coverage, imposes a duty to confer in good faith on "wages, hours and other conditions of employment." The Connecticut Teacher Negotiation Act, however, requires bargaining on "salaries and conditions of employment," significantly omitting the phrase "hours of employment." This omission evidenced a legislative judgment, according to the Court, that "teachers' hours of employment determine students' hours of education and that this is an important matter of educational policy" that should rest exclusively with the school board.[15] Under any definition, observed the Court, the issues of the length of school day and school calendar would be conditions of employment. But inasmuch as they are directly related to "hours of employment," the Court concluded that these items were expressly excluded from the Act, and therefore were not mandatory bargaining subjects.

In directing its attention toward defining the phrase "conditions of employment," the Court commented that many educational policies have an impact on teachers' conditions of employment and the converse is equally true; "there is no unwavering line separating the two categories."[16] But in contrast with the Oregon statute, for instance, which specifically limits negotiations for teachers to "salaries and related economic policies affecting professional services," the Connecticut legislature deliberately chose the broad phrase "and other conditions of employment." On the other hand, Connecticut legislators were not ready to go as far as the Washington lawmakers, who included in their statute a long list of negotiable items, such as curriculum, textbook selection, in-service training, hiring and assignment practices, to name but a few. According to the Connecticut Supreme Court:

The use of the phrase "conditions of employment" reflects a judgment that the scope of negotiations should be relatively broad, but sufficiently flexible to accommodate the changing needs of the parties.[17]

Referring to the private sector, the Court noted that the scope of bargaining has consistently been expanded by the NLRB and the courts. In Fibreboard,[18] however, Justice Potter Stewart, in his concurring opinion, emphasized that decisions lying at the "core of entrepreneurial control" were not mandatorily negotiable. According to the Connecticut Supreme Court, "The notion that decisions concerning the 'core of entrepreneurial control' are solely the business of the employer appears to have a special kind of validity in the public sector."[19] In teacher-school board relations, educational policy parallels the private sector concept of decisions lying at the "core of entrepreneurial control." At the least, stated Judge Ryan, matters of educational policy are those that are "fundamental to the existence, discretion and operation of the enterprise."[20]

Bearing this in mind, one must also consider the policies underlying the Teacher Negotiation Act. The Court made it clear that the collective bargaining act divests boards of education of some of the discretion that they otherwise could exercise. Through this enactment the legislature "expressed the view that the state's best interest will be served" in that the need for teachers to resort to illegal and disruptive tactics would be reduced.

The Court emphasized that the statute does not force the parties to agree or make concessions. The school board retains the power to say "no"—as long as it does not bargain in bad faith. "But, by submitting matters to the mediating influence of negotiations, it is more likely that disputes will be resolved. . . ." This, stated the Court, was the theory behind the Act.

Having developed this background, Judge Ryan turned to the question of class size and teacher load.* The school board argued that both of these subjects were matters of policy within the exclusive province of the board of education. The Court agreed that "policy questions" were involved in these subjects, but stated that this was not decisive:

> Class size and teacher load chiefly define the amount of work expected of a teacher, a traditional indicator of whether an item is a "condition of employment." Further,

---

*The stipulation defined class size as the number of pupils assigned to a class. Teacher load meant the number of teaching classes per day or per week and the number of different preparations per day or per week.

we see from the stipulation that of the ninety-six group teacher contracts negotiated in Connecticut, sixty-one have class size provisions and forty-one have provisions dealing with teacher load. The legislative intent is clear that class size and teacher load are mandatory subjects of negotiation.[21]

WASHOE COUNTY SCHOOL DISTRICT

Under Nevada's Local Government Employee Relations Act, enacted in 1969, local government employers are obligated to negotiate in good faith with employee organizations on wages, hours, and conditions of employment. The Act contains, however, a management rights clause that recognizes that public employers maintain the responsibility under appropriate situations to direct employees; to hire, promote, suspend or terminate employees; to maintain efficiency of governmental operations; "and to otherwise proceed to do such things, without reference to negotiation or any negotiated agreement which, if not done, would seriously infringe upon the local government employer's duty to the taxpayers. . . ."[22]

In The Matter of the Washoe County School District and The Washoe County Teachers Association,[23] the Nevada Local Government Employee-Management Relations Board was called upon to determine the negotiability of several issues including class size.*

The school board urged a very strict interpretation of the statutory management prerogatives provisions, one that would have precluded negotiations on matters related to wages, hours, and working conditions if these matters also involved any items enumerated under the management prerogatives clause. Unpersuaded by this argument, the Employee-Management Relations Board concluded that the legislature did not intend such an interpretation of the law:

> Public employees by this Act have been denied perhaps their most valuable right—the right to strike. On the other hand, the local government employer has retained

---

*The issues were class size, professional improvement, student discipline, school calendar, teacher performance, special student program, differentiated staffing, teacher load, and instructional supplies. All of the contested issues were found negotiable except special student program. The Board did not categorize subjects as either mandatory or permissive. Its decision implies, however, that a negotiable item is one about which the parties must bargain at one another's request.

the right to define and recognize particular bargaining units, the right to exercise its management prerogative without reference to negotiation or any prior negotiated agreement.[24]

The Board reasoned that any matter significantly related to wages, hours, and working conditions is negotiable, "whether or not said matters also relate to questions of management prerogative."[25]

The Board's discussion of each contested item was extremely brief; and with respect to class size, it tersely noted that class size was "significantly" related to wages, hours, and working conditions because student density "directly affects a teacher's workload including the required hours of preparation and post-class evaluation."[26] Class size also related to working conditions, inasmuch as it affects the teacher's control and discipline problems, teaching and communication techniques, and the total amount of work required for a fixed compensation.

Having offered this succinct discussion, the Board simply held that class size was a negotiable subject. The decision is interesting, nevertheless, in that the Nevada Employee-Management Relations Board, even though mindful of the state law's management rights clause, saw class size quite clearly as a bargaining subject. In contrast, the Connecticut Supreme Court, despite its decision upholding the negotiability of class size, admitted that the issue was a hybrid one, falling in the "gray area" between clearly negotiable and nonnegotiable subjects.

Moreover, as is demonstrated by the cases discussed below, at least some public employee relations boards and state courts view class size as a subject too tightly intertwined with educational policy to impose upon the employer a duty to negotiate on it.

HAWAII STATE TEACHERS ASSOCIATION AND DEPARTMENT OF EDUCATION

One of the more complex decisions concerning class size was rendered by the Hawaii Public Employment Relations Board (HERB) in Hawaii State Teachers Association and Department of Education.[27] In this case HERB was called upon to resolve the parties' dispute over the interpretation and implementation of an article in their collective agreement. Because the precise contract language was crucial in the decision, relevant excerpts are presented here:

A. Class Size Committee
1. A joint class size committee shall be established within four weeks after the execution date of this

agreement. . . .[T]he committee is authorized to
hear and investigate complaints regarding class size
and make recommendations to the Superintendent
regarding such complaints.
2. Beginning with the 1972-73 school year, the Employer agrees to reduce the average class size ratio
by approximately one student. Based on current Employer practices, this would require a minimum of
250 positions for the 1972-73 school year. These
positions shall be in addition to presently allocated
positions, additional positions required by increased
student enrollment and additional teaching positions
created in the preparation time and duty-free lunch
provisions of this Agreement.
The current proportion (15%) of these positions
shall be used to increase the number of counselors
and bargaining unit supportive positions. . . .
3. It is recognized in fulfilling the obligations set
forth . . . that bargaining unit positions allocated
for the school year 1972-73 shall not be reduced
to implement said articles.
4. The committee established . . . above shall have
the authority to recommend to the Superintendent
specific changes to be made to accomplish the
objectives set forth in Sections A-2 and A-3. . . .[28]

The Department of Education, without prior negotiation or consultation with the Hawaii State Teachers Association (HSTA), began
to move 169.5 classroom positions, used as "support" positions,
back into the classroom.* The Department maintained that its plan
was a partial implementation of the agreement to reduce the classroom teacher:pupil ratio. HSTA, however, filed a prohibited practice
charge against the Department of Education (DOE), alleging that
DOE violated the terms of the agreement, and thereby interfered
with, restrained, and coerced its employees in the exercise of rights
guaranteed under Chapter 89 of the Hawaii Public Employment Relations Act.† HSTA's specific contentions were that (1) Article VI A(2)
required that 250 new teaching positions be hired in order to decrease
the average class size ratio by approximately one student; (2) DOE's
intentions to abolish the 169.5 supportive positions in order to place

---

*"Support" positions were counselors, traveling art and music
teachers, and other supportive services to regular classroom
teachers.
†Under the Hawaii bargaining law, violation of the terms of a
collective bargaining agreement is a prohibited practice.

the teachers occupying them into classroom teaching positions would not satisfy the contract language calling for 250 new positions; (3) such DOE action would violate Article VI A(3) of the contract; and (4) the elimination of temporary support positions, which were used as a means to provide preparation periods or duty-free lunch periods, would adversely alter the working conditions of many teachers and would violate Article VI, X and Y of the contract, which provided for preparation periods and duty-free lunches, as well as Article XX C, which provided for maintenance of teacher benefits existing prior to the effective date of the agreement.

The DOE contended that there had been no breach of Article VI, since that article interfered with the employer's rights and responsibilities and was, therefore, void and in violation of Section 89-9(d) of the bargaining law and the state constitution. Section 89-9(d) provides, in part:

> Excluded from the subjects of negotiations are matters of classification and reclassification, retirement benefits and the salary ranges and the number of incremental and longevity steps now provided by law. . . . The employer and the exclusive representative shall not agree to any proposal which would be inconsistent with merit principles . . ., or which would interfere with the rights of a public employers to (1) direct employees; (2) determine qualification, standards for work, the nature and contents of the examinations, hire, promote, transfer, assign, and retain employees in positions and suspend, demote, discharge, or take other disciplinary action against employees for proper cause; (3) relieve an employee from duties because of lack of work or other legitimate reason; (4) maintain efficiency of government operations; (5) determine methods, means, and personnel by which the employer's operations are to be conducted; and take such actions as may be necessary to carry out the missions of the employer in cases of emergencies.

The constitutional provision in question states:

> The board of education shall have power, in accordance with law, to formulate policy, and to exercise control over the public school system through its executive officer, the superintendent. . . .

Additionally, the DOE argued that HSTA's interpretation of the contract language on class size was invalid because it would have involved a "cost item" under Section 89-2, which required legislative approval and appropriation of funds. The DOE also denied violation of other contract articles.

HERB was initially faced with a jurisdictional problem: Could it rule in a case involving interpretation and application of an agreement that itself provided for final and binding arbitration? After reviewing the bargaining act and legislative intent behind it, HERB concluded that it had jurisdiction over prohibited practices, including those involving alleged breaches of contracts. The Board then added that it would be its policy "to attempt to foster the peaceful settlement of disputes, wherever appropriate, by deferral of matters concerning contractual interpretation and application to the arbitration process agreed to by the parties."*

But the key issue in the case was whether the contractual provision in question violated the bargaining act, which limits the scope of bargaining. In interpreting Section 89-9, the Board noted that the legislative intent was expressed in Section 89-1, wherein it was stated:

> The legislature finds that joint decision-making is the modern way of administering government. Where public employees have been granted the right to share in the decision-making process affecting wages and working conditions, they have become more responsive and better able to exchange ideas and information on operations with their administrators.[29]

Section 89-9(a) mandates negotiations on wages, hours, and other terms and conditions of employment. But 89-9(c) and 9(d) indicate that the legislature did not intend the scope of bargaining to be unrestricted. Section 89-9(c) states that all matters affecting employee relations, especially those not considered wages, hours, or terms and conditions of employment, are subject to consultation with employee representatives. Additionally, the employer shall make "every reasonable effort to consult with the exclusive representatives prior to effecting changes in any major policy affecting employee relations." Section 89-9(d) is the broad management prerogatives provision.

---

*The Board also said:

It is clear that when it provided for grievance arbitration, the Legislature hoped to foster resolution of disputes by arbitration. . . . But it is apparent that the Legislature did not intend, by providing for such arbitration, to oust the Board of jurisdiction over violations of section 89-13 (a)(8) and (b)(5) [prohibited practices]. Rather, it is clear that the Legislature intended to place the duty of resolving prohibited practice cases squarely on the shoulders of the Board.

Having considered the complex interrelationship among Sections 89-9(a), (c), and (d), and the expressed intent of the legislature regarding public sector labor relations, the Board concluded:

. . . that all matters affecting wages, hours, and conditions of employment, even those which may overlap with employer rights as enumerated in Section 89-9(d), are now shared rights up to the point where mutual determinations respecting such matters interfere with employer rights which, of necessity, cannot be relinquished because they are matters of policy "which are fundamental to the existence, direction and operation of the enterprise." West Hartford Educ. Assn. v. DeCourcy.30

Turning to the class size provision, HERB took note of the Connecticut, Nevada, and Pennsylvania decisions on this subject and emphasized again that class size is a hybrid issue involving and affecting both policy and working conditions. In the instant case the purpose of the contract provision was to reduce the average class size ratio by approximately one student. "It is obvious, following the reasoning in the decisions on class size in other jurisdictions, that the provision on average class size ratio significantly affects conditions of employment, particularly work load." The Board added that the DOE did not present any evidence to show that the reduction of average class size ratio by one pupil would, in fact, interfere with its rights pursuant to Section 89-9(d). Accordingly, the Board found that the reduction in average class size ratio was negotiable, and that such agreement did not violate Section 89-9(d).*
But, HERB continued:

The issue of class size ratio, insofar as it involves overall policy dealing with the level of quality in education desired by our Legislature and developed by the DOE is . . . a management prerogative not to be interfered with by the HSTA. [Only] insofar as the average class size ratio constitutes a significant condition of employment, we believe that the matter is negotiable. . . .31

In light of this conclusion, contract language requiring the hiring of 250 teachers and the assignment of 15 percent of them to counselor and supportive staff positions impinged upon the employer's right to

---

*
Having determined that the average class size ratio at the time of the agreement was 26.4, HERB ordered the employer to reduce this ratio by approximately one student.

262

hire, transfer, and assign employees and to determine the methods, means, and personnel by which school operations were to be conducted. HERB emphasized:

> . . . while we hold that average class size ratio is a condition of employment, negotiation upon which does not per se interfere with employer rights under Section 89-9(d), we are of the opinion that the manner of implementing the reduction in average class size ratio involves decisions of inherent managerial policy and is not a proper subject of negotiation.[32]

As for the transfer of 169.5 temporary support positions, the Board found that this was a change in the employer's policy affecting employee relations.* Therefore, DOE's failure to consult on this major change violated Section 89-9(c). HERB emphasized, however, that DOE was not obligated to bargain on the transfers, because they were outside the scope of bargaining.

HERB also determined that the horizontal transfers did not violate the provision against reduction of the number of bargaining unit positions. Nor was there evidence that teachers who had enjoyed preparation periods and duty-free lunches prior to the execution of the agreement relinquished these benefits as a direct result of the transfers, which would have been a violation of the agreement.[33]

The transfers did, however, breach a section of the contract stating that nothing in the contract should be construed so as to "eliminate, reduce, or otherwise diminish any teacher benefit existing prior to its effective date." The temporary support jobs were originally allocated as classroom teaching positions; when these positions were changed to support positions, such staff services and benefits as preparation periods and free lunch periods were increased. Although the DOE had the "ultimate right" to transfer employees, the Board held that its past practice of changing teacher positions to supportive jobs "was construed as a benefit at the time of the negotiation and execution of the agreement." Since the reconversion of the support positions resulted in a decrease in staff services existing at the time of agreement, the transfers were in violation of the agreement.[34] DOE was therefore ordered to start implementing the class size provision, to reconvert temporary support positions where the transfers had caused loss of benefits,

---

*The record indicated that the employer's practice had been to assign originally allocated classroom teaching positions to various temporary support positions.

and to consult HSTA on major policy changes affecting employee relations.*

Shortly after it rendered its class size decision, HERB resolved another scope-of-bargaining controversy between HSTA and the Hawaii Board of Education concerning their current contract. HERB declared a state of impasse in negotiations under the contract's reopener provision.[35] It also held as nonnegotiable HSTA's proposals that preparation periods for teachers be scheduled "within the students' instructional day" and that daily work loads be limited to responsibility for specific maximum numbers of students.[36]

Relying on HERB's earlier decision in which reduction of average class size ratio was held to be a negotiable subject, HSTA argued that work load was directly related to class size and, therefore, negotiable. As to preparation time, the Association noted that in the past these periods had been scheduled during the students' school day. Additionally, HSTA contended, preparation periods did affect working hours and the teachers' ability to performing teaching functions.

The Board of Education, on the other hand, contended that both the maximum work load and preparation period demands violated its statutory and constitutional rights.†

HERB decided that the work load proposal, unlike an average class size restriction, would "interfere substantially" with the school board's right to direct its operations, pursuant to Section 89-9(d) of the public employee bargaining law. And although HERB conceded that preparation periods are a condition of employment,

---

*There was one dissenting opinion. Board member Guntert believed that the subject of teacher:pupil ratio was not negotiable and, consequently, that the contract provision was illegal. He contended that the DOE was not guilty of committing any prohibited practices.

†The Board of Education stated that the work load provision would necessitate the hiring of additional teachers, which in turn would result in "very small" work loads and inefficient use of personnel. In addition, the Board argued that it would be impossible to provide expanded facilities for an enlarged work force. Implementation of the work load provision also might force the school system to bus students to other schools that could accommodate the extra students when the work load maximum had been reached at their regular school.

With respect to the preparation time demand, the Board contended that it was not practical to schedule such periods within the students' instructional day, since school days vary among the schools and additional teachers would have to be hired to allow the preparation time.

it found that the scheduling of such time amounted to the scheduling of work, which is also a management right under the law.

Referring to its previous decision regarding the reduction of average class size ratio, HERB stated that in that case, it had "balanced the employer's right to manage against the impact of class size on working conditions":

> Notwithstanding its admitted relation to educational policy, we found in that instance that the element of impact on teachers' working conditions was great, while the imposition of an average, statewide class size ratio had minimum impact on the [DOE's] right to establish educational policy.[37]

HERB distinguished the class size decision from the work load issue. It held that the latter would "rigidly fix" the maximum number of students for a particular class and would force the school board to hire personnel and expand facilities "regardless of its rights and duty to maintain efficiency of operations." The Board admitted that work load was a "significant term and condition of employment," but determined that:

> [W]hen the [Board of Education] is required to utilize methods which would cause deterioration of the learning environment . . ., such as, placing two teachers in the same classroom or increasing team teaching regardless of a teacher's ability to team teach, it becomes obvious that the [Board's] right and duty to provide the best educational system possible is being interfered with.[38]

NEA v. BOARD OF EDUCATION OF SHAWNEE MISSION

Under Kansas' Professional Negotiations Act of 1970, teacher representatives and school boards are required to negotiate in good faith on terms and conditions of professional service. In NEA v. Board of Education of Shawnee Mission,[39] the Kansas Supreme Court was called upon to interpret the meaning of good faith negotiations and to define the scope of bargaining under the Act.

Not all aspects of the Court's decision are relevant for the discussion herein. By way of background, however, the case involved a set of negotiations in which the school board contended that all matters, whether or not legally negotiable, that constituted board "policies" remained subject to unilateral managerial action. The employer refused to enter into a written agreement on terms of professional service; and while it agreed to "lend a respectful ear" to teachers' suggestions on policies, it reserved final say on both formulating and changing policy. The NEA had submitted contract demands on a broad range of subjects including class size, and insisted that agreed-upon policies affecting terms and conditions of service at least be incorporated in individual teaching contracts.

In dealing with the duty to negotiate in good faith, the Kansas Supreme Court stated that a fundamental issue of dispute between the parties was their conflicting view of the Act's objective. NEA considered the Act a "collective bargaining" law, under which the parties must reach a binding agreement; the school board, on the other hand, termed the Act a "meet and confer" statute, under which the board's obligation was merely to listen to teachers before acting unilaterally.

After reviewing the Act's provisions, the Supreme Court concluded that "professional negotiations" means not only meeting and conferring but doing so "in a good faith effort by both parties to reach agreement." And if agreement is reached, the parties must commit it to writing and be bound by it.

The more provocative points of the Court's decision were made in its analysis of the statutory scope of negotiations. The Court noted that the lower court had excluded matters of basic educational policy but had included salaries, hours and amounts of work, vacations, holidays, sick and other leaves, retirement, insurance, wearing apparel, overtime pay, jury duty, grievance procedure, and "such other areas that directly or by implication involve these factors."

The NEA, however, argued that "terms and conditions of professional service" encompassed any matter affecting teachers' working conditions. In particular it pointed to two lists of items contained in their original proposal to the school board that were not covered by the lower court's definition of the scope of professional negotiations. The first list contained items that the board of education had stipulated were negotiable—although only in its limited concept of negotiability: probationary period, transfers, teacher appraisal procedure, disciplinary procedure, and resignations and terminations of contracts. But the second NEA list contained matters that the board vehemently argued were nonnegotiable: class size, curriculum, payroll mechanics, use of paraprofessionals, use and duties of substitutes, teachers' ethics, and academic freedom.

Because the legislature did not define the phrase "terms and conditions of professional service" or list the subjects it considered negotiable, the Court looked for guidance in the legislative history of the Act, particularly at two teacher bargaining bills that were introduced in the 1969 legislature. One of these bills contained a very broad scope of bargaining, in that it would have authorized negotiations not only on terms and conditions of professional service but also on "other matters of mutual concern." Because this language was stricken from the 1970 statute, the Supreme Court concluded that the legislature did not intend that those matters on the NEA's second list be negotiable. While issues such as curriculum and class size may be of "concern to the teacher, we see the legislative action as a deliberate effort to remove such concepts from the area of negotiability."[40]

On the other hand, the second 1969 bill, which would have allowed negotiations only on "wages, hours, and other economic conditions of employment," also was rejected by the Kansas legislature. The 1970 Professional Negotiations Act was, therefore, a compromise between labor and management. In light of this history, the Court determined that the items on NEA's first list fell within the phrase "terms and conditions of professional service" and were therefore negotiable.

The Court concluded its analysis of the subjects for negotiation with a reference to Justice Potter Stewart's concurring opinion in Fibreboard and a suggestion as to how problems of negotiability might be approached:

It does little good, we think, to speak of negotiability in terms of "policy." Salaries are a matter of policy, and so are vacation and sick leaves. Yet we cannot doubt the authority of the Board to negotiate and bind itself on these questions. The key, as we see it, is how direct the impact of an issue is on the well-being of the individual teacher, as opposed to its effect on the operation of the school system as a whole. The line may be hard to draw, but in the absence of more assistance from the legislature the courts must do the best they can.[41]

STATE COLLEGE AREA SCHOOL DISTRICT

Also contrasting with the decisions handed down in Connecticut and Nevada was the Pennsylvania Labor Relations Board (PLRB) ruling in State College Area School District.[42] The case grew out of an unfair practices charge filed by the State College Area Education Association, alleging that the Board of School Directors of State College Area School District refused to negotiate on 21 bargainable demands, including a provision for maximum class sizes. The Board of Directors, in its answer to the charge, admitted its refusal to bargain on the Association's demands, on the ground that they were matters of inherent managerial policy over which it was not obligated to bargain by virtue of Section 702 of the Public Employee Relations Act.

Article VII of the Act, entitled "Scope of Bargaining," contains three fundamental provisions. Section 701 requires the parties to "meet at reasonable times and confer in good faith with respect to wages, hours and other terms and conditions of employment, or the negotiation of an agreement or any question arising thereunder and the execution of a written contract. . . ." Under Section 702 public employers are not required to bargain over matters of "inherent managerial policy, which shall include but shall not be limited to such areas of discretion or policy as the functions and programs of the public employer, standards of services, its overall budget, utilization of technology, the organizational structure and selection and direction of personnel. Public employers, however, shall be required to meet and discuss on policy matters affecting wages, hours and terms and conditions of employment as well as the impact thereon. . . ." Section 703 states that the parties "shall not effect or implement a provision in a collective bargaining agreement if the implementation of that provision would be in violation of, or inconsistent with, or in conflict with any statute" enacted by the state legislature or the provisions of municipal home rule charters.

The real task for the Board in this case was to define the scope of public employee bargaining pursuant to Article VII of the Act. In its discussion the PLRB noted that school teachers have a "dual status"—one as employees having an employment relationship with their employer, and the other as professionals enjoying a relationship with their "clients," the students. If teachers are viewed in this way, concluded the PLRB,

> . . . it appears quite clear that the Act intended to speak to their employee status with consideration being given to their professional status by the use of their professional expertise in meet and discuss matters.
> Albeit that teachers are professionals . . ., they are nevertheless employees within the four corners of the Act and are to be considered as such in its application to them.[43]

The purpose of the Act was to promote orderly and constructive relationships between public employers and employees, subject to the paramount right of the public to keep inviolate the guarantees for their health, safety, and welfare. In fulfillment of this purpose, the Act imposes the duty to bargain in good faith over wages, hours, and other terms and conditions of employment—but excludes from the scope of bargaining matters of inherent managerial policy. These matters include, but are not limited to, "the functions and programs of the public employer, standards of services, its overall budget, utilization of technology, the organizational structure and selection and direction of personnel."[44] The scope of bargaining is further limited by Section 703, which prohibits effectuation of negotiated provisions that conflict with preexisting laws. An employer does,

268

however, have to meet and discuss policy matters affecting wages, hours, and working conditions as well as the impact thereon, upon request by the public employee representative.

By virtue of the powers conferred upon school boards, the policy-making function, emphasized the Board, belongs solely to the Board of School Directors. The Directors have been granted broad discretionary powers in order that they may operate an efficient school system. "Any erosion of these powers should be strictly constructed on the basis that the public interest is paramount." Moreover, it has long been recognized that school officials may not "divest themselves of the powers which have been conferred upon them for a public purpose."

The PLRB thus concluded that the State College Area School Board of Directors was not obligated to negotiate over matters that were the responsibility and prerogative of government; the school board did, however, have the duty of meeting and discussing policy matters affecting or having an impact on wages, hours, and working conditions.

With respect to the Association's demand for a contract clause on maximum class size, the PLRB determined that the subject was not negotiable. In a brief statement the Board held that maximum class size was "within the scope of inherent managerial policy, specifically within the areas of standards of services, functions and programs, and the overall budget of the Respondent."[45]

The PLRB's decision, rendered in October 1971, was not the last word on the case. The Association filed exceptions, and in June 1972 a differently composed Board reconsidered the case and issued a final order holding that 5 of the 21 demands—pertaining to assignments, cafeteria duty, files, chaperoning, and preholiday closings—were negotiable but that the other 16 items were within the scope of managerial policy and, therefore, not bargainable.

Both the Board of School Directors and Education Association petitioned the Centre County Common Pleas Court for review of the PLRB order, and the lower court held that all 21 items were nonnegotiable—thus upholding the original October 1971 PLRB decision. The Association and PLRB appealed to the Pennsylvania Commonwealth Court, which handed down its decision on June 6, 1973. In a four-to-three decision, the Commonwealth Court upheld the lower court, ruling that all 21 items fell within the scope of inherent managerial policy and were not mandatory subjects of negotiation.

Writing the majority opinion, Judge Glenn Mencer noted that Section 701 of the Act expressly mandates good faith bargaining on wages, hours, and terms and conditions of employment. Assuming that a proposed bargaining demand does involve such matters, the "further and controlling question" is "whether the item also involves matters of inherent managerial policy," and if so, the item

269

is not bargainable under Section 702 "... [T]he controlling provision ... is that under Section 702 a public employer is not required to bargain on any policy matter notwithstanding the effect or impact that it may have on wages, hours, and terms and conditions of employment."[46] Judge Mencer added that the responsibilities and rights granted to a school board under the Public School Code of 1949 cannot be the subject of collective bargaining because of the restriction and prohibition contained in Section 703.

Reviewing school board authority under the law, Judge Mencer concluded that these boards have been given broad powers by the legislature to operate schools. "If Act 195 [the PERA] represents a departure from the traditional principle of our public schools' being operated and managed by school boards, it would be a sharp departure not to be presumed but the result of clear legislative declaration. A statute is never presumed to deprive the state of any prerogative or right unless the intention to do so is clearly manifest, either by express terms or necessary implications."[47]

The policy matters enumerated in Section 702 are not exhaustive, continued Judge Mencer. Matters of inherent managerial policy, over which employers need not bargain, are those that belong to the public employer as a "natural prerogative or essential element of the right (1) to manage the affairs of its business, operation or activity and (2) to make decisions that determine the policy and direction that the business, operation or activity shall pursue."[48]

Having developed this definition of managerial policy matters, the decision clarifies the meaning of "wages, hours, and other items and conditions of employment." "Wages" represent the remuneration one receives for his labor. Clearly this is not a policy matter, for it is inherent in the establishment and continuation of the threshold relationship of employer and employee. The term "hours" generally encompasses the total number of hours worked, the periods of time covered, the starting and ending times, and rest periods. Under Section 701 these items are mandatorily bargainable.*

The Court acknowledged that the phrase "other items and conditions of employment" is susceptible to both broad and narrow interpretations. It determined, however, that the term refers to such subjects as the physical conditions of one's working surroundings, the quantity and quality of work required, the safety practices

---

*Indicating how narrowly the court defines "hours," Judge Mencer suggested, as an example of a nonmandatory "hours" item, a school board's decision as to whether a teacher shall be present at a parent-teacher meeting held in the evening. Such a "policy" affecting hours would be subject only to the meet-and-discuss requirement of Section 702 of the Act.

at and near the job site, sick and hospital benefits, and retirement benefits.

Thus, Judge Mencer concluded that Sections 701, 702, and 703 produced the following criteria with respect to the scope of bargaining:

1. The required bargainable items of Section 701 are of a limited nature.
2. Any item of wages, hours, and other items and conditions of employment, if affected by a policy determination, is not a bargainable item.
3. Any item involving matters of inherent managerial policy is a nonbargainable item by virtue of Section 702.
4. Duties and responsibilities imposed upon and granted to public employers by statutes or the provisions of municipal home rule charters are not subject to collective bargaining by virtue of Section 703.
5. The legislature has vested broad powers in school boards to administer the public school system and to determine policy pertaining thereto.
6. Any statutory departure from the school board's traditional role of operating and managing our public schools must be the result of clear legislative declaration.
7. Inherent managerial policy is a broad term and includes the right to manage and to make decisions that determine policy.[49]

Applying these criteria, the court found the 21 contested demands to be nonmandatory subjects of bargaining.* With respect to the

---

*Despite the very restrictive language of the State College Area decision, a 1974 Commonwealth Court decision suggests that the scope of public sector bargaining in Pennsylvania may not be as narrow as State College Area implied. In Canon-McMillan School Board v. Commonwealth of Pennsylvania (544 GERR B-14 [Mar. 4, 1974]), the Pennsylvania Commonwealth Court affirmed a finding by the PLRB that the Canon-McMillan School Board committed an unfair labor practice in refusing to bargain with the education association regarding teacher pay for performing extracurricular duties.

The court's opinion was written by Judge Genevieve Blatt and was joined in by Judges James Bowman, James Crumlish, Jr., Harry Kramer, and Roy Wilkinson. Judge Mencer dissented, along with Judge Theodore Rogers.

The school board alleged that extracurricular pay fell in the area of meet-and-discuss issues, under Section 702 of the Act. But

Association's demand for a contract provision on maximum class size, the Court held that it was not bargainable because it was within the scope of inherent managerial policy, specifically in the areas of public employer's functions, programs, standards of services, and overall budget.

In a dissenting opinion, Judge Harry Kramer warned that general interpretations of the bargaining act could dissipate employment rights that the legislature intended to confer. He suggested:

It seems to me that the board and the courts will have to evaluate each item as it is presented and strike a balance. If the item directly affects the "inherent managerial policy" of the school district as it applies to its mandate to provide an education system, then it is not subject to collective bargaining. If the item directly affects a teacher's personal rights, as it relates to wages, hours, and conditions of employment, then it is subject to collective bargaining. In between these two ends of the spectrum are varying shades, which are not subject to any prospective rule-making.[50]

The Commonwealth Court's decision in State College Area has been appealed to the Pennsylvania Supreme Court, the state's highest court. At the time of this writing, a decision has not yet been handed down.

WEST IRONDEQUOIT

In July 1974 the New York State Court of Appeals decided West Irondequoit Teachers Association v. Robert Helsby, et al.[51] In this decision it affirmed the Appellate Division of the State Supreme

---

the court concluded "that the clear wording and meaning of the entire Article VII of Act 195 require different interpretation." Section 701, which mandates bargaining on wages, makes no exceptions. And although Section 702 provides for meeting and discussing policy matters that might relate to wages, "in this case we do not have a policy matter at issue which might affect wages, for the policy matter has already been decided by the school board, but an issue of wages itself, and this issue necessarily comes under the bargaining provision requirements of Section 701."

In his dissenting opinion Judge Mencer cited State College Area and concluded that in the instant case, the majority reached "a diametrically opposite conclusion."

Court, which, a year earlier, had upheld the Public Employment Relations Board ruling that class size limitations were not a mandatory subject of bargaining. Although the court's decision was unanimous and brief, the case itself had been hard-fought for almost four years, and its history warrants discussion.

The facts of the case were not in dispute. During the 1970 contract negotiations, the West Irondequoit school board submitted to the Association a contract proposal that provided for administrative flexibility in determining class size. The Association proposed a contract provision containing specific numerical limitations on class size. The school board argued that such limitations were not a term and condition of employment but, rather, decisions that were the nondelegable responsibility of the school board to make.

On these facts the Association filed improper practice charges with PERB, alleging that the school board violated Section 209-a of the Taylor Law by refusing to negotiate in good faith. The hearing officer's decision[52] adopted the approach of the National Labor Relations Act, which holds that any subject with a "significant or material" relationship to conditions of employment constitutes a term or condition of employment, unless it involves decisions pertaining to the basic goals and directions of the employer. The hearing officer tried to strike a balance between the responsibility of the elected officials to make decisions and the statutory rights of employees to bargain on subjects affecting their terms and conditions of employment. The decision held that class size had a "major and tangible impact" on teachers' working conditions, especially work load. The hearing officer stated that class size was ". . . an integral component of the working environment" and not an expression of a primary policy goal or basic school board direction. Thus class size was held to be a term and condition of employment.

In ruling on the lawfulness of the Association's class size proposal, the hearing officer stated:

There is nothing in the Education Law that prohibits the parties from jointly determining minimum, maximum or optimum standards for class size. This does not mean that an employer must accede to a proposal containing "numbers"; but it does mean that the respondent cannot, out-of-hand, reject such a proposal as non-negotiable.[53]

The hearing officer concluded that the school board was obligated to negotiate on standards for class size, and recommended that it be ordered to negotiate about that matter.

PERB, however, did not adopt the findings of the hearing officer.[54] Relying heavily on its decision in City School District of the City of New Rochelle v. New Rochelle Federation of Teachers,[55] PERB determined that a public employer should not be required to delegate the responsibility of determining the manner and means by which educational services are to be provided and what the extent of such services should be. PERB thus found that class size was a basic element of educational policy, comparing that subject with budgetary cuts (and accompanying job eliminations) that were held to be nonnegotiable in New Rochelle. PERB concluded that such decisions may be made unilaterally by a public employer but that the employer must bargain with the employee representative regarding the impact of such decisions on the terms and conditions of employment.*

Board member George Fowler dissented, stating:

> In my judgment, the impact of numerical limitations of class size upon teaching load is so direct as to make a line of demarcation impossible. Just as my colleagues have determined that an employer must negotiate over demands relating to work load, I feel that an employer must negotiate over demands which impose numerical limitations for class size.[56]

The Association moved for reargument before PERB. In its motion, it urged that PERB had overlooked the extraordinary impact of class size on the work load of elementary school teachers. The Association argued that although the totality of the work load of high school teachers "is a function of class size, number of classes, number of preparations, length of class periods and length of school day, the work load of elementary school teachers consists of only two major elements, class size and length of school day." Because of the "interesting proposition" raised by the motion, PERB granted reargument.[57] At the reargument, however, the Association withdrew from the position it took in making its motion and reasserted that the impact of class size upon elementary school teachers was not greater than the impact upon secondary teachers, elaborating on the same arguments it had set forth in its original presentation. The majority of PERB found these arguments no more persuasive than they did in the first hearing and reaffirmed the Board's prior decision.

The Association thereupon commenced a proceeding, pursuant to CPLR Article 78, to review a decision of the PERB. On January 4, 1972, the matter was transferred to the Appellate Division by the

---

*Although PERB recognized that ". . . the line of demarcation between a basic policy decision and the impact on terms and conditions of employment may not always be clear," class size decisions were policy matters and determinations made in light of district resources and the needs of the public.

Special Term of the Albany Supreme Court, in accordance with the provisions of CPLR Section 7804 (g). The Association's petition sought a court order (1) annulling PERB's decision, (2) declaring that the school board had a statutory obligation to negotiate with the Association on class size, (3) declaring that the refusal to negotiate class size was an improper practice, and (4) ordering the school board to begin collective negotiations with the Association on class size.

In its brief the petitioner Association urged that class size directly affected hours of work and was a condition of employment. Teaching, it argued, could be broken into various activities—teaching, testing, supervising, and disciplining pupils—and class size had a "direct influence on each area."[58]

The Association relied heavily on the New York Court of Appeals' Huntington decision,[59] which held that a public employer must negotiate with its employees on all terms and conditions of employment unless prohibited from doing so by a specific statutory provision. The Association argued that there is no statutory provision in the Education Law prohibiting a collective bargaining agreement from dealing with maximum class size. Moreover, boards of education are given broad powers under Sections 1804 and 1709 of the Education Law to assign pupils and make provision for their instruction. "However, the existence of these broad powers does not negate the duties imposed by [the Taylor Law], but rather enabled the board to fulfill said duties. Only if negotiations concerning class size directly conflicted with some provision of statute would that subject be exempt from bargaining. . . ."[60]

The Association's brief also referred to the class size decisions of other jurisdictions, such as Hawaii and Connecticut, to support its contention that class size was a condition of employment and a mandatory bargaining subject. In addition petitioner cited Irving Sabghir's study (discussed in Chapter 11) on the scope of public sector bargaining, which indicated that class size provisions appear in 56 percent of the New York teacher-school board contracts analyzed in his report.[61] Class size, the Association asserted, was thus a "common subject" in public sector collective agreements.

The Association also urged that private sector experience held that items such as class size are mandatorily negotiable. Under Fibreboard,[62] petitioner argued, subjects are nonmandatory only when they impinge upon the basic structure of the enterprise. Changes not going to the heart of an operation must be negotiated.

Finally, the petitioner contended that the "mission"-terms of employment dichotomy set forth in several PERB cases was inapplicable to school boards. "Boards have no powers equivalent to the management prerogative of a private industry to change the products manufactured, to close a plant and subcontract work or to relocate plants. Boards must carry out the educational mission imposed upon them by statute."[63] School boards have little discretion in establishing missions; they are merely granted powers under the Education Law to carry out the state's purpose of educating children. And issues such as class size are peripheral to the statutorily mandated services that the school board is obligated to provide. Thus the West Irondequoit board of education, according to the Association, was obligated to negotiate class size pursuant to the Taylor Law, and "PERB erred in holding that the board had a managerial interest or special 'mission' exempting it from the broad duty to negotiate on subjects such as class size."

PERB, in response to the Association's arguments, contended that the Taylor Law was designed to regulate the relationship between governments and their employees without destroying the ability of governments to perform their basic function of determining the manner in which they will discharge their obligations to the public. The basic policies and mission of government agencies, "their raison d'etre, are matters between governments and their constituents and were not intended by the Taylor Law to be negotiated with employee organizations. PERB has, therefore, taken the view that not every governmental decision affecting employees' working conditions is required to be negotiated."[64]

PERB also argued that its decision in West Irondequoit recognized that any decision on class size necessarily affects basic decisions about the type of educational program the school board will provide the community. Class size decisions directly affect the ability to innovate and introduce new teaching techniques, as well as the facilities and number of classrooms needed. The negotiation of class size therefore may constitute negotiation of capital investment in school equipment and plant and may influence the quality of the school system.

PERB cited its other scope-of-bargaining decisions—New Rochelle, Oswego Principals, White Plains Fire Fighters.[65] It noted:

> . . . each decision of PERB has been made on a case by case basis, with PERB applying the provisions of the Taylor Law to the facts before it in each case. While it may be that under certain circumstances the workload element of class size outweighs the educational elements, warranting the issuance of an order by PERB compelling negotiation of class size, . . . the record in the instant proceedings supports PERB's refusal to issue the far reaching decision and order which the petitioner herein seeks, to wit, that class size, per se, is a negotiable term and condition of employment.[66]

PERB also looked to the decisions of the NLRB and courts under the NLRA to support the soundness of its class size decision. Private sector decisions have adopted the concept that the negotiability of a particular subject may depend on the context in which it occurs. Additionally, employers in private employment have not been required to negotiate on matters that would "significantly abridge [their] freedom to manage the business."[67] In numerous cases following Fibreboard, PERB added, federal courts have held that basic policy decisions of management are not negotiable. And, especially in the public sector, it is "important that employers, who have been charged with fulfilling governmental duties to their electorates, not be compelled to negotiate on subjects which "significantly abridge [their] freedom to manage the business."[68]

PERB forcefully argued that although the line between issues primarily affecting terms and conditions of employment and those that are primarily affairs of government is a fine one: "Where PERB's determinations have warrant in the record and a reasonable basis in law, they should not be disturbed by the court."[69] PERB cited Matter of Howard v. Wyman.[70] In it the court restated the limits of judicial review:

> It is well settled that the construction given statutes and regulations by the agency responsible for their administration, if not irrational or unreasonable, should be upheld. . . . As this court wrote in the Mounting & Finishing Co. case . . . , statutory construction is the function of the courts, but where the question is one of specific application of a broad statutory term in a proceeding in which the agency administering the statute must determine it initially, the reviewing court's function is limited. (Board v. Hearst Publications, 322 U.S. 11, 131).[71]

As to the Association's reliance on Huntington to establish that PERB's West Irondequoit decision no longer had reasonable basis in law, PERB argued that in Huntington, the Court of Appeals held that Section 1709 of the Education Law, in combination with the Taylor Law, authorizes and requires negotiation of terms and conditions of employment unless there is some statutory provision explicitly and definitively prohibiting an agreement on the particular term of employment. PERB pointed out, however, that the Court in Huntington was dealing with the negotiability of subjects that "no one disputed were terms and conditions of employment." It dealt only with the authority of a board to agree to admitted terms and conditions of employment.

> The court in Huntington did not have before it and did not decide the question of whether a public employer can be compelled by PERB to negotiate on a subject which is basic to its governmental mission but only tangentially related to terms and conditions of

employment. Nor did PERB have before it in the instant case, evidence to conclude under what circumstances, if any, class size is a term and condition of employment.[72]

In Chapter 6, it was emphasized that Huntington, for all its expansive language, required that an item first be found to be a term and condition of employment before it can be defined as a mandatory subject of bargaining. PERB seized on this point in defending its West Irondequoit decision, and apparently the Appellate Division was persuaded that class size is not a term or condition of employment.

In its succinct decision the Court first cited Fibreboard and commented that in the private sector, an employer is not required to bargain about matters that would significantly hinder his ability to operate the enterprise. "Mandatory negotiation of numerical class size would necessarily involve mandatory determinations of the number of classes, and ultimately it would constitute negotiation of capital construction." The Court's decision did not preclude bargaining on the impact of decisions on class size, but it affirmed PERB's ruling that final determination of class size must be a permissive subject of bargaining.

Second, the Court considered Huntington and agreed with PERB that the Court of Appeals' decision was distinguishable from the instant case. In Huntington,

... the parties had agreed that five subject items were terms and conditions of employment and sought a determination whether specific statutory authority was required before a board of education could act, whereas in the instant matter we are asked to determine whether or not numerical class size is a term and condition of employment.

The Teachers' Association appealed the Appellate Division's decision to the state's highest court, only to be rebuffed by a unanimous decision affirming the lower court.[73]

Writing for the Court, Judge Gabrielli framed the issue: Is class size a term or condition of employment, so as to be a mandatory bargaining subject, or is the question of class size one of educational policy susceptible of unilateral action by the employer?

In answering the question, Judge Gabrielli turned briefly to Fibreboard, and noted that four Supreme Court justices had concurred in a separate opinion in that case because they believed the majority language was too broad and because decisions regarding commitment of investment capital and the basic scope of the enterprise were not mandatorily negotiable. Subsequent NLRB and court decisions interpreting Fibreboard were not binding in the instant case, continued Judge Gabrielli, nor were they especially persuasive "except as they suggest that there is an area of non-negotiable policy making left to the employer."

The Court of Appeals decision emphasized that its task as a reviewing court was merely to determine whether PERB's decision was affected by an error of law, or was an arbitrary or capricious decision, or was an abuse of discretion. Its role was not to substitute its judgment for PERB's, based upon consideration of what the NLRB or federal courts might do in a similar matter. Inasmuch as the legislature under the Taylor Law delegated to PERB the power to settle disputes arising out of negotiations, that agency's construction of the statutory scheme must be accepted if it was not unreasonable.

As to the Association's substantive arguments, the Court was not persuaded that PERB's decisions in Oswego Principals[74] and West Irondequoit were inconsistent, as alleged by the teachers. In the former case, in which PERB held that the employer's decision to change the length of the working year was a condition of employment, and therefore a mandatory bargaining topic, the contested action directly affected only the employer-employee relationship. But in West Irondequoit, explained Judge Gabrielli, PERB "was free to find that class size is a basic element of educational policy bearing on the extent and quality of the service rendered."[75] The Court stressed that its decision in no way relieved the employer of its obligation to bargain on the impact of class size on teachers. An employer's decision, for example, that sections of the fourth grade should contain 25, 28, or 32 pupils should be a nonnegotiable policy matter. But, continued the Court, "whether teachers responsible for the sections are to receive varying consideration and benefits depending on the ultimate size of each section as so determined is mandatorily negotiable. . . ."[76]

Finally, the Court agreed with PERB and the Appellate Division that the Association's reliance on Huntington was misplaced because in that case the disputed subjects were clearly terms and conditions of employment. The question posed for judicial determination was whether the employer was limited by the Education Law as to the terms and conditions it could negotiate, or whether the Taylor Law gave the employer unqualified authority to bargain freely on such terms and conditions without regard to express authority under the Education Law. In contrast, the question posed in West Irondequoit was whether class size is a term and condition of employment at all. PERB, held the Court, developed sufficient rationale for answering that question in the negative.

PERB had developed, in earlier scope-of-bargaining decisions, a negotiability "test" that required a party "to negotiate an item that constitutes a term or condition of employment unless (a) it is deemed to be a matter of managerial prerogative. . . . or (b) the negotiability of the item has been prohibited" by the constitution, law, or judicial fiat. This test was rigorous, especially because under its standards, not all terms and conditions of employment were mandatory bargaining items, regardless of the Taylor Law's broad language. Under Huntington, however, all terms and conditions of employment are mandatory subjects of bargaining unless they are "explicitly and definitively" prohibited by law. PERB's test, therefore, conflicted with the standard enunciated by the state's highest court.

In effect, however, the two tests have now been merged and any difference has become one of semantics. Implicit in PERB's arguments before the courts in West Irondequoit was the application of another test, developed in the private sector and used by PERB's hearing officer in Rochester Administrators:[77] "Any subject with a significant or material relationship to conditions of employment constitutes a term and condition of employment unless it involves decisions concerning basic goals and directions of employers." Unlike PERB's earlier test, this stops short of saying that a term or condition of employment may not be mandatorily bargainable, yet accomplishes the same purpose by requiring that an item meet a more stringent requirement in order to be defined as a "term and condition of employment." Since class size, held the Court of Appeals, affects educational policy matters, the mission of the employer, and decisions regarding capital outlays, it is not a term or condition of employment. Its effect on working conditions is negotiable, but class size per se is a permissive, rather than a mandatory, subject of bargaining.

THE IMPACT OF WEST IRONDEQUOIT ON HUNTINGTON

The Court of Appeals' decision in West Irondequoit is significant not only because it resolves a hotly debated issue in school negotiations but also because it adds a new dimension to Huntington, which generally has been viewed as an expansive interpretation of the statutory scope of bargaining. West Irondequoit illustrates, however, that there are certain subjects that affect working conditions and are not prohibited by law but, nevertheless, are not negotiable because they are primarily issues of managerial policy. Under Huntington an employer must bargain on wages, hours, and all terms and conditions of employment, unless specifically limited by law; but under West Irondequoit the statutory phrase "terms and conditions of employment" does not include policy decisions as to the direction and implementation of the mission of a government agency.

Read together, Huntington and West Irondequoit provide the standard against which negotiability disputes can be resolved on a case-by-case basis. And PERB apparently has been given a judicial "go-ahead" to continue applying the tests it has developed for distinguishing between policy matters and working conditions.

APPLYING WEST IRONDEQUOIT: THE YORKTOWN CASE

In West Irondequoit, PERB and the courts emphasized that the impact of class size decisions and the issue of teacher work load are mandatory bargaining subjects, to be distinguished from the employer's independent determination of numerical class size limitations. In other words, it was suggested that one could separate an employer's unilateral decisions on educational policy matters from the effects of those decisions on employees in the bargaining unit. Only dissenting PERB member George Fowler expressed concern about the difficulty in drawing a line of demarcation between class size decisions and their effects on teacher work loads.

Fowler's concern may have been well-founded, however. In a recent case where the meaning and applicability of West Irondequoit were at issue, PERB and its hearing officer expressed different interpretations of the landmark class size decision. In Yorktown Faculty Association v. Yorktown Central School District No. 2,[78] a school employer denied the negotiability of several faculty association demands, including one that pertained to "professional loads."*

The latter demand would have limited each teacher's work load to a maximum of 22,000 student contact minutes per week (WSCM). WSCM was to be computed by multiplying five factors: (1) contact periods per day per teacher by (2) length of contact period by (3) number of students per contact period (class size) by (4) number of contact periods per week by (5) weighting factor. The weighting factor was a formula for assigning different values to different classes.

In ruling on the negotiability of the WSCM demand, the hearing officer acknowledged that under West Irondequoit, class size was

---

*The employer also refuted the negotiability of teacher demands that the district bargain on job eliminations; demands for a greater role in the making of decisions related to curriculum development, evaluation of plans, and assignment of paraprofessionals; demands for a greater role in the formulation of policy relating to student guidance in high school; demands that each student have a specific number of contact periods in various subjects with teacher specialists; and demands concerning the salary and job assignment of per-diem substitutes who were not in the bargaining unit.

not negotiable but teacher work load was a mandatory bargaining subject. Referring to West Irondequoit, the hearing officer noted that PERB had recognized that "the line of demarcation between a basic policy decision and the impact on terms and conditions of employment may not always be clear. . . . At first look, class size and teaching load may seem the same, but as we see them, they are not."79

The hearing officer concluded that PERB had anticipated just the type of interrelationship between class size and teacher load that was envisioned by the Yorktown Teachers' Association proposed formula. In the instant case a limit on class size was an essential element of the teachers' demand. Because of the inclusion of a nonmandatory subject as a factor in the proposal, the hearing officer found that the employer had not refused to bargain in good faith.

On appeal PERB held that the demand for a limitation on the WSCM was negotiable. Suggesting that the hearing officer misread West Irondequoit, PERB stated:

> Class size is but one factor in the calculation of WSCM; a demand for limitations on the WSCM is a workload demand and a mandatory subject of negotiations. The formula for the determination of WSCM includes not only class size, but also hours of work and the number of teaching periods which we ruled were mandatory subjects of negotiations in Matter of West Irondequoit Board of Education 80

Yorktown reemphasizes that although class size is not a mandatory subject of bargaining, work load demands related to and stemming from class size decisions are negotiable. Moreover, teacher proposals to limit work loads may even include class size as a factor. PERB's decision in Yorktown raises the possibility that shrewd teacher representatives will be able to bargain effectively, albeit indirectly, on proposals that include class size limitations. And school districts, now compelled to bargain, on request, about WSCM-type demands, may well find themselves in some way bilaterally negotiating class size even though this issue is per se a permissive subject of bargaining.

SUMMARY

The class size decisions discussed in this chapter reflect the difficulty, not only of labor and management but also of the boards and courts, in defining the scope of bargaining for professional employees. Even in jurisdictions with similarly constructed bargaining statutes, there are significant variations in interpretation of law and legislative intent. The Connecticut Teacher Negotiation Act and the Taylor Law contain similarly broad statutory definitions of the bargaining area, and neither includes management prerogatives clauses. In Connecticut, however, the Supreme Court held that the number of students assigned to a class was a term and condition of employment, whereas the New York Appellate Court disagreed. The Kansas Teachers Act provides for negotiation on terms and conditions of professional service, implying a legislative recognition of the professional status of teachers and the broad areas of professional concern. The Kansas Supreme Court, however, excluded class size, curriculum, and use of paraprofessionals and substitutes from the scope of negotiations. Also contrasting were the views of the Hawaii and Nevada public employment relations boards and the Pennsylvania Labor Relations Board and Commonwealth Court with respect to the interpretation of similar management rights clauses. In Hawaii and Nevada, it was reasoned that matters related to wages, hours, and terms and conditions of employment were negotiable, even if such matters also involved certain areas of management prerogatives. Although the Hawaii Employment Relations Board qualified this holding somewhat,* the thrust of its decision was that the phrase "wages, hours, and conditions of employment" was to be interpreted narrowly. In contrast, the Pennsylvania Commonwealth Court held that if a bargaining demand related to wages, hours, and terms and conditions of employment, but also involved matters of managerial policy, the item was "not bargainable under Section 702" of the PERA. This provision was controlling, ruled the Court; and under its language a public employer need not bargain on any policy matter, despite its effect on wages, hours, and terms and conditions of employment. The Court held: "The required bargainable items of Section 701 are of a limited nature. Any item of wages, hours, and other terms and conditions of employment, if affected by a policy determination, is not a bargainable item."[81]

Reviewing the decisional history of class size provides one avenue of exploring the issue. But another avenue, especially in

---

*To reiterate, the Hawaii Employment Relations Board said:

. . . all matters affecting wages, hours, and conditions of employment, even those which may overlap with employer rights as enumerated in Section 89-9(d), are now shared rights up to the point where mutual determinations respecting such matters interfere with employer rights which, of necessity, cannot be relinquished because they are matters . . . "fundamental to the existence, direction, and operation of the enterprise."

light of the discrepant judicial opinions, is through an analysis of the actual bargaining experiences of the parties. Chapter 11 presents the empirical findings of a field research project on class size.

NOTES

1. David Selden, "Class Size and the New York Contract," Phi Kappa Deltan, Mar. 1964, p. 286.
2. Albert Shanker, quoted in Allan J. Mayer, "Who's in Charge?-Public Employe Unions Press for Policy Role; States and Cities Balk," Wall Street Journal, Sept. 7, 1972, p. 1.
3. Robert E. Doherty, "Letter to a School Board," Phi Delta Kappan 48, no. 6 (Feb. 1967): 275, also printed as ILR Reprint Series, no. 208 (Ithaca: New York State School of Industrial and Labor Relations, Cornell University).
4. New York Public Schools Boards Association, PSBA Bulletin, "Class Size and Pupil-Teacher Ratio: An Annotated Bibliography," Sept.-Oct. 1971, p. 10.
5. Ibid.
6. National Education Association, "Class Size," NEA Research Bulletin, Washington, D.C., May 1968, p. 36.
7. New York State Teachers Association, Report of the Special Committee on the Duties of Teachers, Albany, Aug. 1968, p. 4.
8. W. Sawadsky, with assistance of Susan Walz, British Columbia School Trustees Association research report, findings reported in PSBA Bulletin, Sept.-Oct. 1971.
9. National Education Association, op. cit., p. 35.
10. Selden, op. cit., p. 283.
11. 295 A.2d 526 (1972).
12. "Section 10-221 of the General Statutes provides that boards of education shall 'prescribe rules for the management, studies, classification and discipline of the public schools and subject to the control of the state board of education, the textbooks to be used.' "
. . ." 295 A.2d 526, at 532.
13. 138 Conn. 269, 83 A.2d 482 (1951).
14. Ibid. at 533.
15. Ibid. at 534.
16. Ibid.
17. Ibid. at 535.
18. 379 U.S. 203 (1964).
19. 138 Conn. 269, 83 A.2d 482 (1951).
20. Ibid. at 536.
21. Ibid. at 537. With respect to extracurricular activities, the Court noted that under Connecticut law, "boards of education shall maintain . . . good public elementary and secondary schools, imple-

ment the educational interests of the state . . . and provide such
other educational activities as in their judgment will best serve the
interests of the town." In light of this language, the Court held that
the West Hartford school board alone was empowered to decide
whether there should be extracurricular activities and what such
activities should be. Issues involving assignment of teachers to
such activities and questions of compensation for such activities,
however, affect salaries and other conditions of employment and,
to that extent, were held to be mandatory subjects of bargaining.
The Court also struck down the school board's arguments against
negotiating binding arbitration of grievances into the contract. The
Court held that although under Norwalk and the Teacher Negotiation
Act, a school board may not abdicate its responsibility to an arbitrator in the drafting of a collective agreement, a public employer
that is authorized to execute a contract necessarily has the power
to agree on a method for settling disputes arising under the contract.
Thus binding arbitration of grievances was held to be a mandatory
subject of bargaining.

22. In the Matter of the Washoe County School District and
Washoe County Teachers Association, Item #3, Oct. 1971, at 3-1.

23. Ibid.

24. Ibid.

25. Ibid. at 3-2.

26. Ibid.

27. 480 GERR E-1 (Nov. 27, 1972).

28. Collective Bargaining Agreement between the Hawaii State
Teachers Association and Department of Education, entered into on
February 29, 1972, Article VI: Teaching Conditions and Hours,
quoted in 480 GERR E-1 (Nov. 27, 1972).

29. Ibid. at E-4.

30. Ibid. at E-5. Emphasis added.

31. Ibid. at E-6.

32. Ibid.

33. Ibid. at B- .

34. HERB quickly added, however, that its determination should
not be read to require the employer to keep 169.5 teachers in support positions should the need for the level of supportive services
provided at the time of the agreement decrease or become subject
to accommodation through some other means. "Moreover, nothing
in this opinion should be regarded as dictating how the support
services are to be provided as long as they are continued. We do
not intend herein to dictate what types of qualifications persons used
to continue the subject benefits must possess." Ibid. at E-7.

35. Board of Education, State of Hawaii, and Hawaii State Teachers Association, HPERB Case no. CU-05-9, Dec. no. 24, Dec. 21,
1972, reported in 487 GERR B-9 (Jan. 22, 1973).

36. Petition for Declaratory Ruling by the Department of Education, HPERB case no. DR-05-5, Dec. no. 26, Jan. 12, 1973; reported in 487 GERR B-9 (Jan. 22, 1973).

37. 487 GERR B-13 (Jan. 22, 1973).

38. Ibid.

39. 512 P.2d 426, 84 LRRM 2223 (1973).

40. 84 LRRM 2223, at 2230.

41. Ibid. In a similar vein the Nebraska Supreme Court, in Seward Educ. Ass'n. v. School Dist. of Seward (199 N.W.2d 752, 80 LRRM 3393 [1972]), held that "terms and conditions of employment" does not include areas "predominantly matters of educational policy, management prerogatives, or statutory duties" of school boards. It concluded that the statutory standard "can be interpreted to include only those matters directly affecting the teacher's welfare." Thus, in dicta, it excluded class size, curriculum, assignment, and work schedule from the scope of negotiations. In South Dakota the public employee law provides for bargaining on "rates of pay, wages, hours of employment, or other conditions of employment." In Aberdeen Educ. Ass'n. v. Board of Educ. (82 LRRM 2287 [S.D. Cir. Ct., 1972]), a South Dakota Court used a similar test to remove class size, use of teacher aides, planning periods, and conference time, as well as other issues, from the scope of bargaining.

42. Case no. PERA-C-929-C, 1971, reported in 426 GERR F-1 (Nov. 8, 1971).

43. 426 GERR F-2 (Nov. 8, 1971).

44. The PLRB continued: "Matters of 'inherent managerial policy' over which public employers are not obligated to bargain are such matters that are firmly fixed and belong to the employer as a right or permanent and inseparable element, quality or attribute involved in the constitution or essential character of the employer, and incapable of being surrendered or transferred where specifically prohibited by statute." Ibid.

45. Ibid.

46. 510 GERR E-3 (July 2, 1973).

47. Ibid.

48. Ibid.

49. Ibid. at E-4.

50. Ibid. at E-5. It perhaps is noteworthy that the court split along party lines. Three Republican judges concurred with Judge Mencer, while the three dissenters were Democrats.

51. 42 A.D.2d 808, 346 N.Y.S.2d 418 (1973), aff'd., 35 N.Y.2d 46 (1974).

52. 4 PERB 4511, at 4606 (1971).

53. Ibid. at 4608.

54. 4 PERB 3070, at 3725 (1971).

55. 4 PERB 3060, at 3704 (1971).

56. 4 PERB 3070, at 3728 (1971).

57. 4 PERB 3089, at 3753 (1971).

58. Brief on behalf of petitioner, in the Matter of the Application of the West Irondequoit Teachers Association Against Robert Helsby, et al., Constituting PERB, Sneeringer and Rowley, attorneys for petitioner, Albany, New York, at 24.

59. 30 N.Y.2d 122 (1972).

60. Brief on behalf of petitioner, at 28. The petitioner's brief noted that under Section 1709, Education Law, school boards are granted ". . .all the powers . . . necessary to exercise powers granted expressly or by implication and to discharge duties imposed by this chapter or other statutes." This language, it was asserted, "surely gives such boards the powers to fulfill the duty imposed by Article 14, CSL [Taylor Law] and collectively negotiate with their employees concerning such terms and conditions of employment as class size." Ibid. at 33.

61. Irving Sabghir, The Scope of Bargaining in Public Sector Collective Bargaining, report sponsored by PERB, Oct. 1970.

62. Fibreboard Paper Products Corp. v. NLRB, 379 U.S. 203 (1964).

63. Brief on behalf of petitioner, at 45.

64. Brief of respondent Public Employment Relations Board, in the Matter of the Application of the West Irondequoit Teachers Association Against Robert Helsby, et al., Martin L. Barr, attorney for repondents, Albany, New York, at 11.

65. 4 PERB 3060, at 3704 (1971); 5 PERB 3011, at 3023 (1972); 4 PERB 3074, at 3732 (1971).

66. Brief of respondent, at 19-20.

67. Fibreboard Paper Products Corp. v. NLRB, 379 U.S. 203 (1964).

68. Brief of respondent, at 24.

69. Ibid. at 26.

70. 28 N.Y.2d 434, at 438 (1971).

71. Brief of respondent, at 26.

72. Ibid. at 27-28.

73. In the Matter of the West Irondequoit Teachers Association v. Robert Helsby, et al.

74. City School District of Oswego v. Association of Administrative Personnel, 5 PERB 3011, at 3023 (1972).

75. In the Matter of the West Irondequoit Teachers Association v. Robert Helsby, et al., 35 N.Y.2d 46 at 51.

76. Ibid. at 51-52.

77. 4 PERB 4509, at 4599 (1971).

78. 7 PERB 3030 (1974).

79. 7 PERB 4503 at 4514 (1974).

80. Yorktown Faculty Association v. Yorktown Central School District No. 2, 7 PERB 3030 at 3053.

81. 510 GERR E-4 (July 2, 1973).

THE ISSUE OF
CLASS SIZE IN
NEW YORK STATE

In the preceding chapter a test, rooted in the Fibreboard decision, was developed to determine, on an issue-by-issue basis, the scope of public sector bargaining. Simply stated, this test focused on two questions: (1) the bargaining practices, or experience, concerning a proposed subject, and (2) the appropriateness of the collective bargaining process to settle a disputed issue. The validity of this Fibreboard-based formula was tested by applying it to the uniquely public sector issue of class size—which, it was concluded, satisfied both prongs of the negotiability test. This conclusion was substantiated by the results of an empirical study on the class size issue, a discussion of which follows.

BACKGROUND

The complexity, individuality, and fluctuating nature of teacher-school board labor relations pose a significant problem for the researcher. On the one hand, to be able to make some meaningful generalizations and conclusions, however limited and tentative, data must be collected about a broad sample of bargaining (or nonbargaining) relationships. This need for a large sample requires some type of information-gathering instrument, such as a questionnaire, that permits the researcher to maximize the number of subjects being investigated given fixed research resources. On the other hand, teacher labor relations, just like labor relations in most occupations, are highly individualized, both to the locality which the labor-management interactions occur and to the specific issues that form the basis for such interaction. Thus, to be able to analyze teacher labor relations accurately, the investigator must collect a large volume of contextual, or issue-specific, data.

In 1970 the New York State Public Employment Relations Board sponsored a study, conducted by Irving Sabghir, on the scope of bargaining in the public sector.[1] Professor Sabghir studied a broad range of contracts covering various occupations in the public sector in New York state. He based his analysis on a 10 percent sample of both teaching and nonteaching contracts, and he explored many aspects of the scope of bargaining in order to gain a broad overview of the three-year bargaining experience under the Taylor Law.

After studying the scope of teacher bargaining, Sabghir reported that the issue of class size was "clearly [one of] the most important matters specifically discussed by the parties."[2] This writer's own experience in working with and representing local teacher organizations in negotiations, although limited, also had indicated that class size was becoming an increasingly significant issue in discussions and negotiations between teachers and school boards. This experience, plus a keen interest generated by increasing litigation throughout the country concerning the negotiability of class size, led this researcher to embark on an "issue-specific," follow-up study of the Sabghir report on the scope of public sector bargaining. Although this study was focused primarily on a general analysis of the legal, political, and sociological aspects of determining the scope of public sector bargaining, it was determined that an in-depth analysis of the class size issue would provide a useful "case in point"—an indication of whether the scope of bargaining as set forth in the Taylor Law was proving troublesome, as well as a guide toward the consideration of other "hybrid" subjects whose negotiability also is controversial. In addition, it was hoped that a study of the class size bargaining experience would provide new information for legislators and members of PERB who must make and interpret law on the scope of negotiations, and would help teachers and school boards gain a better understanding of how class size problems are being resolved throughout the state.

RESEARCH DESIGN

One research design framework classifies field study designs according to the purposes for which data are collected.[3] Three design types are set forth: exploratory, descriptive, and hypothesis-testing. The exploratory study is best used to become familiar with a problem or to suggest directions for future resarch. Descriptive studies examine the characteristics of the object being studied or determine the frequency of various occurrences and examine the interrelations. Hypothesis-testing studies gather data in order to confirm or deny specific hypotheses. The researcher engaged in an exploratory or descriptive study is likely to collect as much information as possible about his subjects, in contrast to the hypothesis tester, who is concerned only with the information germane to his hypotheses.[4]

Under this categorization of research designs, this study presents findings of an exploratory-descriptive investigation. Although, as will be set forth below, some fundamental hypotheses were tested, it was aimed primarily at exploring several broad questions and describing the bargaining parties' experiences in coping with a controversial issue.

A questionnaire was used to elicit specific information from both teachers and school administrators in an effort to answer the following broad questions:

1. Is class size a significant issue in teacher-school board labor relations?
2. Do teachers and school administrators have strongly divergent views regarding the negotiability of class size and the existence of class size problems in their districts? Do their interests and objectives overlap or conflict?
3. Does class size lend itself to resolution through collective bargaining, unilateral managerial policy, informal faculty-administration discussions—or a combination of all of these means?
4. Do the parties view class size as essentially an issue of educational policy, professional concern, or working conditions—or as a combination of all three? And based on these views, how are class size problems most effectively handled?
5. Has third party assistance been widely used to resolve contract disputes on class size?
6. How have the parties reacted to PERB's decision in the West Irondequoit case?
7. Are there major differences in attitudes, experiences, and problems between districts with contracts containing class size provisions and those whose contracts are silent on the issue?
8. What kinds of class size provisions are being negotiated and included in collective bargaining agreements? Is there variation in their nature and in the goals they seek to satisfy?

The only hypotheses posed for testing concerned the relationship between types of school districts and the frequency of class size provisions in contracts. Thus, it was hypothesized that:

1. Class size provisions would be more prevalent in the contracts of large school districts than in the contracts of small districts.
2. Class size provisions would be more prevalent in the contracts of urban and suburban districts than in the contracts of small districts.
3. The prevalence of class size provisions in contracts would increase with the number of years in which collective bargaining occurred in school districts.

DATA-GATHERING

A detailed questionnaire was sent to the presidents of local teacher organizations and to the superintendents (or supervising principals in central school districts) in each of 431 school districts throughout the state. Different, though very similar, questionnaires were sent to teachers and administrators. Each recipient was asked to give the questionnaire to the teacher(s) or administrator(s) most directly involved in recent negotiations, since many of the questions were directed toward the bargaining experience of the parties.

A sample was selected from two populations.* The first population was composed of the 627 school districts that had filed with the New York State Teachers Association a copy of their 1971-72 collective bargaining agreement.† Within this population there were two subpopulations: 305 districts whose contracts contained class size provisions and 322 districts whose contracts did not. Inasmuch as one of the purposes of this study was to compare and contrast the experiences of districts whose collective agreements contain class size language with those districts that have not included class size in their agreements, the sample was controlled by randomly selecting two-thirds of the districts from each of these subpopulations.

The second population consisted of the 13 school districts outside New York City that had been organized by local organizations of the American Federation of Teachers (AFT) as opposed to the

---

*Sampling was necessitated by a lack of financial resources to send a questionnaire to the entire population.

†To this writer's understanding, 640 districts represent over 90 percent of the school districts in New York state. The balance of these districts, however, may not have negotiated a collective bargaining agreement or had one on file with an agency to which this writer had access. Therefore, 627 made up the total population of collective bargaining agreements available.

New York State Teachers Association (NYSTA). Because this population was relatively small, questionnaires were sent to teachers and administrators in all 13 districts, 10 of which had contracts containing class size language. The purpose of separating and identifying the NYSTA and AFT districts was to enable the researcher to see if any striking similarities or differences existed in their contracts or bargaining experiences.

From this sample of 431 districts, completed questionnaires were received from 381 respondents. Approximately 55 percent (208) of these respondents reported that their contracts contained class size provisions, and 45 percent (173) stated that their contracts did not. 183 teachers and 198 superintendents (or supervising principals) responded. In 85 districts only teachers responded, and in 100 districts only superintendents responded. In 98 districts, however, questionnaires were completed and returned by both teachers and superintendents. All told, therefore, a total of 283 districts responded.

HIGHLIGHTS OF THE FINDINGS

Significance of the Issue

1. Is class size a significant issue in school labor relations?

The survey responses have been organized under the eight broad questions underlying the study. Thus, the first inquiry—Is class size a significant issue?—can be answered, at least in part, by analyzing the respondents' answers to such survey questions as the following: (a) When and how often has class size been discussed both in negotiations and in other forums? (b) Have negotiated class size provisions generated problems, and if so, what kind? (c) Is class size a troublesome issue in districts without class size language in the collective agreement? (d) Do teachers file many grievances on class size?

With respect to the first indicator, in districts with class size provisions, 59 percent of the respondents reported that class size had been discussed in negotiations in at least four of the past six years, and an additional 12 percent responded that class size had been discussed in negotiations in at least three of the last six years. In districts whose contracts did not contain class size language, approximately 32 percent reported that class size language was proposed by the teachers in three out of the last five years. An additional 11 percent said that teachers proposed class size in at least two out of the last five years. In districts both with and

292

without class size in their contracts, the frequency of negotiations over class size increased after 1970.*
When asked if the class size language in their contracts had generated any problems, 42 percent of the respondents answered this question affirmatively; 59 percent said no. Almost 33 percent of the respondents in districts without negotiated class size provisions answered that class size had presented problems. (The specific nature of these problems is discussed below.) Interestingly, 83 percent of all respondents said no grievances concerning class size had been raised in their districts; almost 8 percent said one grievance; 3 percent reported six or more grievances, indicating that most districts have no grievance history regarding class size and a few districts have had relatively many grievances concerning this subject. Only 2 percent of all grievances on class size had gone up through the last step of the grievance procedure in their districts.

Approximately half of the teachers responding to the questionnaire indicated that they were planning to bargain on class size, specifically for more rigid contract provisions, during the next round of negotiations.

The data with respect to the first broad study question, therefore, indicates that class size is a significant issue that frequently was a subject of negotiations, especially after 1970. Additionally, class size problems have arisen in districts both with class size provisions in their agreements and without it. A significant number of teacher respondents evidenced intentions to make class size demands at the bargaining table during the next round of contract negotiations.

Objectives and Views Regarding Class Size
and Its Negotiability

2. Do teachers and school administrators have divergent views regarding the negotiability of class size and the existence of class size problems in their districts? Do their interests and objectives overlap or conflict?

Teachers and administrators expressed contrasting views on the negotiability of class size and different concerns relating to the inclusion of class size provisions in collective bargaining agreements. The vast majority of teacher respondents (89 percent)

---

*Findings also showed that the smaller the number of teachers in a bargaining unit, the more likely they were never to have proposed class size for inclusion in the collective agreement.

believed that there should be no restraints on the negotiability of class size. The remaining teacher respondents favored statutory numerical limits for class sizes. In contrast, 64 percent of the responding school administrators stated that there should be no legal requirement on the public employer to bargain over class size.* A significant minority, however, (28 percent) said the law should not impose constraints on the negotiation of class size. In urban districts, in particular, employers favored no restraints on the negotiability of class size; 62 percent of urban employers, as opposed to 47 percent and 45 percent of suburban and urban employers, respectively, expressed this attitude. In actual collective bargaining sessions, approximately 53 percent of the employers adopted the position that class size was nonnegotiable under the Taylor Law, the Education Law, or both.† The remaining 47 percent of the employers reported that they never contended in bargaining that class size was not negotiable under these laws.‡

Teachers in school districts both with and without class size clauses in their contracts were asked whether class size had created "problems" in their districts. Interestingly, 43 percent of the teachers and 66 percent of the administrators in districts with negotiated contract provisions on class size reported that such contract language had not generated any problems. Where problems were specified, teachers felt the most significant ones pertained to difficulty in interpreting the contract language and the lack of adequate classroom space. The problem of adequate classroom space also was checked frequently by administrators as one of their class size problems. Administrators, however, most frequently responded that their most important problem was that contractual class size provisions had increased district costs. The second most significant problem pertained to difficulty in interpreting the contract language on class size. Apparently the problem of interpretation was of concern to both employees and employers in districts with class size provisions in their agreement.

---

*This percentage remained constant throughout the eight regions into which, for study purposes, the study was divided: Long Island, Westchester, Albany, St. Lawrence, Syracuse, Binghamton, Rochester, and Buffalo.

†Approximately 11 percent said Taylor Law; 13 percent said Education Law; and 30 percent said both laws. The findings also indicated that in all regions except Long Island and Buffalo, there was a 50 percent likelihood that an employer had argued that class size was nonnegotiable. In Long Island and Buffalo, the likelihood was 32 and 37 percent, respectively.

‡Teachers also reported that approximately half of their employers had never contested the negotiability of class size.

Teachers and administrators also responded to a question asking them to evaluate the class size language in their contracts. Of the teacher respondents, 19 percent reported that the contract language satisfied their goals, 24 percent said the language failed to satisfy their goals, and 57 percent said the language partially satisfied their goals. On the other hand, 57 percent of the employer respondents indicated satisfaction with the contractual class size language, 14 percent said the language failed to satisfy their goals, and 29 percent said the contract provisions were partially satisfactory.* Three-fourths of the employers also reported that they were not having any difficulty in adhering to the negotiated class size provisions.† Seventy-seven percent of the teachers responded that generally the class size provisions in their agreement were being adhered to by their employers.

In districts without class size language in their contracts, approximately 20 percent of the teachers and 43 percent of the administrators indicated that class size was not a problem. The problems most frequently specified by teachers were that large classes were hindering their ability to give individualized instruction and that wide variations in class sizes existed among different subject areas and grade levels in their schools. This latter problem also was considered by teachers to be their most significant one with respect to class size.

Teachers and administrators were questioned about their interests, objectives, and arguments in collective bargaining over class size. Of the 81 teacher respondents reporting that their current contracts were silent on class size, 59 indicated that class size proposals had been presented in collective negotiations. The content of these proposals most often pertained to establishing specific numerical limitations on class size.‡

---

*In every region except Rochester, the most frequently selected employer response regarding contract satisfaction was that the class size language satisfied their goals. It also was found that employers who viewed class size as a working condition were more likely to be satisfied with the contract language on the subject than were employers who viewed class size as either a professional or a managerial issue.

†As one might expect, most of the employers (62 percent) reporting difficulty in adhering to the contract also said the language failed to satisfy their goals.

‡Administrators in districts without class size contract language affirmed that the most frequently presented teacher proposal related to the establishment of specific class size limits in the agreement.

All teachers were asked what their underlying objectives and interests were in negotiating on class size. The most significant and most frequently checked answers were increased opportunity for individualized instruction, a belief that small classes improve education in general, and improvement in pupil:teacher ratios.[*] In describing their interests and objectives in negotiations on class size, administrators most often responded: "maintaining flexibility in making teaching assignments." Of those employers ranking their objectives, most said that preserving managerial flexibility was their most important objective. A significant number of administrators also reported that "the financial constraints" were their most important interest in collective bargaining over class size.[†]

As to arguments that employers raised against including or modifying class size language in collective agreements, the one most frequently adopted was that "there is no conclusive evidence that class size limitations result in more effective teaching or increased pupil achievement."[‡] Two other positions often adopted by employers at the bargaining table were that class size was a management prerogative and that class size limitations would result in increased costs for the district. The employers who ranked their arguments in order of importance selected with equal frequency the "management prerogative" stance and the "no-evidence-on-benefits" position.[§]

---

[*] The data indicated that as classroom pupil:teacher ratios increased, there was a corresponding increase in the percentage of teachers adopting improvement of pupil:teacher ratios as their most important bargaining objective. As the pupil:teacher ratio in districts increased, the likelihood of teachers seeking opportunity for individual instruction as the most important goal also increased.

[†] Moreover, cross-tabulations showed that there apparently was no relationship between an employer's most important interest/objective and the region, the number of teachers in the bargaining unit, the number of years of formal bargaining, pupil:teacher ratios, and the type of class size provision in the contract. Thus, notwithstanding the fact that "maintaining flexibility" and the "financial constraints" were the two most important interests/objectives generally, it appears that employers' interests and objectives also reflect the particular problems, issues, and attitudes in their districts during any given set of negotiations.

[‡] Approximately 74 percent of the employers made this argument in response to teachers' bargaining demands.

[§] Cross-tabulations also indicated that those employers saying that there should be no requirement to bargain on class size were most likely to adopt the "management prerogative" argument as their most important. Additionally, where the administrator

296

To summarize, although two-thirds of the administrator respondents would prefer not to be compelled by law to bargain on class size, almost half of the employers had not adopted the position that class size is legally nonnegotiable. Significantly, in districts where class size had been negotiated into contracts, a greater percentage of administrators than teachers stated that the contract language had not generated any problems. Moreover, 75 percent of the administrators said they were having no trouble adhering to their contract provisions on class size. In districts without negotiated class size clauses, again more administrators than teachers reported "no problems." Also worth noting was the fact that where class size was included in the collective agreement, more administrators than teachers said the contract language satisfied or at least partially satisfied their goals. This employer satisfaction is perhaps attributable to the belief of some administrators that their contract clauses were "weak" or not overly restrictive. What is important for discussion here, however, is the suggestion that the mere negotiation and inclusion of class size in a collective agreement has not resulted in deep employer dissatisfaction or in management's inability to direct school operations.

Teachers and administrators frequently identified similar problems, but their emphases differed. Administrators, although admitting, for example, wide variations in class sizes within their districts, were particularly concerned with financial limitations and the fiscal ramifications of negotiating class size. They also desired to preserve their "management right" to make assignments. Teachers, on the other hand, expressed greater concern about the educational aspects of class size. According to questionnaire responses, class size demands were presented much less with an eye toward reducing work loads or protecting job security than with a desire to improve pupil:teacher ratios in order that more individualized instruction could be given in the classroom. Although some may argue that employees' motives are actually more selfish than teachers care to admit, the teacher responses to this questionnaire reflect the complexity of bargaining in the professional services.

Procedures for Resolving Class Size Problems

3. Does class size lend itself to resolution through collective bargaining, unilateral managerial policy, joint

---

reported that the "management prerogatives" argument was his most important, there was a greater likelihood of his district's having either no class size in the contract or a weaker provision than where the administrator noted other arguments as his most significant.

297

faculty-administration discussions—or a combination of these procedures?

Over 75 percent of the respondents whose contracts contained class size language reached agreement on the inclusion of such language in their agreements prior to mediation or fact-finding. An additional 10 percent reached agreement on class size language during mediation, and an additional 4 percent reached accord after mediation but before fact-finding. Only 10 percent determined their class size provisions during or after fact-finding. Admittedly, the sample used in this study was controlled for the presence of class size provisions in approximately half of the collective agreements. However, the high percentage of parties who were able to reach accord on their contractual language at the bargaining table and without third party assistance arguably is one indication that this issue is capable of being resolved through collective bargaining.

Perhaps a second indication is the fact that approximately 86 percent of the superintendents and 77 percent of the teachers with contracts containing class size clauses reported that their agreements either partially or substantially satisfied their goals with respect to the issue.[*]

Practitioners of public sector labor relations frequently suggest that the "gray area" issues, those with both working conditions aspects and managerial policy implications, be resolved through "meet and confer" procedures rather than full collective bargaining. The questionnaire used in this study therefore asked the parties to express their views on and experiences with informal faculty-administration discussions on class size. 35 percent of the employers and 43 percent of the teachers said no informal joint discussions regarding class size had taken place. Where they had occurred, more administrators than teachers found them productive: 19 percent of the superintendents said these joint discussions were very productive, 41 percent said they were productive to a limited degree, and 5 percent said they were unproductive. In contrast, no teachers said these discussions were very productive, 31 percent said they were productive to a limited degree, and 26 percent said they were unproductive.

The grievance experience of bargaining parties regarding subjects they have negotiated into their agreements also may indicate whether or not such issues are successfully handled through collective negotiations or better resolved in other forums. Although

---

[*] One also may argue that class size can be satisfactorily resolved through collective bargaining because of the substantial percentage (60 percent) of administrators who responded that their contracts' class size language had not generated any problems.

the propensity of teachers to file grievances may rest on many factors other than (or in addition to) whether or not class size provisions of their contracts actually are being violated or misapplied, it is arguably significant that the respondents reported very few grievances being filed in their districts on this subject. Over 83 percent indicated no grievances had ever been filed on class size, approximately 8 percent reported one grievance, and 3 percent reported six or more.* At the risk of being too speculative, one may suggest that bargaining about class size, and even negotiating it into collective agreements, does not necessarily mean that many grievances are the inevitable result. Class size problems are being resolved through bargaining, and yet employers have not been deluged with grievances. The lack of grievances may also reflect the fact that school employers have been able to negotiate class size provisions that are not excessively binding. In other words, the contract clauses may contain employer "escape hatches" making it difficult for teachers to grieve successfully that administrators are guilty of noncompliance. Perhaps one implication of these findings is that even "gray area" issues, such as class size, do lend themselves to determination at the bargaining table—especially if public employers bargain hard to protect their prerogatives where policy questions are involved. Public employees have great faith in the collective bargaining process and eventually find ways to place issues that they consider important on the bargaining table. Employers need not be mortally weakened, however, by the negotiations mechanism. As more and more government employers are learning, collective bargaining is a give-and-take process through which management, as well as employees, can press for and stand pat on their own demands, particularly those that affect the mission and direction of their agencies.

The Essence of the Class Size Issue

4. Do the parties view class size essentially as an issue of educational policy, professional concern, or working conditions? And based on these views, how is class size most effectively handled?

This question is a corollary to the previous inquiry, but it approaches from a different vantage point a fundamental question

---

*When considering this 83 percent, it should, however, be borne in mind that 45 percent of the respondents reported contracts without class size language.

underlying this survey—should class size be within the scope of mandatory bargaining?

To reiterate two relevant findings, a little more than half of the employer respondents had taken the position in negotiations that class size was nonnegotiable under the Education Law, the Taylor Law, or both. The remaining 47 percent had never argued that legislation precluded bargaining on class size. Additionally, almost two-thirds of the employers stated that there should be statutory restraints on the negotiation of class size; specifically, there should be no legal requirement to bargain on the subject. Almost 30 percent of the administrators and 90 percent of the teachers disagreed, however; they did not favor any restraints on the negotiability of class size.

When asked to characterize the issue of class size, 42 percent of the teachers said it was an issue of "professional concern"; 31 percent said it was a working condition; and 26 percent said it was a combination of professional concern and working conditions.* Only 1 percent believed it was a subject for managerial control. Of the administrators responding, 49 percent believed class size was a professional issue; 7 percent said it was a working condition; and 31 percent said it was a policy issue for managerial control. An additional 12 percent said it was a combined issue of professional and managerial concern, and 2 percent said it represented a combination of working conditions and professional aspects.

Respondents also were asked their opinions on the most effective means of dealing with class size. Not surprisingly, few employers said "collective bargaining." Almost 21 percent said the subject was best handled through unilateral managerial policy, and 71 percent favored faculty-administration study committees. One-third of the teacher respondents also favored joint study committees, but 53 percent said collective bargaining was the best method; 13 percent opted for a combination of collective bargaining and joint study committees.

There was a tendency for teachers increasingly to favor collective bargaining as urbanity and bargaining unit size increased. In rural and small districts (less than 200 teachers), there was a greater percentage of teachers favoring joint study committees

---

*Teachers who believed class size was a professional issue were more likely than teachers who viewed the issue as a working condition to report that small classes improve education in general as their most important interest. In other words, they were more highly motivated to bargain on class size because of a belief in the educational value of small classes, whereas the latter group of teachers tended to express more pragmatic goals: increased opportunity to give individual instruction and improvement of pupil: teacher ratios in the classroom.

300

than in larger districts (201 or more teachers) and districts located in suburban and urban areas. The study also indicated that the smaller the classroom pupil:teacher ratio, the more likely it was that teachers favored joint study committees, whereas, as ratios increased, teachers showed greater preference for collective bargaining. Two-thirds of the teachers who defined class size as a working condition said collective bargaining was the most effective means of dealing with the issue. The majority of teachers characterizing class size as a professional issue favored joint study committees.

On the whole, most teachers favor collective bargaining on class size and do not wish to see restraints on the negotiability of this issue. A significant number, however, believe that because class size is a hybrid subject with educational policy implications, it may best be handled through faculty-administration committees, away from the bargaining table.*

Most administrators would prefer not to be statutorily obligated to negotiate on class size, and a significant minority believe the matter should be determined solely by school management. Many employers, however, identified class size as an issue of professional concern, or at least a subject of both professional and managerial interest. In light of these views, it was not surprising that 71 percent of the administrators favored faculty-administration study committees as the most effective means of dealing with class size. Moreover, such committees often lack the power to make binding recommendations, and employers find them helpful as a forum through which teachers can make suggestions rather than demands. Clearly, unless these committees are authorized (for instance, through collective bargaining) to make and implement class size or other educational policies, they are much less threatening to managerial prerogatives than collective negotiations on policy-related issues.

---

*The author, however, has reservations about the real implications of these findings, because relatively few teachers whose districts had experienced joint class size discussions away from collective bargaining found them to be productive. Moreover, 73 percent of those teachers who had reported unproductive discussions with administrators on class size favored collective bargaining as the best means of dealing with the topic, as compared with 48 percent of the entire population that favored collective bargaining.

301

5. Has third party assistance been widely used to resolve contract disputes on class size?

Over 70 percent of the survey respondents reported that the issue of class size had never been presented to either a mediator or a fact-finder; 19 percent said the issue had been submitted to both mediation and fact-finding; 6 percent reported submission only to mediation; and 3 percent reported submission only to fact-finding. Where third party assistance was reported with respect to the class size issue, it was more frequently used in 1970 and subsequent years than during the period 1967-69.

In addition to analyzing the aggregate response to this question, the experiences of districts with class size in their contracts and without it were studied separately. The analysis indicated that third party assistance on the issue of class size was more frequently used in districts with contract language on class size than in districts without it. One-fourth of the respondents with class size in their agreements, as opposed to 12 percent of those with contracts silent on the issue, had submitted the issue to both mediation and fact-finding. Whereas 64 percent of the respondents with class size reported that the subject had never been submitted to either mediation or fact-finding, 79 percent of the respondents with no class size contract language reported that neither form of third party assistance had been used.* This finding suggested that although class size had not been widely submitted to mediation and/or fact-finding in either type of district, in those districts with collective agreements including class size provisions, third party assistance might have been instrumental in bringing about this inclusion.

Respondents were asked: "If mediation occurred, was the neutral helpful either in discussing or facilitating agreement on the class size issue?" Over 70 percent reported that mediation was not helpful. Moreover, this percentage remained constant when the answers of teachers and administrators were analyzed separately. There was a difference, however, between the responses of teachers and administrators in districts with class size in their contracts, and the answers of teachers and administrators in districts without

---

*In districts with class size provisions, 7 percent of the respondents reported use of mediation on the issue, and 4 percent reported use of fact-finding on class size. In districts without class size contract language, less than 5 percent reported that the issue had been submitted to mediation, and 2 percent said it had been presented to a fact-finder.

class size contract language. In the latter category 19 percent of the respondents said mediation on class size was helpful; in the former, 35 percent reported that mediation was helpful.

Although relatively few respondents reported that class size had been submitted to fact-finding, more respondents in districts with contract language stated that the fact-finder made recommendations on the issue than did respondents without class size provisions in their contracts.* 42 percent of the respondents reporting that their districts received a fact-finding recommendation on class size said that the fact-finder's recommendation was accepted.† There was a slightly higher percentage of acceptances, however, in districts with class size in their contracts than in districts without contract language—44 percent compared with 38 percent. ‡

All told, 33 respondents reported that fact-finding recommendations on class size had been rejected in their districts. Answers to a question on the reasons for these rejections were not especially significant, however, because many respondents chose not to reply.§ In districts both with and without contract provisions on class size, most respondents reported that rejected fact-finding recommendations on this issue were not used as a basis for further bargaining or for compromise.

The third party assistance discussed so far has pertained to mediation and fact-finding in contract disputes on class size. Parties also were asked about their experience with grievance arbitration on class size.

As noted above, over 80 percent of the survey respondents indicated that no grievances concerning class size had ever been filed

---

*69 percent of the respondents with class size language, as opposed to 61 percent of those without contract language, said the fact-finder had made recommendations on the issue.

†58 percent of the respondents receiving fact-finding recommendations on class size rejected them; 33 percent reported that the employer rejected the recommendations, 14 percent reported that the teachers rejected them, and 11 percent reported that both parties rejected them.

‡The breakdown with respect to who rejected the recommendations on class size was similar even when the answers of respondents in districts with and without contract provisions on class size were studied separately.

§Of those that did offer reasons, 18 percent said that the fact-finding recommendation was rejected because of a belief that fact-finders should not decide the issue of class size. 15 percent stated that the fact-finding recommendation was either too high or too low. An additional 15 percent said rejection was due to a lack of specificity in the fact-finder's recommendation.

in their districts. The experience with grievance arbitration on class size, therefore, was extremely limited; only 2 percent reported grievance arbitration on this issue. As might have been expected, however, respondents in districts with class size provisions in their contracts did report a somewhat higher number of grievances on the issue. Whereas 95 percent of respondents in districts without contract class size provisions reported "zero" grievances, 73 percent of the respondents whose contracts had class size language reported no grievances on this topic. This finding might have been expected, inasmuch as most contracts define grievances as violations, misapplications, or misinterpretations of specific contract terms. Where there is no contract clause covering class size, it is difficult for teachers to present formal grievances on the subject.

One might anticipate that where negotiations occur over hybrid issues, such as class size, the parties, particularly management, would exhibit much "hard bargaining." In other words, the employer would cling more tenaciously to his bargaining position in efforts to protect the inherent managerial interests in these subjects. But if resort to neutrals in bargaining deadlocks is any indication of hardness of bargaining, which some believe it is,[5] then class size may not be one of the most hotly or stubbornly negotiated items on bargaining agendas. This study has indicated that third party assistance may have been somewhat responsible for the inclusion of class size clauses in the contracts of several districts. This suggestion rests on the fact that respondents in districts with class size in their contracts reported a higher level of use of neutrals and greater satisfaction with third party assistance than did respondents in districts without class size language in their agreements. But in light of the fact that over three-fourths of the parties who negotiated class size into their contracts did so without the help of neutrals, it would appear that this issue, though hybrid, is conducive to resolution through collective bargaining.

The Impact of West Irondequoit

6. How did the parties react to PERB's West Irondequoit decision?

Approximately 50 percent of both teachers and administrators had not read either the West Irondequoit decision or a summary of it.[*]

---

[*] 53.1 percent of the teachers and 48 percent of the administrators had read nothing of the case. This percentage remained constant in both districts with and without class size provisions in their contracts.

20 percent of both the teachers and administrators indicated that they had read West Irondequoit, or at least about it, but were unsure of what effect the decision would have on their future negotiations. 15 percent (26) of the teachers indicating they had read either the decision or a summary reported that the decision would affect future negotiations; 13 percent said it would not affect negotiations. 18 percent (36) of the employers having knowledge of West Irondequoit indicated it would affect future negotiations; 13 percent said it would not. Essentially, 70 percent of both teacher and superintendent respondents, therefore, either had no familiarity with this case or were uncertain as to what influence it would have on future collective bargaining.

Teachers and administrators indicating that West Irondequoit would affect future negotiations were asked to predict the nature of the decision's effect. Teachers answering this question frequently responded that they would ignore PERB's decision and attempt to bargain on class size per se.* The next most popular answer was that teachers would bargain on the impact, or effect, of class size— a response that basically was what PERB's ruling authorized.†

Administrators who anticipated that West Irondequoit would affect their future negotiations also were asked to describe this expected effect. Almost twice that number, however, answered this question, a situation that, though somewhat confusing, deserves consideration. Fifty employer respondents stated that they would bargain on the impact of class size, but not on class size per se. Eighteen employers said that they would bargain on class size per se even though it is a permissive subject of bargaining.‡

This questionnaire was completed by study participants during March, April, and May 1972—approximately six months after PERB rendered its West Irondequoit decision. The New York State Teachers Association (NYSTA) considered the decision to be very significant, and it promptly sought rehearing of the case. Following its

---

*Twenty teachers gave this answer, which, to a considerable extent, may also have reflected the attitude of the 13 percent who said that West Irondequoit would not affect their future bargaining.

†Fifteen teacher respondents selected this answer. The remaining respondents spread their choices over the following alternatives: maintain current contract language, bargain for decreased pupil: teacher ratios, negotiate more preparation periods.

‡Here, too, several employers selecting this response may have shared, to some extent, the beliefs of that proportion of the 13 percent who may have bargained on class size in the past and who indicated that PERB's decision would not affect their future negotiations.

unsuccessful attempt to win a reversal of the decision, NYSTA began proceedings to appeal PERB's decision in court. The newsletters of both NYSTA and the New York State School Boards Association reported West Irondequoit. Apparently, however, half of the teachers and administrators in responsible negotiating positions had not read even a summary of the decision, and a significant percentage of those who had knowledge of the case could not discuss what effect it might have on bargaining. It is difficult to make a value judgment on this finding, although PERB members and neutrals on PERB's impasse panels, who are greatly concerned about the large number of bargaining impasses and the excessive number of issues that frequently are submitted to third parties for resolution, probably will find it significant that so many teacher and school board negotiators could potentially face each other at the bargaining table uninformed about a crucial PERB decision—one that might be dispositive of an issue in dispute. If a substantial number of teacher representatives and school administrators were unenlightened about West Irondequoit, then it is not far-fetched to suggest that an equally significant number of teachers and district administrators might have had little knowledge about the existence or meaning of other important scope-of-bargaining decisions that have gradually defined the rights and duties of parties at the bargaining table.

Comparison Between Districts With and Without Class Size Contract Provisions

7. Are there major differences in attitudes, experiences, and problems between districts whose contracts contain class size provisions and those that do not?

The survey indicated that the class size issue, though raised frequently in collective bargaining in both types of districts, had been negotiated more often in districts with contracts containing class size provisions than in districts whose contracts were silent on the topic. In addition, 32 percent of the respondents in districts without class size provisions said that teachers had never proposed or demanded such a contract provision during bargaining. In light of this finding, it is not surprising that 33 percent of the respondents in districts without class size language in their contracts reported that this subject was not a "problem" in their districts. The suggestion is that when class size becomes a genuine "problem," the teachers' bargaining representative generally raises the matter in collective bargaining.

Attitudes toward the issue of class size in districts with and without contract provisions showed both similarities and differences.

Significantly, 50 percent of the respondents in each type of district agreed that joint study committees provided the most effective way of resolving the class size issue. In districts with negotiated clauses, however, over 30 percent of the respondents believed collective bargaining was the best means of handling the issue, and only 8 percent believed that unilateral control by management was the most effective means. In contrast, in districts without contract language, 22 percent checked collective bargaining and 14 percent said class size is best determined through unilateral managerial policy.* On a related question, 60 percent of the respondents in districts where class size had been negotiated into the agreement stated that there should be no restraints on the negotiation of the issue; only 52 percent of the respondents without class size provisions agreed.

In response to a question asking the parties to characterize the class size issue, a sizable and similar percentage of respondents in districts with and without contract provisions (43 and 48 percent, respectively) defined class size as an issue of "professional concern." But 23 percent in districts with contract language, as opposed to 14 percent in districts without contract language, described class size as a working condition; and 12 percent in districts with contract provisions, in contrast with 21 percent in districts without such provisions, defined class size as a managerial issue.

Thus, although the differences in views between respondents in districts with and without negotiated class size clauses were not startling, parties in the former category tended to express more "liberal" attitudes toward the negotiability of class size. Similarities were apparent in that over 40 percent of the parties in each type of district saw class size as a professional issue and over half said joint faculty-administration committees provided the best means of handling the subject. In addition, in both types of districts, where employers opposed the inclusion of class size language in the collective agreement, they tended to use the same arguments in the same order of frequency. The two most often used contentions were that class size was a management prerogative and that class size language in the contract would lead to increased district costs.

Experiences with third party assistance have already been described; essentially, respondents with contracts containing class size language during the period of this study reported more frequent resort to neutrals regarding the issue and greater satisfaction with

---

*Teachers whose contracts had class size language were more likely to favor collective bargaining than teachers whose contracts were silent on the issue. Teachers in the latter category showed a slightly stronger preference for joint study committees than did those with class size in their contracts.

dispute settlement assistance than did respondents without class size contract language.

As to familiarity with the West Irondequoit decision, respondents with class size contracts more frequently reported knowledge of the case and certainty as to its effect on their future negotiations.[*] Although there are several possible explanations for this finding, a plausible one is that parties who had bargained on class size and included it in their agreement might have been more aware of the experiences of other school districts regarding the issue and more cognizant of legal developments affecting its negotiability.

The presence and absence of contractual class size provisions were cross-tabulated with other variables to determine if certain relationships existed between districts whose agreements had specific language and other variables. It was hypothesized that relationships would exist between the presence of class size clauses in a contract and the size of a district, the type of area in which the district was located, and the number of years in which the parties had engaged in formal collective bargaining. In addition, other variables were cross-tabulated with the presence/absence of contract language to explore other possible relationships that were not originally hypothesized.

Cross-Tabulation Findings

District size was measured by the number of teachers in the bargaining unit; the greater the number of teachers, the larger the district. The survey indicated that in bargaining units of less than 50 teachers, only 29 percent had class size in their contracts. At least 50 percent of the bargaining units containing more than 50 teachers, however, had class size language in their agreements. This percentage ranged from 53 percent in the districts with 50-100 teachers up to 80 percent in districts with more than 500 teachers. This relationship persisted even when one controlled for region of the state.

Respondents were asked to answer whether their districts were located in urban, suburban, or rural areas. The findings indicated that 85 percent of the urban districts, 59 percent of the suburban districts, and 48 percent of the rural districts had class size provisions in their contracts. Thus, there was a greater likelihood of finding negotiated class size provisions in the contracts of urban

---

[*] 43 percent of the respondents with class size provisions, as compared with almost 60 percent of those without contract language, said they had not read the case or a summary of it.

districts than in the contracts of suburban districts, and a greater likelihood of finding contract language on class size in agreements of suburban districts than in agreements of rural districts.

In considering the relationship between presence of class size contract provisions and the number of years of bargaining, it was found that very few (15) districts had been bargaining for only one or two years. In these districts, 12 and 28 percent, respectively, had written class size provisions into their contracts. It was not until three years of bargaining that the number of districts with class size provisions increased to 49 percent, reflecting (approximately) the sample as a whole. Even at the four- and five-year levels, however, the likelihood of a district having class size contract language was 50 percent. In other words, the percentage of districts with class size provisions hovered around 50 percent regardless of whether the parties had been bargaining three, four, or five or more years.

Interesting, though unanticipated, results were obtained when the presence/absence of class size variable was cross-tabulated with classroom pupil:teacher ratio and average number of pupils per day (for secondary teachers). In districts where the pupil:teacher ratio was less than 15:1, the incidence of class size contract language was only 11 percent. In all ranges greater than 15:1, however,[*] the incidence of class size in the contract was between 50 and 60 percent, with the percentage of agreements with contract language increasing from 50 percent to 60 percent as pupil:teacher ratio increased. Thus contract language did not preclude pupil:teacher ratios of 31:1-35:1. This finding implies that class size contract language does not necessarily reflect or impose small class sizes. Moreover, teachers in districts already enjoying very small pupil:teacher ratios—less than 15:1—probably feel no need to bargain on the item.

Similar findings were obtained when presence/absence of class size contract language was cross-tabulated with the average number of pupils per day of secondary school teachers. Where the average number of pupils per day per teacher was 75-100, only 26 percent of the contracts had class size language. Where the average number of pupils per day was 101-25, 126-50, or 151-75, approximately 60 percent of the contracts had class size provisions. Apparently, where overall teaching loads, in terms of the daily number of students assigned to a teacher, are small, there is less need to negotiate on class size. Moreover, the results indicate that contract language certainly does not "cause" small ratios and teaching loads. Class size provisions in collective agreements may

---

[*] The ranges were less than 15:1, 15:1-20:1, 21:1-25:1, 26:1-30:1, 31:1-35:1.

memorialize existing conditions, specify limits, or bring about reductions; but the questionnaire results show that the smallest class sizes, ratios, and teaching loads exist in districts without written class size provisions.

Types of Class Size Provisions

8. What kinds of class size provisions are being negotiated into contracts? Are there variations in their nature and in the goals they seek to achieve?

Knowing the content of a contract's class size provision is as important as knowing whether any contract provision on this subject exists at all. In fact, the real impact of negotiating over class size can best be measured by studying the precise language to which parties have agreed to bind themselves.

To accomplish this, the class size contract provisions of all districts whose agreements contained class size clauses were collected. The class size provisions were then ranked on a scale of 1-5, according to their degree of rigidity and specificity.

The number 1 was assigned to contract language that established mandatory class size maxima, minima, ranges, or averages. The following contract provisions, for example, were assigned a number 1:

Article VI. Teacher-Pupil Ratio and Class Size:
No teacher shall be required to teach more than 25 periods per week or more than 29 students in 1970/71, or more than 28 students in 1971/72 for enriched and regular classes, or more than 23 in 1970/71, or more than 22 in 1971/72 for modified classes except for new transfers into the District after September 1st, or a total of more than 145 in 1970/71 or more than 140 in 1971/72. Each teacher may have one class of 30 regular or enriched, or 24 modified but not more than the total limits. Gym classes shall be limited to 50 students per class.

Conditions of Employment

A. Staffing and Teaching Conditions

1. Level of Staffing

There shall be a district-wide ratio of not less than 50 professional employees to each 1,000 pupils.

310

2. Maximum Class Size

Effective Date	Grades	Maximum Class Size
Sept., 1969	1-12	33
	Kdgn.	
Sept., 1970	2-12	33
	Kdgn.-1st grade	30
Sept., 1971	2-12	30
	Kdgn.-1st grade	28

In instances when class size as set forth above is exceeded by one child per class or per grade level in a building, an additional cluster aide shall be employed to assist all classes affected. Such cluster aide shall be employed for a minimum of two hours daily plus an additional hour for each child above two to a maximum of six hours daily.

The number 2 was assigned to contract provisions that were mandatory but that included certain recognized and specific exceptions to the mandatory requirements. For example:

Article VII. Class Size

A. The Board and the Association agree that classes of moderate size tend to produce teaching loads designed to enable teachers to be more effective in their teaching.

. . . . . .

C. Therefore, it is agreed that, within the physical facilities available, the following shall be the maximum class sizes:

Grades K-3	25
Grades 4-6	26
Jr. High Schools	27
Sr. High Schools	28

D. It is further agreed that in the secondary schools exceptions to the junior and senior high schools maximums listed above will be limited to the following: physical education, typewriting, band, orchestra, and chorus. In addition, in the senior high schools only, biology, chemistry, physics and earth science will be permitted a class maximum of 31 where the teacher teaches no more than three classes of 21 periods per week.

311

The number 3 was assigned to what were termed "nonmandatory" provisions. These clauses did not actually tightly bind the employer to do more than "make efforts" to adhere to "guidelines" or to establish certain "goals" regarding class size, "whenever possible." The following provisions are examples of this "escape hatch" language:

It is the goal of the Board of Education, insofar as administratively feasible, to maintain class sizes within the following limits:
K   20-25
1-3   20-25
4-6   25-30
7-12 25-30

Maximum Class Size

a. The following criteria shall be regarded as the goal in setting the limit on class size. Every reasonable effort shall be made by the Board of Education in holding to these limits where possible and in achieving the conditions to make them possible as rapidly as is feasible. . . .

The number 4 was given to contract language that stipulated merely that the employer would "consult" with teachers or their bargaining representative regarding class size. Such provisions did not commit the employer to accept teacher recommendations. Generally, they either established formal consultation committees or provided for informal communication on class size. The following language was considered consultative:

The Board will adhere to its policy on class size and will strive to achieve mutually acceptable ratios of class load as far as administratively feasible. The Board and the Administration will consult with a teacher committee when policy or class size is considered.

Article IV. Class Size.

The Board of Education recognizes the fact that class size may play an important role in our total instructional program. Therefore, it shall periodically evaluate the class size structure and will seek advice from the professional staff of this school district in that evaluation.

The number 5 was assigned to the least binding or specific type of class size provision. The language in this type of provision tended to be rhetorical, with emphasis on keeping class sizes consistent with "quality education." Frequently, rhetorical provisions also expressed a need for further study and evaluation of class size problems. The following provisions were given a number 5:

D Class Size

    a. It is agreed that classes of moderate size enable teachers to be more effective in their teaching.
    b. The Board recognizes the concept of flexible scheduling in terms of class and group size as a means through which optimum educational benefits for children may be achieved. . . .
    c. The Board and the Association agree:
        1. Small classes generally offer opportunity for teachers to know their students better.
        2. Smaller classes provide the opportunity to use more effectively a greater variety of instructional materials and methods. . . .
        3. Experimentation, innovation and invention are more likely to occur in small classes.
    d. Where a class size is inconsistent with the above and does not meet the needs of students, the Administration shall take reasonable measures to alleviate the situation, such as providing extra instructional personnel.

Class Size. The Board shall continue to make every effort to establish class sizes consistent with sound educational practices.

54.6 percent of questionnaire respondents reported collective agreements containing some class size language. The most frequently negotiated type of provision was number 3—the nonmandatory, or "escape hatch," language. This was true regardless of the size of the district, the type of area in which it was located, and the number of years in which the parties had bargained. The types of clauses and their approximate percentages are shown below.

Percent	Type of Clause
45	No class size provision in the contract
27	Nonmandatory language (#3)
8	Mandatory language with stipulated exceptions (#2)
6	Mandatory language (#1)

5	Rhetorical language (#5)
4	Consultative language (#4)
5	Contract language not available to researcher

When the variable concerning type of class size provision was cross-tabulated with the number of teachers in the bargaining unit, the districts with more than 500 teachers had the highest percentage of mandatory contract language. Districts with less than 100 teachers, in contrast, had the greatest percentage of rhetorical language. This finding suggests that in small districts, rhetorical language may have been sufficient to satisfy the parties' interests, whereas in the largest districts, most of which were in urban areas, class size was too important an issue to be disposed of through philosophical contract language. In small districts, even if class size were a problematical issue, the teachers might have also lacked sufficient numerical strength to negotiate more stringent provisions.[*]

"Maintaining flexibility" was the most frequent and most significan administrator objective in negotiations on class size. The analysis concerning types of class size provisions appearing in contracts indicates that employers have enjoyed considerable success in fulfilling this bargaining objective. The teachers' primary bargaining goal pertained to increasing their opportunity to provide individualized instruction. Apparently they have, in many cases, agreed to contract language that, though permitting the employer a degree of latitude in determining overall policy and making assignments, acknowledges their commitment to decreasing class sizes and recognizes that enlarged opportunity for individual instruction is a worthwhile and mutually shared education objective.[6]

Admittedly, "weak" contract provisions can, over time, be strengthened, especially if employees exert sufficient pressure. This "foot-in-the-door" tactic may, understandably, be feared by public employers. Interestingly, however, teacher responses to a question asking if they intended to make a class size demand in the next round of negotiations were not overwhelmingly affirmative: 43 percent stated that they intended to bargain for a more rigid class size contract provision. But almost as many, 41 percent, stated that they did not intend to present any proposals on class size; and an additional 10 percent said they were uncertain.

---

[*]In addition, as type of class size provision increased in rigidity and/or specificity, there was a greater propensity for teachers to favor collective bargaining. In contrast, as the type of class size provision became weaker, an increasing number of teachers favored joint study committees. In fact, those teachers with rhetorical language showed particularly strong preference for joint study committees rather than collective bargaining as the most effective means for handling class size.

NYSTA Versus AFT Districts

Inasmuch as only 12 questionnaires were returned from districts in which the AFT was the exclusive bargaining representative, it was practically impossible to make any valid comparisons between these districts and those in which NYSTA locals bargained for the employees. Probably the most significant conclusion one can draw from the data analysis is that, based on the sample used here, there are few differences between both teacher and administrator respondents in NYSTA and AFT districts with respect to their attitudes, goals, and experiences concerning class size. Although NYSTA and the UFT have recently merged in New York and become the New York State United Teachers, a broader sample of historically AFT districts and an equal sample of former NYSTA districts could be used in the future to analyze certain tendencies that the questionnaire suggested: that a higher percentage of administrators in AFT districts (57 percent) than in NYSTA districts (46 percent) believed class size was negotiable; that those AFT districts with contract language on class size had only types 1, 2, or 3, whereas almost 10 percent of the NYSTA districts had types 4 and 5; and that AFT districts had a greater propensity to use third party assistance to resolve contract disputes on class size than did NYSTA districts.

SUMMARY

Most teachers and a significant number of administrators do not favor the adoption of legal restrictions on the negotiability of class size. They believe the law should allow the parties flexibility and creativity in handling class size problems. In some districts this may be accomplished through collective bargaining, and in others through the establishment of joint study committees. In some schools a combination of techniques may prove most effective. Even those employers who do not consider class size a mandatory subject of bargaining frequently recognize it as a professional issue that should not be determined exclusively by school management. And teachers, though cognizant of the policy implications of class size, believe strongly that the subject is too much a professional interest and too directly a part of their classroom working conditions to be excluded from the bargaining table.

Overall, there have been few serious problems in negotiating class size provisions into collective agreements. School employers are concerned about sharing managerial prerogatives with teacher representatives, and they also fear the financial consequences of including tight class size language in their agreements. The study indicates, however, that employers have demonstrated considerable success in negotiating flexible provisions into their contracts that give them latitude in establishing class sizes and making teaching assignments. Moreover, over two-thirds of those administrators with class size contract provisions reported "no problems"; 57 percent said their contract language fully satisfied their goals; and over three-fourths said they experienced no difficulty in adhering to the specific contract clauses on class size. Additionally, in districts with class size in their contracts, the percentage of teachers filing grievances was extremely low.

Urban and large district administrators were notably liberal in their attitude toward the bargainability of class size. Their questionnaire responses, as well as more elaborate explanations that several administrators attached to their questionnaires, expressed their conviction that limitations on the negotiability of class size would be unrealistic. Small, rural districts had more limited experience in negotiating this issue, and respondents frequently expressed the belief that class size problems could be worked out through faculty-administration committees away from the bargaining table. In the rural and small districts, however, class size quite often had not presented any problems, nor had it ever been proposed as a bargaining demand. Few class size difficulties, plus traditionally amicable teacher-school board relations in these districts, may have led teachers to believe that contract language on the issue was not necessary.

In general, the questionnaire evidenced no strong employer interest in pressing for legislative exclusion of class size from the scope of bargaining. Although some employers believed that class size was inappropriate for mandatory negotiations, most administrators seemed to have reconciled themselves to collective bargaining and appeared willing to deal with such matters as class size in a bilateral process. The evidence on the type of class size language that has actually been included in agreements, as well as employer comments about the objectives they sought to accomplish in negotiations and the managerial interests they strove to protect, reflect a managerial awareness of the obstacles and danger points in bargaining and a confidence that issues such as class size can be negotiated without managerial abrogation of policy responsibilities.

NOTES

1. Irving Sabghir, The Scope of Bargaining in Public Sector Collective Bargaining, report sponsored by PERB, Oct. 1970.
2. Ibid., p. 64.

3. Claire Sellitz, Marie Jahoda, Morton Deutsch, and S. W. Cook, Research Methods in Social Relations (rev. ed.; New York: Holt, 1959), as reported in W. Richard Scott, "Field Methods in the Study of Organizations," James G. March, ed., Handbook of Organizations (Chicago: Rand McNally, 1965).

4. Peter Feuille, "Police Union Power," manuscript of doctoral dissertation (University of California, Berkeley, 1973), p. 13.

5. David Lipsky and John Drotning, forthcoming bargaining study (Ithaca: New York State School of Industrial and Labor Relations, Cornell University.)

6. Charles Perry and Wesley Wildman also did a study of teacher-school board agreements, and their findings with respect to class size substantiate what was found here regarding types of class size contract provisions. They write: "In short, the inclusion of a class size clause in a negotiations agreement is more often a procedural or symbolic rather than substantive victory for a teacher organization." The Impact of Negotiations in Public Education (Worthington, Ohio: Jones, 1970), p. 207.

CHAPTER

12

CONCLUDING
OBSERVATIONS:
THE SCOPE OF
BARGAINING AND
THE PUBLIC INTEREST

The institution of collective bargaining in public employment is frequently viewed as beneficial to the public employees but also as making present government services more costly to the taxpayers. Extensive changes in the relationships between public employers and their employees are to be expected, as well as changes in the relationship between these government agencies and the public; but whether or not this improves the quality of government services remains to be seen.[1]

Some critics contend that public sector collective bargaining, especially on a wide scope of issues, jeopardizes the public interest by giving unions an excessive share of political power. Harry Wellington and Ralph Winter, for instance, have expressed concern that

> . . . demands of public sector unions do have effects that go beyond the parties to the agreement. All of us have a stake in how school children are disciplined. Expansion of the subjects of bargaining in the public sector, therefore, may increase the total quantum of union power in the political process.[2]

Wellington and Winter emphasize differences between private and public sector collective bargaining. They suggest that public sector negotiations impose on society not only a potential misallocation of resources through restrictions on economic output, as in private employment, but also misallocations of political power. A full transplant of private sector collective bargaining into government service

> . . . would, in many cases, institutionalize the power of public employee unions in a way that would leave competing groups in the political process at a permanent and substantial disadvantage.[3]

318

There are, they say, three reasons for this. First, some government services are so essential that any prolonged disruption would menace public health and safety. Second, the demand for many government services is relatively inelastic, especially since there is a lack of close substitutes. The third reason for fearing a full transplant is the extent to which the disruption of a government service inconveniences municipal taxpayers, particularly since most politicians are vulnerable to both union and political pressures and are often forced to think in terms of the short-run, rather than the long-run, impact of labor settlements.

Other students of public sector labor relations, including this writer, do not believe that comprehensive public employee collective bargaining and the public interest are incompatible. The structure of government and the political process can protect the commonweal against potential misallocations of power resulting from collective bargaining.

In most jurisdictions, collective bargaining agreements are not self-implementing. New York's Taylor Law and New York City Collective Bargaining Law, for example, recognize the ultimate responsibility of the legislative process with respect to determination of public policy and allocation of resources. Both laws provide that terms of any agreement or impasse panel decision requiring legislative approval may not be effectuated until such approval is secured—or, in the case of New York City—until a law is enacted.

The recently amended Wisconsin Employment Relations Act covering state employees is unique in that it clearly identifies and fixes the bargaining responsibility in the executive, but recognizes the legislature as the final repository of authority. Tentative agreements reached between state agencies and unions, however, must be submitted to a joint legislative committee, which conducts a public hearing and then approves or disapproves the agreement. This committee is composed of the speaker of the Assembly, president pro tem of the Senate, the majority and minority leaders, and cochairmen of the Committee on Finance. Once the committee has approved the agreement, it introduces bills in both houses to implement those provisions of the agreement, such as wages and fringe benefits, that require legislative action. If the committee does not approve the tentative agreement, it is returned to the parties for further negotiations. Thus, in Wisconsin the legislature not only implements public sector collective agreements but, through a committee, participates in the bargaining process as well.[4] As the elected representatives of the public, the legislature is thus able to ride close herd on the progress of negotiations and make its influence felt.

In Milwaukee a legislative committee of the City Council has the responsibility for employer bargaining. The bargaining team is employed by and reports to the Council's Committee on Personnel and Finance. In New York City a Labor Policy Committee has been established to advise and guide the director of the Office of Labor Relations in bargaining with public employee unions. Two deputy mayors, a budget director, personnel director, corporation counsel, and labor relations director serve as the mayor's labor relations policy-making team. Such coordination places responsibility on the executive and reduces the possibility of "end runs" by union leaders to other governmental authority.[5]

These procedures operate in the public interest. They prevent unions from playing the executive and legislative branches against one another but, more important, they recognize that although employer negotiators must have authority to engage in meaningful bargaining, the legislature holds the budget and taxing powers. And, as a practical matter, there are statutory and political constraints on the willingness of lawmakers to impose higher taxes to implement collective bargaining agreements. As Arvid Anderson writes:

> The political reality of legislative power, even if a statute does not expressly provide for legislative approval of . . . collective agreements, can be relied on to prevent the execution of agreements . . . which are regarded as too costly or without regard to the public interest.[6]

Wellington and Winter are doubtful that taxpayer resistance or the determination of municipal government, or both, will substantially offset union power. In New York, however, one example of the way in which public pressure can affect the scope of bargaining concerns public employee pensions. Essentially, mounting public displeasure with the level of pension benefits recently resulted in legislation that removes pensions from the scope of bargaining until 1976. Additionally, a special session of the legislature adopted pension legislation classifying public employees for pension benefits and limiting the level of pensions of newly hired employees. In the long run, removing pensions from the scope of bargaining may prove to be a mistake,* but at least in the short run the "public" has claimed a victory over the bargaining power of several large and influential public unions.

---

*Many believe that pensions are a basic ingredient of the entire economic package in collective bargaining. Removing pensions from the scope of bargaining does not eliminate the issue; it merely results in legislative determination of pension benefits. The consequences may well be that pensions become a political football and that public employee unions increase other economic demands at the bargaining table to compensate for denial of pension bargaining rights.

The public interest is preserved not only by the force of collective opinion but also by the operation of public employment relations boards. As has been demonstrated throughout this study, in most jurisdictions these boards have the responsibility in the first instance to resolve scope-of-bargaining disputes through the application of consistent criteria that balance employee rights against the responsibility of public management to operate government agencies in the public interest. Frank Zeidler, in his essay "The Public as Third Party," also recognizes labor boards as a guardian of the public interest:

> Boards exercise authority over employee-employer relations in the public service, and see that the third party interests of the public as embodied in state or federal law are observed. They see that fair practices are followed and that the rights of all the parties are protected. Such boards also employ methods such as mediation, conciliation, fact finding, and arbitration to keep the heat of disputes at a manageable point. In this way they tend to reduce public anxiety over what is happening in labor-management relations. The public is beginning to regard such boards as the first line defense against either management or employees.[7]

George Hildebrand has written that in a democracy, the quest for and use of political power by diverse interest groups are an integral part of government and, if employed properly for lawful purposes, a legitimate endeavor. Public employee collective bargaining under statutes that define rights and responsibilities is such a legitimate activity, and one that need not subordinate the public interest as long as the community possesses and uses the "ultimate periodic safeguard of electoral challenge and review of the acts of its chosen officers."[8] Moreover, just as collective bargaining in private employment is subject to the constraints of the marketplace, so should collective negotiations in the public sector be fashioned under the structure of political democracy and its governmental processes. As George Taylor wrote, "The objective of collective negotiations is not to provide employees with power 'to write their own ticket' but to provide for their effective participation . . . in the establishment of their terms and conditions of employment."[9]

One aspect of political democracy pertains to the right of citizens to participate in government affairs. Just as employees seek a role in the determination of wages and working conditions, today concerned taxpayers increasingly seek involvement in the decision-making activities of local government agencies. Traditionally, however, collective bargaining has been a bilateral rather than a multilateral process. Over the next decade efforts must be devoted to designing ways that will give the electorate the opportunity to make itself heard in governmental decision-making while simultaneously preserving a viable scope of employer-employee collective bargaining. Decisions concerning such issues as school decentralization, school integration, establishment of civilian police review boards, and the level of welfare services to be provided involve more than just managerial prerogatives and employee working conditions. Certainly the resolution of these questions affects employer-employee relations; but they are, first and foremost, matters of public policy with great impact on the community. The taxpayers have a right to participate in the formulation of such policies.

Several public participation schemes have been suggested, some of which would debilitate the collective bargaining mechanism.[10] One plan that may promote the public interest and yet not harm the integrity of the bargaining process would establish several citizens' committees representing different viewpoints in the community with respect to various governmental services. These committees could meet with labor and management negotiators prior to and during bargaining to discuss the sentiments of the public on issues being negotiated. Such meetings might benefit the public employer by providing it with public opinion before it reaches final agreement on issues important to the electorate. Unions also might welcome the meetings because they could indicate to the employer public support for the union's demands (where such support exists). And, most important, establishment of these citizens groups would give the public a sense of participation in decision-making, which it is hoped would generate community support for the final agreement reached by the bargaining parties.[11] This proposed plan stops short of suggesting that negotiations be conducted in a "goldfish bowl"—a highly ineffective procedure. It does, however, acknowledge that the public has a right to know of and participate in matters of public policy.

Today the major question concerning the scope of public sector bargaining relates to what impact the negotiating process will have on legislative and executive decision-making and on the allocation of resources and power. Collective bargaining, like other social experiments, carries certain risks. But weakening the process in order to avoid the risks will not alleviate the labor-management issues that need to be resolved in mutually satisfactory ways. I do not think that there is an ideal collective bargaining scheme; different procedures may work well in different environments. I do believe, however, that a fluid and flexible scope of bargaining will facilitate the resolution of labor-management problems and adapt itself more easily to the changing needs of the parties and the public they serve.

NOTES

1. George Taylor, "The Public Interest in Collective Negotiations in Education," in Stanley Elam, Myron Lieberman, and Michael Moskow, eds., Readings on Collective Negotiations in Public Education (Chicago: Rand McNally, 1967), p. 13.

2. Harry H. Wellington and Ralph K. Winter, The Unions and the Cities (Washington, D.C.: Brookings Institution, 1971), p. 23.

3. Ibid., p. 30.

4. Arvid Anderson, with the assistance of Joan Weitzman, "The Impact of Public Sector Collective Bargaining," 1973 Wisconsin Law Review 986 (1973).

5. Ibid.

6. Ibid.

7. Frank Zeidler, "The Public as Third Party," Public Personnel Administration (Englewood Cliffs, N.J.: Prentice-Hall, 1973).

8. George Hildebrand, "The Public Sector," in John Dunlop and Neil Chamberlain, eds., Frontiers of Collective Bargaining (New York: Harper and Row, 1967), p. 133.

9. Taylor, op. cit., p. 17.

10. Wellington and Winter, op. cit., pp. 150-53.

11. Frederick R. Livingston, "Collective Bargaining and the School Board," in Sam Zagoria, ed., Public Workers and Public Unions (Englewood Cliffs, N.J.: Prentice-Hall, 1972), p. 75.

APPENDIXES

COLLECTIVE BARGAINING BY PUBLIC EMPLOYEES—
A SUMMARY OF STATE AUTHORIZATIONS

State	Employees Covered	Authorization
Alabama	Fire fighters	Ala. Code tit. 37, § 450 (Supp. 1967)
Alaska	Public employees	Alaska Stat. §§23.40.070-260 (1972)
	Teachers	Alaska Stat. §§14.20.550-610 (1970), as amended
California	Local employees	Cal. Gov't. Code §§3500-11, Tit. 1,2, Div. 4, Ch. 10 (1961), as amended
	Fire fighters	Cal. Gov't. Code §§3525-36, Tit. 1, Div. 4, Ch. 10.5 (1971), as amended
	Teachers	Cal. Educ. Code §§13080-90, Art. 5, Div. 10, Ch. 1 (1965), as amended
	Employees of Los Angeles County	Los Angeles County Employee Relations Ordinance (1968)
	Employees of San Francisco City and County	San Francisco Administrative Code, Art. XIa (1973)
Connecticut	Municipal employees	Conn. Gen. Stat. Rev. §§7-467 to 478 (1965), as amended
	Teachers	Conn. Gen. Stat. Rev. §10-153 a-h (1967), as amended (Supp. 1969)
District of Columbia	All employees	Order of Commissioner HO. 70-229, (1970)
Delaware	Public employees	Del. Code Ann. tit. 19, §§1301-12 (Supp. 1968), as added by S.B. 660, (1970) L

State	Employees Covered	Authorization
[Delaware]	Teachers	Del. Code Ann. tit. 14, §§4001-13 (1969)
Florida	Fire fighters	Fla. Stat. Ann. §§447.20-35 (1972)
	Teachers (Hillsborough County)	Ch. 71-686 (1971)
	Teachers (Pinellas County)	Ch. 71-875 (1971)
Georgia	Firemen	Code of Ga. Ann. Title 54, Ch. 54-13, §§54-1301-1315 (1971)
Hawaii	Public employees	Haw. Rev. Stat., Ch. 89, §§89-1 to 20 (1970), as amended
Idaho	Municipal employees	Attorney General Opinion, Mar. 18, 1959
	Firemen	Idaho Code, §§44-1801 to 12, Ch. 18 (1970)
	Teachers	Idaho Code, §§33-1271 to 76, Ch. 12 (1971)
Illinois	State employees	Executive Order (1973)
	Firemen	Ill. Rev. Stat. Ch. 24, §§10-3-8 to 10-3-11, (1965)
Indiana	Teachers	Ind. Stat. Ann., Code Ed., Tit. 20, §§20-7.5-11 to 14 (1973)
Iowa	Public employees	
Kansas	Public employees	Kan. Stat. Ann., §§75-4321 to 37, Ch. 75, Art. 43 (1971), as amended
	Teachers	Kan. Stat. Ann., §§72-5413 to 25, Ch. 72, Art. 54 (1970)
Kentucky	Firemen	Ky. Rev. Stat., Ch. 345, §§345.010-130 (1972)
	Police	Ky. Rev. Stat., Ch. 78, §§78.400, 78.470, 78.480 (1972)
Maine	Municipal employees	Me. Rev. Stat. Ann. Tit. 26, Ch. 9-A, §§961-72 (1969), as amended

State	Employees Covered	Authorization
[Maine]	State employees	Me. Rev. Stat. Ann. Tit. 5, §§751-53 (Supp. 1970)
Maryland	Teachers	Md. Ann. Code, Art. 77, §160, Ch. 14.5 (1969), as amended
	Local employees	Baltimore City Code, Art. I, §§110-24 (1968)
	Local employees	Prince Georges Code of Ordinances and Resolutions, Ch. 13a (1973)
Massachusetts	Public employees	Mass. Gen. Laws Ann., Ch. 150E, §§1-15 (1973)
Michigan	Public employees (except state)	Mich. Comp. Laws Ann., §§423.201-216 (1947), as amended
	Police, firemen	Mich. Comp. Laws Ann., §§423.231-247 (1969), as amended
Minnesota	Public employees	Minn. Stat. Ann., §§179.61-76 (1971), as amended
Missouri	Public employees	Ann. Mo. Stat., §§105.500-530 (1967), as amended
	Teachers	Attorney General Opinion, Dec. 12, 1968
Montana	Nurses	Rev. Codes of Mont., Tit. 41, §§41-2201 to 2209 (1969)
	Teachers	Rev. Codes of Mont., Tit. 75, §§75-6115 to 6128 (1971)
	Public employees	Rev. Codes of Mont., Tit. 59, §§59-1600 to 1616 (1973)
Nebraska	Public employees	Neb. Rev. Stat., Ch. 48, Art. 8, §§48-801 to 837 (1947), as amended
	Teachers	Neb. Rev. Stat., Ch. 79, §§79-1287 to 1295 (1967)
Nevada	Local government employees	Nev. Rev. Stat., Ch. 288, §§288.010-280 (1969)

State	Employees Covered	Authorization
New Hampshire	State employees	N.H. Rev. Stat. Ann., Ch. 98-C, §§98-C:1 to C:7 (1969)
	Police	N.H. Rev. Stat. Ann., Ch. 105-B:1 to B:14 (1972)
New Jersey	Public employees	N.J. Stat. Ann., Tit. 34, Ch. 13A, §§34:13A-13 (1941), as amended
New Mexico	Public employees	Attorney General Opinion, Apr. 14, 1971
New York	Public employees	Consolidated Laws of N.Y. Ann., Civil Service, Art. 14, §§200-14 (1967), as amended
New York City	Local employees	N.Y.C. Admin. Code, Ch. 54 (1967), as amended
North Dakota	Public employees	N.D. Cent. Code, Tit. 34, Ch. 34-11, §§34-11-01 to 05 (1960)
	Teachers	N.D. Cent. Code, Tit. 15, Ch. 15-38.1, §§15-38.1-01 to 15 (1969)
Oklahoma	Police and firemen	Okla. Stat. Ann., Tit. 11, §§548.1-14 (1971), as amended
	Teachers	Okla. Stat. Ann., Tit. 70, §§509.1-10 (1971)
Oregon	Public employees	Ore. Rev. Stat., Ch. 243, §§243.650-782 (1963), as amended
	Portland employees	Code of City of Portland, Ordinance no. 128058, §§3-2202, 3-2203, 3-2208 (1968)
	Eugene employees	Eugene Code, 1971, §§2.875-876 (1971)
Pennsylvania	Public employees	Pa. Stat. Ann., Tit. 43, §§1101.101-2301 (1970)
	Police and firemen	Pa. Stat. Ann., Tit. 43, §§217.1-10 (1968)

State	Employees Covered	Authorization
[Pennsylvania]	Municipal transit employees	Pa. Stat. Ann., Tit. 53, §39951, Art. IV(a-e) (1967)
Rhode Island	State employees	R.I. Gen. Laws Ann., §§36-11-1 to 11, Tit. 36, Ch. 11 (1958), as amended
	Municipal employees	R.I. Gen. Laws Ann., §§28-9.4-1 to 19, Tit. 28, Ch. 9.4 (1967)
	Teachers	R.I. Gen. Laws Ann., §§28-9.3-1 to 16, Tit. 28, Ch. 9.3 (1966)
	Fire fighters	R.I. Gen. Laws Ann., §§28-9.1-1 to 14, Tit. 28, Ch. 9.2 (1961), as amended
	Policemen	R.I. Gen. Laws Ann., §§28-9.2-1 to 14, Tit. 28, Ch. 9.2 (1963), as amended
South Dakota	Public employees	S.D. Comp. Laws 1967, Tit. 3, Ch. 3-18, §§3-18-1 to 17 (1969), as amended
	Police, firemen	S.D. Comp. Laws 1967, Tit. 9, Ch. 9-14A, §§9-14A-1 to 2 (1971)
Texas	Police, firemen	Tex. Civil Statutes, Art. 51540, 1, Tit. 83, §§1-20 (1973)
Utah	State employees	Attorney General Opinion, Jan. 12, 1960
	Municipal employees	Attorney General Opinion, Oct. 1, 1945
Vermont	State employees	Vt. Stat. Ann., Tit. 3, §§901-1007, Ch. 27 (1969), as amended
	Municipal employees	Vt. Stat. Ann., Tit. 21, §§1721-34, Ch. 22 (1973)
	Teachers	Vt. Stat. Ann., Tit. 16, §§1981-2010, Ch. 57 (1969)
Virginia	Municipal employees	Attorney General Opinion, July 30, 1962 Attorney General Opinion, Feb. 18, 1970

State	Employees Covered	Authorization
Washington	Local employees	Wash. Rev. Code Ann., Tit. 41, Ch. 41.56, §§41.56.010-950 (1967), as amended
	Teachers	Wash. Rev. Code Ann., Tit. 28A, Ch. 28A.72, §§28A.72.010-100 (1965), as amended
	Community college academic employees	Wash. Rev. Code Ann., Tit. 28, Ch. 28B.52, §§28B.52.010-200 (1971), as amended
	State university system classified employees	Wash. Rev. Code Ann., Tit. 28, §28B.16.100 (1969), as amended
	Port district employees	Wash. Rev. Code Ann., Tit. 53, Ch. 53.18, §§53.18.010-060 (1967)
West Virginia	Public employees	Attorney General Opinion, July 1962
Wisconsin	State employees	Wis. Stat. Ann., §§111.80-97 (1966), as amended
	Municipal employees	Wis. Stat. Ann., §§111.70, 111.71 (1959), as amended
Wyoming	Fire fighters	Wyo. Stat. Ann., Tit. 27, §§27-265 to 273, Ch. 14 (1965)

THE SCOPE OF BARGAINING IN PUBLIC EMPLOYMENT—A SUMMARY OF STATE LAWS[*]

State	Employees Covered	Bargaining Rights	Scope of Bargaining	Restrictions on Scope
Alabama	Firemen	Employees may present proposals	Salaries, other conditions of employment	None
Alaska	Public[†]	Collective negotiations permitted, but not required	Terms or conditions of employment, grievance procedure, mutual aid or protection	None
	Teachers	Parties must bargain in good faith	Matters pertaining to employment and fulfillment of professional duties	Act not to be construed as an abrogation or delegation of legal responsibilities, powers, and duties of school board, including right to make final decisions on policies
California	Public	State and municipalities must meet and confer with employees	Wages, hours, other terms and conditions of employment	No bargaining allowed on services or activities provided by law or executive order, charters, ordinances, and rules of local public agencies that establish

[*]Laws applicable to transit and port employees are not summarized.
[†]Unless otherwise specified, the word "public" (under "Employees Covered") means all public employees.

State	Employees Covered	Bargaining Rights	Scope of Bargaining	Restrictions on Scope
[California]				a merit system or that provide for alternative means of administering employer-employee relations
	Teachers	School boards must meet and confer with employee organization	Wages, hours, salaries, and other terms and conditions of employment; definition of educational objectives; content of courses and curricula; textbook selection; other aspects of instructional program within employer's discretion	Tenure rules and regulations; merit or civil service system that provides for other ways of administering employer-employee relations
	Firemen	Employees may present and discuss their recommendations with the employer	Wages, salaries, hours, working conditions	None
Connecticut	Municipal	Parties must bargain collectively (terms of agreements prevail over existing laws and regulations)	Wages, hours, conditions of employment, dues deduction procedures	Conduct and grading of merit exams; rating of candidates; establishment of lists based on merit exams and appointment from such lists; provisions of municipal charters regarding political activities of municipal employees
	Teachers	Parties must bargain collectively	Salaries and other conditions of employment	None

State	Employee group	Requirement	Scope	Comments
Delaware	Public	Parties must bargain collectively and sign agreements	Wages, salaries, hours, vacations, sick leave, grievance procedures, other terms and conditions of employment	None
	Teachers	School boards and employee representatives must negotiate in good faith	Salaries, employee benefits, working conditions	Contractual provisions for binding arbitration are prohibited; right of public through elected or appointed school boards not negotiable
District of Columbia	Public[a]	Employees may organize and bargain	Terms and conditions of employment	None
Florida	Fire fighters	Employees may present proposals	Terms and conditions of employment	None
	Teachers (Hillsborough County)	School board must meet and confer with employees; agreements reached must be put in writing	Salaries, hours, wages, rates of benefits, other items of employment, curriculum, discipline, personnel policies, items affecting rights and responsibilities of teachers	None
	Teachers (Pinellas County)	Parties must bargain	Terms and conditions of professional service and other matters of mutual concern	None
Georgia	Fire fighters[b]	Parties shall meet and confer if employee organization so requests	Wages, rates of pay, hours, working conditions, all other terms and conditions of employment	None

State	Employees Covered	Bargaining Rights	Scope of Bargaining	Restrictions on Scope
Hawaii	Public	Parties must bargain collectively	Wages, hours, working conditions, other terms and conditions of employment	Scope excludes matters of classification and reclassification, retirement benefits, and the salary ranges and number of incremental and longevity steps provided by law.[c] Parties not allowed to agree to any proposal inconsistent with merit principles or the principle of equal pay for equal work. Also excluded are management rights.[d]
Idaho	Municipal	Employers may bargain and sign agreements with employee representatives	Undefined	None
	Firemen	Firemen granted right to bargain collectively	Wages, rates of pay, working conditions, all other terms and conditions of employment	None
	Teachers	Parties must negotiate and reach agreement	Those matters specified in any negotiations agreement between the parties	None[e]
Indiana	Teachers	School employers must bargain with employees	Salary, wages, hours, salary- and wage-related fringe benefits,	Management rights.[f] No contract may include provisions in conflict

	procedure; parties to "meet and discuss" subjects not within scope of bargaining, including curriculum, textbook selection, teaching methods, assignment and promotion of personnel, discipline, pupil:teacher ratio, class size, budget appropriations		...law, school employee rights as defined in Sec. 7(a) [employer unfair practices] or school employer rights as defined in Sec. 7(b) [employee organization unfair practices]. Employers not allowed to enter into contracts that would put them in a position of deficit financing
Public (Attorney General Opinion)	Employers may consult with employee representatives unless otherwise prohibited by law	Wages, hours, and working conditions	None
Firemen	Arbitration of disputes	None	None
State (Executive Order) (State police and university employees are not covered)	Employees may organize and bargain with state agencies	Wages, hours, terms and conditions of employment	State need not bargain on merit principle and competitive examination principle; agency policies, programs, and statutory functions; budget and structure; decisions on standard, scope, and delivery of service; use of technology; the state retirement system; life and health insurance; and "anything" required or prohibited by law
Illinois			

State	Employees Covered	Bargaining Rights	Scope of Bargaining	Restrictions on Scope
Iowa	Public	Parties must bargain collectively in good faith	Wages, hours, vacations, insurance, holidays, leaves of absence, shift differentials, overtime compensation, supplemental pay, transfer procedures, seniority, job classifications, health and safety, evaluation procedures, procedures for staff reduction, other matters mutually agreed on	Law does not diminish authority of the merit employment department, board of regents' merit system, or any civil service commission established to recruit, test, and rate employees and candidates for promotion or for other matters of classification
Kansas	Public	Parties must meet and confer in good faith	Conditions of employment	Excluded are management rights,[g] merit principle, and civil service system
	Teachers	Parties shall engage in professional negotiations	Terms and conditions of professional service	Nothing in the Act shall change or affect any right or duty conferred or imposed by law upon any board of education
Kentucky	Fire fighters (in cities of over 300,000)	Parties must negotiate in good faith	Wages, hours, and other conditions of employment	None
	Police (in counties of over 300,000)	Employees may organize and bargain	Wages, hours, terms and conditions of employment	Employer need not bargain over matters of inherent managerial policy

State	Employee group	Requirement	Scope of bargaining	Restrictions/Exclusions
Maine	Municipal	Parties must bargain collectively	Wages, hours, working conditions, and contract grievance arbitration[h]	Conduct and grading of merit exams, establishment of lists from such exams, rating of candidates, education policies[i]
Maryland	Teachers	Parties must bargain collectively	Salaries, wages, hours, working conditions, and binding arbitration of grievances	Employer renders final decision on all matters that were the subject of negotiation; nothing in bargaining law supersedes rules of employer that regulate tenure Management rights[j]
	Baltimore employees	Parties must bargain	Terms and conditions of employment	
	Prince Georges County employees	Parties must negotiate in good faith	Wages, hours, and other terms and conditions of employment that are subject to negotiation under law	Employer need not bargain on county-wide matters that must be uniform for all employees unless a labor organization represents more than half of all employees; civil service system; merit principle
Massachusetts	Public	Employer must meet and negotiate with exclusive representative	Wages, hours, standards of productivity and performance, and any other terms and conditions of employment	None
Michigan	Public	Parties must bargain collectively	Wages, hours, terms and conditions of employment	None
	Police, firemen	Arbitration of disputes	—	—

State	Employees Covered	Bargaining Rights	Scope of Bargaining	Restrictions on Scope
Minnesota	Public	Parties must negotiate in good faith	Grievance procedures and terms and conditions of employment, including hours of employment, compensation, fringe benefits, personnel policies affecting employee working conditions; in the case of professional employees: hours, compensation, and economic aspects relating to employment, but not educational policies[k]	Employers not required to bargain on matters of inherent managerial policy, which include, but are not limited to, functions and programs of the employer, overall budget, utilization of technology, organizational structure, and selection, direction, and number of personnel[l]
Missouri	Public[m]	Parties must meet and confer; results of conferences must be written in the form of ordinances, resolutions, or bills, which must become legal contracts when approved by appropriate body	Salaries and other conditions of employment	None
Montana	Teachers	Parties must bargain collectively	Matters relating directly to employer-teacher relationship, such as salary, hours, and other terms of employment	Excluded are matters of curriculum, policy of operation, selection of teachers and other personnel, physical plant of school; nothing in act shall impair employer's right to hire

State	Category	Bargaining requirement	Scope of bargaining	Exceptions
	Public	Parties must bargain collectively	Wages, hours, fringe benefits, and other conditions of employment	or discharge teachers for cause consistent with other state laws[n] Management prerogatives[o]
	Nurses in public and private facilities	Parties must bargain collectively	Establishment and maintenance of desirable employment practices	None
Nebraska	Public	Employers bargain collectively	Grievance procedures, terms and conditions of employment	None
	Teachers	Employers may meet with employee organizations if they so choose; if negotiations occur, parties must execute written agreements	Subjects requested by employee organizations	None
Nevada	Local	Parties must bargain collectively	Wages, hours, conditions of employment	Management rights[p]
New Hampshire	State	Parties must bargain to reach agreement	Conditions of employment, which can include establishment of procedures for adjustment of grievances (including arbitration), conferences on recommendations to improve personnel policies, and mediation or fact-finding	Management rights[q]
	Police	Employers must meet and confer	Matters of salaries, wages, or other benefits	Management rights[r]

State	Employees Covered	Bargaining Rights	Scope of Bargaining	Restrictions on Scope
New Jersey	Public	Parties must bargain collectively and sign agreements	Terms and conditions of employment, grievance procedures (with provisions for binding arbitration)	Law states that nothing contained within it shall be construed as interfering with, impeding, or diminishing in any way any right guaranteed by law or federal or state constitutions
New Mexico	Public (Attorney General Opinion, Apr. 14, 1971)	Parties may confer and/or bargain collectively	Rules and regulations of New Mexico State Personnel Board[s]	Retained management rights;[t] agency shop clauses prohibited
New York	Public	Parties must bargain in good faith and enter into written agreements	Salaries, wages, hours, other terms and conditions of employment	None
New York City	Local	Parties must bargain in good faith	Wages (including but not limited to wage rates, pensions, health and welfare benefits, uniform allowances, and shift premiums), hours (including but not limited to overtime and time and leave benefits), and working conditions	Management rights[u]
North Dakota	Teachers	Parties must bargain collectively in good faith	Terms and conditions of employment; employer-employee relations, including but not limited to salary, hours, other terms and condi-	Law states: "Nothing contained herein is intended or shall conflict with, contravene, abrogate, or diminish the powers, authority

State	Employee group	Bargaining requirement	Subjects of bargaining	Exclusions
			tions of employment, provisions for binding arbitration	duties . . . vested in boards of education by the statutes and laws. . . ."
Oklahoma	Firemen, police	Parties must meet and confer	Wages, hours, and other conditions of employment	None
	School employees	Parties must negotiate in good faith	Items affecting performance of professional services	None
Oregon	Public	Parties must bargain in good faith	Matters concerning "employment relations," including fair share agreements and binding arbitration procedures	None
	City of Eugene employees	Parties must negotiate in good faith	Wages, hours, and other terms and conditions of employment	None
Pennsylvania	Public	Parties must bargain and enter into written agreements	Wages, hours, terms and conditions of employment	Negotiation not required over matters of inherent managerial policy, such as standards of service, budget, utilization of technology, organizational structure, selection and direction of personnel
	Police, firemen	Employees have right to bargain collectively	Terms and conditions of employment, including compensation, hours, working conditions, retirement, pensions, other benefits	None

343

State	Employees Covered	Bargaining Rights	Scope of Bargaining	Restrictions on Scope
Rhode Island	State[v]	Parties must bargain and execute written agreements	Wages, hours, working conditions within officials' budgetary control, and agency shop provisions	None
	Municipal	Parties must meet and confer and enter into written agreements[w]	Salaries, hours, working conditions, other terms of employment	None
	Police, firemen	Parties must bargain and enter into written agreements	Wages, rates of pay, hours, working conditions, other terms and conditions of employment	None
	Teachers	Parties must meet and confer collectively	Salaries, hours, and all other terms and conditions of professional employment	None
South Dakota	Public	Employers must bargain and execute agreements with employee representatives	Grievance procedures and conditions of employment	None
	Police, firemen	Law provides for binding arbitration of bargaining impasses	—	—
Texas	Police, firemen[x]	Parties must bargain collectively	Wages, hours, and other terms and conditions of employment	Management rights[y]
Utah	Municipal (Attorney General Opinions, 10/1/45 and 1/12/60)	Employer may bargain collectively with employees	Undefined	Governmental powers

Jurisdiction	Requirement	Scope	Limitations
	confer in good faith	relationship between employers and employees, including wages and salary; work schedules, relating to assigned hours and days of the week; use of vacation or sick leave; general working conditions; overtime practices; and rules and regulations of the personnel board	nothing contained in the law is to be construed to contravene or derogate the merit system principles and personnel laws
Municipal (includes fire fighters)	Parties must bargain collectively	Wages, hours, terms and conditions of employment, execution of written agreement	Parties not compelled to bargain on managerial prerogatives, i.e., matters of "inherent managerial policy"
Teachers	Parties must bargain and enter into written agreements	Salaries, related economic conditions of employment; grievance procedures; and any mutually agreed-upon matter not in conflict with the laws of Vermont	Matters conflicting with statutes and laws of Vermont are not negotiable
Virginia Municipal (Attorney General Opinion)	Cities may bargain but are not required to do so	Undefined	None
Washington Local government	Parties must bargain collectively for written agreements	Grievance procedures, personnel matters, wages, hours, working conditions	Any matter that, by ordinance, resolution, or charter, has been delegated to any civil service commission or personnel board

345

State	Employees Covered	Bargaining Rights	Scope of Bargaining	Restrictions on Scope
[Washington]	Teachers	Employee organizations are granted the right to meet, confer, and negotiate with employers; the latter, however, make final decisions	School policies, including curricula, textbook selection, in-service training, student programs, personnel, hiring and assignment practices, leaves of absence, salaries and salary schedules, and noninstructional duties	None
	Community college employees	Parties are authorized to meet, confer, and negotiate; employers, however, make final decisions	School policies, including curricula, textbook selection, in-service training, student programs, personnel, hiring and assignment practices, leaves of absence, salaries, salary schedules, noninstructional duties	None
	State university system classified employees	Law requires higher education personnel board to adopt and promulgate rules and regulations regarding the basis for, and procedures to be followed for, among other matters, agreements between institutions and related boards	Personnel matters	—
	Port district employees	Port districts are authorized to enter into agreements	Matters of employment relations	No labor agreement shall restrict right of port district in its discretion

State	Category	Obligation	Scope of Bargaining	Exclusions / Notes
				to hire; limit right of port to secure its regular employees from the local community; and include within the same agreements port security personnel or port supervisory personnel
West Virginia	Public (Attorney General Opinion)	Public employees may join unions and discuss wages, hours, and working conditions with employers	Wages, hours, working conditions	Final decision made by governmental authorities and cannot be delegated away
Wisconsin	State	Parties must bargain collectively and enter into written agreements	Grievance procedures; application of seniority rights; work schedules relating to assigned hours and days of the week and shift assignments; scheduling of vacations and other time off; use of sick leave; application and interpretation of work rules; health and safety practices; transfers	Management rights;[aa] promotions, layoffs, position classifications, compensation and fringe benefits, examinations, discipline, merit salary determination policy
	Municipal	Parties must negotiate collectively	Wages, hours, conditions of employment, fair share agreements	Management rights[bb]
Wyoming	Firemen	Parties must meet and confer and enter into written agreements	Wages, rates of pay, working conditions, all other terms and conditions of employment	None

Notes to Appendix B

aTeachers not covered.

bThis law applies only to cities of more than 20,000 population, provided that a city's governing authority passes an ordinance bringing the city under coverage.

cHowever, the amount of wages to be paid in each range and step and the length of service necessary for the incremental and longevity step are negotiable.

dThese include public employer's right to direct employees; determine qualification standards for work, the nature and contents of examinations, hire, promote, transfer, assign, and retain, suspend, demote, discharge, or take other disciplinary action for proper causes; relieve an employee because of lack of work or for other legitimate reason; maintain efficiency of government operations; determine the methods, means, and personnel by which operations are to be conducted; and take such actions as are necessary to carry out the missions of the employer in cases of emergency. However, the law also states:

Except as otherwise provided herein, all matters affecting employee relations, including those that are, or may be, the subject of a regulation promulgated by the employer or any personnel director, are subject to consultation. . . . The employer shall make every reasonable effort to consult with the exclusive representatives prior to effecting changes in any major policy affecting employee relations.

eHowever, the law states that nothing contained within it is intended to conflict with or abrogate the powers and duties vested by the laws of Idaho in the legislature, state board of education, and boards of trustees of school districts. Each school district may, without negotiations, take action necessary to carry out its responsibility due to situations of emergency or acts of God.

fSchool employers retain responsibility to direct work of employees; establish policy; hire, promote, demote, transfer, assign, and retain employees; suspend or discharge employees in accordance with law; maintain efficiency of school operations; relieve employees from duties because of lack of work or other legitimate reason; take actions necessary to carry out the mission of public schools.

gPublic employers retain the right to direct work of employees; hire, promote, demote, transfer, assign, and retain employees; suspend or discharge employees for cause; maintain the efficiency of government operations; relieve employees because of lack of work or other legitimate reason; take necessary action to carry out the agency's mission in emergencies; and determine the methods, means, and personnel by which operations are to be carried on.

hContract provisions concerning binding arbitration on demotion, layoff, reinstatement, suspension, removal, discharge, or disciplinary action of any public employee shall be controlling in the event they conflict with the authority and power of a municipal civil service commission.

348

iEmployers are prohibited from negotiating with teachers on educational policies. However, they must meet and confer concerning them.

jEmployers retain right to determine mission of agencies; set standards of services; exercise control and discretion over agency organization and operations; direct employees; hire, promote, transfer, assign, or retain employees; establish work rules; suspend, demote, discharge, or take other disciplinary action for just cause in accordance with civil service laws; relieve employees from duty in the event of lack of work or for other legitimate reasons.

kHowever, a public employer must meet and confer with professional employees to discuss policies and those matters relating to their employment not included under the definition of terms and conditions of employment.

lAny contract provision that conflicts with or violates any state statute or regulation, or ordinance of a municipal home rule charter, or a rule of a board or agency governing licensure or registration of an employee shall be returned to the arbitrator for an amendment to make the provision consistent with the statute, rule, regulation, charter, or ordinance.

mState police and teachers are excluded.

nHowever, it is the duty of an employer to meet and confer on proposals not considered terms and conditions of employment, as long as such proposals do not amend the terms of the agreement.

o"Public employees and their representatives shall recognize the prerogatives of public employers to operate and manage their affairs in such areas but not limited to:
(a) direct employees; (b) hire, promote, transfer, assign, and retain employees; (c) relieve employees from duties because of lack of work or funds or under conditions where continuation of such work be inefficient and nonproductive; (d) maintain the efficiency of government operations; (e) determine the methods, means, job classifications, and personnel by which government operations are to be conducted; (f) take whatever actions may be necessary to carry out the mission of the agency in situations of emergency; (g) establish the methods and processes by which work is performed."

pPublic employer retains the right to direct employees; hire, promote, classify, transfer, assign, retain, suspend, demote, discharge, or take disciplinary action against any employee; relieve employees from duty because of lack of work or any other legitimate reasons; maintain the efficiency of governmental operations; and determine the methods, means, and personnel by which operations are to be conducted.

qThe state retains the right to direct and supervise the work force; appoint, promote, discharge, transfer, or demote employees; lay off unnecessary employees; maintain the efficiency of operations; determine methods, means, and personnel by which operations shall be conducted; take whatever action is necessary to carry out the mission of the agency in emergencies. Every agreement is subject to approval by the attorney general as to form and legality.

rThe statute contains no language concerning management rights other than a reference to it in the section covering prohibited practices of employees and employee organizations: "It shall be a prohibited practice for police officers or employee organizations willfully to . . . (b) interfere with, restrain, or coerce a board with respect to management rights granted in this chapter. . . ."

sNew Mexico does not have any legislation authorizing collective bargaining for public employees. In April 1971, however, the attorney general of New Mexico issued two opinions stating that state employers could enter into either bargaining or consultation relationships with employee organizations, if they so chose. Shortly thereafter, the New Mexico State Personnel Board issued regulations, effective July 1, 1971, to provide guidelines for those employers electing to bargain or consult with representatives of their employees. Under the Personnel Board regulations, bargaining is permitted on terms and conditions of employment, which are defined as "subjects of interest to employees which are not specifically covered by statute, executive order, Board rules or management rights and are within the discretionary power of the negotiating official.

tAll collective bargaining agreements must contain the following clause: "Agreements reached herein shall not impinge upon or diminish the rights and obligations of management officials in accordance with applicable laws and regulations to exercise their basic responsibilities which include but are not limited to the following: maintain the efficiency of the operations; determine the methods, means, and numbers and kinds of personnel by which operations are to be conducted; provide reasonable standards and rules for employees' safety . . .; direct employees; hire, promote, demote, transfer, assign and retain employees, and to suspend or discharge employees for proper cause, or to take other disciplinary action against employees; relieve employees from duties because of lack of work or other legitimate reasons.'' All collective bargaining agreements also must state the parties' recognition that they are governed by existing or future statutes, laws, legal regulations, executive orders, and rules of the Board, and agency policies in existence at the time their negotiated agreement was approved. All collective bargaining agreements must be limited to matters that are under the delegated authority and control of the agency or manager involved in the negotiations. Agreements must not contain provisions that compel the agency to commit funds for programs or purposes for which funds have not been appropriated by the legislature.

u''. . . b. It is the right of the city, or any other public employer, acting through its agencies, to determine the standards of services to be offered by its agencies; determine the standards of selection for employment; direct its employees; take disciplinary action; relieve its employees from duty because of lack of work or for other legitimate reasons; maintain the efficiency of governmental operations; determine the methods, means and personnel by which government operations are to be conducted; determine the content of job classifications; take all necessary actions to carry out its mission in emergencies; and exercise complete control and discretion over its organization and the technology of performing its work.'' Decisions of the city or any other public employer on those matters are not within the scope of collective bargaining, but questions concerning the practical impact that decisions on the above matters have on employees, such as questions of work load or manning, are within the scope of collective bargaining.

vState police are excluded.

wTeachers, police, and firemen are excluded.

xLaw applies only in local jurisdictions where voters petition their municipal governments for a referendum and adopt the law by a majority vote.

y"Nothing contained in this Act shall be deemed a limitation on the authority of a fire chief or police chief . . ., except to the extent the parties through collective bargaining shall agree to modify such authority."

zManagement's rights include the right to carry out the statutory mandate and goals of any agency or college; to utilize personnel, methods, and means in the most appropriate manner possible; and to take necessary action to carry out the mission of any agency in an emergency.

aaManagement retains the right to carry out the statutory mandate and goals of the agency utilizing personnel, methods, and means more appropriate and efficient; to manage employees of the agency; to hire, promote, transfer, and assign or retain employees; to establish reasonable work rules; to suspend, demote, discharge, or take other appropriate disciplinary action; and to lay off employees in the event of lack of work or funds, or under conditions where continuation of such work would be inefficient or nonproductive.

bb"The employer shall not be required to bargain on subjects reserved to management and direction of the governmental unit except insofar as the manner of exercise of such functions affects the wages, hours, and conditions of employment of the employees. In creating this subchapter the legislature recognizes that the public employer must exercise its powers and responsibilities to act for the government and good order of the municipality, its commercial benefit and the health, safety and welfare of the public to assure orderly operations and functions within its jurisdiction, subject to those rights secured to public employees in the constitution of this state and of the United States and by this subchapter."

351

QUESTIONNAIRE TO LOCAL TEACHERS' ORGANIZATIONS
ON THE ISSUE OF CLASS SIZE

This study is being conducted by Joan Weitzman of the New York State School of Industrial and Labor Relations at Cornell University. The purpose of this study is to analyze the experience of local teachers' organizations and school boards in negotiating the issue of class size. This questionnaire should be completed only by those individuals who are or were responsible for the negotiation of collective bargaining agreements.

INSTRUCTIONS: Please answer the following questions. If there is more than one possible answer, check all which you think may apply. If there are any additional comments or explanations you may wish to make, they would be appreciated, and you may attach an additional page for this purpose.

SECTION 1. BACKGROUND DATA

1. Name of the school district:

2. Name of the teacher organization:

3. Number of teachers in the bargaining unit:

4. My school district is in a(n) (check one): Urban area __
   Suburban area __   Rural area __

5. How many years have the above parties engaged in formal collective bargaining for a written agreement: 1 year __   2 years __
   3 years __   4 years __   5 years or more __

6. Pupil/classroom teacher ratio (exclude specialists and noncertified personnel): below 15:1 __   15:1-20:1 __   21:1-25:1 __
   26:1-30:1 __   31:1-35:1 __   over 36:1 __

7. (a) Average class load of secondary-level instructional staff:
   3 periods __   4 period __   5 periods __   6 periods __
   over 6 periods __

(b) Average number of pupils assigned to secondary-level teachers per day: 75-100 __ 101-125 __ 126-150 __ 151-175 __ over 175 __

SECTION II. BARGAINING HISTORY

If your collective bargaining agreement CONTAINS a class size provision(s), answer all questions in this section EXCEPT numbers 13, 14, and 15.

If your collective bargaining agreement DOES NOT contain a class size provision(s), OMIT questions 8 through 12, and begin this section with question 13.

8. Check each year you remember class size being discussed in negotiations: before 1967 __ 1967 __ 1968 __ 1969 __ 1970 __ 1971 __ 1972 __

9. When did a class size provision(s) first appear in the agreement: before 1967 __ 1967 __ 1968 __ 1969 __ 1970 __ 1971 __ 1972 __

10. Class size proposal(s) first initiated by: Teachers' Organization __ Employer __

11. Is the class size provision(s) in your current agreement a modification of an earlier contractual class size provision(s): Yes __ No __

    If "yes," how has the class size provision(s) been modified (please specify below briefly):

12. When did the employer agree to the inclusion of class size language in the agreement: Before mediation __ During mediation __ After mediation but before fact-finding __ During fact-finding __ After fact-finding __

    THOSE DISTRICTS WHOSE CONTRACTS DO NOT CONTAIN CLASS SIZE PROVISIONS BEGIN THIS SECTION HERE

13. Has the teachers' organization ever proposed a class size clause in negotiations: Yes __ No __

    If "yes," when (check all applicable): before 1969 __ 1969 __ 1970 __ 1971 __ 1972 __

353

14. If you answered question 13 affirmatively, did the contents of the teachers' most recent class size proposal (check all applicable; if you check more than one answer, mark a number "1" next to the response most closely resembling your proposal):

__ attempt to establish class size averages for each grade, cluster of grades, school building, or district
__ attempt to establish specific numerical limitations on class size
__ meet the recommendations of the commissioner of education with respect to class size
__ urge the board of education to make "reasonable efforts" to reduce class size
__ other (please specify) _____

15. Has the employer ever initiated a class size proposal for inclusion in the contract: Yes __ No __

If "yes," when (check all applicable):
before 1969 __ 1969 __ 1970 __ 1971 __ 1972 __

If "yes," was this class size proposal (check all applicable; if you check more than one answer, mark a number "1" next to the response most closely resembling the employer's proposal):

__ part of a broader "management rights" proposal
__ stated in terms of specific numerical limitations or averages with respect to class size
__ an offer to keep class sizes "reasonable"
__ a pledge to make "reasonable efforts" to keep class sizes small or stable
__ other (please specify)

ALL RESPONDENTS ANSWER REMAINING QUESTIONS
IN THIS SECTION

16. Did the employer ever (in either negotiations or grievance arbitration) take the position that class size was a nonnegotiable item under either the Education Law or the Taylor Law, or both: Yes __ No __

If "yes," which law(s): Education __ Taylor __ Both __

17. During the negotiations on class size, were you very concerned with the community's attitude toward this issue: Yes __ No __ Somewhat __

During the negotiations on class size, how much support do you
think the teachers had from the community with respect to this
issue: Much support __ Moderate support __ Little support __
No support __ Uncertain __

18. During the most recent negotiations over the question of class
size, did the employer raise any of the following arguments
against the inclusion or modification of class size provision(s)
in the agreement (check all applicable; if you check more than
one answer, mark a number "1" next to the employer's principal argument):

__ "Class size is a management prerogative"
__ "Class size provisions will reduce managerial flexibility"
__ "Class size limitations will result in increased costs for
the district"
__ "The teachers' proposal on class size is objectionable on the
basis of the specific numerical limitations proposed"
__ "There is no conclusive evidence that class size limitations
result in more effective teaching or increased pupil achiev-
ment"
__ other (please specify) _____

19. In the most recent negotiations in which a class size provision(s)
was proposed, were the objectives of the teachers' organization
any of the following (check all applicable; if you check more than
one answer, mark a number "1" next to your most important
objective):
__ reduced work loads
__ improvement of pupil:teacher ratios
__ increased opportunity to give individualized instruction in
the classroom
__ belief that small classes improve education in general
__ gaining guarantees with respect to maximum class sizes
permissible
__ other (please specify) _____

20. Was class size an issue presented to a: Mediator __
Fact-finder __ Both __

If "yes," when (check all applicable): before 1969 __ 1969 __
1970 __ 1971 __

21. If mediation occurred, was the neutral helpful in discussing
and/or facilitating agreement between the parties on the class
size issue: Yes __ No __

22. If, during 1971, class size was an issue presented to a fact-finder, did the fact-finder make a recommendation on the issue: Yes __ No __

23. (a) Did either party, or both, reject the fact-finder's recommendation on class size: Employer __ Teachers' organization__ Both __

    (b) If "yes," on what grounds was the recommendation rejected (check all applicable; if you check more than one answer, mark a number "1" next to the most important reason):

    __ belief that fact-finders should not decide issue of class size
    __ fact-finder's recommendation on class size maxima (or averages) was too high or too low
    __ class size recommendation required no commitment from the school board to do anything specific
    __ recommendation was not comprehensive enough; did not cover all situations
    __ other (specify) _____

    (c) If rejected, was the fact-finding recommendation on class size nevertheless used by the parties as a basis for: Further bargaining __ Compromise __ Neither __

SECTION III. EVALUATION OF THE CLASS SIZE ISSUE

If your collective bargaining agreement CONTAINS a class size provision(s), answer all questions in this section EXCEPT numbers 27, 28, and 29.

If your collective bargaining agreement DOES NOT contain a class size provision(s), OMIT questions 24, 25, and 26, and begin this section with number 27.

24. How do you evaluate your agreement's class size language in terms of the organization's original objectives in negotiating class size:

    __ contractual language satisfies goals
    __ contractual language fails to satisfy goals
    __ contractual language partially satisfies goals

25. Has the class size language in your agreement generated any of the following problems between the administration and the teachers? For example, has the class size language (check all

applicable; if you check more than one answer, mark a number "1" next to the most significant problem):

___ been too rigid, not allowed innovations (e.g., team teaching)
___ been difficult to administer fairly
___ been difficult to interpret
___ involved increased costs for the district
___ created problems with respect to adequate classroom space
___ other (specify) _____
___ no problems

26. In general, is the class size provision(s) of your current agreement being adhered to by the employer: Yes ___ No ___

THOSE DISTRICTS WHOSE AGREEMENTS DO NOT CONTAIN
CLASS SIZE PROVISIONS BEGIN THIS SECTION HERE

27. Is class size a problem in your district? For example (check all applicable; if you check more than one answer, mark a number "1" next to the most significant problem):

___ class sizes excessively large
___ wide variations in class sizes among the different grade levels
___ wide variations in class sizes among the different subject areas
___ large class sizes, resulting in heavy teacher work loads
___ large class sizes, reducing teachers' ability to give individualized instruction
___ employer claims financial constraints make it impossible to reduce class sizes
___ other (specify) _____

28. Have organization and administration representatives ever discussed class size in informal meetings outside of negotiations or grievance hearings (for example, through liaison or joint study committees): Yes ___ No ___

29. If "yes," how would you evaluate these meetings:
Very productive ___ Unproductive ___ Productive to a limited degree ___

ALL RESPONDENTS ANSWER REMAINING QUESTIONS

30. (a) Since 1969, how many grievances on class size have been filed: 0 ___ 1 ___ 2 ___ 3 ___ 4 ___ 5 ___ 6 or more ___

357

(b) If your answer is 1 or more, how many grievances went to the last step of the grievance procedure (advisory arbitration, binding arbitration, or school board decision):
0 __ 1 __ 2 __ 3 __ 4 __ 5 __ 6 or more __

If 1 or more grievances on class size went to arbitration, please list the arbitrator's(s') name(s): _____

31. In your opinion, should the law impose any constraints on the negotiation of class size: Yes __ No __

    If "yes," should these constraints be:

    __ no requirement on the employer to negotiate on class size
    __ numerical limitations with respect to class size minima, maxima, or both
    __ other (please specify) _____

32. In your opinion, class size is most effectively dealt with:
    __ through collective bargaining
    __ through unilateral managerial policy
    __ through joint faculty-administration study committees
    __ other (specify) _____

33. Do you intend to (or have you already begun to) propose clauses on class size in this year's negotiations: Yes __ No __ Uncertain __

34. If "yes," what provisions will the organization attempt to negotiate into the contract (be brief):

35. Have you read either a summary of or the entire PERB decision in the Matter of West Irondequoit Board of Education and West Irondequoit Teachers' Association (the leading decision on class size): Yes __ No __ Unsure __

36. If "yes," do you think the West Irondequoit decision will affect your future negotiations with respect to class size: Yes __ No __ Uncertain __

If "yes," how (check all applicable; if you check more than one answer, mark a number "1" next to your most important response):

___ will ignore decision and attempt to bargain on class size per se
___ will bargain on the impacts or effects of class size
___ will bargain for decreased pupil:teacher ratio
___ will bargain for increased preparation periods
___ other (specify) _____

37. In your opinion, class size is principally
___ a working conditions issue
___ an issue of professional concern
___ an issue for managerial control

_____
Position/title of person filling out
this questionnaire

QUESTIONNAIRE TO SCHOOL SUPERINTENDENTS ON CLASS SIZE

This study is being conducted by Joan Weitzman of the New York State School of Industrial and Labor Relations at Cornell University. The purpose of this study is to analyze the experience of local teachers' organizations and school boards in negotiating the issue of class size. This questionnaire should be completed only by those individuals who are or were responsible for the negotiation of collective bargaining agreements.

INSTRUCTIONS: Please answer the following questions. If there is more than one possible answer, check all which you think may apply. If there are any additional comments or explanations you may wish to make, they would be appreciated, and you may add an additional page for this purpose.

SECTION I. BACKGROUND DATA

1. Name of the district:

2. Name of the teacher organization:

3. Number of teachers in the bargaining unit:

4. My school district is in a(n) (check one): Urban area __
   Suburban area __ Rural area __

5. How many years have the above parties engaged in formal collective bargaining for a written agreement: 1 year __ 2 years __
   3 years __ 4 years __ 5 years or more __

6. Pupil/classroom teacher ratio (exclude specialists and noncertified personnel): below 15:1 __ 15:1-20:1 __ 21:1-25:1 __
   26:1-30:1 __ 31:1-35:1 __ over 36:1 __

7. (a) Average class load of secondary-level instructional staff:
   3 periods __ 4 periods __ 5 periods __ 6 periods __
   over 6 periods __

(b) Average number of pupils assigned to secondary-level teachers per day: 75-100 __ 101-125 __ 126-150 __ 151-175 __ Over 175 __

SECTION II. BARGAINING HISTORY

If your collective bargaining agreement CONTAINS a class size provision(s), answer all questions in this section EXCEPT numbers 13, 14, and 15.

If your collective bargaining agreement DOES NOT contain a class size provision(s), OMIT questions 8 through 12, and begin this section with question 13.

8. Check each year you remember class size being discussed in negotiations: before 1967 __ 1967 __ 1968 __ 1969 __ 1970 __ 1971 __ 1972 __

9. When did a class size provision(s) first appear in the agreement? before 1967 __ 1967 __ 1968 __ 1969 __ 1970 __ 1971 __ 1972 __

10. Class size proposal(s) first initiated by: Teachers' organization __ Employer __

11. Is the class size provision(s) in your current agreement a modification of an earlier contractual class size provision(s): Yes __ No __

    If "yes," how has the class size provision(s) been modified (please specify briefly):

12. When did the employer agree to the inclusion of class size language in the agreement: Before mediation __ During mediation __ After mediation but before fact-finding __ During fact-finding __ After fact-finding __

    THOSE DISTRICTS WHOSE AGREEMENTS DO NOT CONTAIN CLASS SIZE PROVISIONS BEGIN THIS SECTION HERE

13. Has the teachers' organization ever proposed a class size clause in negotiations: Yes __ No __

    If "yes," when (check all years applicable): before 1969 __ 1969 __ 1970 __ 1971 __ 1972 __

14. If you answered question 13 affirmatively, did the contents of the teachers' most recent class size proposal (check all applicable; if you check more than one answer, mark a number "1" next to the response most closely resembling the teachers' proposal):

__ attempt to establish class size averages for each grade, cluster of grades, school building, or district

__ attempt to establish specific numerical limitations on class size

__ meet the recommendations of the commissioner of education with respect to class size

__ urge the board of education to make "reasonable efforts" to reduce class size

__ other (please specify) _____

15. Has the employer ever initiated a class size proposal for inclusion in the agreement: Yes __ No __

If "yes," when (check all applicable):
before 1969 __ 1969 __ 1970 __ 1971 __ 1972 __

If "yes," was this class size proposal (check all applicable; if you check more than one answer, mark a number "1" next to the response most closely resembling your proposal):

__ part of a broader "management rights" proposal

__ stated in terms of specific numerical limitations or averages

__ a pledge to make "reasonable efforts" to keep class sizes small or stable

__ an offer to keep class sizes "reasonable"

__ other (please specify) _____

ALL RESPONDENTS ANSWER REMAINING QUESTIONS
IN THIS SECTION

16. Did you ever (either in negotiations or grievance arbitration) take the position that class size was a nonnegotiable item under either the Education Law or the Taylor Law, or both:
Yes __ No __

If "yes," which law(s): Education __ Taylor __ Both __

17. During the negotiations on class size, were you very concerned with the community's attitude toward this issue: Yes __ No __ Somewhat __

During the negotiations on class size, how much community support do you think you had on your position: Much support __ Moderate support __ Little support __ No support __ Uncertain __

18. During the most recent negotiations over the question of class size, did you raise any of the following arguments against the inclusion or modification of class size provision(s) in the agreement (check all applicable; if you check more than one answer, mark a number "1" next to your principal argument):
    __ "Class size is a management prerogative"
    __ "Class size provisions will reduce managerial flexibility"
    __ "Class size limitations will result in increased costs for the district"
    __ "The teachers' proposal on class size is objectionable on the basis of the specific numerical limitations proposed"
    __ "There is no conclusive evidence that class size limitations result in more effective teaching or increased pupil achievement"
    __ other (please specify) _____

19. In the most recent negotiations over the question of class size, what were your objectives and/or interests (check all applicable; if you check more than one answer, mark a number "1" next to your most important interest):
    __ the financial constraints
    __ maintaining maximum flexibility in making teaching assignments
    __ providing the opportunity for individualized classroom instruction
    __ preventing the teachers from encroaching upon managerial prerogatives
    __ other (please specify) _____

20. Was class size an issue presented to a: Mediator __ Fact-finder __ Both __

    If "yes," when (check all applicable): before 1969 __ 1969 __ 1970 __ 1971 __

21. If mediation occurred, was the neutral helpful in discussing and/or facilitating agreement between the parties on the class size issue: Yes __ No __

363

22. If, during 1971, class size was an issue presented to a fact-finder, did the fact-finder make a recommendation on the issue: Yes __ No __

23. (a) Did either party, or both, reject the fact-finder's recommendation on class size: Employer __ Teachers __ Both __

    (b) If "yes," on what grounds was the recommendation rejected (check all applicable; if you check more than one answer, mark a number "1" next to the most important reason):
    __ belief that fact-finders should not decide issue of class size
    __ fact-finder's recommendations on class size maxima were too high or too low
    __ class size recommendation was too generally worded
    __ class size recommendation was not comprehensive enough
    __ other (please specify) _____

    (c) If rejected, was the fact-finding recommendation on class size nevertheless used by the parties as a basis for:
    Further bargaining __ Compromise __ Neither __

SECTION III. EVALUATION OF THE CLASS SIZE ISSUE

If your collective bargaining agreement CONTAINS a class size provision(s), answer all the questions in this section EXCEPT numbers 27, 28, and 29.

If your collective bargaining agreement DOES NOT contain a class size provision(s), OMIT questions 24, 25, and 26, and begin this section with question 27.

24. How do you evaluate your agreement's class size language in terms of your objectives in negotiating class size:
    __ contractual language satisfies goals
    __ contractual language fails to satisfy goals
    __ contractual language partially satisfies goals

25. Has the class size language in your agreement generated any of the following problems between the administration and the teachers? For example, has the class language (check all applicable; if you check more than one answer, mark a number "1" next to the most significant problem):

___ been too rigid, not allowed innovations (e.g., team teaching)
___ been difficult to administer fairly
___ been difficult to interpret
___ involved increased costs for the district
___ created problems with respect to adequate classroom space
___ other (specify) _____
___ no problems

26. In general, are you having difficulty adhering to the negotiated class size provision(s) in your agreement: Yes ___ No ___

THOSE DISTRICTS WHOSE AGREEMENTS DO NOT CONTAIN CLASS SIZE PROVISIONS BEGIN THIS SECTION HERE

27. Is class size a problem in your district? For example (check all applicable; if you check more than one answer, mark a number "1" next to the most significant problem):
___ teachers believe class size is excessively large
___ wide variations in class sizes among the different grade levels
___ wide variations in class sizes among the different subject areas
___ employer believes class sizes too small
___ teachers complain of heavy work loads
___ financial constraints limit employer's ability to reduce class sizes
___ other (specify) _____

28. Have organization and administration representatives ever discussed class size in informal meetings outside of negotiations or grievance hearings (for example, through liaison or joint study committees): Yes ___ No ___

29. If "yes," how would you evaluate these meetings:
Very productive ___ Unproductive ___ Productive to a limited degree ___

ALL RESPONDENTS ANSWER REMAINING QUESTIONS

30. (a) Since 1969, how many grievances on class size have been filed: 0 ___ 1 ___ 2 ___ 3 ___ 4 ___ 5 ___ 6 or more ___

(b) If your answer is 1 or more, how many grievances went to the last step of the grievance procedure (advisory arbitration, binding arbitration, or school board decision):
0 ___ 1 ___ 2 ___ 3 ___ 4 ___ 5 ___ 6 or more ___

If 1 or more grievances on class size went to arbitration, please list the arbitrator's (s') name(s): _____

---

31. In your opinion, should the law impose any constraints on the negotiations of class size: Yes __ No __

    If "yes," should these constraints be:
    __ no requirement on the employer to negotiate class size
    __ numerical limitations on class size minima or maxima, or both
    __ other (please specify) _____

32. In your opinion, class size is most effectively dealt with:
    __ through collective bargaining
    __ through joint faculty-administration study committees
    __ through unilateral managerial policy
    __ other (please specify) _____

33. Have you read either a summary of or the entire PERB decision in the Matter of West Irondequoit Board of Education and West Irondequoit Teachers' Association (the leading case on class size): Yes __ No __

34. If "yes," do you think that the West Irondequoit decision will affect your future negotiations with respect to class size: Yes __ No __ Unsure __

    If "yes," how (check all applicable; if you check more than one answer, mark a number "1" next to your most important response):
    __ employer will bargain on impact or effects of class size, but not on class size itself
    __ employer will file improper practice charge if teachers insist upon bargaining on class size per se
    __ employer will bargain on class size even though permissive subject of bargaining
    __ other (please specify) _____

35. In your opinion, class size is principally
    __ a working conditions issue
    __ an issue of professional concern
    __ an issue for managerial control

    _____
    Position/title of person filling out
    this questionnaire

366

MEAN CLASS SIZE FOR SELECTED SUBJECT AREAS
IN PUBLIC SCHOOLS, NEW YORK STATE,
EXCLUSIVE OF NEW YORK CITY,
1967-68 AND 1970-71

Subject Area	Mean Class Size	
	1967-68	1970-71
Elementary 1-6	25.9	25.7
English 7	25.5	26.5
Math 7	25.4	26.8
General science 7	26.0	26.6
Social studies 7[a]	25.8	26.9
English 9	24.7	24.7
General science 9	25.5	25.4
Math 9 (algebra 1 yr.)	25.4	26.7
Math 9 (basic)	22.1	21.8
Introduction to business	22.6	22.8
Business arithmetic	23.0	23.7
Distributive education (1 yr.)	23.6	22.9
French 1	21.4	21.3
Spanish 1	23.8	24.3
Asian and African culture	25.1	25.3
Biology (Regents)	25.1	25.7
European culture studies[b]	25.6	25.5
Math 11	23.5	22.8
Chemistry (Regents)	22.7	23.9
Physics (Regents)	18.7	20.6
American studies[c]	24.2	25.0
English 12	23.4	23.8

Note: Mean computed by dividing number of students by number
of classes.
[a]Called Our Community and State in 1967-68, or Our Cultural
Heritage in 1970-71.
[b]Called world history in 1967-68.
[c]Called American history in 1967-68.
Source: New York State Education Department, unpublished
data from Basic Educational Data System.

MEAN CLASS SIZE FOR SELECTED SUBJECT AREAS IN NEW YORK STATE, EXCLUSIVE OF NEW YORK CITY, BY ECONOMIC AREA, 1970-71

Subject Area	Mean Class Size					
	Total	Binghamton Area	Buffalo Area	Capital District	Elmira Area	Long Island
Elementary 1-6	25.7	24.0	25.8	25.5	26.5	25.9
English 7	26.5	25.1	27.8	26.1	24.6	26.4
Math 7	26.8	25.9	29.2	29.6	25.0	25.9
General science 7	26.6	24.8	27.4	26.1	28.6	26.5
Our Cultural Heritage	26.9	29.6	27.4	26.6	26.3	26.4
English 9	24.7	24.8	25.5	24.7	23.3	24.7
General science 9	25.4	26.1	26.7	25.8	23.5	25.5
Math 9 (algebra 1 yr.)	26.7	24.5	27.0	25.4	32.4	27.5
Math 9 (basic)	21.8	20.8	24.3	22.1	21.2	20.4
Introduction to business	22.8	20.4	25.6	22.3	21.8	23.0
Business arithmetic	23.7	20.9	24.6	22.7	23.0	25.4
Distributive education (1 yr.)	22.9	17.5	23.9	23.4	22.4	24.1
French 1	21.3	19.1	23.1	21.3	18.4	22.3
Spanish 1	24.3	20.9	24.0	27.3	18.9	25.1
Asian and African culture	25.3	25.3	26.3	25.4	24.0	25.2
Biology (Regents)	25.7	28.7	25.1	25.3	25.1	25.9
European culture studies	25.5	25.0	26.0	24.9	24.4	26.0
Math 11	22.8	22.1	23.8	21.9	20.5	23.8
Chemistry (Regents)	23.9	21.9	28.5	22.9	24.8	23.8
Physics	20.6	20.7	23.0	21.6	19.1	21.6
American studies	25.0	26.4	25.6	21.1		

English 7	24.9	26.3	25.8	27.6	25.9	28.5
Math 7	24.9	25.7	25.0	28.1	26.5	26.6
General science 7	24.9	26.4	26.3	28.6	26.2	25.6
Our Cultural Heritage	29.2	25.8	25.5	27.2	27.2	25.9
English 9	23.9	23.6	25.2	25.1	24.4	24.4
General science 9	25.4	25.1	23.8	25.1	25.1	25.3
Math 9 (algebra 1 yr.)	25.3	24.0	23.8	28.2	25.8	26.5
Math 9 (basic)	21.5	21.3	20.6	23.0	20.0	22.0
Introduction to business	22.5	21.6	20.1	22.9	21.1	24.1
Business arithmetic	24.3	22.9	21.1	23.2	21.2	25.6
Distributive education (1 yr.)	23.1	23.2	15.4	21.4	17.3	23.8
French 1	19.1	20.1	20.2	22.0	21.2	21.7
Spanish 1	23.4	22.5	19.2	25.2	24.6	25.2
Asian and African culture	24.2	24.4	24.9	27.4	24.6	24.9
Biology (Regents)	23.9	23.9	26.1	25.8	26.8	25.9
European culture studies	23.7	24.2	23.9	26.6	25.4	25.7
Math 11	20.9	20.6	19.1	22.8	23.7	24.4
Chemistry (Regents)	21.8	22.6	21.9	24.0	23.6	24.9
Physics	16.5	19.4	16.6	20.5	22.2	19.8
American studies	22.1	23.4	23.1	24.8	24.1	26.3
English 12	22.0	22.7	23.0	23.3	23.4	24.8

Note: Mean computed by dividing the number of students by the number of classes.

Source: New York State Education Department, Information Center on Education, unpublished data from Basic Educational Data System, 1970-71.

Ackerly, Robert L., and W. Stanfield Johnson. Critical Issues in Negotiations Legislation. Washington, D.C.: National Association of Secondary School Principals, 1969.

Advisory Commission on Intergovernmental Relations. Labor-Management Policies for State and Local Government. 101 GERR Reference File 101. Washington, D.C.: Bureau of National Affairs, March 1970.

"AFL-CIO Criticizes ACIR Report as 'Backward Step' in Bargaining." 343 GERR, B-12, April 6, 1970.

American Association of School Administrators. School Administrators View Professional Negotiation. Washington, D.C.: the Association, 1966.

——The School Administrator and Negotiation. Washington, D.C.: the Association, 1968.

Anderson, Arvid. "Personnel Opinions." Public Personnel Review 27 (1966): 52.

——"Public Employees and Collective Bargaining: Comparative and Local Experience." In Proceedings of New York University Twenty-First Annual Conference on Labor, May 1968. Edited by Thomas Christensen. New York: Matthew Bender, 1969.

——"The Structure of Public Sector Bargaining." In Public Workers and Public Unions. Edited by Sam Zagoria. Englewood Cliffs, N.J.: Prentice-Hall, 1972.

——with the assistance of Joan Weitzman. "The Impact of Public Sector Bargaining." 1973 Wisconsin Law Review 986 (1973).

Andree, Robert G. Collective Negotiations. Lexington, Mass.: D. C. Heath, 1970.

Bakke, E. Wright. "Teachers, School Boards and the Employment Relationship." In Employer-Employee Relations in the Public Schools. Edited by Robert Doherty. Ithaca: New York State School of Industrial and Labor Relations, Cornell University, 1967.

Ben-David. "Professionals and Unions in Israel." Industrial Relations 5 (1965): 48.

Bendiner, Robert. The Politics of Schools, pp. 85-123. New York: Harper and Row, 1969.

Benson, Charles S. "Economic Problems of Education Associated with Collective Negotiations." In The Changing Employment Relationship in Public Schools. Edited by Robert Doherty, Joan Egner, and William Lowe. Ithaca: New York State School of Industrial and Labor Relations, Cornell University, 1966.

Blair, Patricia N. "State Legislative Control over the Conditions of Public Employment: Defining the Scope of Collective Bargaining for State and Municipal Employees." 26 Vanderbilt Law Review 1 (1973).

Bok, Derek, and John Dunlop. "Collective Bargaining the the Public Sector." In Labor and the American Community. New York: Simon and Schuster, 1970.

Carlton, Patrick W., and Harold I. Goodwin. The Collective Dilemma: Negotiations in Education. Worthington, Ohio: Charles A. Jones Publishing Co., 1969.

Clary, Jack R. "Labor Law." 18 Wayne Law Review 371 (1972).

"Class Size and Pupil:Teacher Ratio: An Annotated Bibliography." PSBA Bulletin, September-October 1971, pp. 10-13.

"Class Size, Workload, Binding Arbitration of Grievances Are Mandatory Bargaining Subjects, Connecticut Court Rules," 473 GERR B-13 (October 9, 1972).

Cogen, Charles. "Changing Patterns of Employment Relations." In The Changing Employment Relationship in Public Schools. Edited by Robert Doherty, Joan Egner, and William Lowe. Ithaca: New York State School of Industrial and Labor Relations, 1966.

"Collective Bargaining and the Professional Employee." 69 Columbia Law Review 277 (1969).

Colorado Legislative Council. Public Employee Negotiations. Report to the Colorado General Assembly. Research Publication no. 142. December 1968.

Committee on Executive Management and Fiscal Affairs, National
Governors' Conference. 1969 Supplement to Report of Task
Force on State and Local Government Labor Relations. Chicago:
Public Personnel Association, 1969.

———1970 Supplement to Report of Task Force on State and Local
Government Labor Relations. Chicago: Public Personnel Association, 1971.

Connecticut Commission on Collective Bargaining by Municipalities.
"Text of Report." 81 GERR, D-1 (March 29, 1965).

Connery, Robert, and William V. Farr, eds. "Unionization of Municipal Employees," Proceedings of the Academy of Political Science
30, no. 2 (December 1970).

"Court Restricts Pa. Teacher Bargaining Rights to Wages, Hours,
and Working Terms Not Affected by Board Policies." 510 GERR
B-5 (July 2, 1973).

Cox, Archibald, and John Dunlop. "Regulation of Collective Bargaining by the National Labor Relations Board." 63 Harvard Law
Review 389 (1950).

Craver, Charles. "Bargaining in the Federal Sector." 19 Labor
Law Journal 569 (1968).

Crispo, John H. G., ed. Collective Bargaining and the Professional
Employee. Toronto: Center for Industrial Relations, University
of Toronto, 1966.

Derber, Milton. "Labor-Management Policy for Public Employees
in Illinois: The Experience of the Governor's Commission,
1966-67." Industrial and Labor Relations Review 21 (1968): 541.

Doherty, Robert E. "The Impact of Teacher Organizations upon
Setting School Policies." Clearing House 40, no. 9 (May 1966):
515-24; also published as ILR Reprint Series no. 193, New York
State School of Industrial and Labor Relations, Cornell University.

———ed. Employer-Employee Relations in the Public Schools. Ithaca:
New York State School of Industrial and Labor Relations, Cornell University, 1967.

———"Letter to a School Board." Phi Delta Kappan 48, no. 6 (February 1967): 272-77; also published as ILR Reprint Series

no. 208, New York State School of Industrial and Labor Relations, Cornell University.

Doherty, Robert E. "Teacher Bargaining, Resource Allocation and Representative Rule." Industrial Relations Research Association, Proceedings, Winter 1969, pp. 248-56.

———"Negotiation Issues in Public Education." In Collective Negotiations and Public Administration, pp. 44-48. Conference Series no. 15. Iowa City: Center for Labor and Management, University of Iowa, 1970.

———Joan R. Egner, and William T. Lowe, eds. The Changing Employment Relationship in Public Schools. Ithaca: New York State School of Industrial and Labor Relations, Cornell University, 1966.

———and Walter E. Oberer. Teachers, School Boards, and Collective Bargaining: A Changing of the Guard. Ithaca: New York State School of Industrial and Labor Relations, Cornell University, 1967.

Donovan, Bernard. "Speaking for Management." In Readings on Negotiations in Education, pp. 287-90. Edited by Stanley Elam, Myron Lieberman, and Michael Moskow. Chicago: Rand McNally, 1967.

Duvin, Robert P. "The Duty to Bargain: Law in Search of Policy." 64 Columbia Law Review 248 (1964).

Edwards, Harry T. "The Emerging Duty to Bargain in the Public Sector." 71 Michigan Law Review 885 (1973).

Elam, Stanley M., Myron Lieberman, and Michael H. Moskow, eds. Readings on Collective Negotiations in Public Education. Chicago: Rand McNally, 1967.

Epstein, Benjamin. What is Negotiable? Washington, D.C.: National Association of Secondary School Principals, 1969.

Etzioni, Amitai. Modern Organizations. Englewood Cliffs, N.J.: Prentice-Hall, 1964.

Feuille, Peter. "Police Union Power." Doctoral dissertation, University of California, Berkeley, 1973.

Flexner, Abraham. "Is Social Work a Profession?" In Education as a Profession. Edited by Myron Lieberman. Englewood Cliffs, N.J.: Prentice-Hall, 1956.

Garbarino, Joseph W. "Professional Negotiations in Education." Industrial Relations 93 (1968).

Garber, Philip E. "The Scope of Negotiations in the Public Sector." Preliminary draft. Extension Division, New York State School of Industrial and Labor Relations, Cornell University, 1971.

Gerhart, Paul F. The Scope of Bargaining in Local Government Labor Negotiations. Reprint Series no. 211, Institute of Labor and Industrial Relations, University of Illinois, 1969.

Gilroy, Thomas P., and Anthony V. Sinicropi, eds. Collective Negotiations and Public Administration. Conference Series no. 15. Iowa City: Center for Labor and Management, University of Iowa, 1970.

Goldberg, Joseph P. "Changing Policies in Public Employee Labor Relations." Monthly Labor Review 93 (July 1970): 5.

———"Recent Statutes Covering Public Employees." Monthly Labor Review 93 (December 1970): 31.

———"Public Employee Developments in 1971." Monthly Labor Review 95 (January 1972): 56.

Gould, William B. "The New York Taylor Law: A Preliminary Assessment." 18 Labor Law Journal 323 (1967).

Governor's Commission to Revise the Public Employee Law of Pennsylvania. "Text of Report." 251 GERR, E-1 (July 1, 1968).

Governor's Committee on Public Employee Relations, State of New York. Final Report. March 31, 1966.

———Interim Report. June 17, 1968.

———Report of January 23, 1969.

Greenwood, Ernest. "Attributes of a Profession." In Howard Vollmer and Donald Mills, Professionalization, pp. 10-19. Englewood Cliffs, N.J.: Prentice-Hall, 1966.

374

Haber, Herbert L. "Productivity Bargaining." Presented at Productivity Conference: The New York City Approach to Improving Productivity in the Public Sector, March 19, 1973; also excerpted in LMRS Newsletter 4, no. 6 (June 1973).

Hamilton, Edward K. Productivity Program: Annual Summary Fiscal Year 1972-1973. New York: Office of the Mayor, 1973.

Hanslowe, Kurt L. The Emerging Law of Labor Relations in Public Employment. Ithaca: New York State School of Industrial and Labor Relations, Cornell University, 1967.

——and Walter E. Oberer. "Determining the Scope of Negotiations Under Public Employment Relations Statutes." Industrial and Labor Relations Review 24 (1971): 432.

Hart, Wilson R. Collective Bargaining in the Federal Service. New York: Harper & Row, 1961.

"Hawaii Board Declares Impasse in Teacher Bargaining, Says Workload, Prep Time Scheduling Are Not Negotiable," 487 GERR B-9 (January 27, 1973).

Helsby, Robert. "Impact of the Taylor Law on Public Schools, 1968-1970." 1 Journal of Collective Negotiations in the Public Sector 3 (February 1972).

Hildebrand, George. "The Public Sector." In Frontiers of Collective Bargaining. Edited by John Dunlop and Neil Chamberlain. New York: Harper & Row, 1967.

Howlett, Robert G. "Scope of Collective Bargaining in Public Employment." In Government Employees and Collective Bargaining, Hawaii PERB: Year One, pp. 25-40. Edited by John B. Ferguson and Joyce M. Najita. Honolulu: Industrial Relations Center, University of Hawaii, April 1971.

——"State Experience." In Collective Bargaining Today. Washington, D.C.: Bureau of National Affairs, 1971.

Illinois Advisory Commission on Labor-Management Policy for Employees. "Text of Report." 184 GERR, D-1 (March 20, 1967).

Institute of Industrial Relations, University of California, Los Angeles. Scope of Bargaining in the Public Sector—Concept and Problems. Report submitted to U.S. Department of Labor, August 1971.

375

Jackson, J. A., ed. Professions and Professionalization. Cambridge: Cambridge University Press, 1970.

Jencks, C. "Private Schools for Black Children." New York Times Magazine, November 3, 1968, p. 30.

Joint Legislative Committee on the Taylor Law (Public Employees' Fair Employment Act). 1972 Report. State of New York, Legislative Document (1972) no. 25.

Kilberg, William J. "Appropriate Subjects for Bargaining in Local Government Labor Relations." 30 Maryland Law Review 179 (1970).

Klaus, Ida. "The Evolution of a Collective Bargaining Relationship in Public Education: New York City's Seven-Year History." 67 Michigan Law Review 1033 (1969).

Klein, Paul E., and Janet Axelrod. "The Taylor Law and Public Schools: A Look at the Areas of Representation and Improper Practices." Labor Law Journal 21 (1970): 420.

Kleingartner, Archie. Professionalism and Salaried Worker Organization. Madison: Industrial Relations Research Institute, University of Wisconsin, 1967.

——"Impact of Professionalism on Scope of Bargaining in the Public Sector." In Scope of Bargaining in the Public Sector—Concepts and Problems. Report submitted to United States Department of Labor by Institute of Industrial Relations, University of California, Los Angeles, August 1971.

Koretz, Robert F., and Rober J. Rabin. "Labor Relations Law." 23 Syracuse Law Review 531 (1972).

Lefkowitz, Jerome. "Unionism in the Human Services Industries." 36 Albany Law Review 603 (1972).

Legislative Research Committee, State of Maine. Report on Collective Bargaining by Municipalities to the Second Special Session of the 103rd Legislature. Publication 103-18. January 1968.

Lieberman, Myron. "Collective Negotiations by Teachers." In Myron Lieberman and Thomas Patten, When School Districts Bargain. PERL 5. Chicago: Public Personnel Association, 1968.

___ The Impact of the Taylor Act upon the Governance and Administration of Elementary and Secondary Education. Report to Fleischmann Commission. June 1971.

——"Why Teachers Will Oppose Tenure Laws." Saturday Review, March 4, 1972.

——and Michael H. Moskow. Collective Negotiations for Teachers. Chicago: Rand McNally, 1966.

Lindsay, John V. "Overview of the New York City Productivity Program." Address given at Productivity Conference: The New York City Approach to Improving Productivity in the Public Sector, March 19, 1973.

Livingston, Frederick R. "Collective Bargaining and the School Board. In Public Workers and Public Unions. Edited by Sam Zagoria. Englewood Cliffs, N.J.: Prentice-Hall, 1972.

Love, Thomas M. "Joint Committees: Their Role in the Development of Teacher Bargaining." 20 Labor Law Journal 174 (1969).

——and George T. Sulzner. "Political Implications of Public Employee Bargaining." Industrial Relations 18 (1972).

McCulloch, Frank. "Role of Federal Government in Labor Relations: Labor Relations Philosophy of Kennedy Administration NLRB." 49 LRRM 74 (1962).

McGivern, Bernard T. New York State School Boards Association, Inc., Position Statement. New York: Negotiations Management Institute, 1971.

McHugh, William F. "New York's Experiment in Public Employee Relations: The Public Employees' Fair Employment Act." 32 Albany Law Review 58 (1967-68).

Male, Raymond F. "Labor Crises and the Role of Management." Developments in Public Employee Relations. Chicago: Public Personnel Association, 1965.

Maryland, Report and Recommendations of the Governor's Task Force on Public Employee Labor Relations. 278 GERR, AA-3 (January 6, 1969).

Mayer, Allan J. "Who's in Charge?—Public Employee Unions Press for Policy Role; States and Cities Balk." Wall Street Journal, September 7, 1972, p. 1.

"Meany, Wurf, Howlett, and St. Antoine Address Collective Bargaining Forum in New York." 350 GERR, B-6 (May 25, 1970).

Michigan Advisory Committee on Public Employee Relations. "Text of Report." 181 GERR, F-1 (February 28, 1967).

Moberly, Robert B. "Causes of Impasse in School Board-Teacher Negotiations." 366 GERR, F-1 (September 14, 1970).

Morris, Charles J., ed. The Developing Labor Law. Washington, D.C.: Bureau of National Affairs, 1971.

Morse, Muriel. "Shall We Bargain Away the Merit System?" In Developments in Public Employee Relations: Legislative, Judicial, Administrative. Edited by Kenneth O. Warner. Chicago: Public Personnel Association, 1965.

Moskow, Michael H. Teachers and Unions. Philadelphia: Wharton School of Finance and Commerce, University of Pennsylvania, 1966.

——J. Joseph Loewenberg, and Edward Clifford Koziara. Collective Bargaining in Public Employment. New York: Random House, 1970.

National Education Association. Addresses and Proceedings of the 103rd Annual Meeting. Washington, D.C.: NEA, 1965.

——Guidelines for Professional Negotiation. Washington, D.C.: NEA, 1965.

——"Class Size in Large School Systems." NEA Research Bulletin, October 1967, pp. 78-80.

——"Class Size." NEA Research Bulletin, May 1968, pp. 35-36.

——"School Board and Administrative Policy on Class Size and Teacher-Pupil Ratio." Research Summary 1968-S1, Class Size, pp. 39-49. Washington, D.C.: NEA, 1968.

New Jersey Public and School Employees' Grievance Procedures Study Commission. "Text of Report." 229 GERR, D-7 (January 29, 1968).

New York State Public Employment Relations Board. PERB News: 3, no. 2 (February 1970); 4, no. 1 (January 1971); 4, no. 5 (May 1971); 4, no. 7 (July 1971); 4, no. 8 (August 1971); 4, no. 9 (September 1971); 5, no. 2 (February 1972); 5, no. 3 (March 1972).

New York State Teachers Association. Recent Research on Class Size. Albany: the Association, 1971.

Newman, Barry. "The Vise Squad: New York City Seeks 'More Bang for Buck,' Pushes for Efficiency." Wall Street Journal, April 12, 1973, p. 1.

Nigro, Felix A. Management-Employee Relations in the Public Service. Chicago: Public Personnel Association, 1969.

———"Collective Bargaining and the Merit System." In Unionization of Municipal Employees, Proceedings of the Academy of Political Science 30, no. 2 (December 1970). Edited by Robert Connery and William Farr.

Oberer, Walter E. "The Future of Collective Bargaining in Public Employment." 20 Labor Law Journal 777 (1969).

———Kurt L. Hanslowe, and Robert E. Doherty. The Taylor Act: A Primer for School Personnel. Bulletin 59, New York State School of Industrial and Labor Relations, Cornell University, 1968.

———The Taylor Act Amendments of 1969: A Primer for School Personnel. Bulletin 62, New York State School of Industrial and Labor Relations, Cornell University, 1970.

Ocheltree, Keith, ed. Perspective in Public Employee Negotiation. Chicago: Public Personnel Association, 1969.

Ohio Legislative Service Commission. Public Employee Labor Relations. Report no. 96. February 1969.

Pendleton, Edwin C. "Collective Bargaining in the Public Sector: Scope of Bargaining." Reports, Industrial Relations Center, University of Hawaii, January-February 1971.

"Pennsylvania Board Narrows Scope of Teacher Negotiations with Exclusion of 21 Noneconomic 'Managerial Policy' Items," 426 GERR, B-11 (November 8, 1971).

"PERB Decides School Board Must Negotiate on Impact of Budget Reductions but Not on Cuts Themselves." 409 GERR, B-9 (July 21, 1971).

Perry, Charles R., and Wesley A. Wildman. The Impact of Negotiations in Public Education. Worthington, Ohio: Charles A. Jones Publishing Co., 1970.

Platt, Elihu. "The Duty to Bargain as Applied to Management Decisions." 19 Labor Law Journal 143 (1968).

"PLRB Changes Stand on Negotiability of Certain Teacher Demands, Orders Bargaining on Assignments, Files, Cafeteria, Chaperoning." 464 GERR, B-2 (August 7, 1972).

Plunkett, Thomas J. "Rethinking Management Relations in the Public Service." In Collective Bargaining in the Public Service: Theory and Practice. Edited by Kenneth O. Warner. Chicago: Public Personnel Association, 1967.

——"The Seminar in Retrospect." In Collective Bargaining in the Public Service: Theory and Practice. Edited by Kenneth O. Warner. Chicago: Public Personnel Association, 1967.

Rabin, Robert J. "Fibreboard and the Termination of Bargaining Unit Work: The Search for Standards in Defining the Scope of the Duty to Bargain." 71 Columbia Law Review 802 (1971).

Rains, Harry H. "New York Public Employee Relations Laws Pros and Cons on Proposed Amendments—Stalemate Procedures, Strikes and Penalties." 20 Labor Law Journal 264 (1969).

Rehmus, Charles M. "Constraints on Local Governments in Public Employee Bargaining." 67 Michigan Law Review 919 (1969).

Rentfro, William E., ed. Collective Negotiations in Public Employment—Which Way? Boulder: Center for Labor Education and Research, University of Colorado, 1968.

Repas, Robert F. Collective Bargaining in Federal Employment. Honolulu: Industrial Relations Center, University of Hawaii, 1970.

Roberts, Harold S. Labor-Management Relations in the Public Service. Honolulu: Industrial Relations Center, University of Hawaii, 1968.

—— and John B. Ferguson, eds. Collective Bargaining and Dispute
   Settlement in the Public and Private Sectors. Honolulu: Industrial Relations Center, University of Hawaii, 1969.

Sabghir, Irving H. The Scope of Bargaining in Public Sector Collective Bargaining. Report sponsored by New York State Public
   Employment Relations Board, October 1970.

Scott, Richard. "Field Methods in the Study of Organizations." In
   Handbook of Organizations. Edited by James G. March. Chicago:
   Rand McNally, 1965.

Seidman, Joel. "State Legislation on Collective Bargaining by Public
   Employees." 22 Labor Law Journal 13 (971).

Seitz, Reynolds C. "School Board Authority and the Right of the
   Public School Teachers to Negotiate—A Legal Analysis,"
   22 Vanderbilt Law Review 239 (1969).

Selden, David. "Class Size and the New York Contract." Phi Kappa
   Deltan, March 1964, pp. 283-87.

Select Joint Legislative Committee on Public Employee Relations.
   1969 Report. State of New York, Legislative Document (1969)
   no. 14.

Shaw, Lee C. "The Development of State and Federal Laws." In
   Public Workers and Public Unions. Edited by Sam Zagoria.
   Englewood Cliffs, N.J.: Prentice-Hall, 1972.

Shils, Edward B., and C. Taylor Whittier. Teachers, Administrators
   and Collective Bargaining. New York: Thomas Y. Crowell Co.,
   1968.

Smith, Russell. "State and Local Advisory Reports on Public Employment Labor Legislation: A Comparative Analysis." 67
   Michigan Law Review 891 (1969).

Special Committee on the Duties of Teachers. The Duties of Teachers, pp. 4-10. Albany: New York State Teachers Association,
   1968.

St. Antoine, Theodore J. "The Consent of the Governed—Public
   Employee Unions and the Law." In Collective Bargaining Today.
   Washington, D.C.: Bureau of National Affairs, 1971.

Stanley, David T. "What Are Unions Doing to Merit Systems?" Public Personnel Review 31 (1970): 108.

——Managing Local Government Under Union Pressure. Washington, D.C.: Brookings Institution, 1972.

State Legislative Research Council, State of South Dakota. "Labor-Management Relations in Public Employment." Staff memorandum. December 1, 1969.

Stetson, Damon. Productivity: More Work for a Day's Pay. Labor Management Relations Service, 1972.

Stinnett, T. M., Jack H. Kleinmann, and Martha L. Ware. Professional Negotiation in Public Education. New York: Macmillan, 1966.

Sullivan, Daniel P. "Subjects of Collective Bargaining in Public Service: Not Really Collective Bargaining." 33 Missouri Law Review 409 (1968).

Task Force on Public Employee Labor Relations, State of Maryland. "Text of Report." 278 GERR, AA-3 (January 6, 1969).

Taylor, George W. "The Public Interest in Collective Negotiations in Education." In Readings on Collective Negotiations in Education. Edited by Stanley Elam, Myron Lieberman, and Michael Moskow. Chicago: Rand McNally, 1967.

Tennessee Legislative Council Committee. Study on Public Employer-Employee Relations 1970. Nashville, 1971.

"The Development of the Fibreboard Doctrine: The Duty to Bargain Over Economically Motivated Subcontracting Decisions." 33 University of Chicago Law Review 315 (1965).

The Relevance of Private Sector Experience to Public Sector Collective Bargaining. New Brunswick, N.J.: Institute of Management and Labor Relations, Rutgers University, 1968.

"The Scope of Collective Bargaining," 74 Yale Law Journal 1472 (1965).

Twentieth Century Fund. Pickets at City Hall—Report and Recommendations of the Twentieth Century Fund Task Force on Labor Disputes in Public Employment, 1970, GERR Reference File, 51: 151, BNA, Washington, D.C.

"Union May Not Use Unfair Labor Practice Proceeding to Challenge Agency's Negotiability Determination." 394 GERR, A-11 (March 29, 1971).

U.S. Labor Management Services Administration. Scope of Bargaining in the Public Sector—Concepts and Problems, Report, by Paul Prasow and others. Washington: U.S. Government Printing Office, 1972.

Vollmer, Howard M., and Donald L. Mills. Professionalization. Englewood Cliffs, N.J.: Prentice-Hall, 1966.

Warner, Kenneth O., ed. Developments in Public Employee Relations. Chicago: Public Personnel Association, 1965.

"Weinberg Advocates 'Hard Bargaining' Rather Than More Experiments to Solve Future Public Sector Labor Disputes." 486 GERR, B-11 (January 15, 1973).

Weisenfeld, Allan. "Public Employees—First or Second Class Citizens." 16 Labor Law Journal 685 (1965).

——"Collective Bargaining by Public Employees in the U.S." In Industrial Relations Research Association, Collective Bargaining in the Public Service. Proceedings of Spring meeting, 1966.

Weitzman, Joan P. "The Professional Test: Can Teachers Pass?" Industrial and Labor Relations Forum 7 (December 1971): 1.

Wellington, Harry H. Labor and the Legal Process. New Haven: Yale University Press, 1968.

——and Ralph K. Winter. "Structuring Collective Bargaining in Public Employment." 79 Yale Law Journal 805 (1970).

——The Unions and the Cities. Washington, D.C.: Brookings Institution, 1971.

Werne, Benjamin. "Collective Bargaining in the Public Sector," 22 Vanderbilt Law Review 833 (1969).

Winter, Ralph K., and Harry H. Wellington. "The Limits of Collective Bargaining in Public Employment." 78 Yale Law Journal 1107 (1969).

Wollett, Donald H. "The Coming Revolution in Public School Management." 67 Michigan Law Review 1017 (1969).

—— and Robert H. Chanin. "The Public Employee at the Bargaining Table." 15 Labor Law Journal 8 (1964).

——The Law and Practice in Teacher Negotiations. Washington, D.C.: Bureau of National Affairs, 1970.

Zeidler, Frank P. "The Public as Third Party." In Public Personnel Administration. Englewood Cliffs, N.J.: Prentice-Hall, 1973.

JOAN PARKER WEITZMAN is a trial examiner and the executive assistant to the chairman of the New York City Office of Collective Bargaining. In addition, she teaches in the Cornell University credit program at the Labor College in New York City.

She has served as a professional negotiator in teacher-school board negotiations in upstate New York. Her article "The Professional Test: Can Teachers Pass?" appeared in the December 1971 issue of Industrial and Labor Relations Forum.

Dr. Weitzman studied at the School of Industrial and Labor Relations, Cornell University, receiving her Bachelor of Science degree in 1970 and her Master of Science degree in 1972. She received her Ph.D in January of 1974.

INTERNATIONAL MANUAL ON COLLECTIVE
BARGAINING FOR PUBLIC EMPLOYEES
edited by
Seymour P. Kaye
and Arthur Marsh

POSITION CLASSIFICATION: A Behavioral
Analysis for the Public Service
Jay M. Shafritz

PUBLIC SERVICE EMPLOYMENT: An Analysis
of Its History, Problems, and Prospects
edited by
Alan Gartner, Russell A. Nixon,
and Frank Riessman

TRADE UNION WOMEN
Barbara Werthiemer
and Anne Nelson